Critical Paths

B L A K E   A N D   T H E

Edited by

Duke University Press   Durham and London

CRITICAL PATHS

ARGUMENT OF METHOD

Dan Miller, Mark Bracher, and Donald Ault

1987

Permissions for reproducing the following
illustrations are gratefully acknowledged:
H. Ramberg and P. S. Martini, *The Exhibition of the Royal Academy, 1787,* by
permission of the Trustees of the British
Museum; Maerten van Heemskerck, *Ecce
Homo,* by permission of Bob Jones University Art Gallery and Museum; William
Blake, *Visions of the Daughters of Albion*
(copy G), plate i (frontispiece), by permission of the Houghton Library, Harvard
University; Henry Fuseli, *The Nightmare,*
by permission of the Frankfurter Goethe-
Museum, Frankfurt am Main; William
Blake, *Visions of the Daughters of Albion*
(copy I), plates 1 and 3, by permission of
the Yale Center for British Art, Paul Mellon
Collection; William Blake, *Visions of the
Daughters of Albion* (copy J), plates iii, 1,
and 3, by permission of the Lessing J.
Rosenwald Collection, Rare Books and Spe-
cial Collections Division of the Library of
Congress; William Blake, *The Marriage of
Heaven and Hell* (copy H), pl. 1, by permis-
sion of the Fitzwilliam Museum, Cambridge,
England; William Blake, *The Soldiers Casting Lots for Christ's Garments,* by permis-
sion of the Fitzwilliam Museum, Cambridge,
England.

For Martin K. Nurmi and John E. Grant,
who may agree with little here,
but who led the way.

Contents

Illustrations

Key to References

All Blake quotations are from *The Complete Poetry and Prose of William Blake,* edited by David V. Erdman, commentary by Harold Bloom, newly revised edition (Garden City, NY: Anchor Press–Doubleday, 1982), abbreviated as E. Citations generally note plate (or page) number, line numbers, and then page numbers in the Erdman edition. Citations for *The Four Zoas* list Night, page in Blake's text, lines, and page in the Erdman edition: *FZ*IX:118:7–16, E387 means *The Four Zoas,* Night IX, page 118, lines 7–16, page 387 in Erdman. In essays devoted to single works, page references to Erdman have been omitted. The following abbreviations are used:

A	*America a Prophecy*
ARO	*All Religions are One*
DC	*A Descriptive Catalogue of Pictures*
Eur	*Europe a Prophecy*
EG	*The Everlasting Gospel*
FR	*The French Revolution*
FZ	*The Four Zoas*
J	*Jerusalem*
L	*The Song of Los*
M	*Milton*
MHH	*The Marriage of Heaven and Hell*
NNR[a][b]	*There is No Natural Religion* [a] [b]
SE	*Songs of Experience*
T	*Tiriel*
Th	*The Book of Thel*
U	*The [First] Book of Urizen*
VDA	*Visions of the Daughters of Albion*
VLJ	*A Vision of the Last Judgment*

Acknowledgments

The editors thank the departments of English at their respective universities for assistance of many kinds, direct and indirect, in bringing this project to completion. We thank Carol Palmquist at Iowa State University for her invaluable help with word processing, which got the project underway. Terry Abbott and Cheryl Kamps also aided us greatly. We would also like to acknowledge the support given by Professor Frank Haggard, chair, Department of English, Iowa State University. At North Carolina State University, Carol Sharpe's excellent typing helped bring the project to completion, and N. Charlene Turner generously stepped in at the last minute to replace pages obliterated by an errant computer.

Joanne Ferguson, assistant director and editor-in-chief at Duke University Press, guided the editors through publication with expertise and infinite patience. Nancy H. Margolis undertook the impossible task of copyediting order out of chaos; her careful hand helped shape this book.

Introduction

Dan Miller

The present is a time of crisis and chaos in philosophy. The exceptional diffi-culty which modern philosophers find in accepting each other's conclusions, and even in understanding each other's arguments, is a necessary consequence of their failure to agree upon principles of method, or even to find out how they differ; this only is clear, that the old methods are no longer followed, and every one is free to invent a new one of his own. This is a state of things natural and proper to an age when new movements are in the making; but if it lasts too long discouragement and indifference will take the place of enterprise, and the new movement will be rotten before it is ripe.
—R. G. Collingwood, *An Essay in Philosophical Method*

Method, etymology argues, has to do with following paths and pursu-ing ways. To get from here to there, take this road, proceed a certain distance, turn at a particular point, again at another point, and you will reach your destination. Method suggests that a specific path is in some sense optimal: there may be other routes, but they will not lead to your goal, or if they do go to the right place, they are longer or more arduous or less easily followed. One particular road, one *hodos,* is the proper path. And if you are called upon to repeat the journey, the right way remains the same. With method, means lead to an end, through distinct steps set out in invariable order, by an indefinitely repeatable and ra-tionally justifiable procedure. Take *this* road, for others have followed it to your destination and vouched it safe and sure. The way is open, and the journey assured.

In practice, however, following a path usually proves difficult. Way-farers asking directions from the local inhabitants often have to suffer through lengthy debate about how best to get from here to there, whether you can get there from here, or even whether *there* is where you really want to go. Even more often, problems of itinerary arise. When there are many travelers, roads multiply until the well-known and frequently traveled path is no longer the only or best route. Crowded

roads make for slow trips. And with sufficiently many roads, even experienced pilgrims will have to consider, at each point along the way,
when and where to turn. Traveling becomes a complex business, requiring guidebooks, maps, and compasses. Too many paths make a
maze.

Blake himself considered the problem of methodical ways, sometimes
directly—as in his annotations to Reynolds's *Discourses*—and other
times indirectly—as in *The Marriage of Heaven and Hell,* that oblique
exploration of paths and roads. Blake opens *The Marriage* with "The
Argument," a gnomic verse fable about a "just man" who follows "a
perilous path" through the "vale of death" and pursues his course with
such justice that the wilderness flowers. Once the desert is transformed,
the "villain" leaves his "paths of ease, / To walk in the perilous paths,
and drive / The just man into barren climes" and into "the wilds /
Where lions roam" (*MHH*2:3–5, 14–20, E33). The just man still
roams the wilderness, but once his way has been usurped, there are
no paths to guide him. He becomes Rintrah, the wrathful prophet, led
only by his own visionary promptings. The *topos* of two paths, one
more difficult than the other, carries with it a long literary and religious history, but Blake varies the traditional image by making the
just man's path doubly dangerous. The route not only passes through
the valley of death but leads, if followed successfully, to failure. Though
the strenuous way becomes productive—roses blossom among the thorns,
and "honey bees" flourish "on the barren heath" (2:7–8)—that fruit-
fulness draws those who seek to avoid effort and to profit from the labor of others. Blake's fable tells of the perversion of paths; it suggests
that the right way is all too easily taken over and altered, so that the
just man must pursue a pathless route.

As if in response to the problem of failed paths, the "Proverbs of
Hell" advance what might be called a method of just indirection. They
have been frequently quoted and admired, yet they are rarely taken as
guides for reading Blake. This is probably for the best: a reader faced
with texts as inherently difficult as Blake's will find that a celebration
of indirect, transgressive ways only compounds the difficulty. And yet
the advice is clearly there: "The road of excess leads to the palace of
wisdom"; "If the fool would persist in his folly he would become
wise"; "Improvement makes strait roads, but the crooked roads without Improvement, are roads of Genius" (*MHH*7–10, E35–38). Blake's
maxims for travelers suggest that, though roads and methods are neces-

sary, the most obvious and common way will, of necessity, miss its destination. Hence, if there is a truly Blakean methodology—one that could be applied to the reading of Blake's own works and serve as a touchstone to test critical methods—it may be necessary to approach it tangentially. Some paths require detours.

At the conclusion of her review of modern Blake criticism, Mary Lynn Johnson writes, "The old order passes; the rough beast slouches. . . . If a major shift is occurring in Blake studies, as it seems to be, it does not pivot on any one new work, and no new paradigm is in evidence."[1] Johnson has accurately assessed the present state of Blake criticism, and her allusion to Yeats expresses something of the current unease about it. Something is about to be born, but no one knows what the new dispensation will be. Concern grows that Blake studies have arrived at a crossroads and that a tangle of ways hides the right path. We hear echoes of Collingwood's worry about the proliferation of methods; new and competing procedures bring new possibilities, but they may also result in a Babel of different languages that will endanger the entire philosophic (or, in our case, scholarly and critical) enterprise. Readers of Blake have always known his works pose special problems for critical method, and the field has seen its share of methodological innovation, but the critical path (the term is Northrop Frye's) has been fairly well charted and, with some exceptions, faithfully followed. That consensus seems on the verge of disintegration, and in its place comes a plethora of critical approaches inspired by seemingly unBlakean theories. Recent years have seen the appearance of studies whose concerns and approaches are psychoanalytic (Brenda S. Webster's *Blake's Prophetic Psychology*; Diana Hume George's *Blake and Freud*), Marxist (Heather Glen's *Vision and Disenchantment*; Jackie DiSalvo's *War of Titans*; David Aers, Jon Cook, and David Punter's *Romanticism and Ideology*), semiotic (Nelson Hilton's *Literal Imagination*), and deconstructive (*Unnam'd Forms: Blake and Textuality*, edited by Hilton and Thomas A. Vogler).[2] As newer methods contest the established critical path and their adherents argue vigorously with one another, we may confront, as Collingwood did fifty years ago, a crisis in method.

The present volume of essays responds to that perception of crisis. The editors conceived it as a forum in which the major shift in Blake studies could be described, gauged, analyzed, and assayed. Some of the contributors take up the issue of method itself; others consider how Blake studies can proceed in a world of conflicting and competing methods; others investigate and perform those methods that are transforming the field. Readers will find several points of agreement among the various essays, but they will discover more points of disagreement, explicit or implicit. If Blake studies are indeed in transition, this lack of unanimity is appropriate. Though not all the critical approaches currently emerging will prove viable, many of them will, and the disciplinary coherence we have previously known will probably never return. Some lament that loss, but others, including the contributors to this volume, embrace it as the occasion for new understandings of Blake and for a methodological self-awareness that can only improve criticism. But multiple paths do bring certain risks—the fragmentation of critical discourse, methodological insularity, and sterile debate. This volume accepts those risks, and gambles that the gains far outweigh the possible losses.

What paths has Blake criticism taken to arrive at this crossroads? Method as such has not posed a major problem in Blake studies until now, and for good reason. Critics had to make sense of works that seemed to make little sense, and asking *how* that sense got made would have only complicated an already complex undertaking. The first major task, of course, was to cut through the tangle of bibliographic and textual problems in order to get some sense of the lay of the land. The initial and overriding consideration was simply that there be a reasonably good path. Thus, in the 1920s, Geoffrey Keynes provided the prerequisites for any reading of the poetry: a census of Blake's works as comprehensive as was then possible (*A Bibliography of William Blake*), a complete standard edition (the three-volume *Writings of William Blake*), and a more usable edition that put Blake before a wider audience (the single-volume *Poetry and Prose of William Blake*).[3] But Keynes's methods, based on accepted editorial procedures of the time, led him to standardize Blake's texts, altering punctuation and spelling in order to convert the idiosyncrasies of Blake's hand-printed page into conventional typographic form. Keynes's editions served their purposes admirably until both were supplanted by his *Complete Writings of William Blake* in 1957,[4] but serious readers soon felt the need for a text that was closer to Blake's own in punctuation, grammar, and even visual impact. That need was partially met by David V. Erdman's

Poetry and Prose of William Blake (1965), which went through several editions and eventually became *The Complete Poetry and Prose of William Blake* (1982), now the edition officially approved by the MLA.[5] Erdman's intent was to produce "a text as close as possible to Blake's own, even in punctuation" (E786), and he succeeded in producing great accuracy, even to the extent of recovering lines Blake excised from the copperplate. However, Erdman arrived at his texts by comparing and collating all existing copies of each work, so a poem as it appears in his edition does not necessarily correspond to any poem that Blake himself ever produced. In this regard, Erdman's edition differs significantly from G. E. Bentley's *William Blake's Writings* (1978), a two-volume work that attempts to draw even nearer to Blake by selecting one particular copy of each work as copy text, by supplying black-and-white reproductions of most of the designs, and by editorially marking changes in punctuation within the text.[6] The possibility and even the desirability of anything like an approved edition has been challenged, most recently by the Santa Cruz Study Group, whose review of Erdman's latest edition points out the ways in which it tends to regularize both line and meaning.[7] The pioneering of Keynes and the refining of Erdman and Bentley have made it clear that, in addition to the facsimiles of individual works, more than one edition of Blake may be necessary for scholarship. Though there will always be a standard or, at least, a commonly used edition, the progress of textual scholarship has tended to increase, not decrease, the number of editorial problems in Blake studies. The very successes of Blake's editors have made a single editorial path impossible.

Just as textual scholarship cut a trail out of and then back into the wilderness of Blake's multiple copies, so has interpretation made sufficiently good sense of Blake that we now begin to ask how we arrived at that sense. As early as Ellis and Yeats, critics treated the poetry as if it were in a code that required deciphering, usually by means of some "key"—a central dogma or a set of occult sources or a knowledge of esoteric traditions—that was to be found outside the texts and used to unlock encrypted meaning.[8] S. Foster Damon's early work turns upon the claim of Blake's "mysticism," as does D. J. Sloss and J. P. R. Wallis's interpretive concordance of Blakean symbolic terms.[9] Though not as burdened by the assumption of Blake's mysticism as his first writings, Damon's *A Blake Dictionary*, an immensely useful critical resource, moves along the same exegetic path: the prophecies can be read once the code is cracked. In his introduction, Damon speaks of a system that "must be discovered," of "clues" to Blake's meaning that are "broadcast throughout his writings" and must be assembled, of a "prodigious jigsaw puzzle" that, once fitted together, "makes amazing good sense which might have been obvious from the first."[10] From this perspective, Blake's "sense" is not a critical problem, only the discourse in which that sense is articulated; interpretation becomes the act of solving a semiotic puzzle, and the bits and pieces of the puzzle serve simply the purpose of joining together to form the larger message. The Sloss-Wallis and Damon undertakings, much like the early Keynes editions, work to regularize. They assume that Blake's symbols have relatively invariant meanings, that translation from symbol to symbolized is adequate exegesis, and that meaning remains more or less stable and coherent throughout the canon. Similar methodology informs George Mills Harper's and Kathleen Raines's readings of Blake through hermetic, Neoplatonic traditions.[11] Because of the pressing need to determine some legible sense, these readings all move quickly from symbol to meaning, leaving largely unexamined the motives for symbolization. Interpretation-as-decipherment has been responsible for genuine scholarly discoveries, but once a puzzle has been reasonably well solved, we wonder why it was a puzzle in the first place.

With some guides to the territory in hand, Blake studies could begin to range more widely, and the 1940s brought readings of Blake focused on social and intellectual context. Jacob Bronowski and Mark Schorer describe the historical and idelogical backgrounds that allow us to understand Blake's poetry as political and philosophic statement.[12] This approach culminates in Erdman's *Blake: Prophet against Empire* (1954), a work of painstaking historical research that demonstrates the very specific references of Blake's social and political allegory.[13] In one book, Erdman fully establishes the historical dimensions of Blake's art and the political commentary pervading it. Though Erdman lays the foundations for an historical-political reading of Blake, until very recently few critics have followed this line of investigation. In addition, though nearly all of Erdman's commentaries offer powerful insights, too often interpretation ends with the discovery of a particular allusion to a contemporary event. That Blake was heavily involved with events and political debates of the day is now beyond doubt, but this version of contextualism, based on a rather empiricist mode of historiography, tends to resolve poetry into history. Contex-

tualism offers a needed balance to interpretive decoding, but the discovery of allusions functions much as does code breaking, and reading
becomes commentary.

The major methodological change in Blake studies before Erdman
came with Northrop Frye's *Fearful Symmetry* (1947), which led to
Anatomy of Criticism and an entire school of criticism whose tenets
and history are well known. With Frye, the interpretive relation turns
around: no longer are keys imported from outside to unlock meaning,
but now the texts themselves, if rightly read, provide all the terms necessary for their own interpretation. Blake himself becomes the key to
an entire literary universe. In the closing chapter of *Fearful Symmetry*, Frye quotes Blake's claim, "All had originally one language,
and one religion" (*DC*44, E543), and remarks that once "we follow
his own method, and interpret this in imaginative rather than historical terms, we have the doctrine that all symbolism in all art and all
religion is mutually intelligible among all men, and that there is such
a thing as an iconography of the imagination."[14] For Frye, this iconography is stable and coherent throughout Blake, universal and consistent
throughout literature. This stability and consistency makes possible a
return to the metaphor of deciphering: in *The Critical Path* Frye reflects on writing *Fearful Symmetry* at a time when there were "many
paths, some well trodden and equipped with signposts, but all pointing
in what for me were the wrong directions"—toward esotericism, sociology, and psychology—and then remarks that "my task was the specific one of trying to crack Blake's symbolic code, and I had the feeling
that the way led directly through literature itself."[15] As Harold Bloom,
Peter F. Fisher, and others followed his lead, Frye's path has itself
come to be very well traveled and posted.[16] Critical practice during
the 1960s and 1970s, the period in which the "Blake industry" flourished, generally confined itself to the mode of commentary established
by Frye.

This brief survey of critical paths has left much uncharted, particularly the surge of interest in Blake's visual art and its methodological
insistence that no reading of poetry is adequate without attention to
the illuminations and to the special nature of Blake's composite art
as a whole. Some of this work has served to disturb traditional methodology, but much of it has followed roughly the same interpretive
paths, simply extending the deciphering impulse from the text into
the field of Blake's designs. Given this critical consensus, other meth-

ods will naturally be seen as alien, intrusive, and even destructive. For example, in a special issue of *Studies in Romanticism*,[17] several noted scholars evaluate the past achievements of Blake criticism and, with a mixture of anticipation and foreboding, attempt to gauge its future. Like Johnson, W. J. T. Mitchell speaks of a "major shift that seems to be occurring in the study of Blake" and then characterizes it as a change that "will replace twenty years of attempts to justify Blake as a great formal artist" with "a kind of criticism that tends to deface the monument we have erected" (412). In the same issue, Robert Essick anticipates a fundamental alteration of critical approach: the *"intrinsic* approach" based on "a point of view and a critical vocabulary taken from Blake himself" has been able to tell us "what Blake 'meant,' " and we should expect "admittedly *extrinsic* methodologies that . . . pose questions which have not been generated by the intrinsic approach" (397). Pervading the comments of these critics is the sense that an era of Blake studies is coming to an end, and another is beginning. Some of the prophets embrace the changes they foresee. Essick allows that new methods "can open up this closed system" of Blake criticism based exclusively on Blakean axioms (397), and Hazard Adams suggests that current investigations of "the rhetorical aspects of literary works" may help us better understand Blake's longer prophecies (402). But most of these writers in the mainstream of Blake studies also sense a danger in the entry of theoretically informed methods: Adams warns of a critical faddishness that forgets "the futility . . . of theory *as practice*" (402); Essick asks that "the methodological sophisticates stay in close contact with traditional scholarship" (339); and Morton Paley fears a "remystification of the texts" and cautions that "the best writers on Blake will assimilate post-structuralist theory to their own critical sensibilities" (426). If a new dispensation is at hand, many imagine it as a very rough beast.

Most of these writers assume that new methods are less closely linked to Blake's text (or to his meaning or to his own method) than those of the past—that they are, in Essick's terms, extrinsic as opposed to intrinsic methods—and are therefore inherently more dangerous procedures. Having a method, it seems, means giving up the grounds and guarantees of criticism organically linked to its object. Method appears extrinsic and artificial: a psychoanalytic or Marxist study may prove interesting in some respects, but since Blake was neither Freudian nor Marxist, such approaches miss the essential nature of Blake's poetry.

Hence, any method requires the discipline of "traditional scholarship" or "critical sensibilities" (which are themselves either not methods or methods so fully validated as to escape the dangers of methodology) to tie it to the text we already know and prevent it from remaking the text in its own image. Viewed in this light, method opens the possibility of solipsism: a text given over to a method previously shaped by an independent literary theory is a text made liable to distortion.

Such distrust of method makes sense only if we can know texts without method or by some critical method fully mandated by the text itself. But the first possibility is illusory and the second doubtful. Methods that have given us a knowledge of "what Blake 'meant' " are no less methods than those that replace them. It is arguable whether Frye did or could read Blake on purely literary and internal grounds. All methods are to a certain degree extrinsic, and all bring with them the danger of solipsism. Knowledge of Blake's poetic method will help refine any critical approach, but the decision to base interpretation solely on Blakean principles is itself a methodological decision made on extrinsic grounds. In addition, the attempt to read along the lines articulated by the text itself involves a peculiar paradox: to know how to read requires that the reader already know what he or she needs to interpret. The appearance of new methods shows that what once seemed methodologically neutral or innocent was in fact not so. When some methods appear not to be methods and others seem only extrinsic, we may have lost sight of what method really is.

In both literary criticism and philosophy, the history of method shows the progressive impoverishment of a once rich and powerful concept. Though the term has come to mean, rather exclusively, scientific method, for most of that history method has been linked much more closely to the arts than the sciences. Plato associates *methodos* with *techne:* method is the rational means of acquiring an art, a way of gaining a skill that involves real understanding rather than chance or simple intuition or repetitive practice. Method discovers the true ends of a particular art (such as the art of medicine or the art of rhetoric, the two exemplary cases in the *Phaedrus*) and then organizes parts of the *techne* in light of their functions in attaining that end. For Plato, the preeminent method is dialectic, the "way of inquiry that attempts systematically and in all cases to determine what each thing is" (*Republic* 7:533c). Dialectic is universal method, an art that has as its object not the knowledge involved in any particular skill, but the proper understanding of all arts. Yet dialectic remains a particular *techne* and is not *theoria;* it is a specific art or skill, though universal in its results, and remains distinct from philosophic knowledge proper. Platonic method is clearly a determinate operation with stages set out in fixed order, but while an art leads to restricted knowledge (the art of medicine to knowledge of the body, rhethoric to knowledge of human opinion), method ranges more widely. The problem of how best to come to know about the body or human opinion requires a degree of procedural self-consciousness not necessarily required by particular arts. For modern thought, theory and practice stand in sterile opposition, but Platonic dialectic operates in the space between the two. Our inability to conceive method as anything but an imposition (of theory on practice) or a specific art (of critical practice based on "Blake's own method") means we have lost the very domain of method.

Further, Plato treats the method of dialectic as a method of discourse, a way of conducting discussion, of advancing and qualifying hypotheses, of moving through questions and answers. At its first appearance, method joins knowledge and language: the method proper to any art emerges when that art is properly described and discussed.[18] Only with Aristotle does method begin to distinguish itself from both art and discourse to become a universally valid procedure for all undertakings. Plato's dialectic is the method of thought within language; Aristotle's dialectical method is much closer to a simple mode of operation. When Heidegger meditates on thinking as the tracing of a path within language, he seeks to move from the scientific definition of method, developed from Aristotle, to the more powerful Socratic notion.

After Aristotle, the path of method moves through Stoic aesthetics and Galenian medicine (rhetoric and healing still accompanying the concept) and eventually becomes the subject of considerable controversy during the Renaissance. Vives, Ramus, and other Renaissance Humanists advance a specifically pedagogical and rhetorical notion of method: the writer or teacher who is able to set out his subject in the most systematic and economical manner and who can transmit knowledge through set procedures has succeeded in making knowledge methodical. Opponents of the Humanists appeal to the authority of Aristotle and insist that the sole purpose of method is capacity to produce and test knowledge.[19] Medicine and rhetoric part ways, and they divide the functions of method between them: Galenian medicine, proclaimed by traditionalists as the paradigmatic method, leads toward the Cartesian search for rigorous, scientific methodology; while rhetoricians like Ramus enlist the systematicity of method in the cause of pedagogical efficiency and, more importantly, discursive power. The Platonic dialectic, which unites methodical knowledge and discourse, splits into "true" method and "mere" method, into the stringent procedures required by science and the seemingly idiosyncratic procedures of the humanities.[20]

Given this history, it should not be surprising to find widespread hostility to method among literary critics and theorists. Opposition to method comes from both sides of the current critical spectrum: it is denounced both in the name of the text and in the name of the reader. Richard E. Palmer offers a case in point of the first: "Method is an effort to measure and control from the side of the interpreter; it is the opposite of letting the phenomenon lead. The openness of 'experience'—which alters the interpreter from the side of the text— is antithetical to method. Thus method is in reality a form of dogmatism, separating the interpreter from the work, standing between him and it, and barring him from experiencing the work in its fullness."[21] For Palmer, method seeks to master the text by bringing it under the rule of previously defined analytic categories, an act motivated by the "modern technological way of thinking and the will-to-power that lies at its root" (247). When reading gives up method and lets itself be taken over by "the language event of experiencing the work itself," then it joins "the inner movement of the thing that is unfolding" (248). When the reader allows the literary work to speak with its own voice, a dialogue between text and reader replaces the one-sided interrogation conducted by methodology.

Palmer's discourse against method is as much ethical as it is theoretical: method attempts to gain power over the text and to defend against its experiential force. Openness and respect stand directly opposed to closure and violence. On one hand, a properly hermeneutic experience of the literary work breaks down interpretive categories, transforms the reader, and engenders original meanings; on the other, methods "tend not to call into question their own guiding presuppositions but rather to operate within a system, so that the answer" to any critical inquiry "is always potentially present and expected within the system" (233). Of course, Palmer's *Hermeneutics,* one of the first introductions of that interpretive theory for the American critical community, does itself advance a definite methodology, but the most substantial role Palmer grants method is a negative one. Proper method is merely that "discipline" that restrains the reader's "will to master" (209) and maintains reading in the posture of openness to experience that transcends any methodological appropriation of the work.

Palmer's charges are not wholly unfounded, for method does always carry with it the possibility of interpretive violence. Method also aspires to systematicity and maximum formalization. The routine tracing of invariable pathways suggested by the etymology of "method" can all too easily become all that method offers. In addition, method always defines its object and interpretive categories beforehand. But if method involves this kind of violence, so does all interpretation. Though methods necessarily limit and totalize, the threat of violence cannot be avoided by recourse to an experience apart from or beyond prior categories. Experience has its own interpretive forms, terms, and categories, and method is precisely the attempt to reflect critically on them. The refusal to run the risks of method only courts the greater danger of falling prey to unrecognized and uncriticized methodology. Method can easily disintegrate into the mechanical technique Palmer rightly deplores, and a degree of formalization inheres in any developed methodology, but the antidote to systematizing blindness can come only from the self-reflections of method upon itself.

In *The Reach of Criticism*, Paul H. Fry launches an attack on method from the opposite direction. Though he allows that all interpretation necessarily involves method, consciously articulated or not, Fry focuses on the failure inherent in any methodological project. Fry argues that all critical and, more generally, epistemological undertakings by nature occlude their own methods: "the structural properties of knowledge and of its objects are just what will always remain, to one indeterminate degree or another, obscured by the activity of knowing."[22] Method, Fry argues, can never become sufficiently self-reflexive to know or govern the conditions within which it actually operates, and the successes of methodical activity usually arise when that blindness is most acute and systematicity breaks down. Fry approves Paul de Man's contention that critics' strongest "findings about the structure of texts contradict the general conceptions they use as their model" and that they "owe their best insights to the assumptions these insights disprove."[23] Fry specifies the causes of error: method can never succeed because of "the necessarily incommensurable implication of the interpreter in the interpreted" and the inescapable temporality of any "representation of experience (Fry 4). In Fry's view, method tries to purify reading of subjective factors that can never be purged and then to render in static, formal categories an interpretive process that is fundamentally temporal.

We have moved from Palmer's imperative that the work be allowed to unfold itself within the reader's receptive experience to Fry's epistemological skepticism that asserts the uncontrollable heterogeneity of reading. In the first case, method fails because it betrays the work to an imposed reading; in the second, it fails to the degree that it seeks to regulate the ungovernable process of interpretation. For Fry, "the work of art is intended in irreconcilable ways by consciousness and by the coercive manifold that comprises the unconscious" (170–71). Fry makes the historicity of interpretation so extreme that no method can hope to know or control the historical contingencies that hedge it. The historically determined assumptions we bring to any act of reading can never be transcended because history offers no vantage point for a critique of its own determinisms. Fry does not, however, conclude that literary meaning is unknowable; in place of methodical knowing, he offers "more radical alternatives—the sublime, the 'grace' beyond the reach of art, and modes of recognition that are themselves dislocations of form" (3). Making a virtue of inevitability, Fry embraces the error that plagues all interpretive efforts and celebrates it as the source of uncontrollable and unpredictable insight. When method reaches its limits, knowledge begins. Fry proposes a hermeneutics of distraction, an interpretive practice that liberates "the necessarily wandering course of attention which no critical theory has ever taken into account" (170).

Though Fry invokes de Man, the latter's argument is significantly different and points out the shortcomings of Fry's attack on method. Where Fry makes value judgments (of antimethodical insight against methodological blindness, of literary meaning against critical formalization), de Man avoids them: certain critics "can be called 'literary' in the full sense of the term, because of their blindness, not in spite of it" (de Man 141). De Man's is the more extreme position, for he identifies error with reading as such, makes no distinction between methodical and aberrant readings, and refuses to distinguish literary from critical practices. Method inevitably misconstrues, but there is no escape. De Man's strongest assertion, the one that shows most clearly the limits of Fry's argument, is that the struggle between "method-ological dogma" and "literary insight" goes on *within* method: "this interplay between methodology and literature develops in turn the highly literary rhetoric of what could be called criticism" (139). For de Man, blindness and insight are so inseparably linked that any prac-tical escape, however distracted, from the dilemma is impossible.[24]

Predictably, Palmer and Fry end in agreement. In seeking to evade method, both embrace a number of Romantic themes—the spontaneity and unpredictability of experience, nonmethodical creativity (whether of the work or the reader), the moment of sublimity and possession—originally set out by Romantics such as Blake with much more irony and sophistication. As much as Palmer and Fry might want to lay claim to Blake's meditation on roads in *The Marriage*, they are effec-tively seeking to straighten paths that ought to remain crooked. Both critics aspire to a moment of reading that escapes methodology and methodological violence. Palmer looks toward a pure self-unfolding of the work itself, and Fry toward the unpredictable insight produced by the vagaries of reading, but the two share a hope that somehow there may be interpretation that is not interpretation. An ideal of reading free of procedure, categorization, system, and formalism probably informs all acts of interpretation, but the strength of that ideal mea-sures the degree to which reading remains blind to its own method.

We began with the possibility that in such texts as *The Marriage of Heaven and Hell* Blake offers some principles, however paradoxical, that could shape a method of reading Blake. But our detours have dis-covered no escape from methodology. Critical method always precedes and defines its object. Does this disqualify any advice Blake may have to give us about reading? Yes and no. Because Blake's advice can reach us only through acts of reading shaped by method, it cannot govern method beforehand. But, as our method has led us to read Blake's proverbial wisdom, he has held that excessiveness and crooked-ness are methodological virtues. This view accepts the necessity of roads and goes on to suggest that the best way will be the most self-complicating path. Some roads are straight and easily traveled; others take surprising turns. Some methods can be quickly usurped; others resist villains. These differences are all that matter, not the differences between method as such and something beyond method. It has been observed that "language can only indefinitely tend toward justice by acknowledging and practicing the violence within it. Violence against violence."[25] In our terms, method against method. Method never gains complete control of its own operations, but some methods work strategically against their own limitations and others do not. The fool who becomes wise does so by persisting in his folly, not by being given the gift of wisdom from some exterior source.

The issue, then, is not *whether* method but *which* methods. And though we should not expect a clear-cut resolution of the present crisis in Blake studies, the debates concerning method will eventually take us in some direction. These arguments have very real consequences for the teaching and other cultural uses of Blake, so there must be, in the long run, winners and losers. In this volume, we fight some of the battles and attempt to rethink the logic of critical paths.

The two opening essays address the problem of critical method directly. In "Methods and Limitations," Stephen D. Cox responds to a factionalized, methodologically plural world that promotes either unhappy scepticism or complacent relativism. Drawing on the Chicago Critics, Karl Popper, and E. D. Hirsch, Cox argues for a carefully restricted pluralism in which each critically useful method will specify its range of application: the kinds of texts that fall within its purview, the types of problems it can take up, and above all the forms of evidence that can support or falsify its claims. In "Synecdoche and Method," Hazard Adams shares Cox's desire for a common ground to support critical exchange. But while Cox works to establish that ground from the outside, Adams builds from within, from Blake's own poetic method, in order to establish a methodological "circumference" for Blake studies generally. Adams sees "radical synecdoche," the core of Blake's poetic method, as a dynamic, progressive movement of identification that forges links between part and whole, microcosm and macrocosm, signifier and signified, sign and significance—and continually forges them anew.

We move next to essays that take up particular critical methods, the first of which is Gnostic revisionary interpretation. In "Blake's Revisionism: Gnostic Interpretation and Critical Methodology," William Dennis Horn argues that Blake's revisionism is itself part of a Gnostic tradition whose latest embodiment is Harold Bloom's revisionary theory of poetic influence. Horn sees both Blake and Bloom as inheritors of Gnostic techniques of reading against manifest or intended meaning to reveal greater truth. But, for Horn, Blake represents the fulfill-

ment of the tradition, and Bloom its collapse. Nelson Hilton's "Literal/
Tiriel/Material" offers a version of strong reading (though not Bloom-
ean reading) in practice. Hilton's critical path has taken him to
language at its most fundamental level: to the graphic shapes of
Blake's engraved letters, to the sounds of Blakean phrases and their
potential for pun and unexpected associations, and to the cultural histories that Blake's words carry with them and weave into dazzling
webs of allusions. For Hilton, *Tiriel* is a tissue of semantic and semiotic fibers, and the design in the cloth varies as the light strikes it:
literal imagination belongs to both author and reader.

Cox invokes the Chicago Critics, Adams and Horn, the Gnostic procedures of rereading myth; Hilton, the literal matter of language. All
these elements figure in Donald Ault's "Blake's De-Formation of Neo-
Aristotelianism," a critique of Chicago School analytic methods and,
as a result of subjecting those methods to the pressure of Blake's *Book
of Urizen*, a "transgressive rewriting of Neo-Aristotelianism." Ault
argues that Blake's reflexive plotting collapses the Neo-Aristotelian
distinctions between formal and final causes, objects imitated and
mimetic intention, narrated event and event of narration. As Ault unfolds *The Book of Urizen*, the perspective defining each character finds
itself progressively decomposed, restricted, inverted, and linked to
other points of view, so that Blake's plot reveals the "incommensurability" of competing perspectives. Similar paradoxes in critical method
emerge in the following essay, "Blake and the Deconstructive Interlude," which shows that Derridean deconstruction adheres to all the
classical criteria for method but departs from classical methods of
reading in its object: discourse as textuality is a field of conflicts,
strictly regulated by a logic, but that logic necessarily obscures itself
in producing discourse. Here method becomes absolute strategy or, in
Derrida's words, "strategy finally without finality," and reading becomes fundamentally provisional, largely self-canceling, and yet interminable. On this intentionally uncertain basis, I outline one course
a deconstructive reading of Blake might take.

Psychoanalytic approaches appear next in a pair of essays that make
contrary uses of the method. The first, Mark Bracher's "Rouzing the
Faculties: Lacanian Psychoanalysis and the Marriage of Heaven and
Hell in the Reader," adopts Jacques Lacan's model of the psyche and
language to illustrate how literary texts, particularly Blake's, can bring
about fundamental transformations of their readers. Departing from

more familiar critical uses of Freud, Bracher employs psychoanalytic categories to describe not the text itself or its author but the interactions between text and reader. A work such as *The Marriage of Heaven and Hell* articulates a linguistic code that, although initially alien to the reader, has the power to remake the reader's subjectivity and lived world, both of which Lacan defines as functions of symbolic systems. In sharp contrast to Bracher's use of psychoanalysis, Brenda S. Webster applies Freudian methods to Blake's poetry and to Blake himself. Webster's "Blake, Women, and Sexuality" also opens a feminist reading of Blake, as she asks us to suspend our "efforts to normalize Blake" long enough to confront the "radical sexual ideas and fantasies" that pervade his work. She then focuses on Blake's often disturbing attitudes toward sexuality and women, attitudes that previous criticism has tended "either to ignore . . . or to recast . . . in terms of official theologies or ideologies."

In "Blake's Feminist Revision of Literary Tradition in 'The SICK ROSE,' " Elizabeth Langland argues that, of the several modes of feminist investigation, a feminist critique that analyzes the ideological assumptions of both texts and readings offers the greatest possibility for arriving at a theoretical consensus. More specifically, her method is "formal-feminist"—feminist in that it pursues ideological redefinitions and antipatriarchal meanings, formal in that it focuses on "the poem itself as an allegory of its own interpretation." The result is an illumination of the "ideological bias that pervades a work's inception, its production, and its critical reception." David Aers's "Representations of Revolution: From *The French Revolution* to *The Four Zoas*" also demands that critics confront the political consequences of critical method. Aers shows that only a vision of the literary work "as a social text created in specific circumstances" and an understanding of literary language as shaped by "socio-ideological meaning" (Bakhtin) can restore the critical ability to respond humanly to Blake's art. Aers surveys Blake's strategies for representing revolution, its potential agents and possible forms, and he finds that Blake repeatedly encounters the same political and linguistic impasse: by describing a world in which "the ruling class's values have gained such control that they pervade all areas of being" and by representing the oppressed in an "homogenized" language that merges various classes and different genders into a single, absolutely dominated group, Blake allows little possibility for revolutionary agents or change.

Thomas A. Vogler's " 'in vain the Eloquent tongue': An Un-Reading of *VISIONS of the Daughters of Albion*" expands two themes that appear repeatedly in preceding essays: interpretation that finds itself anticipated and dramatized by the poem that the critic seeks to read, and the literary work that stands within larger social discourses that also contain and govern the act of critical reading. Vogler pursues an unreading that avoids fixing the Truth of Blake's poem and instead treats it "as a text 'about' the production of Truth." Reading the poem through the cultural systems of representation that make all interpretation possible leads to, in Vogler's words, "a nonmethod that challenges the adequacy of the interpretive mastery that claims to speak a discourse of a Truth undefiled by . . . rhetorical strategies and fictions." Finally, David Wagenknecht's "Afterword" offers a last, but not final, word. Written after and in response to all the essays, this epilogue crosses Blake and Derrida, interweaves iconicity and the Freudian unconscious, and points toward "a radically different Blake, quite beyond the reach of deconstruction, who would hardly offer us the Christ and the anti-Christ in the same breath without expecting us to choose between them." Wagenknecht closes the volume by insisting on that dimension of critical method that could be called (though Wagenknecht does not use the term) "ethical" in its most fundamental sense—the need to choose. The paths traced in this collection of routes end, where this introduction began, at a crossroads.

Methods and Limitations

Stephen D. Cox

In thinking about problems of critical method, it is helpful, I believe, to keep three facts in mind from the beginning. First, literary critics almost automatically follow some kind of "method," whether they want to regard themselves as doing so or not. Second, critical methods are evaluative and not merely descriptive—if only because the choices they indicate at the most basic level of consideration, choices of what to notice in a text and what to ignore, are types of evaluation. Third, even a comparatively simple text can be viewed from so many perspectives, and be subjected to so many kinds of evaluation, that virtually any critical method can be used to interpret some aspect of the text.

These ideas are suggested by my own experience in reading literary texts and in reading criticism, but I think they will agree with other people's experience as well. The problem is what to make of them. On the one hand, they can provide the basis for a despairing skepticism—for a feeling that because all interpretation is tainted by critics' acts of judgment, no interpretation can be considered authoritative. I have not discovered, however, that any practicing critic has ever actually operated with so thorough a skepticism. On the other hand, such ideas can, and commonly do, provide the basis for an optimistic relativism—for a conviction that because all types of criticism are involved with ideology as well as with texts, and because all critical methods have their interpretive uses, all applications of method can be regarded as equally legitimate. I am not aware, however, of any critic who, holding this conviction about the works of others, has not insinuated the idea that his or her own method is to be valued, not simply as an expression of ideology, but as a superior instrument for analyzing texts.

A type of criticism exists that is, indeed, less analytical than expres-

sive, whether of a critical ideology or of a critical personality. Blake
engages in this form of criticism in some of his polemical annotations
to the texts of others. Jorge Luis Borges has written a story, "The Immortals," that satirizes "the English rancher don Guillermo Blake, who
devotes his energies not only to the breeding of sheep but also to the
ramblings of the world-famous Plato and to the latest and more freak-
ish experiments in the field of surgical medicine."[1] Although this
Blake isn't quite the same one that we find in the Erdman edition,
Borges's exercise in expressive criticism is a masterly work of literature. I will have more to say about the expressive function of criticism
later. Right now, I want to consider criticism's analytical rather than
expressive function, and to discover what may be said—because or in
spite of the premises I have just listed—about the legitimacy of analytical methods: those that seek to justify themselves by their ability to
explain, read, deconstruct, contextualize, historicize, or otherwise persuasively examine something in or about literary texts.

According to my premises, literary texts permit multiple responses;
each critic must, of course, decide on the methodological response to be
made to any particular aspect of a text. The critic is free to choose any
sort of approach whatever, but some choice is going to be made, and
it can be a purposeful choice only if the critic defines (hence, restricts) the problems under consideration and carefully defines the
kind of problems to which each available method of interpretation can
usefully be addressed. Conscious control over one's own methods demands a conscious definition of each method's range of application.
None of this is compatible with either pure relativism or unlimited
skepticism, both of which, by viewing all critical methods and assumptions in the same way, deny the possibility of meaningful choices—
including (this is the absurdity) the choice of pure relativism or unlimited skepticism.

So far, I suspect, most of my Blakean audience is still with me. Most
Blakeans recognize—at least in a general way that offers little danger
of interference with their own immediate practice—that no single
method of criticism is likely to result in a comprehensive response to
the problems of a complex Blakean text. The issue of methodological
limitations is routinely mentioned in the introductory and concluding
chapters of critical studies of Blake. The discussion usually takes the
form of a concession to pluralism, in which the critic generously ad-
mits that more than one method can be used to study Blake, that the

method followed in the current study must be supplemented by the use of others, and so forth. Who among us has not made such gracious but sometimes empty concessions—concessions that come as easily from determined advocates of highly inclusive systems as from hesitant employers of shy, ad hoc approaches? Lately a new version of the concession to pluralism has become common, taking the form of a helpful but often unspecific endorsement of "contemporary" theories and methods that can be used to provide "alternative" interpretations to those supplied by "traditional" methods. But how shall we go about defining, in a way that is precise enough to give direction to further work, the appropriate range of each particular alternative response to a text?

I would suggest that a method is more usefully defined by its potential failures than by its perceived successes. Critics should, of course, be able to state in positive terms the nature and advantages of their methods. But if we cannot say what a method is not, how can we say what it is? If we cannot tell when a method is not working, how can we tell when it is? And how can we make informed choices of method without being able to tell such things about the various methods available? It is insufficient in determining even the nature of a method to assert—or to demonstrate—that it is capable of interpreting certain features of a text; one must also raise to full consciousness what the method does *not* do, the kind of circumstances that are *least* hospitable to it, and the kind of evidence that would be *least* likely to support its various assumptions and interpretations. At the point at which such evidence is actually found, the method should, to use the Blakean term, start submitting to "self-annihilation." Although the usefulness of the method may not previously have been placed in doubt, this is the point from which further theoretical investigation should begin. If no such difficulties are discovered, then the method has received a powerful legitimation within a wide range of application. No interpretive method, however, can be legitimated by a priori assumptions about its range of application.

This test by attempted limitation or falsification cannot, obviously, be used by critics who employ methods in a universalizing manner, who assume that their chosen methods will yield uniformly positive results for all texts or problems to which they are applied. No limitations posed by contesting or falsifying evidence can be hypothesized for methods presumed in advance to be of unlimited application.[2] Here one must be sure to distinguish a priori assumptions used to validate a method from predictions or generalizations submitted to tests by specific evidence. We may notice, for instance, that issues of social class impinge repeatedly on the works of certain authors; we may make assertions, subject to the possibility that falsifying evidence may be discovered, about the forms that such issues assume in these authors and even in literature generally; further, we may predict (while we are looking for falsifying evidence) that the interpretive methods we have found useful in understanding the literary relations of these issues will continue to be useful wherever such issues appear. But this is quite different from assuming that all literature is necessarily structured in certain ways by issues of social class, and that a particular method of interpretation designed to deal with such issues is necessarily useful in whatever context it is applied. Every method of thinking probably involves some kind of basic a priori assumptions; problems of credibility develop when such assumptions so fully constitute a method that its users have difficulty imagining and testing its limitations.

Now, a priori assumptions, like generalizations or predictions from evidence, may happen to be correct. And neither the making of generalizations from evidence nor the application of a priori assumptions is a cost-free activity. Literary criticism depending on the first is always in danger of having its conclusions falsified; criticism depending on the second is always in danger of being scorned or ignored, regardless of its real merits, by everyone who does not already happen to accept its ideological presuppositions. Outsiders will be inclined to view a method based on a priori assumptions with greater skepticism the larger its interpretive aspirations become, suspecting, as Hazard Adams has said, that "every theory of interpretation (or anti-interpretation) constitutes any text it chooses as an allegory of its own theory." "For a while," he observes, "all poems were metapoetic in the New Critical sense. Now they deconstruct themselves."[3] I don't think that every interpretive theory behaves in just this way, but theories that derive largely from a priori assumptions are likely to do so, and universalizing theories can hardly be prevented from doing so. "Seek, and ye shall find" is after all very bad advice for literary critics, because without benefit of self-limitations we will too easily find what we are looking for in any text we consider.

Not a new observation, of course. One remembers those graduate-seminar experiments that discovered the fallacy of New Critical assumptions about every real work of literature constituting an organic whole: when students imbued with New Critical ideas were offered passages from the telephone directory, they easily managed to uncover all sorts of organic principles in the merely alphabetical listings (the time taken to do this averaged, I believe, about fifteen minutes). Thomas E. Lewis, a Marxist critic, has protested that the charge of reductionism "is usually directed against those disciplines (Marxism, semiotics, psychoanalysis) that embody the greatest explanatory power."[4] This is naive. Almost any conceivable method, wise or foolish, can acquire practically complete explanatory power—in the eyes of those who employ it with complete confidence. Almost any method, that is to say, can, if applied without limitations, give unlimited expression to the assumptions of its users. The method of Ellis and Yeats, for example, can exert as much explanatory power over Blake as any Marxist or Freudian method—if it is employed with adequate confidence.

Discussing the relation of evidence to interpretive procedures, David Hackett Fischer, the critic of historical method, has argued that because the purpose of intellectual inquiry "is not to vindicate a method," one's "criteria of significance should not be methodological, but substantive in nature. They should always be grounded in the nature of the problem itself and not in the tools of problem solving."[5] The explanatory power of an interpretive method cannot really be measured unless it is always undergoing trial by the most difficult aspects of the problems it faces—by those aspects of the text and its various contexts that may not be effectively or efficiently addressed by the method.[6] This implies no mystification of the text (however one defines that controversial entity), such as would result from the insistence that all legitimate interpretations must evaluate it in just the same way, the way miraculously imposed by an omnipotent set of textual signs: "nothing," as Fischer says, "is literally self-explanatory."[7] It implies, rather, that methods can legitimate their analytical functions only when they are brought in contact with substantive evidence that they have not themselves produced, and that is allowed the possibility of contesting their assumptions, generalizations, or specific interpretations.[8]

When Blake's text is not granted enough extramethodological power to exclude certain interpretations, every critic acquires an unlimited ability to create personal systems of meaning. To clear away all the old obstructions erected by ideas of a substantial, evidentiary text is also to clear away the foundations of sharable meaning. But (to quote E. D. Hirsch, Jr.) "at the last ditch few would . . . be so eccentric as to deny the sharability of meaning. To whom and to what purpose would they address their denial?"[9] This is not just a humorous remark at the expense of idle speculation; the political, let alone the literary, results of dispensing with substantial texts are too unpleasant to make light of. Methods that can operate unchecked by extramethodological facts surrender apparently complete power over Blake to every critic who employs them.[10] Yet that power is a very questionable commodity. It must be maintained not by reference to any enduring text, but by rhetorical flash or by the academic prestige derived from a favorable location on a "cutting edge," or at the "center" of some "tradition."

Blake was right in suggesting that "mystery" produces unjustifiable power relations—and we as critics have a tendency to produce the mysteries that give us power. To assume that texts, because of their historicity or multisignation, or the diverse perspectives of members of their audience, cannot be used as methodologically limiting evidence is to render them just as mysterious as they are made by a reverence for all-powerful and self-explanatory textual signs. As I indicated at the beginning, critical methods are ways of choosing and evaluating textual evidence. If they are to acquire analytical authority, however, they must possess the self-corrective ability to recognize—even actively to seek out—the evidence that might contest or modify their assumptions. This is a difficult but hardly an impossible requirement. The only alternative to meeting it is to proceed as if every analytical method can legitimately act with unlimited freedom in relation to evidence, to proceed as if every method can act, for all practical purposes, as its own final evidence. Such a procedure, of course, works against its own logic, since it obscures the crucial distinction between method and evidence on which any concept of the hegemony of method over evidence must be based.

To expand my argument, I need to cite specific examples of what I consider real problems in the works of real critics. These citations are not meant to indicate disapproval of any critic's total work. Such is the complexity of Blake's text that no work of Blake criticism that I can recall depends for its authority on only one line of argument or set of methodological assumptions. Clarity is an important consideration in my choice of examples, and the critics whom I cite tend to be those who are admirably forthright in their use of method. To specify an example, then, of the problems involved in methods that advance universal a priori assumptions about Blake, I will mention a recent book that offers many insights into the prophecies, Nelson Hilton's *Literal Imagination: Blake's Vision of Words*. Hilton advances the theory, based on his study of linguistics, psychoanalysis, and anthropology, that every word in a text has an unlimited range of meanings: "The word depends on how it is perceived. . . . Every word has unlimited potential. . . . every time we use a word (or any other sign) we cannot possibly truly know all we are saying—or, put another way, we always mean more than we think and read more than we see."[11] Hilton does not of course study a great variety of words and discover that every word always and necessarily has one more meaning than the meanings he can perceive: that would not be possible. His is a universal a priori assumption rather than a generalization to be tested by evidence. Like other universal assumptions, this one has an ironically constricting effect: it depends on the discounting of something. Hilton's assumption requires that he discount the possibility of any simple or limited meanings; so, for instance, when Blake refers to the "Litteral expression" of the "Divine Revelation" (*M*42:14, E143), Hilton argues that "Litteral" does not refer to "actual" or "straightforward" expressions.[12] The crucial word, then, does not have an "unlimited potential"; Hilton's interpretation relies, not on his universal assumption about words, but on the history of this particular word's spelling and on Hilton's understanding of Blake's philosophy of language as expressed in other passages. In one important case, Hilton's assumption about the unlimited meanings of Blake's words has been shown to be incapable of an un-self-contradictory interpretation of Blake's text. Facts of this sort might be used in the further development of Hilton's linguistic theory, for they indicate points at which his ideas concerning plurisignation need to be supplemented by theories of contextual or philological inquiry.

Unlimited a priori assumptions are no less influential in the older than in the newer interpretations of Blake, and they exist in many forms. They may be assumptions about the nature of Blake's concepts and symbols, such as Kathleen Raine's assumption that "traditional metaphysics" is so extensively relevant to Blake's ideas that his works "can be understood" "only in the light of" that metaphysics.[13] They may be assumptions about the organizing principles of Blake's work, such as Northrop Frye's assumption that "the engraved poems of Blake form a canon" and that "anything admitted to that canon, whatever its date, not only belongs in a unified scheme but is in accord with a permanent structure of ideas."[14] They may be assumptions about a particular concept that is given a general rather than a restrictive or limiting definition. A restrictive definition reduces the number of meanings that may be assigned to a word and limits the number of interpretive contexts in which it can appropriately be used. A general definition, however, can be used to justify almost any interpretation. "Dialectic," as it is frequently employed in Blake criticism, is a good example of a concept without a sufficiently limiting definition. An a priori assumption is made that Blake is a pervasively dialectical poet, and because few, if any, limitations are imposed on the possible meanings of the term, dialectics are easily located virtually everywhere in his writings—in every kind of duality, parallel, contrast, and apparent contradiction. When one employs a nonrestrictive working definition, one cannot easily determine what sort of pairing would *not* constitute a dialectic.[15] Nonrestrictive definitions and unlimited assumptions can sometimes lead to interpretive success, because they can encourage one to look closely for, and actually to discover, elements in a text that confirm them; they can also lead one to confuse confirmation with the results of an unduly general treatment of words and concepts.

My way of thinking about these issues has important precedents in the work of the Chicago Critics, a group of writers who have had remarkably little effect on Blake criticism.[16] There are a number of possible reasons for this. The Chicago Critics are especially concerned with combating the fallacies of the New Criticism, a method that, in its severer moods, has never been widely used to interpret Blake; his work can scarcely be analyzed without studying political, religious, and historical questions that the New Critics often consider extraneous. Also, the Chicago Critics themselves sometimes concentrate too intensely for Blakean purposes on the discovery of distinctively literary "forms"; the foreground of their work is often occupied, naturally enough, by consideration of those formal aspects of literature that their particular method seeks to identify, while consideration of the means to be employed in judging and legitimating the array of methods available for other purposes recedes into the background.[17] Nevertheless, the criticism of the Chicago school offers powerful arguments for the use of empirical procedures in testing hypotheses and weighing the advantages of methods. It may be this fact, more than any other, that has warned Blakeans away from the Chicago Critics. Blake has some hard things to say against empirical reason, though he often uses it well; and the safest prediction about any new commentary on his works is that it will argue uncompromisingly against "reason" and "experiment"—and that its argument will emphasize its own superior rationality.

Under these circumstances, it would be helpful to have some fresh studies aimed at clarifying the various things that reason means to Blake and to Blakeans. Still more helpful, however, would be a fresh look at the practical techniques that can be used to test critics' ideas about the role of reason or of anything else in Blake's text. Techniques that need to be fully understood, rather than dismissed as the products of some false, rationalistic religion, include (1) the reduction of a priori assumptions to the minimum necessary to begin explanation of a text (not to guarantee a successful conclusion); (2) the formation of restrictive (rather than general) definitions; (3) the formation of competing interpretive hypotheses that are valued for their ability to be refuted (not just supported) by evidence that might actually be discovered; (4) the abandonment, modification, or reconstruction (on the basis of newly discovered evidence) of interpretations that have already been falsified in some respect; (5) the consequent identification, with increasing precision, both of the effective limits of the interpretive methods employed and of the problems that lie beyond those limits and that need to be investigated with new or revised methods.

I do not mean to suggest, amid all these remarks about methods, hypotheses, and evidence, that every study of Blake should contain lengthy reviews of testing procedures, discarded hypotheses, and so on; or that every critic should find a good method and stick Urizenically within its carefully tested range ($U4:36-40$, E72); or that we need to survey every piece of evidence we have about Blake before we can start to interpret a single passage—no intuitions allowed. On the contrary: most of the self-testing that I have been discussing should go on before the typewriter is ever plugged in, and readers will usually be quite able to see if it has; every critic of Blake should be cognizant of many more methods than one, if only because hypotheses are difficult to evaluate if alternative hypotheses cannot be imagined;[18] and no combination of methods will accomplish much if it cannot build on educated intuitions about particular texts.

Vigorous objections may nevertheless be made to my emphasis on the testing techniques I've outlined. Two such objections arose when the preceding pages were first read by other people interested in interpretive theory. The two objections were nicely balanced: one group of colleagues argued that there is little reason to insist on techniques that critics will probably not, in fact, be able or willing to use effectively; another group argued that there is little reason to insist on techniques that are already in general use, little point in emphasizing conventional precepts not specially relevant to the present or future needs of Blake studies.

The first objection is based on the idea that critics who formally adopt the techniques I advocate can find ways of keeping them from having any important influence on their work; they may, for instance, seek to legitimate their favorite methods by "testing" them merely against straw-man hypotheses. And, of course, critics can usually be depended upon to refuse to reach agreement with one another even about their restrictive definitions of such terms as "dialectic." True enough: no set of critical procedures will ever drive the ridiculous from life, or induce universal harmony. But it does not follow that more modest, but nevertheless very important, goals are unattainable. Critics who do not wish to test their methods fairly can hardly show us what the use of testing procedures can accomplish; but critics who do perceive a positive value in the search for methodological limitations can employ procedures to indicate what may and may not authoritatively be said within the boundaries of various critical languages, and to reveal relationships between methodological assumption and textual meaning that are something besides a presumed identity.

If the first objection suggests a counsel of despair, the second suggests a far too reassuring view of the exigencies of current literary study in general and of Blake studies in particular. Never before has academic discourse been so factionalized among contending schools of theory-derived criticism, and every school stands ready to offer a systematic interpretation of Blake's text. When this sort of factionalization develops, critics competing in the academic marketplace understandably emphasize the breadth and ambition of their chosen theories and the ability of those theories to supply new, "powerful," and provocative interpretations; they shrink at submitting their methods to tests meant to reveal their limitations. Jonathan Culler has noted with approval the tendency of current literary theories to provide "the source of intellectual youth's attempt to differentiate itself from the past"; theories recommend themselves by their "persuasive novelty."[19] But if Culler is right, this is the time to pay particularly close attention to basic techniques that enable one to judge the analytical persuasiveness actually achieved by each of the many novelties available.

Unfortunately, the present state of Blake studies gives special encouragement to theoretical speculation of the aggressively unlimited kind. Blake has been splendidly edited; his life and times have been carefully investigated; his symbolism has ceased to seem mysterious. Study in these areas will continue, but fundamental reconstitutions of his text are less likely to come from patient research than from the application of innovative critical theories—and in this work, boldness will earn a premium of attention. The theories to which Blake's text is most vulnerable are globally unifying ones. His text is exceptionally varied and complicated; its sources and implications are exceptionally diverse; yet it is obviously the product of a single, strong intelligence, an intelligence continually producing its own global theories. Critics of Blake, who normally confront his work with great sympathy, must suffer an exceptionally powerful temptation to find a single, powerful theory that can assert the unity of the text and still account for all its variations and complexities. Under these circumstances, only an emphasis on the importance of techniques that can promote a wide array of consciously limited approaches to the text can keep Blake studies from fragmenting into a peculiar jumble of contradictory yet ostensibly global interpretations.

In order to consider some of the ways in which multiple responses to a particular text can be generated and then made to reveal their limitations, I have chosen a brief passage from Blake, one that has not attracted a great deal of commentary—perhaps simply because it is capable of prompting some annoying questions about the degree to which we understand its author's methods. Toward the end of *The Marriage of Heaven and Hell,* a Blakean devil informs a Blakean angel that

> if Jesus Christ is the greatest man, you ought to love him in the greatest degree; now hear how he has given his sanction to the law of ten commandments: did he not mock at the sabbath, and so mock the sabbaths God? murder those who were murderd because of him? turn away the law from the woman taken in adultery? steal the labor of others to support him? bear false witness

when he omitted making a defence before Pilate? covet when he pray'd for his disciples, and when he bid them shake off the dust of their feet against such as refused to lodge them? I tell you, no virtue can exist without breaking these ten commandments: Jesus was all virtue, and acted from impulse: not from rules. (*MHH*23–24, E43)

On the meaning of this passage, and on its significance in the context of *The Marriage*, practitioners of many types of criticism will be likely, if pressed, to have something to say. The literary historian, for example, can be expected to point out an important fact: the Biblical Jesus hardly acted in the "murderous" and "covetous" spirit of the Jesus in *MHH*23; further, Blake knew this to be the case, because, as the literary historian is delighted to show you by copious quotations from other sections of Blake's works, he had a thorough knowledge of the Bible. Wishing to improve on this limited insight, the literary historian may conclude that *MHH*23 is clearly ironic in one of that word's many senses. This conclusion is supported by the presence of numerous apparent ironies in *The Marriage*, and by the arguments of numerous commentators who believe that Blake refuses to identify his own ideas completely with the devilish ideas presented in the work.[20] Our critic will perhaps decide that *MHH*23 is part of a consistently ironic discourse, or—desiring to be as specific as possible about this vague business of irony—present the passage as an extreme example of the manner in which Blake separates himself from his spokesman when he wants to arouse his audience in a special way. Harold Bloom's reading of *MHH*23 may be brought in here: "Blake is resorting again to the rhetoric of shock. . . . As argument, this last Memorable Fancy is weak, but we are not intended to take it as more than a fiery polemic, uttered for its fire and not its light."[21] Such interpretations offer some falsifiable hypotheses, one of which—that concerning the ironic consistency of *The Marriage* or of its "hellish" passages—is easily falsified by a look at those devilish expressions that, if judged to be ironic, are ironic in a sense that counteracts the ironic thrust of *MHH*23: "The cut worm forgives the plow. . . . The most sublime act is to set another before you" (*MHH*7, 8; E35, 36). If it is correct to assume that Blake's devilry is consistently ironic, then the irony stems from inconsistent ideas: at one time, Jesus is ironically praised for violent rebelliousness; at another, both worms and people are ironically praised for conduct that looks suspiciously like a mild obedience to the Sermon on the Mount. But suppose that *MHH*23 is meant to be taken with a large quantity of salt because it contains shocking, polemical, and cavalier arguments. This suggests the falsifiable implication that Blake is not fully serious whenever he is writing in this vein—an hypothesis for which contesting evidence is readily available.

Let us consider, then, whether we can take *MHH*23 completely straight. A Marxist critic provides a strong statement to this effect, seeing the passage as an "antinomian" attack on "middle-class moralism," and allying it with the spirit of the seventeenth-century Ranters.[22] This gives a wider, and possibly richer, context to the passage, yet the analysis is in certain ways difficult to legitimate. There is a problem of definition. If the middle-class moralism that Blake attacks can be recognized by its opposition to such things as murder, theft, and bearing false witness, then virtually all systems of morality are middle-class, and virtually all attacks on moralism can be regarded as attacks on the middle-class variety. Yet this is to give "middle class" so broad a meaning that it will be hard to determine when it is used inappropriately. Once we have a restrictive definition of "middle class," of course, we can construct testable hypotheses about the degree of importance, if any, that *The Marriage* gives to the concept of the middle class: if it is an important concept, it will probably not only appear in some form but be reiterated or otherwise emphasized by identifiable literary devices. Another problem, however, lies in the attempt to support the straight interpretation by placing *MHH*23 in the revolutionary tradition of the Ranters. We can read texts in the light of a tradition only if we already have a fairly good idea of what they mean and can estimate fairly precisely their degree of affinity with a tradition and its significant variants. When a text makes clearly identifiable references to figures, documents, or ideas within a tradition (such as this text makes to Jesus, the Bible, and the concepts of the Mosaic law), we will have an easier time making testable hypotheses about the nature of the relationship than we will when a text makes no such references and we have to select for ourselves the relevant figures and documents and speculate about what tradition, and how much of it, best fits the text. Relation in time may be important; Blake's implicit references to contemporary figures and ideas are sometimes (though certainly not always) more clearly identifiable than his implicit references to phenomena of the distant past. In the case of *MHH*23, the critic's allusion to the radical tradition of the Ranters has interpretive suggestiveness but not interpretive authority, since *MHH*23 can be read in such a way as to show in a similarly plausible manner its affinity or lack of affinity with a variety of ethical or antiethical traditions of which Blake may or may not have been aware.

But surely it is proper to be concerned, not just about the intended meaning of a particular text, but also about the nature of the mind that produced it, especially when the argument of the text, if it is not ironic, appears at least highly idiosyncratic. The psychoanalytic interpreter may suggest, for instance, that the subconscious logic of *MHH*23 is that of an attempt to involve Jesus in Blake's own Oedipal conflicts: "Blake's outrageous argument is forced on him by the need to identify Jesus completely with the rebel son." This interpretation reminds us that not all conflicts are intellectual or political, and its reading of Blake's emotional temperature is supported by the apparent fact that "elsewhere in *Marriage,* he identifies with the aggressor."[23] But how far can we take this insight as a guide to Blake's psychological structure as manifested in *The Marriage?* If Blake insistently identified with the aggressor, then we would not expect to find the kind of aphorisms, already mentioned, in which he appears to recommend forgiveness and acquiescence. We may explain his attitude in such passages as aggression reassuring itself "against fears of retaliation."[24] We may be right. But this logic will make it hard to hypothesize any evidence that might falsify or modify our general assumption about Blake's aggressive impulses. The interpretations that result from this assumption may be suggestive about certain features of the text, but they will not be accepted as generally authoritative by people who are not predisposed to find the assumption true.

Here the critic who is concerned more with the verbal structures of the text than with its background in Blake's ideas or personality will protest that everyone else has missed the joke: Blake's devil is addressing solemn people like us with the sort of verbal play that, empty in itself, is taken for reality by empty angelic minds. The devil uses highly charged ethical terms such as "murder" and "false witness" as if he were giving angels the kind of discourse—a sermon—that they evidently most enjoy, but he is purposely stripping these terms of meaning. "Murder" and "false witness" are signs with no more actual signification than the reference to a Biblical "Jesus"; if they point to anything, it is only to the nullity of all conventional moral discourse.

This method of interpretation certainly accounts for the seeming out-
rageousness of Blake's words and links them with the dramatic context
of the devil and his audience, but can it show why it should be used on
this passage and not on others? Difficulties arise when one tests its
logic on the discourse in other parts of *The Marriage*. Elsewhere, "Ezekiel," "Jeremiah," "the Devil," and "Blake" himself say playful or outrageous things, but these are not all apparently without conventionally
serious signification—unless, that is, we make a universal assumption
that Blake intended all of his verbal signs to be without such signification.

All four of the above methods of interpretation have limitations, but
when considered together they can contribute something to the investigation of *MHH*23. One of their contributions is a revelation of the real
difficulty of a passage that may appear very simple to the single vision
provided by single critical methods; if Blake attempted a joke, perhaps
he achieved a conundrum. The conflicting but more or less plausible
interpretations to which the passage can be subjected suggest the need
for further investigation and indicate some directions that it should
take. We need to take a close look at Blakean irony and humor and
try to describe the structures that characteristically distinguish them
from literal, direct, or "serious" statement. We need to make usefully
restrictive definitions of the various ethical systems and traditions that
may be within the range of Blake's allusions, and make testable hypotheses about the ways in which he typically signals his favorable or
unfavorable judgments of such systems. We need to investigate the
possibility of contradictions in Blake's ethical views from one point to
another in *The Marriage* (and other works), define standards by which
we can measure his consistency, and try to refine our procedures for
estimating variations in the quality of his emotional involvement with
his material. In pursuing such questions, we may have recourse to certain forms of the methods I have considered. But even if we do not,
they have been of heuristic use in exposing the problems of the text,
which is a long way from definitive interpretation. The recognition that
it may lie beyond the limit of current explanation should be viewed as
a real addition to knowledge.

I have focused up to now on methodological assumptions operating
at the primary level of evaluation, where they work to determine the
critic's choices of textual or historically contextual elements to consider, to emphasize, to explain away, or to ignore. Assumptions in

which the critic places full confidence can fully determine these choices. But there is another level of evaluation—the level on which the worth of a text or an author is judged; and there is an assumption generated at this higher level that has probably exerted more influence on Blake criticism than has any other. This assumption is substantially as well as instrumentally evaluative: the pervasive assumption of Blake's success as a thinker, poet, artist, or human being. It is an extraordinary fact that every method of criticism so far applied to Blake—theosophic, literary-historical, mythic, psychological, political, semiotic—has been able to produce enthusiastic vindications of his ideas and methods. When the immense Blakean critical literature gets the serious political and sociological study it deserves, this fact should engender a good deal of speculation. Interpretations of particular texts, concepts, and techniques vary wildly in Blake criticism, but the evaluated Blake retains his oracular status. The remarkable uniformity of high-level value judgments in Blake criticism would not be possible without the additional, implicit assumption that there is an unlimited range of agreement between Blake's method of evaluating life, art, and his own texts, and his critics' methods of evaluation, whatever these may be. This assumption has naturally led to a failure, as Adams puts it, "to acknowledge the possibility that things might have gone wrong here and there" with Blake;[25] but the effect on critical reconstitutions of his text is not entirely favorable to the reconstituted "Blake"—for what kind of author is he whose work can be rendered unlimitedly hospitable to positive evaluation by virtually every kind of criticism? The author in question is, in W. J. T. Mitchell's phrase, a "safely canonized" Blake; in Brenda S. Webster's, a "normalised" Blake.[26] In the vocabulary of Hans Robert Jauss, this Blake could be called the author of "culinary" literature—work that (formerly dangerous, perhaps) exerts no power to disturb its readers or change their "horizon of expectations."[27] This is Blake regarded not as an evaluative challenge, but as a pleasant, precooked, preevaluated commodity. As Tzvetan Todorov has said in a direct and insightful essay on the importance of engaging in real "dialogues" with the authors whom one studies, "The only case in which dialogic criticism is impossible is when the critic finds himself in complete agreement with his author: no discussion can then occur. Dialogue is then replaced by apology."[28] And apology is generally incapable of revealing areas where further analytical and evaluative work needs to be done.

Many simple examples of Blake reconstituted in the image of critical desires can be found in commentaries on the area of his life and works where prophecy meets politics. Critical literature of many different kinds has asserted or strongly implied that Blake was a prophet in the mode of his own zealous Ezekiel, intensely studious of raising his fellow-citizens "into a perception of the infinite" and taking "duty to his country" as his "first consideration" (*MHH*13, E39; annotations to Watson, E611). This general understanding is often a major support of specific interpretations, such as those that defend the structure of *Jerusalem* by emphasizing Blake's attempt, through daring manipulations of poetic form, to disturb and redirect his audience's perceptions. The assumption that Blake was intensely interested in his audience has been challenged by questions about his "solipsistic absorption in the silent, solitary obsession with 'Writing' for no audience but [him]self."[29] Such questions are still at variance with common opinion, and common opinion is supported by plenty of positive evidence, the best of which is the prophecies' magnificent calls to the reawakening of Albion, and their identification of Blake's work with the public work of Los. The most powerful contesting evidence lies, of course, in the stubborn fact of the inaccessibility of the great majority of Blake's illuminated books to the contemporary "Public" that he addresses in *Jerusalem* (as distinguished from the late-twentieth-century scholars whom he addresses in his current well-commentaried text). There is something very curious about Blake's denunciation of intricate machinery made to "perplex youth in their outgoings" (*J*65:21–22, E216)—in a work that is merely perplexing, rather than rousing or disturbing, to people who lack specialized training in its own intricate machinery. We cannot ignore this tired and obvious, but politically significant problem: in several ways Blake's works were, indeed, unduly "Expensive to the Buyer" (letter to Dawson Turner 9 June 1818, E771).[30] We should not assume that Blake cared nothing about an audience (we have evidence to the contrary) but we should not analyze him as if his primary concern were usually with the social effect of his works, and not with their artistic and intellectual integrity—a very different thing. If we are to chart this area of competing concerns, our analyses of Blake the social prophet evidently need to be aided by analyses of his artistic theory and psychology. The way is also open for an analysis exploring the difficulties of a subversive thinker impelled by his chosen methods to produce artistic and intellectual luxury goods: Blake is the forerunner of the twentieth-century avant-garde in more ways than one. We aren't likely to get to any of these analyses, however, as long as our methods and judgments are by-products of limitlessly positive assumptions about Blake's political enterprise.

But suppose that all of these analyses have been performed and we have a splendid array of unfalsified hypotheses about Blake's political and prophetic work (and an equally splendid array of hypotheses that have been tested and discarded). Will we have a final evaluative constitution of his text? No. In some respects we will be farther away from it than we are now—and in some respects, luckily. Certain hypotheses (about Blake's psychological processes, for instance) may remain unfalsified simply because we may never have enough evidence to test them fairly; we will, however, have an easier time estimating the probability of these hypotheses, since their context will be provided by a considerably reduced number of *possibly* authoritative ideas about Blake. And, fortunately, we will be in a better position for open debate about high-level value judgments than we are when we are intent on reading our own values directly into the text. One critic's evaluation will, perhaps, offer Blake's text as a warning example of the political impotence of a purist aesthetic creed; another's evaluation will offer a text that illustrates Blake's healthy lack of obsession with politics—about which, this critic thinks, Blake never had very good ideas anyway. These critics will not agree: why should they? At this point, both are engaging in a type of expressive criticism, but this type of criticism can have its own type of legitimacy. We read Blake criticism, not just to have Blake explained to us (often we think we can do a better job of this than any of the critics we read), but to see how other people judge him according to their own systems of values. We have multiple evaluative responses to a critic's text, and within the range of those responses are evaluations—positive or negative—of the critic's expressive work with the text.

A critical method pursued in full conscious awareness of its analytical limitations will still fail to win full acceptance among readers who reject some of its implicit or explicit values. Readers of Blake may, for example, react against those values because they do not consider them "Blakean" enough. But acts of critical evaluation assert the reality of difference: even the supposedly Blakean critic is likely to differ greatly in values and assumptions from the Blake whom the critic attempts to evaluate in accordance with Blakean principles; readers of critical texts are likely to differ greatly from the critics whom they evaluate. This idea is simple enough, but it suggests the related idea that the number and interest of evaluative responses can be increased by making such differences as I have mentioned as clearly apparent as possible. Blake critics have often underemphasized their differences from Blake, and even, despite outbreaks of contentiousness, their differences from one another—perhaps because many people cherish the hidden assumption that everyone else's theories can ultimately be subsumed by their own, more nearly global, notions. Critical methods of many types can work to counteract this tendency, and while so doing can demonstrate their legitimately controversial and expressive functions. To enable their methods to do this, critics should exert a conscious effort to describe for themselves yet another kind of limit besides those mentioned above: they should describe the line that divides what seems uncertain, difficult, or even hopelessly wrong in Blake from what can most easily be translated into the terms of their own texts or appropriated by their own ideologies. Drawing a line of this type is not an exercise in pure objectivity: the Blake under scrutiny is still the Blake of the critic's understanding. But if no such line is drawn, the use of almost any critical method is liable to produce an illegitimate folding together of primary and high-level evaluations, a false sense of identity between Blake and the critic (what Todorov calls "a single, hybrid voice" in which the "respective contributions" of author and analyst "are not clearly distinguished"[31]), and a consequent reduction in the method's ability to provoke complex evaluative responses to the Blake being discussed.

From what I have been saying, it should be clear that my particular method of approaching critical problems is not fully "Blakean" (that is, not fully in accord with Blake's own practices), and that it will probably yield not just descriptions but negative value judgments of some of Blake's text. Blake's idea of a firm "bounding line" or limit between one thing and another is greatly to my critical taste, as is the principled contentiousness implied by his emphasis on "Mental Fight" and warring "contraries." I cannot sympathize, however, with his strong tendency to universalize (it is no accident that "all" is the word of greatest frequency in Erdman's concordance to Blake, and "every" not far behind[32]), with the special pleading in which he engages in some of his criticism of other authors, or with the loose or merely invidious way of defining terms that supports some of his universalizing and special pleading. I doubt that Blake uses the methods of legitimate analytical criticism, for instance, in his attempt to establish, in the annotations to Bishop Watson, that "Tom Paine is a better Christian than the Bishop," whom he considers a mere follower of "State Religion which is the Source of all Cruelty" (E620, 618). My position is, of course, subject to challenge. Someone else may produce effectively contesting evidence or arguments about Blake's critical method in the annotations to Watson, or in other works. In certain cases, I cannot pursue my own investigations of Blake with the high degree of empathy that has often (as "experiment" indicates) recovered riches from passages that I might have considered barren. Where my kind of skeptical inquiry reaches its limits of sympathetic interpretation, other analyses may possibly proceed with great success.

I am sure that other limitations of my analysis will be evident by now. I have excluded certain varieties of relativism and pluralism only to concede to others. I have tried to rule out those invertebrate forms that are prepared to view every analysis as equally acceptable; I have willingly allowed the form that encourages many different interpretive methods to work at solving the many different problems to which they are adapted, and that doubts the ability of any absolutist system to solve them all. I have also allowed the form that grants the interest, often the argumentative stimulation, of a variety of methods that cannot be legitimated strictly in respect to their analytical procedures. Because criticism derives not just from texts, but from critics' values and their experience of the larger life beyond the text, we will never lack interpretations that give us the desire for "mental fight": only let those values be distinct enough, and clearly enough distinguished from Blake's own, to tell us with whom and over what we are fighting.

But to return to the values and assumptions from which my own analysis proceeds—are they not the formations of meager, common-sense empiricism, unaided by many formidable systems of thought that have proven suggestive to other critics? Yes. I have tried to limit my working assumptions to a few that I think most readers of literature share, rather than to reason from those on which one specialized procedure, and no others, may be based. Unfortunately, such assumptions are of limited usefulness: they cannot, by themselves, inform us about Blake's historical context, analyze his psychology, supply the meanings of his symbols, reconstruct or deconstruct his values. They merely suggest methods of checking what we are doing as critics, and of keeping in contact with each other and our wider audience by means of common reference points in a common, though very basic, logic. Most people will agree with Webster when she argues, in justification of the psychoanalytic approach to Blake, that we need "to go beyond . . . commonsense psychology" if we are to understand certain aspects of his work.[33] This is very probably true. No method that consists merely of commonsense procedures will be sufficient for the study of Blake. But it is useful to remember that to go beyond common sense is not necessarily to violate common sense,[34] and that if we do need to violate it, we should clearly specify our grounds for doing so, at least if we want to converse with anyone not in strict ideological affinity with us. Both persuasion and instructive controversy require some sharing of language and concepts, some firm foundation in the "rough basement"[35] of common language, common notions of factuality, and common experience of what it means to explore problems and test assumptions.[36]

This talk about common sense and procedures of limitation may seem dull and limited in the worst sense, because it insists that we inhabit a world (not necessarily a *fallen* one) that is different from the limitless world of certain Blakean visions, and because it imposes a check on some of the creative energy that we might use in perfecting great critical systems. But there are even worse kinds of limitation—including those suggested by Blake's observation, based on what he calls "plain fact," that "Any man of mechanical talents may from the writings of Paracelsus or Jacob Behmen, produce ten thousand volumes of equal value with Swedenborg's"; such mechanical thinkers can, however, only hold "a candle in sunshine." Swedenborg, according to Blake, had trapped himself in an a priori assumption, the idea that "Angels" (including Swedenborg, naturally) are "the only wise." No wonder Swedenborg's interpretations of the visionary world are of strikingly limited value: they originate in "a confident insolence sprouting from systematic reasoning" (*MHH*21–22, E42–43). The analogy is plain. Late-twentieth-century critics can readily produce ten thousand volumes of confident interpretation by applying and con-

Synecdoche and Method

Hazard Adams

In a square foot of paper is contained the boundless space
Lu Chi

To see a World in a Grain of Sand
And a Heaven in a Wild Flower
Hold Infinity in the palm of your Hand
And Eternity in an hour
Blake, "Auguries of Innocence"

Method we tend to identify as opposed to the use of tropes; we would, if we could, sort tropes out of what we would like to constitute as a rigorously logical, antimythical activity.[1] Yet if we are going to speak of poetic method, as we often do, it appears that we shall have to allow tropes to play a role in it. The alternative would seem to be abandonment of the term. Yet Coleridge introduces a trope into the very center of his treatment of method in his essays in *The Friend*. For Coleridge, a man of education is characterized by "the unpremeditated and evidently habitual *arrangement* of his words, grounded on the habit of foreseeing, in each integral part, or (more plainly) in every sentence, the whole that he intends to communicate. However irregular and desultory his talk, there is *method* in the fragments."[2] This trope is synecdoche. Though we usually think of synecdoche spatially (part and whole), here Coleridge speaks of a whole that the part anticipates, thereby introducing a temporal character. Further, what counts is the relation of part to part and part to whole: "Method . . . becomes natural to the mind which has been accustomed to contemplate not things only, or for their own sake alone, but likewise and chiefly the *relation* of things" (451). He notes that the habit of method causes "things the most remote and diverse in time, place, and outward circumstance, [to be] brought into mutual contiguity and succession" (455). Method

($\mu\epsilon\theta o\delta o\varsigma$) means literally in Greek a way or path of transit, and so there comes with it the notion, according to Coleridge, of "progressive transition" and thus of process in time (457). I shall return to the connection of method with temporal process when I discuss William Blake's poetic method as synecdochic and metaphoric and the issues this raises for interpretation or critical reading of his works. Before proceeding, however, it is necessary to consider some difficulties that have arisen in critical theory with respect to the term "synecdoche."

In his remarks, Coleridge is discussing a process of thought not necessarily poetic. His employment of the terms "contiguity" and "succession" suggests those syntagmatic relations with which the trope metonymy has been associated ever since Roman Jakobson's famous essay distinguishing metonymy from metaphor.[3] From the point of view of literary criticism, Jakobson makes a mistake in drawing no distinction of any importance between metonymy and synecdoche. He treats synecdoche merely as a type of metonymy or relation by contiguity. (He may be quite correct with regard to the apparent indifference of the two in matters having to do with aphasia, a phenomenon the observation of which launched him on his subject.) The failure to distinguish is by no means unusual. In a recent book on figures of speech, for example, Arthur Quinn expresses the view that synecdoche is a kind of metonymy, though when he comes around to quoting an example from Blake he becomes uneasy and calls it and certain others "ineffably real synecdoches, if such there be."[4] He then declares such synecdoches to be symbols.

The failure to distinguish is also apparent in Claude Lévi-Strauss's use of the term and in Edmund Leach's accepting commentary.[5] It is also the characteristic behavior of Jacques Lacan.[6] There is a distinction, of course, in psychoanalytic usage between metonymy and synecdoche. The former parallels displacement and the latter condensation of the dream-thought. But both perform the same basic function, and so it is a distinction without a significant difference. In Sigmund Freud's *Interpretation of Dreams*, there is something of a mystery about condensation. Freud remarks:

> One is inclined to regard the dream-thoughts that have been brought to light as complete material, whereas if the work of interpretation is carried further it may reveal still more thoughts concealed behind the dream. I have already had occasion to point

out that it is in fact never possible to be sure that a dream has been completely interpreted. Even if the solution seems satisfactory and without gaps, the possibility always remains that the dream may have yet another meaning. Strictly speaking, then, it is impossible to determine the amount of condensation.[7]

Several comments indicating what Freud implies in this passage are necessary before I proceed:

1. There is a meaning to be discovered behind the manifest dream. Elsewhere Freud rejects the idea that the dream as remembered may inevitably have omissions and that what is left is not strictly speaking a condensation but a congeries of fragments. The manifest dream contains this hidden meaning and is not to be regarded in interpretation as a fragment or set of fragments with some of the fragments missing.

2. Even assuming (as does Freud) a meaning to be reached, the interpreter cannot know whether it has been reached.

3. The manifest dream is a synecdoche of this meaning.

4. This meaning is in some sense there and ideally recoverable, but it may not be in practice fully recoverable in interpretation.

5. Thus condensation is synecdochic in a sense beyond the rhetorical definition of tropes as figures. It is a microcosm, not merely a part that stands for a whole; it is identical to the whole. This I shall call a *radical synecdoche*.

6. Condensation is therefore a relation in which the macrocosm or dream-thought is posited only hypothetically, not fully known, or (to be more accurate) we can never know whether or not it is fully known. We can never be sure of its completeness in interpretation.

7. In that sense, condensation may be called an *open synecdoche*, and, as I shall try to show, it is locked in a negating opposition to a *closed synecdoche* and differs from the kind of synecdoche produced by Blakean method, which is a contrary to this open/closed negation. The differences are that: (a) it is not temporal and progressive as the Blakean is; and (b) as it implies a completed macrocosm somewhere, it also implies that though we might know the macrocosm we can never know that we know it. (It is, in other words, a synecdoche that is probably open.) The Freudian synecdochic relation would properly be examined by a "hermeneutics of suspicion," in Paul Ricoeur's phrase, assuming hidden meaning to be recovered, even if we cannot know that it has been recovered.[8]

8. Insofar as condensation and displacement do the same kind of work and the work is what interests Freud, he need not offer a distinction between synecdoche and metonymy.

Others have made such a distinction. Hayden White describes synecdoche as "integrative," metonymy as "reductive."[9] By reduction he means the identification of two things by treating one thing (the contained, act, effect, etc.) as a manifestation of another thing (container, cause, agent, spirit, essence, etc.). By "integration" he means a relation of "shared qualities." Here White's example is the statement "He is all heart" (34). White sees "heart," itself a word used figuratively, spreading through to the whole of the man as a quality or essence pervading all of him. But then White complicates the matter by suggesting that some statements can be read either as a metonymy or as a synecdoche, as if a trope is defined merely according to the act of reading. In both cases, he distinguishes between what he calls the "literal assertion" and the "figurative understanding," even as he rejects the authority of the assertion in favor of the act of reading. Still, White strives to establish a difference. The outcome seems to be a distinction that, if pressed a little further, claims for synecdoche a relation privileging difference.

Giovanni Battista Vico, White's early-eighteenth-century mentor, identifies the tropes metaphor, metonymy, and synecdoche with primitive man's "poetic logic," characteristic of an age where people were unable to abstract forms and qualities from objects to make "abstract universals" and therefore created "poetic" or concrete universals "by metaphor from the human body and its parts and from the human senses and passions."[10] The reason for this is that "as rational metaphysics teaches that man becomes all things by understanding them (*Homo intelligendo fit omnia*), this imaginative metaphysics shows that man becomes all things by *not* understanding them (*homo non intelligendo fit omnia*); and perhaps the latter proposition is truer than the former, for when man understands he extends his mind and takes in things, but when he does not understand he makes the things out of himself and becomes them by transforming himself into them" (130).

Vico goes on to claim that poetic universals became merely figurative when human beings developed the capacity to make abstract universals: "Words were invented which signified abstract forms or genera comprising their species or relating parts with their wholes" (131). In

Vico, poetic universals privileged identity. But when they became only figurative they privileged difference, difference being now the "truth" about language.

Vico is somewhat ambivalent about the movement of the poetic universal from identity to figurative difference or *standing for*. Blake is not, as the well-known passage from *The Marriage of Heaven and Hell*, plate 11, shows (E38). There Blake describes the evolution of language from creative naming by "ancient poets" to interpretation by a "priesthood." I have discussed this passage elsewhere.[11] Here it is necessary only to remark that the movement noted by both Vico and Blake involves emergence of a new attitude toward tropes, requiring a priesthood of interpreters who hold that there is a hidden meaning behind a word or text or, to put it as White does, a literal surface with a figurative meaning. Introduction of the figurative meaning implies that from that time on the literal surface of a text must be read *through* in order to discover its truth, that language is but a covering over of a prelinguistic or alinguistic thought—something like a Platonic idea perhaps. This view privileges difference, indeed obliterates identity. The literal text has but an arbitrary or allegorical relation to its truth.

Paul de Man's treatment of tropes also privileges difference, not only the difference just discussed, but also a difference arising out of a different—actually a differential view—of language. In "The Rhetoric of Temporality," de Man distinguishes metonymy from synecdoche: a synecdoche is a symbol, and a symbol is a "sensorial equivalence of a more general, ideal meaning," which for de Man means that synecdoches "designate a totality of which they are a part."[12] This totality is the idea, and it is supposedly entirely beyond language. But, of course, de Man denies that this relationship is possible. It is a delusion, for the symbol cannot embody something not linguistic. Indeed, it cannot even embody another linguistic entity. The relationship is always arbitrary between signifier and signified, as Ferdinand de Saussure held, or between word and word, each signified being arbitrarily but another word or set of words. Therefore there is only difference, and difference is a metonymical or syntagmatic relation of contiguity that always knows its arbitrariness, even if its author does not. Allegory is the truth about language; symbol is its illusion; and synecdoche is symbolism implying unity, a closed system in which the word is a delusory entity claiming indifference with the universal idea to which it is supposed to belong.

De Man's argument assumes that synecdoche and symbol imply signifiers that are one with referents outside language and that these referents are purely ideal. He then claims that this is nonsense. Metonymy
and allegory make no such claim and accept the reality of difference, in
which sign and referent never coincide. Indeed, signifier and signified
(components of the sign) can never coincide. The sign itself is differential. Here the notion of language as having some mimetic relation to
nature is completely abandoned. So also is the notion that language as
a creative force can, in a neo-Kantian sense, constitute anything—even
a manifold of sensation—external to it, that language has anything
other than an arbitrary relation to nature, or that any new efforts at expression can refurbish the materials of linguistic culture with which it
works. The argument presumes a hard-and-fast distinction between
words and things (if indeed it can be said that there are things),
and between words and words, taking as its opponent—and regarding
it as absurd—the view that things can be in words or that one word
can be in another.

Blake thought otherwise, but in an unexpected way. He argued for
his own "primitive and original ways" by a contrary mode of thought
that declared the opposition between difference and indifference a negation always privileging one side over the other. This argument requires another term contrary to the negation. Blake's term is "vision."
Elsewhere I have used "identity."[13] The term takes us back again to
Blake's remarks about the "ancient poets" and declares for an antithetical logic that accepts difference and indifference at the same time. It
does not require the other world of the Platonic idea miraculously embodied in language (except as one-half of the opposition to which it is
contrary.) It does accept the notion of language as a force that creates
from the stuff of experience and the decay of linguistic forms a new
linguistic or (as in the case of painting) a new cultural form. This is
accomplished by the poetic antithetical logic of not merely figurative
tropes. A not merely figurative trope declares for both the difference
and indifference of word and thing, word and word. A word never
merely stands for a thing, neither is it merely that thing. The condition
of identity prevents our making either of these assertions alone, because
when alone they belong to another logic. As for the relation of word
and word, the same principle prevails.

But these relations, as we have been observing them, are too stati-
cally spatial. The trope exists only in or as a sentence, which is a dy-

namic form, not an equivalence free of its making and temporal development. A Blakean synecdoche is a dynamic identity (contrary to difference/indifference) of words, but words conceived of as forming new cultural materials from a nature and culture that is only potential until the poet has done something with it. In such antithetical logic each word acts as a "minute particular," but it acts also in a relation of identity to a "larger" word. It is also in relation to some "smaller" word. Both would be particulars. As Blake remarks, "Every Class is Individual" (E648).

This returns us to two distinctions, one of which has already been made in discussion of the passage from Freud and the other implied in the discussion of de Man's privileging of allegory: that between an open and a closed synecdoche, and that between a miraculous and a figurative one. In a *figurative synecdoche* the relation privileges difference and presumes that the part stands for the whole, like White's figure, but that it is really a fragment of the whole. In a *miraculous synecdoche* the part is invaded by a whole that has emanated or shrunk into it. The contrary to this negation is the *radical synecdoche,* in which the part not only is itself but also is the whole, as it would be with Freud's condensation if we could know that whole, or know that we know it.

In a *closed synecdoche* both part and whole are spatially considered as fixed in size. The part, as microcosm, cannot become smaller; the whole, as macrocosm, cannot become larger. Nothing more can come of it. The miraculous, closed synecdoche is the type that de Man calls a symbol and denigrates.

An *open synecdoche* implies a progressive movement or temporality entirely avoiding any suggestion of completed form or what has recently been called "totalization." Such would characterize a synecdoche from the point of view of deconstruction. It would, like the views of Jakobson and Lévi-Strauss, be merely a variety of metonymy with its syntagmatic endlessness, exploited by Jacques Derrida. This is what de Man thinks a synecdoche really is, since it is only, for him, a metonymy trying to be a symbol. The open synecdoche is always in process, and the movement between part and whole continually "supplements," in Derrida's sense, the relationship so as to enlarge it or diminish it. There is no end to this. Rather than creation, however, the activity is always that of differentiation and "dissemination."

The Blakean conception of synecdoche that opposes the negations open/closed and miraculous/figurative I shall call *radical* and *progressive*, adopting the second term from Blake's well-known aphorism "Without Contraries is no progression" (E34). One can attempt a figure to describe the curved space of Einsteinian physics: it proposes an object starting out in a certain direction, holding to it, and returning to its place of origin—but in an infinite length of time. We have come all of this way to meet a paradox. Such space-time would be both infinite and bounded, open and closed. Blake's conception of the synecdochic relation is just this. There is a progression, a supplementation, but rather than rolling out into endless night, it returns infinitely to itself, but always in a new and immeasurably greater—or smaller—form.

Vico said of ancient men that their poetic logic was "the opposite and more sublime thing" (128), though poetic logic was superseded by the logic that followed it and reduced the *radical progressive synecdoche* to the closed figure. The sublimity of progressive synecdoche is its creative possibility. When Immanuel Kant considered the sublime he responded to Edmund Burke's notion that the sublime was overwhelming by arguing that what we discover ultimately in the sublime is the infinitude of the human mind, by which synecdoche he meant the mind's satisfaction in discovering its power. This is where the notion of Derridean supplementation as a movement that always produces more interpretation can be seen as an aspect of progressive synecdoche, but it wanders endlessly into the abyss that Kant rejected.

Blake also rejected the abyss, as in his satirical account in *The Marriage of Heaven and Hell* of a furious but terrified angel who threatens him with it (E41). His notion of language was that it can be constantly creative, shaping what looks like an abyss to the angel and to the pure deconstructionist—the former fearing it and the latter embracing it. Language creates even as it destroys old forms, as in Blake's synecdoche of the spiritual, fourfold London "continually building & continually decaying desolate" (*J*53:19, E203).

The Blakean synecdoche is both closed and open at both ends, and the movement back and forth produces always more and more interpretation. There is, perhaps, something sublime about this. We can consider synecdoche momentarily as a "vertical" relation from small to large and back. Metaphor we can consider as a "horizontal" relation, going out and coming back. Between the two we have what looks like the great egg that W. B. Yeats playfully has Michael Robartes mention in *A Vision*—the world seen in Yeatsian terms as continually turning inside out without breaking its shell.[14] The difference is that this is a whole infinite in all directions and unchartable in terms of directions:

And the Four Points are thus beheld in Great Eternity
West, the Circumference: South, the Zenith: North,
The Nadir: East, the Center
(*J*12:54–56, E156)

or:

And the North is Breadth, the South is Heighth & Depth:
The East is Inwards: & the West is Outwards every way.
(*J*14:29–30, E158)

Here directions are infinite and at the same time they are places; the language itself shapes the world by the oscillation of synecdoche, the world never escaping the words themselves.

To interpret Blake's poetry is to work toward apprehension of an antithetical system in which synecdoche plays a major role. Such criticism is a process that does not end and in practice includes many phases, all of which, except for the containing one with which I am concerned, are part of traditional literary scholarship. Neither the phases nor their order can be prescribed, for then the process would not be a constitutive search, but rather the adoption of an authorized method designed to expose a meaning behind and prior to Blake's text. This would be a meaning kept by a priesthood, guardians of the word and its mystery, and divulged in a fragment only, as if there were a prior whole eventually to be revealed by allegorical interpretation.

E. R. Goodenough has argued that although the term *logos* as employed by Saint John has been translated by the English "word," following the Vulgate latin *verbum,* such meaning is one of the few attributed to it that it never possessed. The Greek for "word" is not *logos* but *ρῆνα* or *ὄγονα.* For Goodenough, *logos* means "primarily the formation and expression of thought in speech."[15] Others have given it various meanings, including "the reasoning mind . . . , a plan, scheme, system . . . , the Platonic Idea of the Good, the Stoic World-Spirit or Reason of God, immanent in creation which it fosters and sustains."[16] In these definitions, the relation of a word to whatever is supposed to lie behind it becomes hazy, and finally the whole relation becomes questionable, mysterious, and quite rightly subject to suspicion. Mysteries require keepers and keys, which imply that, despite the haze or even the possibility of the nothingness of the referent, the text (Blake's or any other) can be passed through to some nonverbal meaning as referent behind it—even if it is a nothingness.

However, the process of synecdoche that I am talking about goes on and on even as it returns. The Blakean sublime is not merely the sublime of magnitude or of dynamism, as in Kant. It is also the sublime of the infinitesimal, the grain of sand and even smaller things. The interpretations produced are never hypothetical reconstructions of something said to lie behind the text awaiting recovery like the Freudian dream-thought. Interpretations are to be made and endlessly remade. So there is a sense after all in which White is right to claim that we can read a text as a synecdoche or as a metonymy, or at least he is correct to say that this is frequently done, correct or not. The difference has to do with what we think reading or criticism or interpretation is all about, what method, if you will, is appropriate.

A reading should want to see a text from its own point of view. This, of course, is strictly speaking impossible, as impossible as de Man claims a symbol to be. But there is, nevertheless, something even more inadequate about sheer impressionism, allegorization, readings as play, and so on. Readings need to bring texts into the range of conversation, where by this mediation they become socially involved. Blake himself beautifully describes what total identification with a text, or in this case a painting, might be:

> If the Spectator could Enter into these Images in his Imagination approaching them on the Fiery Chariot of his Contemplative Thought if he could Enter into Noahs rainbow or into his bosom or could make a Friend & Companion of one of these Images of wonder which always intreats him to leave mortal things as he must know then would he arise from his Grave then would he meet the Lord in the Air & then he would he happy General Knowledge is Remote Knowledge it is in Particulars that Wisdom consists & Happiness too. (*VLJ*82, E560)

But there must always be the return to interpretive assertion for the sake of cultural conversation, and that has its own point of view, even as it tries to capture the moment Blake describes. Such a position, as modern hermeneutics tells us, is always in motion. In spite of this moving on, critical method (as Blakean as it might become), for reasons of its

ironic position, must be allegorical and priestly to some extent. Therefore, the priesthood that publishes in *Blake: An Illustrated Quarterly*
and attends Blake conferences has less than might be imagined to fear
from my insistence on a neo-Blakean critical method that would be the
outer circumference of what they do. The insistence that criticism can
never stand still but must constantly search to reformulate its utterances is only the assertion that it must know itself and the irony of its
situation, which is that criticism requires preconceptions or what
Gadamer calls prejudices and the fictive notion of a certain fixity even
to begin a process always questioning those fixities. Coleridge balanced
such things in his treatment of method, though not so radically as I
have suggested must be done here: "As without continuous transition
there can be no Method, so without a pre-conception there can be no
transition with continuity. The term Method, cannot, therefore otherwise than by abuse, be applied to a mere dead arrangement, containing
in itself no principle of progression" (457).

Criticism of Blake's text seeks to show what Blake does, but to accomplish this it must constitute Blake's doing according to a language
of its own. Such a language is inevitably a set of critical fictions contrary to some extent to the synecdochic antithetical logic of Blake's
text. This criticism works within an ironic system that recognizes its
own fictionality and its own process as a process without end, a process
only, and not the finding of an allegorically represented idea, even
though it sometimes acts as if the allegorical idea is its end and that
end has been achieved. Criticism must have some sort of inner check
against taking its "as ifs" as absolutes. There is required, as I have
suggested, an initial effort to see the text from the text's point of
view—in terms of the text's antithetical logic. This involves a leap to
the opposite, so to speak, and in this case it is the leap to embrace the
synecdochic even though it cannot (though the text can) think synecdochically.

The text I have chosen to discuss is itself a synecdochic part; I shall
make a beginning effort to see to what extent it stands for—no!—*is
identical with,* the whole. The part is plate 10 of Blake's *Europe,* a
poem that Harold Bloom regards as "the subtlest and most difficult of
Blake's works, outside of the three epics, and perhaps the most reward-
ing as a poem."[17] I quote plate 10 in its entirety:

In thoughts perturb'd, they rose from the bright ruins silent fol-
     lowing
The fiery King, who sought his ancient temple serpent-form'd
That stretches out its shady length along the Island white.
Round him roll'd his clouds of war; silent the Angel went,
Along the infinite shores of Thames to golden Verulam.
There stand the venerable porches that high-towering rear
Their oak-surrounded pillars, form'd of massy stones, uncut
With tool; stones precious; such eternal in the heavens,
Of colours twelve, few known on earth, give light in the opake,
Plac'd in the order of the stars, when the five senses whelm'd
In deluge o'er the earth-born man; then turn'd the fluxile eyes
Into two stationary orbs, concentrating all things,
The ever-varying spiral ascents to the heavens of heavens
Were bended downward; and the nostrils golden gates shut
Turn'd outward, barr'd and petrify'd against the infinite.

Thought chang'd the infinite to a serpent, that which pitieth:
To a devouring flame; and man fled from its face and hid
In forests of night; then all the eternal forests were divided
Into earths rolling in circles of space, that like an ocean rush'd
And overwhelmed all except this finite wall of flesh.
Then was the serpent temple form'd, image of infinite
Shut up in finite revolutions, and man became an Angel;
Heaven a mighty circle turning; God a tyrant crown'd.

Now arriv'd the ancient Guardian at the southern porch,
That planted thick with trees of blackest leaf, & in a vale
Obscure, inclos'd the Stone of Night; oblique it stood, o'erhung
With purple flowers and berries red; image of that sweet south,
Once open to the heavens and elevated on the human neck,
Now overgrown with hair and coverd with a stony roof,
Downward 'tis sunk beneath th'attractive north, that round the
     feet
A raging whirlpool draws the dizzy enquirer to his grave:
(*Eur*10:1–30, E63–64)

What work is involved in spinning out the synecdochic nature of
this text? (I acknowledge that in the phrase "synecdochic nature" lies
the irony of critical practice midway between trying to see the text

from its own point of view and trying to constitute it antimythically as a nature or object to a subject. For that matter, "spinning out" is also putting together.) First, I discuss the work of scholarship and learning and the apprehension of how Blake employs a variety of traditionally allegorical conventions of interpretation as material to be reconstituted as myth. I take up five of these interrelated matters as exemplary in no prescribed or prescribable order. My point is that the materials I discuss, some well known, must be subsumed under a theory of Blake's text that recognizes the changes the material has undergone as a result of Blake's method. This is not entirely new, but I believe that in the light of a theory of synecdoche as method it gains a firmer, though paradoxical ground. Second, I add two aspects of method that tend to contain the others. Blake's own vigorous poetic method requires that we emphasize these as absolutely fundamental. A brief discussion of plate 10 follows this.

1. *Gnostic interpretation as a version of antitypical interpretation of Scripture.* One notices in Blake's designs and his poetry the occasional appearance of a serpent hanging on a cross or tree, sometimes crucified, sometimes wrapped around it. The best-known pictorial examples are in the illustrations for *Paradise Lost*, where a serpent is wrapped around the base of a cross on which Jesus is hung, and where Raphael converses with Adam and Eve, a serpent wrapped around a tree in the background. In *America*, one discovers the lines:

> The terror answerd: I am Orc, wreath'd round the accursed tree:
> The times are ended; shadows pass the morning gins to break;
> (*A*8:1–2, E54)

The motif recalls, of course, the serpent of Eden, "more subtil than any beast of the field" (Genesis 3:1). Tradition identifies the serpent with Satan, and Milton has Satan inhabit its body, though the Bible does not do so explicitly. Since in *Europe* the figure of Orc is regarded as a devil by the "angelic" supporters of the "fiery King," we have reason to understand Orc's serpentine form as a Blakean attempt to construct new values for these terms by what looks at first like a kind of verbal violence, especially when it is made abundantly clear that Orc has phallic characteristics. Why Blake puts Orc on a cross or tree or why the biblical serpent was put there may be more difficult to grasp. Blake is drawing on the potentiality of the Gnostic use of the serpent.

To understand this matter, we have recourse to certain references to serpents in the Bible and to some Renaissance occult drawings. In Numbers 21:4–9, Moses raises a serpent up on a pole:

> And the people spoke against God and against Moses. Wherefore have ye brought us up out of Egypt to die in the wilderness? For there is no bread, neither is there any water; and our soul loatheth this light bread.
>
> And the Lord sent fiery serpents among the people, and they bit the people; and much people of Israel died.
>
> Therefore the people came to Moses, and said, We have sinned, for we have spoken against the Lord, and against thee; pray unto the Lord, that he take away the serpents from us. And Moses prayed for the people.
>
> And the Lord said unto Moses, Make thee a fiery serpent, and set it upon a pole: and it shall come to pass, that every one that is bitten, when he looketh upon it, shall live.
>
> And Moses made a serpent of brass, and put it upon a pole, and it came to pass, that if a serpent had bitten any man, when he beheld the serpent of brass he lived.

This event is alluded to in John 3:14, where it is said: "And as Moses lifted up the serpent in the wilderness, even so must the Son of Man be lifted up." Biblical typologists, of whom John was obviously one himself, saw Moses' act and the crucifixion as antitypes; and just as Moses used the serpent on the pole as a magical talisman to ward off evil, so does Christian tradition employ the crucifix. But what justifies this curious relation of Jesus to serpent? Among some Gnostic sects the serpent was transvaluated and worshiped, because the serpent of Genesis created human desire for knowledge, for *gnosis*. Since the Demiurge, not God, had, in Gnostic myth, designed and created the world, the serpent, who urges Eve to disobey the creator, represents a force that rejects the fallen creation and introduces her to real knowledge. As Hans Jonas remarks: "[The serpent] came in a whole group of systems to represent the 'pneumatic' principle from beyond, counteracting the designs of the Demiurge, and thus could become as much a symbol of the powers of redemption as the biblical God had been degraded to a symbol of cosmic oppression."[18] The Genesis story was interpreted as an allegory of man's coming to knowledge via the forbidden fruit and turning away from the lower demonic creator toward the true, transcendent deity. This also makes possible man's being saved in an act expressing love. Man seeking real knowledge could come to transcend the limiting belief that the Demiurge, who created the material world, was the real God. It is a short step from this to the Valentinian Gnostics, who saw a parallel between Jesus and the now-benevolent serpent. For them it was Jesus as serpent who tempted Adam and Eve to eat from the tree and to make knowledge transcending their innocence possible—a knowledge that would bring them to recognition that the Demiurge was not God. And from this point it is not far to the idea that Christ was knowledge and the apple on the tree or the serpent wrapped around it was Christ on the cross. Both were sources of *gnosis*, powerful talismans.

At the same time, there was a competing Gnostic tradition that the serpent with its tail in its mouth is a dragon representing the outer circle or containing form of the fallen creation, identified with Leviathan. One finds this too in Blake, where falling figures are encoiled by serpents, as in the *Book of Urizen*, or where the created Adam is wrapped round by a huge snake. It is noteworthy in this respect that Blake may have engraved for Jacob Bryant's *New System* a serpent wrapped around an egg, which in Blake's own writings is the sleeping world.[19] In any case, the engraving was surely known to him. Blake's use of both of these Gnostic traditions about the serpent expresses in the character of Orc a conflation of what according to antimythical logic seem disparate or contradictory elements.

There is also a curious tradition in alchemy connected with Moses and the serpent. The Gnostic serpent is related to the alchemical dragon or *ouroboros*, the tail-eater. The dragon is "mercurious," the fundamental substance. It is represented in many drawings as an alchemical image of the transmutation of matter, of special knowledge and regeneration, like the serpent on the cross. There is a tradition that Moses, who held up the brass serpent on a pole, was the first alchemist. K. K. Doberer in *The Goldmakers* tells a story averring that Aaron, Moses' brother, may have performed an alchemical trick in a sorcery contest when he "cast down his rod before Pharoah, and before his servants, and it became a serpent." Doberer remarks: "This trick can be performed chemically, without recourse to hypnotism, if the rod is made of a paste of bay-laurel, quicksilver, and sulphur, and stuck together with the gum of the bush Astralogus from Asia Minor. Such a rod, when thrown upon a charcoal fire, turns into a long writhing mass."[20] One finds in C. G. Jung's *Psychology and Alchemy* and Kurt Selig-

mann's *The Mirror of Magic* several representations of crucified serpents and tail-eaters taken from Renaissance alchemical texts.[21]

The crucifixion of Orc in Blake's prophetic books takes up this whole
curious tradition. In the earlier prophetic books Orc is political and
spiritual regeneration. Like Blake's Jesus of *The Everlasting Gospel*,
who violates the law, Blake's Orc appears as a devil to those who represent the status quo. In the later prophetic books, Orc has become a
cyclical concept, tied to linear history, and we find much irony in his
Gnostic connections, his activity being circular and confining like the
tail-eater. Blake's texts are not Gnostic or occultist, but in the crucified
serpent and the tail-eater he employed two venerable devices and took
advantage of the ambiguity that over time they began to harbor. To
read Blake is to discover many such usages, such as the values given
to various numbers, reminiscent of Cabalistic thought and alchemy—
but Blake's texts are not Cabalistic, nor was he an alchemist any more
than he was a Gnostic. The serpent temple of *Europe*, identified with
the body of Albion's thought, has vestiges of the traditions I have mentioned and expresses the connection in Blake's mind between sectar-
ianism and the cyclical figure that the revolutionary Orc eventually
became. Above all, it appears that Blake's intention was to open up
typological method, which traditionally saw its process as expressing
fulfillment in history and closure of the text. Blake's notion was to free
the figure to evoke new possibilities from the vestiges of its typological
usage that are carried into his text. In this sense, Blake's use of typology is a contrary to the type/antitype relation and yet assimilates it as
a part, making us read the part as implying a new sort of whole.

2. Neoplatonic allegorical conventions. It is well known that there
are numerous appearances of Neoplatonic allegorical materials in Blake.
The most frequently cited one is the so-called *Arlington Court Picture*,
which has been interpreted as a visual presentation of Porphyry's interpretation of a passage from *Odyssey* 13. But even here, as Anne Mellor
has shown, Blake departs quite radically from Neoplatonic doctrine,
while illustrating a scene that has been supposed to be Neoplatonic.[22]
He is *using* materials rather than passing on a doctrine under cover of
allegory. Another example is the story of the soul that Kathleen Raine
declares to be in the little-girl-lost-and-found poems from *Songs of Innocence and Experience*.[23] This allegory has to do with the descent of
the soul into matter and its ascent therefrom. There is no question that

Blake was familiar with Porphyry and Neoplatonism, mainly through the contemporary translations of Thomas Taylor, and that he employed their figurative motif; but Blake is concerned with providing the contrary to Platonic concepts. He regards as negations the traditional distinctions between body and soul, matter and the immaterial, and their modern relatives subject and object, and he reworks stories involving them to his own satisfaction, often to parody and criticize their supposed intent. Indeed, in plate 10 of *Europe* such distinctions are regarded as fundamental errors that misled the fiery King and his Angels.

3. *The idea of analogy.* We have already seen an example of antitype and Blake's appropriation of it in the Mosaic serpent on the cross. Blake also used the idea of analogy, that is, the idea of a fallen form of an unfallen truth, but here, as usual there is a creative difference from its usual use, which has Platonic or religious overtones. The most fundamental example is his motif of the upside-down and upright men, which has parallels in Gnosticism and which he steals in part from Dante's vision of Satan at the end of the *Inferno*. It seems also to be a variation on a passage in Plato's *Timaeus* describing man as "a plant whose roots are not in earth, but in the heavens" (90a–b).

In the *Inferno*, Dante and Virgil travel downward through Hell to the center of the earth, where they crawl along the hairy side of the ice-encased body of Satan. Proceeding past the very center of gravity, they discover that what had been downward into Hell is suddenly upward toward Purgatory. Looking back or downward now, they see Satan upside down with his head hanging into the abyss of the sky. In Blake this idea of the upside-down man is applied to Albion, the universal man, who when he is in a fallen condition is upside down. The fallen world contained in Albion's spiritual body is an analogy or demonic parody of his upright state. The idea of analogy, which is the basic principle of the Smaragdine Tablet of Hermes Trismegistus, is that things below copy things above. Things above are spirit; those below, matter. Though Blake uses the idea, he reconstructs it. The whole situation is turned on its side. Things apparently outside parody things inside, and the duality of matter and spirit is declared to be delusion, because matter is a fiction projected by mental activity into externality.

Another example of this symbolism, appropriating the *Timaeus*, occurs in *Europe*, where the nameless shadowy female says,

My roots are brandish'd in the heavens. my fruits in earth be-
    neath
(*Eur* 1:8, E60)

Her statement is platonic, but in Blake her upside-down character is
stressed. She is an upside-down tree, in fact. She is thus identified
metonymically with Eve and the forbidden fruit, the upside-down tree
being fallen nature and a foreboding of the crucifixion, tree being antitype of cross. Elsewhere Blake says that the modern church crucifies
Christ with his head downward, an allusion to the legend surrounding
the crucifixion of Saint Peter and an expression of Blake's view that the
very idea of a church, or the bureaucratization of religion and externalization of God into the abyss of the sky, is a perversion of Jesus'
teaching and thus upside down like the whole modern concept of nature. This idea of upside down as error or the fallen analogy of upright,
turned then on its side to express epistemological error, though it has
its roots in Dante, the *Timaeus*, and Hermeticism, is as far as I know
a purely Blakean construction. We see it at the end of plate 10 of *Europe* as an expression of the state of Albion, where it has the effect
of qualifying or calling in question any interpretation garnered from
its previous usages.

4. *Romantic syncretic mythography.* Two of the most fascinating
and amusing books for the student of Romanticism are Edward B.
Hungerford's *Shores of Darkness* and Ruthven Todd's *Tracks in the
Snow*, which discuss the comparative mythologists who, flourishing in
Blake's day, offered various outlandish theories about the Druids, the
lost tribes of Israel, the location of the source of civilization, and just
about anything else that came to their attention from the past.[24] Blake's
knowledge of some of these writers led to many curiosities in his own
work, such as his statement that human civilization began in England,
that certain mythological or biblical events took place in England, and
that England was a surviving portion of Atlantis.

In reading William Stukeley, Jacob Bryant, or Edward Davies today,
one is struck by their capacity to order large amounts of so-called
knowledge into elegant wholes based on entirely false premises.[25] It has
been pointed out by the recent anthologists Feldman and Richardson
that Bryant (and this would hold good for Davies as well) was a
throwback to late-seventeenth-century polymaths like Bochart.[26] Blake

knew Bryant's *New System;* it seemed to him to attack the rationalist and deistic positions that were so entrenched in his time. (There is, however, some question about how carefully Blake read Bryant.)[27] One is tempted to characterize these works as quasi-artistic, fictive structures, and their authors as Blakean artists using materials from fabulous tradition. There is some similarity between them and the sorts of "anatomies" we find later in Carlyle and Yeats (and even Frye), though the former are totally lacking the irony, satire, and self-conscious fiction making that call upon us to claim a distinction between their work and that of modern "anatomists"—even though the line cannot be strictly drawn anywhere. It must suffice for us to note that the presence of external belief aligns them with the Gnostics on this point and separates their works from the anatomies of Yeats and Carlyle as well as from the poems of Blake, but in the last instance in a somewhat different way.

Much of the syncretic mythographical work was done by those who were seeking to square archeological evidence, such as it was, with Christian tradition as they saw it. Bryant's *New System,* like the work of the early church fathers, assumes that pagan myths were distorted plagiarisms of the Old Testament, and this required the most brilliantly agile approach to chronology and to modes of proof. Bryant was equal to the challenge: as Hungerford has noted, he proved beyond his own doubt that Chatterton did not forge the Rowley poems and that there never had been a Troy.[28] He created a fable of a postdiluvian language called Amonian, which was supposed to have been passed on through the descendants of Ham, son of Noah, who are the gentiles, and which became gradually corrupted. Ham is euhemeristically identified with the sun; and under the domination of Amonion is included everyone except the Jews—Egyptians, Syrians, Phoenicians, Canaanites, etc.

Bryant's method was to pursue a sort of speculative etymology back to a totally imaginary language, Amonian: the family resemblances of all pagan rites and languages were thereby revealed:

> The Deluge was the grand epoch of every ancient kingdom. It is to be observed, that when colonies made anywhere a settlement, they ingrafted their antecedent history upon the subsequent events of the place. And as in those days they could carry up the genealogies of their princes to the very source of all; it will be found,

under whatever title he may come, that the very first king in every country was Noah. For as he was mentioned first in the genealogy of their princes, he was in aftertimes looked upon as a real monarch; and represented as a great traveller, a mighty conquerer, and sovereign of the whole earth. This circumstance will appear even in the annals of the Egyptians: and though their chronology has been supposed to have reached beyond that of any nation, yet it coincides very happily with the accounts given by Moses.[29]

Burton Feldman argues that it was Bryant's absolute disregard for the new rationalists and all progress toward a science of mythography in his own time that appealed to Blake, to whom Bryant's views were "a defense of the true and ancient faith against the corrosive disbelief" of rationalism.[30] Blake uses Bryant as support for his statement about his painting *The Ancient Britons*, now lost. Bryant wrote in a style of absolute self-confidence and dogmatic assurance that probably appealed to Blake as attributes of a "true orator." His tone calls to mind the gestures of a latter-day euhemerist mythographer, Robert Graves. Mixed in with the sanction of Bryant in Blake are traces of the mythological constructions of Stukeley, William Owen Pughe, and Davies.[31]

In two different works, Stukeley explains Avebury and Stonehenge as ancient Druid temples. The story he offers is that of a patriarchal antediluvian religion, not a deistic religion of reason and nature but what he regards as orthodox Christianity itself. He claims the British Druids were direct descendants of the patriarchs who came to Britain before Moses. The Druids are a direct link between those patriarchs and the present Church of England:

> My intent is . . . to promote, as much as I am able, the knowledge and practice of ancient and true Religion; to revive in the minds of the learned the spirit of Christianity, nearly as old as the Creation, which is now languishing among us; to restore the first and great Idea of the Deity, who has carry'd on the same regular and golden chain of Religion from the beginning to this day; to warm our hearts into that true sense of Religion, which keeps the medium between ignorant superstition and learned free-thinking, between slovenly fanaticism and popish pageantry, between enthusiasm and the rational worship of God, which is no where on earth done in my judgment, better than in the Church of England.[32]

Stukeley believed that the temples at Stonehenge and Avebury were serpentine in form, an erroneous judgment; we shall see how Blake used this in *Europe*. Davies's *Celtic Researches*, known to Blake but again read at best only cursorily by him, holds that the antediluvian society was in fact the golden age, in which pre-Noachic people lived to great ages and practiced monotheism. The Druids are traced back to Ashkenez, one of the three sons of Gomer, who was the son of Japheth, one of the three sons of Noah. The Titans were also descended from Ashkenez and after their defeat went to live among the Hyperboreans, who are declared to be the earliest inhabitants of Britain. Thus Britain was the Hell and Paradise of Greek myth. For Davies, in contrast to Stukeley and a number of others, the Old Testament provides the "correct epitome" of the most ancient period of history. Genesis is the key. Hebrew was the original language.

A fundamental difference between Blake's use of these materials and the works of Stukeley, Bryant, and Davies lies in the difference between an attitude and activity that attempts to create the past or all history verbally as a present in a reverse synecdoche and one that seeks only to recover it as a past. I call the former method "internal," the latter "external." The euhemerists regarded their methods as scholarly and leading to external historical fact. It was not a question of their deciding between myth and science, but of their affirming that they had in fact scientifically unraveled texts that had corrupted true history. It is tempting to rescue their works for myth, placing them near the center of a Viconian "poetic logic" as examples of what Northrop Frye calls "symmetrical cosmologies." There is a certain rarefied pleasure in reading them—though they are not to the taste of very many people—but the difference is finally profound. It is fundamentally that between an antimythical externalizing attitude and a mythical one. Blake was not captive to antimythical forms of external belief that have rendered the mythographical efforts of Bryant and others absurd.

Both Hungerford and Ruthven Todd have given attention to Blake's description of his now lost painting, *The Ancient Britons*. In the description of this painting, Blake pictures the three survivors of Arthur's last battle in the West: "In the last Battle of King Arthur only Three Britons escaped, these were the Strongest Man, the Beautifullest Man, and the Ugliest Man; these three marched through the field unsubdued, as Gods, and the Sun of Britain set, but shall arise again with tenfold splendor when Arthur shall awake from sleep, and resume his dominion over earth and ocean (*DC*39, E542). Northrop Frye identifies these three with Tharmas, Luvah, and Urizen, respectively, from Blake's prophetic books.[33] The description Blake proceeds to give of them seems to identify them with the Druids, though an explicit identification is not made. They are the ancient Britons "naked, civilized, learned, studious." They survive Arthur, and Blake constructs his version of the mythic Arthur.

According to Hungerford, Blake's connection of Arthur with Albion, Atlas, and the constellation Boötes (to which belongs Arcturus) indicates his assumption that all of these are corrupt forms of "an original mythological personage."[34] The connection of Atlas with Albion goes back to the erroneous researches of Francis Wilford, who believed that England was the antediluvian seat of all civilization. Appropriating Davies, according to Todd, Blake placed the Druids in England, identified with Atlantis, as early as the time of Abraham, practicing a pre-Christian Christianity.[35] The great strong man of this time was Hercules of Tyre, identified by Stukeley, following Toland's *History of the Druids,* as the actual builder of the stone monuments. Blake derived the idea of his painting from this, from the legend of Arthur, which in his view, appropriating Pughe, is a corruption of the acts of Albion applied to the life of a prince in the fifth century. The vast amount of contemporary mythography, blending together in Blake's fertile imagination, created something entirely new.

Hungerford reconstructs the sources of the relationships Blake made among Albion, Arthur, Boötes, Arcturus, and Atlas and traces the slaying of Albion back to the Greek myth in which a character named Albion is killed by Hercules. But Hungerford ultimately sees no important difference between Blake and his congeries of erroneous sources. With Blake, he claims, "we are plunged into the maddest sort of mythological jumble, in which Blake imposed no limit to his imagination."[36] Todd, who independently located some of the links that Hungerford did, is less willing to be critical of Blake's process.

But Blake's use of these materials is original and coherent, as scholarship subsequent to Hungerford has shown.[37] Perhaps the most important idea that Blake takes from his sources (but with his own twist) is that myths came down to the modern world as corruptions of original visions of identity. The mythographers' aims were to clean up these corrupt versions and to see clearly the reasons for the corruption. Blake's intention was different. In this matter external history was for him utterly of no value. The only important aim was to establish the synecdochic relation. I have spoken of this as "original vision," but it is every bit as potential as original for Blake, and the story of Fall in Blake is reversible to a story of potentiality. Blakean origins and beginnings are not to be merely a receding *then*, separate from the present, but a *then*-slumbering *now*, which is a synecdoche of history and time. Thus, by comparison to many of the Romantic poets there is very little nostalgia in Blake. Blake thought that in our notion of history constituted as external or of time constituted as measured, vision is clouded, so that the true Albion is slain and broken up into pieces, scattered through that cut-up time, some of him being attributed to Arthur, other parts to Atlas, and so on. This is true of Arthur and Atlas as well, who ought to be seen as synecdochic of Albion. The mythic relation among these parts—synecdochic, metaphoric, metonymic—is lost. *The Ancient Britons* is a picture of what survives in this story of cultural decay and cataclysm, present in one version in Arthur's last battle against Rome and in another in the sinking of Atlantis. One original of these versions is not what is to be sought. There is none. What is to be sought is the identity of these versions, or their relation. The relation is one of synecdochic identity between Albion and, say, Arthur. Albion is not then the original of which others are later corruptions, but instead their giant form.

The Arthur version is appropriated by Blake in his picture of three surviving giants. The all-important Blakean fourth is not present. If Frye is right in identifying the three survivors, the missing fourth is Blake's figure for the capacity to form a vision of identity, which would include identity of part and whole. This would be Urthona, or in his working (unmeasured) time-form Los. But he is present as the picture itself or the "originally one man," who appears variously and synecdochically as Albion, Arthur, Atlas.

Blake's remark about England as the seat of the original human creation must be understood mythically and synecdochically as W. B. Yeats understood it. This has not always occurred. Yeats chastised Denis Saurat for an antimythical reading of Blake: "Blake does not think England the place of primitive humanity, or the original wisdom because they were before the flood of time and space—the historical druids he thought degenerate men—'rocky druidism.' He spoke of England and its past because he lived there. In the same way the folklore of the Echte hills in Galway says that the last judgment will be among those hills. Blake sees the near and particular always."[38] England is identical with the world, and this is the way of poetry.

A. L. Owen, who added to our understanding of Blake's use of the Druids, also misunderstood the nature of Blakean belief: "In the Prophetic Books . . . Blake's version of Genesis is so provocative that it hardly lends itself to a willing suspension of disbelief. Nevertheless, it does not affect their central meaning, and if it is disconcerting to see the extent to which Blake was self-deluded, this is partly because his sincerity is so patent."[39] What Owen does not see is that Blake's work demands a distinction between antimythical and mythical forms of belief, forms appropriate to the nature of the utterance, rather than a distinction between belief and suspended disbelief. The antimythical insists on an external historical referent and spatial and temporal differences. The mythical, as Yeats saw, finds every place identical to every other place, every place identical to the whole, implying an ethic of inter-involvement that it regards as more fundamental than external fact. But even Yeats was daunted by the rigor with which Blake kept to this antithetical logic. Yeats called Blake a "too literal realist of the imagination,"[40] and his own reading of Blake resists Blake's determination to construct a mythic world in the spirit of a poetic deliberately not answerable to judgments of verification according to the antimythical logic of the syncretic mythographers he had read. Blake must have seen the work of the mythographers as corrupted efforts to restore mythical thought on an encyclopedic scale, but they proved to be just like the historians he criticized. They did not grasp the appropriate antithetical logic for their work and mistook what they were doing. Blake does not "spirit away" the contents of the Bible—that is, destroy its historicity—as the biblical typologists feared and still fear that allegorical readings, with their Platonizing tendencies, will do. Neither does he, however, externalize the Bible's events purely as history, as typologists desire. He constitutes it as a poetic antithetical logic, exploiting the ethical truth of tropes, so that England and Jerusalem can be in the same place at the same time and we can be in them and they in us and still be ourselves. What Yeats saw in Blake as more fundamental than external fact was an ethic of the trope.

5. *History contained*. The extent of Blake's allegorical use of historical events and personages was not much appreciated until David V. Erdman's *Blake: Prophet against Empire* came out in 1954.[41] There is, no doubt, more to be learned about Blake's historical allegory, and this

information will have to be given its appropriate place in the effort to grasp the antithetical logic of his work. This has not happened to any great extent as yet, for the reading of the historical allegory has tended to be external and reductive. A clear example of historical allegory is plate 10 of *Europe*, where the "fiery King" retreats to his serpent temple. Erdman makes this William Pitt's decision to raise alarms against Jacobins in order to hasten war with France (195–97). Events are actually conflated, since there were three attempts to initiate war in 1787, 1790, and 1791. Indeed, even people are conflated, for surely not only Pitt but also King George III and the members of the government are involved here. Blake speaks not only of the "fiery King," but also of "Albion's Angel" and the "Angels of Albion," as well as the "Ancient Guardian." These are in poetic logic both the same person and several persons. The names contain the allegory, having come first, so to speak; and we are constantly shuffling back and forth from the containing names to the contained historical event that is embodied not as history so much as a synecdochic part of a story that is here and everywhere now, then, and probably (unfortunately) in the future.

The ancient temple of plate 10 is clearly identified with the neolithic remains at Avebury that Stukeley assumed erroneously to be of Druidic origin. It was connected with the site of Verulamium, the ancient Roman town. Blake was interested in the connection between this and Sir Francis Bacon, whose baronial title was Verulam. The opportunity to trope into relation Pitt, Druidism, and Bacon was too much for him not to exploit, for Bacon represented to him the negating domination of empiricism or antimythical externalization. He regarded the Druids as originally the wisest and greatest of men, the earliest true Christians, antedating Jesus himself; but as their religion spread it became codified and sacrificed all that was human to abstraction. The Druid serpent temple, which is Verulam, which is Avebury, which has stretched itself all across England, which is white, or Albion, a giant humanity in a fallen state, stands on the banks of the Thames, itself serpent-shaped, though the river as part is identified as infinite to remind us of the expansion to include everything that is always potential even in the fallen condition of contraction, where everything seems to be thrust outward from a center.

The Druid temple-Verulam-Avebury-serpent-Albion-England is the refuge of Albion's Angel King in debased, codified thought. It is a container, thus a metonym of the Angel King's state of mind, metonymy stringing out the king's thought into external forms. It is closely identified with oak trees, idolized by the Druids. The serpent that lurks here in and as the temple and the river beside it is merely a vestige of the original knowledge it embodied before God cursed it and made it crawl on its belly. It is now merely an image of the infinite, contracted into a circle, which identifies it synecdochically with the circles of the heavenly planets, in turn the mechanical world wound up by a Deistic sky-god. The temple is this world, and when the Ancient Guardian retreats to it, he retreats into the state of mind that created it, and he becomes it. This is a fall into a state of antimythical materialism of the sort invented by Bacon and his coworkers Newton and Locke. Druidism fell similarly, and its vestige is the temple formed as the circle of the constricting tail-eater. The porches of the serpent temple are of stone, surrounded by a forest of oak, and the whole picture is reminiscent of trees on which are hung the serpents of Gnostic lore. Such a crucifix is, of course, a fallen or demonic talisman that succeeds only in warding things off or completing the division of object from the subject.

The ground on which Blake seems to have made the Avebury ruins into a serpent was the research of Stukeley, who in his 1724 book on Avebury erroneously connected it with the Druids and with the serpent. (Stukeley's illustration shows a circle as well as a serpentine line and it is taken up and produced by Blake as such in *Jerusalem* [plate 100].) To the old ruins Stukeley gives the name "Dracontia": " 'The serpent,' says *Maximus of Tyre* Dissert. 38, 'was the great symbol of the deity to most nations, and as such was worshipped by the *Indians*.' The temples of old made in the form of a serpent, were called for that reason *Dracontia*. The universality of this regard for serpents, shews the high antiquity of the symbol, and that it was antediluvian."[42]

Stukeley proceeds to give numerous reasons for the serpent's status, citing Egyptian hieroglyphic use of it and Chinese veneration. Moreover, serpents are beautiful and proceed with a wonderful sinuous motion that Sanchoniathon regarded as spiritual. Moses called the serpent wise. Aristotle called it crafty. Servius noted with admiration that it moved its tongue rapidly. The Gnostic association of Christ with the serpent and Moses' serpent on the pole are invoked. And finally Stukeley employs the principle of analogy and antitype: "Did the devil injure us under the form of a serpent? The like figure is the properest of any to symbolize the remedy, the antidote against poison whereby the devil wrought man's fall. Therefore, naturally, the same is to symbolize the messiah then promised, who is to work man's redemption" (60).

This astonishing example of Mithradatic typologizing Blake seems to have ignored in order to make the temple demonic.[43] Stukeley's Druids were wise men until they disappeared: "When I first began these studies about the Druid antiquities, I plainly discern'd the religion profess'd in these places was the first, simple, patriarchal religion" (1). But Stukeley's single religion of Druidical, Christian common sense Blake does not accept. It is Deism. For him the original religion involved synecdochic vision, and the originally visionary Druids fell into corrupt thought. Blake exploits the ambiguity of the serpent throughout his work, expressing the ambiguity of cyclical Orc and suggesting that the serpent temple is a fallen corrupt vestige of knowledge. Orc's cyclicity is latent in *America* and *Europe,* implying its development in the great longer poems.

6. The literal story. I think of this point and the next as containing the concerns represented by the first five. We should take Blake seriously when he emphasizes that he actually saw his giant forms—the ancient of days on his ceiling, for example. This was Blake's way of emphasizing the literal surface of his works, in addition, of course, to his illustrations, where Albion's Angel has bat's wings and where the serpent temple is a serpent of seven coils and forked tongue and "stretches out its shady length" vertically along the side of plate 10. Blake constantly warns us against reading abstractly toward allegory. This is why it is a fearful mistake to read Blake with a skeleton key that tells us to substitute reason for Urizen, imagination for Urthona, instinct for Tharmas, etc. These creatures and their emanations are giant human forms who argue with each other the way husbands and wives do. They have human failings and strengths. In *Europe,* plate 10, we must not forget the human being who skulks along the Thames to Verulam. He contains allegory but is not allegorical, being a particular.

7. Tropic literality. This phrase emphasizes that there is not only a surface of story that we may too quickly pass through to abstract allegorization but that even this surface is really an internality contained by what Northrop Frye called a pattern of words: words as literally words in relation. The best work bearing this in mind is Nelson Hilton's provocative *Literal Imagination.*[44] Blake causes words to take on worldly bodies and these bodies to form chains of relations based on a variety of possibilities: acronymic, homonymic, punnish, etc. Blake's work is not *Finnegans Wake* because it does not deliberately cut off or frustrate our sense of plot, character, historical allegory, etc. But surely what Aristotle called diction but did not make the principal form of the poem *is* the synecdochic macrocosm, and we must give full attention to all its possibilities.

Thus we find in plate 10 that the appearance of the word "infinite" with both "Thames" and "serpent" sets forth a relation, that Blake's words tend to cluster without center but with equality characterized by their tropological relations.

In the light of past criticism it is not possible, I think, to emphasize the last two points too much.

As plate 10 gets under way, we see that in the temple the acts of the fiery King, Albion's Angel, et al. are identified with what Blake elsewhere calls the worldview of "Bacon, Newton, and Locke." This worldview, he thought, had "ruined England": man's fate, when he becomes enclosed in the self-involving activity of the externalizing reason, is to become serpentine. The fiery King's behavior is a cyclical repetition of the Fall of man, itself an "analogy" of an unfallen state of creativity, where what seems like repetition is identity. To retire to the serpent temple is to replay the temple's creation. This is not, however, quite the best way to put it: what really happens is that there is a movement back and forth between the macrocosmic myth of Fall and the microcosmic part played in particulars by the fiery King et al., who are the "island white" or Albion himself, or "ruined England," or, in turn, man, who is the world that contains him. This movement from part to whole to part to whole is contained in plate 10 itself considered as part identical by implication with the whole of *Europe* and the Blake canon. The shift from the part to the larger myth that occurs, for example, in lines 13ff. may at first appear to be a loss of control over the story characteristic of a garrulous (mad?) narrator. The difference from garrulousness (to say nothing of madness, of which Blake has been accused) is a rigorously synecdochic method that requires constant invocation of the presentness of all history in "visible" particulars as well as the identity of man and men.

And so we are suddenly told of man's enclosure in corporeality, which in Blake is the illusion of materiality separate from imagination. This appears in the form of a great flood, which is also the ancient flood, described as a flood of sense perception, the result of an empirical notion of sense passivity, which petrifies against the infinite or against the principle of synecdoche itself the means of expansion from the alienated, centered individual to man as whole. We soon learn that this petrification is connected with a center of supposed truth called the Stone of Night, fallen Albion's head, and, of course, the Ancient Guardian's.

The flight of man into the forests of night (an oak forest, of course, because the Druids were oak worshippers) is thus identical with the flight of the fiery King et al. to Verulam (to Bacon), who is by metonymy his empiricism surrounded by oak trees. And these flights are not connected merely by a figure of speech, considered as a technical device, but by an avenue of ethical vision according to poetic antithetical logic or myth; for in the very fabric of synecdoche, a warp and woof of infinite magnitude and the infinitesimal as well, there lies everywhere the principal ethical pattern we constitute from Blake's work: the need for annihilation of the self-hood, for sympathetic expansive identity to include the other. As Jesus says to Albion at the beginning of *Jerusalem,* we are involved in identity with each other and must cure ourselves of the illusion of absolute subjectivity, though not of individuality and freedom. We might even conclude that this is the ethical pattern abstractable as idea from myth itself as a way of constituting life and that Blake's canon is a synecdoche of mythmaking.

Beginning at line 24 of plate 10, the southern porch of the serpent temple becomes the head of Albion, and the whole of the temple his body. The porch becomes, as the passage proceeds, the Stone of Night, with its suggestion of a dark immovable center to which all things ought to tend as if it were the word or (deca)*logos.* It ought to be the light of reason, as in Blake's treatment of the unfallen condition, where Urizen is identified with the sun and is in the South or Zenith, supported by the other Zoas with Urthona at the base or North. Instead it is located in a "vale obscure." It is "oblique"—standing inclined, indirect, disingenuous, the dictionary tells us; but the term also hearkens back to *Paradise Lost,* where God's angels

> turn askance
> The poles of earth twice ten degrees and more
> From the sun's axle; they with labor pushed
> Oblique the centric globe.
> (10:668–71)

In Blake's poem the movement is 180 degrees, but particularly important is the dark centering of the sun within and as the head of Albion: as things are thrust out from the mind as objects, so is reason more and more self-enclosed as subject. As the effort to establish an objective center of authority or *logos* becomes more intensified, so does this center become more subjectified as a projection of arbitrary personal power and tyranny. Something is wrong here. The purple flowers and berries are but vestiges of a previous condition of summer; now the sun has departed. This lost light of reason was not then the law, as it is now presumably carved on the Stone of Night, like the tablets of Moses; it was a liberating science. Now everything is reversed: South has become North; Albion's body is upside down, as is the fiery King's, the Angel's, and the Ancient Guardian's, all identified and identical. The head hangs into the abyss of a northern sky. Suddenly we see it, quite properly, as a cavern, because this northern sky, externalized by the fallen reason is really an airy thought contained by Albion's mind. It is also a locked-up sun that can spread no light. Thought is the thought of the subject and the object. Further, the whole of the serpent temple, turned 180 degrees on its axis, also Albion's body, is pulled into this abyss of sky as if the sky were a grave; and we see it sink headfirst, then feet, as if being sucked in by a whirlpool, except that this is a reverse whirlpool that sucks the victim not through the eye of Hell toward Purgatory as Dante went with Virgil, but out into the grave of the abyss. The whirlpool thus continues the notion of everything being reversed or upside down in the fallen state. Caught in this movement, the victim, an inquirer according to the externalizing mode of Bacon, is dizzied. The effort to establish a center by empirical means has resulted in objective/subjective disequilibrium. This story, which begins with the fiery King and expands to include Albion himself, is a synecdoche of the greater story of *The Four Zoas*.

To constitute this text is to become involved in the endless oscillation of synecdoche, where figure expands to become the whole, where whole contracts only to confront a miniscule figure of expansion that expands to become identical with an even larger whole. Plate 10 writes in microcosm the whole of *Europe; Europe* writes *The Four Zoas*, but also "London," "Holy Thursday," and "The Human Abstract." Plate 10 continually progresses out from itself in opposition to the antimythical logic of before/after, here/there, and subject/object.

A neo-Blakean critical method must embody a traditional scholarship that traces the Blakean tropes into odd channels of the past, must read the news of Blake's time, must grasp at the modes of interpretation he may have known, must follow out innumerable hunches; but the results must be enclosed in a discourse that recognizes the Blakean text's synecdochic antithetical logic and discovers ways to make the text's ethical implications, based on this logic, available to conversation. Blake's notion of "Allegory addressd to the Intellectual powers" (E730) was not that its use is the mediated expression of a truth or deity that hides truth even as it speaks in a code of arbitrary signifiers. That would be the detested Romantic allegory addressed to the corporeal understanding. Nor was it that poetry is somehow a miraculous symbolism bringing into existence something lurking in the beyond. That would be delusion. Blake's intellectual allegory shaped by synecdoche is an endlessly exfoliating potentiality of identities, carrying ethical implications of the greatest urgency. Our critical method should not forget the urgency with which he wrote. Our method should be neo-Blakean, lest we detach the ethic from its exfoliation in such a way as to corrupt it into a Stone of Night, constituting ourselves as an antimythical rather than an ironic priesthood.

Blake's Revisionism: Gnostic Interpretation and Critical Methodology

William Dennis Horn

Harold Bloom's revisionary theory[1] is not a methodology so much as a dark vision of the dynamics of poetic creation. A theory of literature, revisionism maps the history of poetry as the history of the imagination. It is concerned not with the poet as personality, but with the imagination as a poetic id that works itself out through the dynamics of ego psychology. Bloom's rhetoric of revisionism describes the pattern by which a poet creates an identity for himself in attempting to deny and then overcome the influence of strongly influential predecessors. Revisionism reduces all literary influence to a psychomachia in which the belated poet must make the work of his strong precursor seem a weaker imitation or prefiguring of his own.[2] The later poet revives the earlier in order to correct his work.

Blake's self-conscious misprision in poems such as *Milton* can help us evaluate revisionist theory. Blake is a key figure in Bloom's creation of a postmodern theory based on ancient Gnostic thought. By examining Blake's relation to his precursors, to Gnosticism, and particularly Gnosticism as filtered through Milton and the Bible, we can achieve a critical perspective on revisionary theory. I propose to examine the roots of Bloom's revisionism in Blake and in ancient Gnosticism. Those roots begin in Blake's preoccupation with rewriting Milton and extend to Blake's absorption of Gnostic techniques for revising the Bible.

Recently, David Fite has shown how Bloomian theory develops from the early *Blake's Apocalypse, Shelley,* and the pivotal *Yeats* through the revisionary criticism of more than a decade.[3] Fite describes how Bloom first formulates revisionism in terms of the Lurianic Kabbalah (*The Anxiety of Influence*) and then develops it in terms of Gnosticism (55–90). Gnosticism grows in Bloomian theory as Bloom uncovers it in Blake and in an entire tradition of revisionist interpretation. To study Blake's use of Gnostic rhetoric is to effect on Bloom a return of the repressed, much in keeping with the critic's own theories. While modeling the form of his revisionary rhetoric in terms of Kabbalah, Bloom increasingly indicates that revisionary theory is specifically Gnostic. Even in *Kabbalah and Criticism* he traces revision to its ultimately Gnostic source: "Whereas Neoplatonism was a rather conventional theory of influence, Gnosticism was a theory of misprision, and so is a necessary model for any contemporary theory of influence as being a creative misunderstanding" (62). And again: "In urging a Kabbalistic model, which means ultimately a Gnostic model, I am in danger of appearing to be like those Valentinian mystagogues whom Plotinus so eloquently condemned" (87). Moreover, in the more recent *Agon* (published in 1982, seven years after *Kabbalah and Criticism*) his references to Kabbalah recede as he speaks of writing "as a Jewish Gnostic, trying to explore and develop a personal gnosis and a possible Gnosticism, perhaps even one available to others" (4). Thus, as Bloom developed his criticism he appealed to older and older sources in tradition. By following his progress, we can come to a better understanding of revisionary theory.

Blake's *Milton* is a central influence on Bloom's rhetoric of revision. In the poem Milton returns to earth as a falling star, entering Blake's left foot (*M*15, E110). This happens so that the later poet can correct the work of the earlier. For Bloom this story stands as a type for the dynamics of influence in which the newcomer can overcome his belatedness only by assimilating and then correcting his precursor, by making the precursor's work a prelude to his own. Though *Milton* represents Blake's most overt expression of revisionism, the revisionist project started early in the poet's work. In *The Marriage of Heaven and Hell*, the voice of the devil argues that "The reason Milton wrote in fetters when he wrote of Angels & God, and at liberty when of Devils & Hell, is because he was a true Poet and of the Devils party without knowing it" (*MHH*6, E35). This standard Romantic attitude toward *Paradise Lost* assumes that a reader, here the devil, interprets a work from perspectives superior to, or at least outside of, those of the author. From the new perspective, the poem means something more or something different from what the poet, in this case Milton, "intended."

In a brief stroke of the pen, Blake foreshadows much modern critical discussion of intentionality and influence. The spirit of his revisionism runs deeper than the critics usually acknowledge. Though Blake finds precedence for revisionism in Milton's own effort to read pagan myths as distorted foreshadowings of true Christian history, his main source lies in a Gnostic tradition of retelling and inverting Jewish scripture. The revisionist project of Blake's poetry springs from early Christian Gnosticism, the effects of which can be found in the New Testament itself.

Historically, Blake critics have acknowledged Blake's Gnosticism with little comment. Henry Crabb Robinson supplies us with the following anecdote: "The eloquent descriptions of Nature in Wordsworth's poems were conclusive proof of Atheism, for whoever believes in Nature said B: disbelieves in God—For Nature is the work of the Devil On my obtaining from him the declaration that the Bible was the work of God, I referred to the commencem^t of Genesis—In the beginning God created the Heaven the Earth—But I gained nothing by this for I was triumphantly told that this God was not Jehovah, but the Elohim, and the doctrine of the Gnostics repeated with sufficient consistency to silence one so unlearned as myself."[4]

Robinson's silence is typical of critical comment on Blake's Gnosticism for the next 120 years. Most major Blake critics mention Gnosticism only to drop the subject. Perhaps this results from criticism's reluctance to deal with what W. J. T. Mitchell calls "the angry, flawed Blake, the crank who knew and repeated just about every bit of nonsense ever thought in the eighteenth century."[5] In his otherwise splendid analysis of *The Book of Urizen*, Mitchell attempts to distinguish between Blake and Gnosticism by arguing that "for Blake, the redemptive energies are in this world, or must be brought into this world. There is no escaping beyond the skies to where the Eternals dwell; they must be brought back to earth, as Blake will make explicit when he has them descend *en masse* as the 'multitudes of Ololon' in *Milton*."[6]

Mitchell has put his finger not on a distinction, but on what Kurt Rudolph cites "as the central idea—the central myth—of Gnosticism: 'the idea of the presence in man of a divine "spark" . . . which has proceeded from the divine world and has fallen into this world of destiny, birth and death and which must be reawakened through its own divine counterpart in order to be finally restored.' "[7] The divine exists in the world, in man, but is ignorant or asleep. Gnosis is an act of awakening the Divine Man, which is the divine in man.[8]

Critics frequently attribute Gnostic elements in Blake's poetry to the

Kabbalist tradition. For example, Sheila Spector[9] takes great pains to reveal where Blake could and could not have learned Kabbalistic lore. The clearest evidence of his knowledge of such myths appears in *Jerusalem*, chapter 2, "To the Jews," where he refers to the Kabbalistic myth of Adam Kadmon (*J*27, E171). But this tradition, like most other evidences of Blake's Kabbalism, is fundamentally Gnostic. Other of Blake's Gnostic stories could not have come from Jewish tradition. His myth of an evil creator and a higher human unity, which is the true God, is specifically Gnostic. Thus in the prose description of *A Vision of the Last Judgment* he says: "Thinking as I do that the Creator of this World is a very Cruel Being & being a Worshipper of Christ I cannot help saying the Son O how unlike the Father" (*VLJ*94, E565). Blake adopts this Gnostic vision of an evil creator as early as *The Marriage of Heaven and Hell* in lines such as the following: "the Jehovah of the Bible being no other than he, who dwells in flaming fire" (*MHH*6, E35), or again in Blake's annotations to Watson's *An Apology for the Bible:* "Wherefore did Christ come was it not to abolish the Jewish Imposture Was not Christ murderd because he taught that God loved all Men & was their father & forbad all contention for Worldly prosperity in opposition to the Jewish Scriptures which are only an Example of the wickedness & deceit of the Jews" (E614).

In *Major Trends in Jewish Mysticism* Gershom Scholem explains why Jewish tradition could not embrace the myth of the evil Genesis God:

> The ancient gnostics of the second and third century distinguished between the hidden and benevolent god, the God of the illuminate whose knowledge they call "gnosis," and the Creator and Lawgiver whom they also call the Jewish God, and to whom they attribute the writings of the Old Testament. The term *Jewish God* or *God of Israel* is abusive and meant to be so. The Gnostics regarded the confusion between the two Gods, the higher loving one, and the lower who is merely just, as a misfortune for religion. It is metaphysical antisemitism in its profoundest and most effective form which has found expression in these ideas and continues to do so.[10]

Blake's version of the Jewish God is Jehovah/Elohim, the lawgiver, who becomes Urizen as the poet's myth matures. This deprecation of the Genesis God is common to many Gnostic texts, but has no real counterpart in the Kabbalah, even in the dualism of Sabbatian theology (Scholem 322–23).

However Blake came to Gnostic thought, he was reinforced in it by his Christianity. Gnosticism exhibits a strong antinomianism and general rejection of Old Testament thought. Blake favored such attitudes and found support for them in the New Testament, especially in the writings of Paul. Moreover, modern scholarship shows that many New Testament documents bear a Gnostic stamp. Though questions of source are entangled, it is clear that Blake appropriated the Gnostic creation myths to his own parody of Enlightenment thought. Ironically, some of the clearest accounts of these myths have come down to us through church fathers such as Justin Martyr, Origen, and Irenaeus who described Gnosticism in order to define and establish orthodoxy in opposition to Gnostic excesses. Their accounts of heresy provide us with much of our understanding of Gnostic practices. Because Blake did not know Latin, he could not have read these accounts directly, but he was acquainted with Joseph Priestley, who wrote, in his support of Unitarianism, at least three histories of the early church, including *A History of the Corruptions of Christianity*.[11] As Stuart Curran indicates, Blake "might easily have encountered lengthy expositions of Gnostic thought in Pierre Bayle's *Dictionary*, Isaac de Beausobre's *Historie Critique de Manichee et Manicheisme*, Nathaniel Lardner's *History of Heretics* and *Credibility of the Gospel History*, Johann Lorenz von Mosheim's *Ecclesiastical History*, Gibbon's *Decline and Fall of the Roman Empire*, and any number of works of the Unitarian theologian Joseph Priestley."[12]

Today, the translation of newly discovered codices has stirred scholarly interest in Gnosticism. Hans Jonas's publication of *The Gnostic Religion* in 1958 gave English-speaking readers a comprehensive view of the role of Gnosticism in Western religious thought. General dissemination of the Nag Hammadi manuscripts (found in 1947 but relatively unpublished and untranslated for more than a quarter century) has made Gnosticism better known outside the arena of biblical scholarship. Elaine Pagels, in a popular evaluation of the new sources, has done much to acquaint English literary critics with Gnosticism as a force in early Christianity.[13] Bolder critics who take seriously Blake's Gnostic attitudes and methodology include Stuart Curran, Leslie Tannenbaum, Harold Bloom, and most recently Norman O. Brown.[14] More conservative critics simply ignore his Gnosticism. Harold Bloom has made it the springboard for his revisionary theory.

The best way to approach Blake's Gnosticism is through a brief look at Gnostic rhetoric. Among the characteristics of the Western or Valentinian form of Gnosticism are numerous writings that retell the creation story of Genesis. In the Gnostic parody (or more specifically, inversion) of Genesis, the world is formed by an evil creator, the demiurge, who mistakenly assumes that he is the only deity; he is ignorant of the deities above him. In this revision of Jewish Scripture, the creator and his creation are evil. A higher, unfallen deity exists in the world as a secret self, a divine spark hidden from a hostile world. His secret name is Adam, or man. Gnostic stories of an evil Genesis creator show how man finds himself thrown into an alien world that is ruled by an alien God. This god mistakenly attempts to assert his authority as the only God with none above him. The creation is frequently described as a succession of emanations resulting in a succession of lower deities. Man is seen as trapped in the world. Though his body and soul are a part of that world, a small spark of deity remains hidden within man. Human alienation is characterized by a nexus of tropes that depict humanity in bondage in a prison cosmos, the lowest dungeon of which is this world. The true man has become drunk or fallen asleep and remains so until awakened by a knowledge ("gnosis") that is supplied by the Gnostic text itself. That knowledge is a revelation of man's true nature.

Blake's *Book of Urizen* revives in theme and trope the Gnostic genre of Genesis parody. As S. Foster Damon indicates, "The central character of this book is Urizen, or Reason, the God of this world. His name in the Bible is Jehovah. Blake seems to have rediscovered, or perhaps adapted for himself, the early Gnostic heresy: 'The evil that is in the world must be due to the Creator of the world.' "[15] At one point in its production, the poem was named *The First Book of Urizen*, echoing the First Book of Moses, or Genesis. In Blake's account, higher deities, the Eternals, watch over an (at first) unnamed lower god who is unaware of their presence. The lower god, who soon receives the name Urizen, asserts an independence based on defiance, after the pattern of Milton's Satan.

We can see that *The Book of Urizen* is fundamentally Gnostic by comparing it to any one of a number of Gnostic revisions of Genesis. For instance, the *Hypostasis of the Archons* includes in its retelling of the Genesis story the following account of an unnamed creator god: "Opening his eyes he saw a vast quantity of Matter without limit; and he became arrogant saying, 'It is I who am God, and there is none other apart from me.' "[16] With all the passion of insecurity, Blake's demiurge creates a material world while mistakenly asserting that he is the sole God of the cosmos. But the world he creates is evil: "The Ox in the slaughter house moans / The Dog at the wintry door" (*U*25:1–2, E82). In a succession of resulting emanations the spirit world is populated. Urizen wanders through the heaven of his new, "dungeon-like" world. This world is inhabited by giants who "shrink from existence" until, as in the Genesis account, they become smaller and live a shorter time than their ancestors. Finally, a Moses figure attempts to free his brothers:

> 8. So Fuzon call'd all together
> The remaining children of Urizen:
> And they left the pendulous earth:
> They called it Egypt, & left it.
>
> 9. And the salt ocean rolled englob'd
> (*U*28:19–23, E83)

The particularly Gnostic flavor of this passage is revealed by a comparison with a passage from Jonas's *The Gnostic Religion:*

> *Sea* or *waters* is a standing Gnostic symbol for the world of matter or of darkness into which the divine has sunk. . . . The Peratae interpreted the Red Sea (Suf-Sea), which has to be passed on the way to or from Egypt, as the "water of corruption," and identified it with Kronos, i.e., "time," and with "becoming."
>
> *Egypt* as a symbol for the material world is very common in Gnosticism (and beyond it). The biblical story of Israel's bondage and liberation lent itself admirably to spiritual interpretation of the type the Gnostics liked. But the biblical story is not the only association which qualified Egypt for its allegorical role. From ancient times Egypt had been regarded as the home of the cult of the dead, and therefore the kingdom of Death; this and other features of Egyptian religion, such as beast-headed gods and the great role of sorcery, inspired the Hebrews and later the Persians with a particular abhorrence and made them see in "Egypt" the

embodiment of a demonic principle. The Gnostics then turned this evaluation into their use of Egypt as a symbol for "this world," that is, the world of matter, of ignorance, and of perverse religion. (117–18)

Though evidence of Gnostic influence in *The Book of Urizen* is large, the early Harold Bloom warns: "Blake never ceased to be a satirist, and even *The Book of Urizen* is more a satire on orthodox theogonies than a serious theogony in its own right."[17] The vehicle of Blake's satire is parodic inversion. Insofar as its target is Genesis, the parody is Gnostic. Blake's Gnostic parody is historically bound; it is a vehicle for the poet's critique of the ascendency of reason in Enlightenment thought. But even here the poet is following a Gnostic habit of revising earlier myth, a habit that accounts for the proliferation of sects despised by the early caretakers of orthodoxy in the church.

Gnostic rhetoric, though never so concentrated as in *The Book of Urizen,* exists throughout Blake's writings. Images of bondage appear as early as *The Marriage of Heaven and Hell:* "The Giants who formed this world into its sensual existence and now seem to live in it in chains; are in truth. the causes of its life & the sources of all activity" (*MHH*16, E40). Here as in *The Book of Urizen,* the giants are actually men, bound by what in the *Songs of Experience* are called "mindforg'd manacles" (E27). Blake's longer works all contain Gnostic rhetoric in their dark images of bondage to the material world. Escape from that bondage, through his much discussed apocalypse, is best described as a "gnosis," or understanding, that the reader achieves by following the text:

> I give you the end of a golden string,
>   Only wind it into a ball:
> It will lead you in at Heavens gate,
>   Built in Jerusalems wall.
> (*J* 77, E231)

In ancient Gnosticism, gnosis referred to a special knowledge possessed by the enlightened or spiritual (pneumatic) man. Gnosis revealed "where we were, wherein we have been thrown; whereto we speed, wherefrom we are redeemed; what is birth and what rebirth" (Jonas 334). The answers to life's fundamental questions were contained in myths drawn primarily from Hebrew and Greek but also from other Mediterranean and Near Eastern cultures. Using syncretic myths to address fundamental questions of existence, Blake sings a Gnostic strain with a burden that is a historically bound attack on the Enlightenment's reification of reason. His post-Enlightenment gnosis answers the Gnostic's fundamental questions somewhat as follows: We are spiritual (i.e., sensory) beings, whose reason (Blake's demiurge) has reduced us to mere bodies. We once lived a giant sensual existence, in an earth as expanded as our imaginations, but now live in a finite globular world defined by weight and measure. Knowledge of our former godlike state can free us from the illusion of bondage to a material existence. We are not our bodies; rather we were born into the world as sensation and desire until our reason reduces our senses to the organs of sensation.

According to Blake's devilish account, the Messiah fell and "formed a heaven of what he stole from the Abyss" (*MHH*6, E35). This "abyss of the five senses" (*MHH*5, E35) is a parody of the Hell that Milton's devils make in their home in *Paradise Lost* (2:522–27 and 546–73ff). The creation of a home in Hell equals the creation of the material world, and of the human body, the instrument of sensation. Sight is reduced to the eyes, "two little orbs . . . fixed in two little caves" (*U*11:13–14, E76). Sound is reduced to "Two Ears in close volutions" (*U*11:21, E76). We can be freed from our shrunken notion of sensation and be reborn in our true nature once we understand who we are. The artist with his sensual works of imagination helps restore us to the life of sensation, life before the assumption of instrumental causality (before we assume that the eyes and ears are the cause of sensation).

This much we can read in the early poems. As his myth matures, Blake reifies the several parts of existence, just as the Enlightenment reified reason. The senses become Tharmas; the sexual, Luvah; and the imagination, Urthona or Los. Together with reason, Urizen, these make up the four fundamental life forms, the Zoas. They are the parts of man not given by the material world, not present in sensation. As such the four Zoas represent the Gnostic divine spark whose secret name is Adam or Man. They are reminiscent of the Gnostic "Four Light-givers, who stand in the presence of the Great Invisible Spirit."[18]

Blake uses Gnostic narrative techniques in the service of his critique of the Enlightenment metaphysics of Newton and Locke. The physical world that is the object of Enlightenment empirical inquiry is for Blake the result of reason's reification (Blake's word is "abstraction") of the entire sensory and intellectual world into static forms: "I have sought for a joy without pain. / For a solid without fluctuation" (*U*4:10–11, E71).

This critique of the material world is similar to Jacques Derrida's critique of the metaphysics of presence. Derrida quotes from Anatole France the following view of philosophy: " 'I think I have at last made you realize one thing, Aristos, that any expression of an abstract idea can only be an analogy. By an odd fate, the very metaphysicians who think to escape the world of appearances are constrained to live perpetually in allegory. A sorry lot of poets, they dim the colours of the ancient fables, and are themselves but gatherers of fables. They produce white mythology.' " For Blake the entire material world is a result of Urizenic abstraction, the creation of entities, while for Derrida the language of Western metaphysics continually relates to an infinite series of referents to which there is neither end nor origin. And just as Derrida insists that he is using logocentric arguments to expose logocentrism, so Blake reifies mental entities to expose the reification process behind our perception of a physical world. Though Blake's critique is aimed at Enlightenment philosophy, it extends to written texts, which continually undercut their narrative frameworks.

Blake's Zoas, then, are a misrepresentation of the forms of humanity. Blake is a humanist positing an essential humanity, but every expression of that humanity partakes of reason's abstraction. Reason, the abstracting power, is a part of that humanity. So is imagination, the power to create. Such forces are primary for Blake; they constitute the human. Blake's myth of unity describes what happens when reason tries to isolate and reify these forces as separately existing entities. Bloom's ego psychology offers a fitting illustration of this error of reason. As Fite expresses it: "Bloom in his application of Freud to the patternings of poetry is *not* concerned with the forces in the poet as a man, but rather solely with the poet as an embattled poetic ego—a nexus of forces within the patterns of force of an internalized literary history" (77). From a Blakean perspective this is a ratio, a specter of imagination narrowed to a solipsistic account of itself. Bloom's misprision of Blake reduces Romanticism to a self-conscious obsession with the dynamics of literary creation. In Blake, the Romantic, self-reflexive preoccupation with poetic identity is embedded in a poetry that wishes to identify humanity with friendship, politics, morality, space, time, sensation, and whatever constitutes our account of human experience. Bloom abstracts a part and chooses to call that the imagination.

Blake's cosmic myth owes much to Gnostic and Neoplatonic emanation theory. Gnostic emanation rhetoric is usually critical and self-conscious. The Gnostic myths, after all, criticize the reification (hypostatization) process by which mythic entities are made substantial. The practice of outrageously inverting a precursor text continually calls into question all textuality. In the same way, Blake's myths of abstraction enact the human ability to abstract and reify at the same time that they parody and condemn. The poet who rages against abstraction is the same who creates and populates a cosmos of his own abstracted deities. He recasts the Gnostic ontological myths in terms of eighteenth-century epistemological concerns. In doing so he creates a misprision of his Gnostic sources. The Gnostics inverted Genesis as a story of man's alienation in a hostile material world (Curran 117). In turn Blake inverts Gnostic myths as the story of reason's growing dominance in Renaissance and Enlightenment thought. Thus, Ialdabaoth, or the Gnostic demiurge, becomes Urizen of "your reason." He is not the creative principle (though he is responsible for creating the material world) as much as he is the God of weight and measure of modern science.

Blake's emanations are the forms that reason and imagination give to the world. They are the modes by which we experience the world: "Los is by mortals nam'd Time Enitharmon is nam'd Space" ($M$24:68, E121). An emanation is a product that reveals the human mental creative or perceptive activity giving rise to it. Apparently, Blake subscribes to an essentially transcendental argument, deducing human characteristics from the undeniable facets of our experience. In Blake's Gnostic account of the cosmos, the entire material world is an emanation of the perceptive faculties of mind (reason or Urizen). Moreover, the products of human endeavor, especially poetry, painting, and music, show the existence of a human creative principle (imagination or Los):

> When in Eternity Man converses with Man they enter
> Into each others Bosom (which are Universes of delight)
> In mutual interchange. and first their Emanations meet . . .
> For Man cannot unite with Man but by their Emanations.
> ($J$88:3–10, E246)

By using emanation rhetoric in a critique exposing the metaphysics of that rhetoric, Blake implies the inescapability of our modes of thought. He expresses this as the fall of reason, his revision of the myth of the fallen man. The myth of the four Zoas depicts a sequence of falls, all of which can be attributed to what reason does when it attempts to reify its own abstracting processes. The account we read is itself fallen for several reasons: (1) The poet creates stasis out of temporal processes by giving a name to the Zoas; he reifies or hypostasizes mental activity. (2) The Zoas are independent beings; reason lays boundaries around interactive mental processes. (3) A single Zoa, reason, begins to see himself as the only human form; not poetry, but abstract philosophy becomes the burden of the poem. (4) The poet must accommodate human reason, as Milton's Raphael accommodates his story to Adam (*Paradise Lost* 5:571–74); the poet puts in the temporal mode of narrative an account of the atemporal structure of human thought. In this way, Blake's fallen poetry insists that a fallen perspective is inescapable.

Blake's emanation rhetoric involves a fundamental choice. Neoplatonism and Gnosticism presented similar theories of creation by emanation, but the two movements were much in opposition, Plotinus's *Enneads* having been written as an extended tractate against Gnosticism. To understand why Blake opted for the Gnostic view is to appreciate a fundamental split in Romanticism that still influences thought in our time. The Neoplatonists believed that the creation was good; the Gnostics believed that the created world and hence its creator were evil. Plotinus's position is generally Stoic insofar as he holds that man must learn to submit to the natural/divine order of the cosmos (Jonas 248–49). The Gnostic, holding that the human is antithetical to the created world, schemes at frustrating the plans of the God of this world. This distinction of attitudes, Stoic and Gnostic, is useful for understanding the history of inversion rhetoric. Ultimately the Stoic position with its commitment to order and its doctrine of acceptance is socially conservative, while Gnosticism, favoring revisionism, individuality, and defiance, undercuts all forms of orthodoxy. Thus, as the early Church codified an oral tradition into a written canon and organized itself, it moved to expel the Christian Gnostics (see Pagels).

In the Romantic misprision of Milton we find this same dichotomy between the conservative submission to the divine order (represented by Milton's Stoic God) and the establishing of a naked self in opposition to the controlling power of the universe (represented by Milton's Satan). However liberal he was for his own time, Milton provides the catalyst for revisionism precisely because he is unbending in his Stoicism. *Paradise Lost* is unrelenting in its insistence that man, angel, and devil must bow to the divine order of the cosmos. Those readers who identify with Satan's plight in the first two books feel smothered under the inexorable force of divine power (necessity) asserted in the remainder of the poem. Blake was such a reader.

Early in his poetic career, in *The Marriage of Heaven and Hell*, Blake proposed a Gnostic inversion of *Paradise Lost* (*MHH* 5 and 6). Here Blake opposed reason to desire, terms that also define a radical Gnostic dichotomy between the man and the world. Desire, the human, is that Gnostic spark that is not of this world. Reason, and the physical universe that reason discovers, or Urizen creates, are an "abyss of the five senses" (*MHH*5, E34). Blake's devil argues that reason restrains desire,

> And being restraind it by degrees becomes passive till it is only the shadow of desire.
> The history of this is written in Paradise Lost. & the Governor of Reason is call'd Messiah.
> And the original Archangel or possessor of the command of the heavenly host, is calld the Devil or Satan and his children are call'd Sin & Death
> But in the Book of Job Miltons Messiah is call'd Satan.
> For this history has been adopted by both parties (*MHH*5, E34)

Thus, Blake suggests two opposing views of human history, or rather two interpretations of the same historical account, depending on which party is doing the interpreting. When Blake's devil claims that "the Messiah fell. & formed a heaven of what he stole from the Abyss" (*MHH*5, E35), he is advancing the Gnostic creation myth that Blake elaborates in *The Book of Urizen*. Thus, Blake draws the battleline between the Stoic view, represented by Milton and orthodox Western tradition, and his own Gnostic view, spoken by the devil. On the one side is Stoicism, reason, restraint, and acceptance; on the other is Gnosticism, desire, exuberance, and defiance.

In Blake especially, and in the darker side of the other Romantic writers,[20] there is a strain of Gnostic defiance that grew in part from the Romantic reaction to Milton. As a Christian poem, *Paradise Lost* champions Stoic submission to this world's God, the cosmos, and historical providence. But Milton's Stoic theme of redemption is played out against Satan's attitude of self-assertion, as painted in the first two books of the poem. When Blake concludes that Milton wrote in "fetters" (*MHH*5, E35), he is invoking a favorite Gnostic image, one that represents bondage to the material world. The true poet, one who has been freed, is Blake's misprision of the pneumatic, the enlightened Gnostic self who is in touch with the divine spark within. The poet's liberty lies not in conforming to a cosmos that in no way resembles him, but in defining himself in opposition to the world.

In Gnosticism, the divine spark that is alien to this world exists within the pneumatic or spiritual man. In Blake's misprision of Gnostic myth, the "Poetic or Prophetic character" (*NNR*[*b*], E3)—later called the imagination—establishes itself by speaking against the natural world. Blake's *The Ghost of Abel* (1822), a response to Byron's *Cain* (1821), begins with this dedication: "To LORD BYRON in the Wilderness: What doest thou here, Elijah? Can a Poet doubt the Visions of Jehovah? Nature has no Outline; but Imagination has. Nature has no Tune; but Imagination has! Nature has no Supernatural & dissolves: Imagination is Eternity" (E270). Like the early tractates entitled "There Is No Natural Religion" (1788), these lines attempt to reveal the spiritual voice in opposition to nature, Blake's eighteenth-century misprision of the Gnostic "cosmos." This voice is responsible on an epistemological level for giving the world the form of human sensory experience. In the longer prophecies the voice is personified as Los. The power that weighs and measures the forms, who relates them in a ratio, is called Urizen, the God of this world.

The theme of Gnostic defiance is expressed in the image of the solitary figure establishing himself by defying the world's power. In Romanticism, the finest examples of this type are Byron's Manfred and Shelley's Prometheus, both modeled on Milton's Satan. Shelley's figure, like Satan, revolts against the existing cosmic order. And like Blake at his most Gnostic, Shelley argues the redeeming effect of a knowledge expressed by the poem. Byron, too, is close to Blake in expressing the Gnostic theme of self-creation through defiance. Throughout Byron's work, but especially in *Childe Harold's Pilgrimage, Manfred,* and *Don Juan,* we find characters who create themselves through acts of defiance.[21] Such Byronic heroes find precedence in the Gnostic figure of Cain. So central was Cain to the Gnostic attitude of defiance that an

entire sect of Cainites arose (Rudolph 17, 256–57, 309). Hans Jonas
sees in this "elevation of Cain" an inversion of traditional values that
comments on the practice of revisionism:

> Perhaps we should speak in such cases, not of allegory at all, but
> of a form of polemics, that is, not of an exegesis of the original
> text, but of its tendentious rewriting. Indeed, the Gnostics in such
> cases hardly *claimed* to bring out the correct meaning of the orig-
> inal, if by "correct" is meant the meaning *intended* by its au-
> thor—seeing that this author, directly or indirectly, was their
> great adversary, the benighted creator-god. Their unspoken claim
> was rather that the blind author had unwittingly embodied some-
> thing of the truth in his partisan version of thing, and that this
> truth can be brought out by turning the intended meaning upside
> down. (95)

In both Gnosticism and Romanticism the rhetoric of defiance speaks
of a character's attempt to bolster an insubstantial self. This concern
with the self helps explain Romanticism's attraction to the defiant
(Gnostic) hero.[22] The Romantics acutely felt the substantiality of the
self eroding in the wake of Enlightenment philosophy. The problem
was best expressed by Hume: "For my part, when I enter most intimately into what I call *myself,* I always stumble on some particular
perception or other, of heat or cold, light or shade, love or hatred, pain
or pleasure. I never can catch *myself* at any time without a perception,
and never can observe anything but the perception. When my perceptions are remov'd for any time, as by sound sleep; so long am I in-
sensible of *myself,* and may truly be said not to exist."[23]

Blake and other Romantic poets inherited the problems of the insubstantial self. One Romantic response (seen particularly in Blake,
Byron, and Shelley) established the self in opposition to an alien
Gnostic cosmos. Another similar response depicted a psychic cosmos
of warring selves that in the aggregate constitute humanity, the human
form. In Blake (and Wordsworth and Shelley, and the other English
Romantics to a lesser extent), the idea of a common human form was
seized to supplement the loss of a personal god on the one hand and
a substantial self on the other. Thus, Blake transforms the Gnostic myth
of the sleeping god to the figure of Albion, symbol of the divine hu-

manity. But even this displacement did not overcome eighteenth-century materialism, which for Blake had reached the lower limit of speculation:

> 10. But Urizen laid in a stony sleep
> Unorganiz'd, rent from Eternity
>
> 11. The Eternals said: What is this? Death
> Urizen is a clod of clay.
> (*U*6:7–10, E74)

Romanticism's more orthodox side holds to the Stoic argument that things will improve if we only bring ourselves into harmony with the natural world. This Stoicism finds a voice in the early Wordsworth,[24] where it is continually mingled with a darker note, as we find in poems such as Wordsworth's "Resolution and Independence." In 1826, Blake indicates something of this in his annotations to Wordsworth's *Poems* (1815): "I see in Wordsworth the Natural Man rising up against the Spiritual Man Continually & then he is No Poet but a Heathen Philosopher at Enmity against all true Poetry or Inspiration" (E665). Here the Natural man is Blake's version of the fleshly or earthly (in Greek *choic* or *hylic*) man. The spiritual man equals the Gnostic pneumatic, who in Blake's rendering is the imagination or poet within the poet; he is everything that cannot be found in the empirical world, the "desire," described in *The Marriage of Heaven and Hell* and the object of desire embodied in the later figure of Jerusalem.

Even epistemology is political. Blake's evil material world justifies a Gnostic defiance, while Wordsworth's benevolent nature begs for Stoic acceptance. The Stoic side of Romanticism developed into meliorism, and at the end of the Victorian period and the beginning of our own, it found its most notable literary form in the works of Thomas Hardy. In the novels, and particularly in the visionary *Dynasts*, the demands of the Stoic view are sharply delineated. Only the strongest Stoic spirit could champion the crushing power of Hardy's fatalistic universe. Passive acceptance of such a world becomes emotionally difficult and politically disastrous. In contrast with this extreme Stoic position, Blake's Gnosticism begins to make sense. Human desires, often inconsequential to the meliorist, emerge as something outside of the natural world. They become the Gnostic spark that is outside the world and yet of it, that divine spark whose secret name is man, that is humanity itself.

Of particular relevance to a consideration of Blake's misprisions is the tendency in the New Testament to interpret the life of Jesus in terms of Jewish scripture (the Old Testament) and to interpret Jewish Scripture in terms of Jesus. Thus, mixing commentary with narrative, Matthew is at pains to show that Jesus is the anointed one spoken of by the prophets, that he was born in Bethlehem, a Nazarene, a son of David, called forth "out of Egypt" and so forth. The Messiah was supposed to be a military leader who would lead the Jews in armed revolt against their enemies. A considerable revaluation of this tradition, much of it in the form of Gnostic revisionism, was required to cast Jesus in the messianic role. While New Testament revisionism may have been a practical and political effort to make Jesus acceptable to the Jews, the rhetoric undermined the authority of sacred texts. The Christian writings were soon canonized as the New Testament, but their treatment of textuality and their fundamental antinomianism undercut their authority. Their misprision of the Old Testament undermines appeals to orthodoxy. It is understandable that they could have been used to support the excesses of Gnosticism, but it is ironic that a dominant established religion was founded on such subversive texts.

Whatever the motivations of the New Testament writers, an identity-creating psychomachia of the kind described by Bloom was probably not among them. These often anonymous writers were not in a struggle to establish literary identity. Clearly, they had other fish to fry. Why then misprision? To understand this is to understand Bloom, to understand what he is repressing.

Typology and homology constitute the most common instruments of New Testament revisionism. Typology reads Old Testament figures such as Adam, the new man, or Joseph, the savior of his brothers, as types of Christ. Homology sees in Old Testament stories complete patterns for New Testament history. The most extreme (and obscure) form of typological reading arises from the early Christian apocalyptic tradition, best represented by Revelation (see Rudolph 277–79), but an excellent small example, the one most critical for understanding Blake, is Paul's allegory of the two Jerusalems in Galatians. Paul attempts to show that arguments over the outward form of worship, the strict observation of Jewish law (often expressed in the synecdoche "circumcision"), miss the spirit of Christianity:

> Tell me, ye that desire to be under the law, do ye not hear the law? For it is written, that Abraham had two sons; the one by a bondmaid, the other by a freewoman. But he who was of the bond-woman was born after the flesh; but he of the freewoman was by promise. Which things are an allegory: for these are the two covenants; the one from the mount Sinai which gendereth to bondage, which is Agar. For this Agar is mount Sinai in Arabia, and answereth to Jerusalem which now is, and is in bondage with her children. But Jerusalem which is above is free, which is the mother of us all. . . . Now we, brethren, as Isaac was, are the children of promise. But as then he that was born after the flesh, persecuted him that was born after the Spirit, even so it is now. (Galatians 4:21–29)

This excellent example of New Testament revisionism divides the world along Gnostic lines, between those who are free and those in bondage, the spiritual (pneumatic) and the earthly (choic). The Gnosticism of this passage, as much as its expression of the Jerusalem ideal, makes it a key to Blake's *Jerusalem,* a poem that describes how the human ideal (Jerusalem) is forgotten when the eternal man (Albion) falls asleep. At the end of the poem, man is awakened when he recovers his vision of an ideal humanity. The Gnostic theme of the sleeping man is thus used by Blake to talk of humanity's loss of the ability to project an ideal for itself.

With its radical misprision of the Hagar/Ishmael story, its severe dichotomy of matter and spirit in terms of slave and elect, its evocation of bondage rhetoric, and its antinomianism, the Galatians passage is particularly Gnostic. It is no accident that Blake's most ambitious work, *Jerusalem: The Emanation of the Giant Albion,* revises Paul's deliberate misprision of the Hagar story. Like Paul, Blake recasts the story in terms of his own epoch. The ideal city Jerusalem becomes the emanation of Albion, Blake's English counterpart to Adam, the eternal man, a Gnostic sign for the supreme deity. Just as *The First Book of Urizen* re-presents the first book of Moses, or Genesis, so the four chapters of *Jerusalem* echo the four gospels. Each book is addressed to a different audience: "To the Public," "To the Jews," "To the Deists,"

"To the Christians." These lines also suggest titles of the New Testament epistles: "to the Romans," "to the Corinthians," "to the Galatians," "to the Hebrews," and so forth. In a characteristic condensation (see Tannenbaum) the four books of *Jerusalem* are Blake's misprision of the entire New Testament.

Scholars identify numerous New Testament passages as being particularly Gnostic. For instance, Kurt Rudolph cites passages as direct borrowings from earlier Gnostic sources (299–306). As Rudolph explains, "The process which is plain from the New Testament itself is twofold, the Christianising of Gnosis and the gnosticising of Christianity. The result of both processes is the canonising of Christianity as an orthodox Church on the one hand, and the elimination of Gnosis as a heresy on the other" (300). The inversion rhetoric that helped found a new religion also threatened to fragment it into a hundred sects. Orthodoxy demanded a single text.

It is significant that Blake found models of revisionist rhetoric in the New Testament and that he favored exactly those passages that were most Gnostic. For instance, he begins *The Four Zoas* (E300) with a verse quoted in Greek and translated in the King James version thus: "For we wrestle not against flesh and blood, but against principalities, against powers, against the rulers of the darkness of this world, against spiritual wickedness in high places" (Ephesians 6:12). The passage— with its archons (*tas archas*) and world-lords (*tous kosmokratoras*), its dark world, and its split between matter (flesh and blood) and spirit— is distinctively Gnostic. The early passage, written before 96 A.D., is quoted in the beginning of the Gnostic *Hypostasis of the Archons* (152–53), written in the third century.

In *The Gnostic Gospels*, Elaine Pagels explains that "both Gnostic and orthodox forms of Christianity could emerge as variant interpretations of the teaching and significance of Christ" (148). Identifying Gnosticism as a concern with the isolated self, Pagels points out that "even the New Testament gospel of Luke includes Jesus's saying that whoever 'does not hate his own father and mother and wife and children and brothers and sisters, yes, and even his own life, he cannot be my disciple'" (148). In contrast, Orthodox Christians could find in the same gospels a more socialized vision of Christ: "Jesus blessed marriage and declared it inviolable; he welcomed the children who surrounded him; he responded with compassion to the most common forms of human suffering, such as fever, blindness, paralysis, and mental illness, and wept when he realized that his people had rejected him" (148). On one side we have a social Christianity emphasizing community and embraced by the orthodox; on the other a personal Christianity emphasizing private experience and embraced by the Gnostic. Significantly, Pagels supports her argument for a twofold reading of the gospels by quoting from Blake's *The Everlasting Gospel:*

> The vision of Christ that thou dost see
> Is my vision's deepest enemy. . . .
> Thine is the friend of all Mankind,
> Mine speaks in parables to the blind:
> Thine loves the same world that mine hates,
> Thy Heaven doors are my Hell gates. . . .
> Both read the Bible day and night
> But thou read'st black where I read white. . . .
> Seeing this False Christ, In fury and passion
> I made my Voice heard all over the Nation.
> (Pagels 148–49; E524, 878)

By interpreting the Bible from a gnostic perspective Blake found a vision of Christ that fit his fierce independence and hatred of the prevailing social order.

Pagels's theory of two Gospels intensifies a problem that has repercussions in our consideration of Bloomian criticism. Blake had in common with Coleridge the assumption that he was restoring the spirit to the dead letter of the canonical texts. The standard modern critical argument, best expressed by Abrams, holds that the Romantics were in fact secularizing the religious metaphors of Western tradition. In his review of *Natural Supernaturalism*, J. Hillis Miller attacks Abrams for being too Romantic,[25] but Abrams might equally be charged with being insufficiently Romantic in denying the Romantic's claim to restore meaning to texts whose meaning has been cloaked in institutional orthodoxies. Abrams and perhaps even Bloom have failed to take seriously enough the Romantic project of restoring meaning to the text, of restoring the spirit to the dead letter. The necessity of the project becomes more apparent as the Gnostic convolutions of traditional interpretation are revealed. As Abrams has shown, enormous changes in social and political perspective extending even beyond the Reformation forced the Romantic poets to reevaluate their religious heritage. In Blake's view, the job was as much a restoration as a reevaluation.

Blake is characteristically Romantic in turning inward toward a personal salvation. Such inward turning reenacts a central move of Christianity. The Jewish Messiah was supposed to bring military salvation to a people. Christ brought personal salvation to the individual. The Gnostic concern with the individual, the self, is expressed even more strongly in Gnostic writings outside the Christian canon (Pagels 119–41; Rudolph 91). But Blake restores to the story of personal salvation the Gnostic myth of social and even cosmic redemption. As Jean-Pierre Mileur indicates, "In his poem *Milton*, William Blake, English literature's greatest student of the ethics of redemption, takes that great poet to task for believing that he can achieve his personal redemption through his disgust with and renunciation of the temporal community and makes the ascetic/solipsistic artist renounce his heaven-for-one in order to return and bend his magnificent will to the task of collective redemption" (47). Blake's rewriting of Milton restores the Gnostic cosmogonic view to Christian soteriology. As Jonas indicates in defining "Gnosticism" in the *Encyclopedia of Philosophy*, "Valentinian speculation inferred that the human individual event of pneumatic knowledge reversed the precosmic universal event of divine ignorance and is in its redeeming effect of the same ontological order. Thus the actualization of knowledge in the person is at the same time an act in the general ground of being" (s.v.). Thus, the salvation at the end of *Jerusalem* recreates a reading of soteriology that Blake hoped to restore to Biblical interpretation.

We have seen how Bloom's theory of misprision is anticipated in Blake's poetic practice and in an entire tradition of interpretation dating back to the early Christian era. It is just this connection with Gnostic thought that keeps Blake central to contemporary critical issues. As Mitchell indicates, "Blake anticipates so many of the strategies of deconstruction, and offers such powerful antidotes to its skeptical and nihilistic tendencies" (416). Thus, we can see Blake as both revisionist and deconstructionist, as when he says: "Both read the Bible day & night / But thou readst black where I read white" (*EG* 33:13–14, E524). These lines play on the figure-background problem to speak of the polysemous nature of the sign and of revisionist tendencies in both first-century biblical authors and the eighteenth-century reader.

In his review of *Natural Supernaturalism*, J. Hillis Miller opposes the "Romantic" view that history proceeds toward a "preordained goal." He suggests instead a Nietzschean vision of the goallessness of human life. The decentered, goalless attitude toward life, Miller hints, is even a theme of Romantic literature itself. It is a partially hidden but persistent view, in Miller's words "an alternative scheme," that contradicts the official stoic belief in reason and order: "This alternative scheme, with its various aspects or motifs, has always been present as a shadow or reversed mirror image within the Western tradition, even in the texts Abrams discusses, for example, in the Platonic dialogues or in *The Prelude*" (13). Miller's alternative scheme is not Gnosticism, but it is Gnostic insofar as it casts a doubtful image of a world that is alien to human desires. Moreover, it is Romanticism, and particularly the Romanticism of Blake, that calls into question visions of a morally and rationally ordered cosmos.

As a Romantic revisionist, Blake offers a version of gnosis that reflects his historical situation; he casts Enlightenment reason (Urizen) in the role of the creator God (Ialdabaoth) of Gnostic parody. The Gnostic primal act of alienation and misrecognition he interprets as a misapprehension of the material world in the mind of an individual. Blake's Gnostic tale in *The Book of Urizen* and elsewhere explains how man comes to ignore everything that is innate to his being (except for what comes through the five senses) in order to adopt this single vision of material creation. In this fallen view everything comes to man from the material world, matter in motion. Blake felt that the Enlightenment tended to focus on reason and the five senses to the exclusion of other innate constituents of human experience. To argue for a more broadly defined human nature Blake resorts to animal imagery, as in the aphorism: "The bird a nest, the spider a web, man friendship" (*MHH*8:31, E36). Such a statement of man's basically social nature might accord with the modern social sciences, but Blake's view includes more. He offers an epistemology that finds all the forms of experience, the very nature of sensations, space and time, to be brought into the world by the fact that it is a human who does the experiencing. Again, Blake puts human nature in the foreground by using animal imagery:

> With what sense is it that the chicken shuns the ravenous hawk?
> With what sense does the tame pigeon measure out the expanse?
> With what sense does the bee form cells? have not the mouse &
>   frog
> Eyes and ears and sense of touch? yet are their habitations.

And their pursuits, as different as their forms and as their joys:
Ask the wild ass why he refuses burdens: and the meek camel
Why he loves man: is it because of eye ear mouth or skin
Or breathing nostrils? No. for these the wolf and tyger have.
Ask the blind worm the secrets of the grave, and why her spires
Love to curl round the bones of death; and ask the rav'nous snake
Where she gets poison: & the wing'd eagle why he loves the sun
And then tell me the thoughts of man, that have been hid of old.
(*VDA*3:2–13, E47)

Thus, human nature can be defined by our bodily form, the way we live, and by what we think, feel, and desire.[26]

Blake's gnosis involves an inclusive vision of human experience, encompassing innate needs for community and the imaginative forms of art. The Blakean apocalypse, like the Gnostic, involves a saving knowledge. For Blake this knowledge redeeems the cosmic vision of a dead material universe by replacing it with a vision of the experiencing human at the center of existence. Blake's saving gnosis occurs when one of man's usurped senses (imagination) is able to tell the Gnostic tale of alienation and thereby reintegrate man to a vision of integrated faculties. The reintegration can occur precisely because imagination in the form of Los—and ultimately Blake himself—is able to create a vision of integration. In producing these "Gnostic" myths Blake recapitulated the soteriology of early Gnostic writings. For Blake, salvation occurs when the individual recognizes the role that reason has in developing the hypothesis of external reality. In this light Blake is very Gnostic indeed. His reading of Gnostic myth is misprision in a Bloomian sense because he identifies Enlightenment reason and empirical science as consolidating the cosmic error about man's nature. And in thus interpreting historical events in a soteriological drama, Blake is following what was for him a most compelling source, the Book of Revelation.

Bloom's misprision of Gnostic and Kabbalistic lore is more boldly revisionary than Blake's insofar as it applies narrowly to the dynamics of literary creation. We are tempted to observe with Blake, "the Son O how unlike Father" (E565). Bloom lives in an age of criticism, and like Blake, he reworks the Gnostic myths in the terms of his historical situation. But Bloom's critical Gnosticism offers no cosmic redemption. As he observes in *Agon*: "In Gnosis the knowledge is neither of eternity nor of this world seen with more spiritual intensity. *The Knowledge is of oneself*" (12). Yet Bloom still holds out the possibility of a communal salvation: "I write this book as a Jewish Gnostic, trying to explore and develop a personal Gnosis and a possible Gnosticism, perhaps even one available to others" (4).

Insofar as Bloom is attempting to salvage literary theory from encroaching nihilism, his gnosis holds the hope of redeeming the social order. In spite of his narrow focus Bloom has retained the crux of Blake's insight into the interconnectedness of human thought. He says of the French poststructuralists: "An empirical thinker, confronted by a text, seeks a meaning. Something in him says: 'If this is a complete and independent text then it *has* a meaning.' It saddens me to say that this apparently commonsensical assumption is not true. Texts don't *have* meanings, except in their relations to other texts, so that there *is* something uneasily dialectical about literary meaning. A single text has only a part of a meaning: it is itself only part of a larger whole including other texts. A text is a relational event, and not a substance to be analyzed."[27] Such a statement is a rather shrunken version of Blake's Gnostic account of fallen experience.

Bloom's central move involves a misreading of Gnosticism, Kabbalah, Blake, Nietzsche and others in such a way that their metaphysical views are transformed into comments on the relationships of literary texts. Thus, in *Kabbalah and Criticism* Nietzsche's "A thing is the sum of its effects, synthetically united by a concept, an image," becomes "A poem is the sum of its effects, synthetically united by a concept, an image" (113). Let us follow Bloom's own practice for a moment to consider a Blakean version of two sentences from Bloom (quoted above): "A single material object has only part of a meaning; it is itself a synecdoche for a larger whole including other objects of experience. An object is a relational event, and not a substance to be analyzed." By replacing "text" with "material object" and "object" we read Bloom as a kind of synecdoche for the Blakean and (Gnostic) concern with the interrelatedness of all creation. Bloom's claim that "Texts don't *have* meanings, except in their relations to other texts," becomes a kind of shrunken version of the Gnostic error of creation: the assumption of independent existence for the self and the objects it perceives.

Thus, Bloom focuses our attention on a subset of the problem of the epistemological (and ontological) status of thingness. If all things are relational, then so are poems. The arena of poetry is appropriate to Bloom's historical moment for three good reasons: (1) Much modern philosophy has focused on language as the vehicle of thought—with deconstructionists arguing that there is no load (tenor, meaning) apart from, within, or behind the vehicle itself. (2) Language has become the center of many structural and poststructural arguments that discuss meaning as relationships among or differences between the objects (signs) of discourse. (3) Literary criticism has found itself involved in such musings precisely because it developed habits of intense textual scrutiny—the closer critics looked, the more problematic (relational) the text became.

The exposure of hypostasis or reification is central to the writing of both Blake and Bloom. True to the epistemology of his age Blake focuses on the role of reification in giving us our concept of the static material object. In his poetry he reifies human attributes, such as reason or imagination, always with the intent of exposing the process of reification: "Visions of these eternal principles or characters of human life appear to poets, in all ages; the Grecian gods were the ancient Cherubim of Phoenicia; but the Greeks, and since them the Moderns, have neglected to subdue the gods of Priam. These Gods are visions of the eternal attributes, or divine names, which, when erected into gods, become destructive to humanity. . . . They ought to be made to sacrifice to Man, and not man compelled to sacrifice to them" (*DC*21–22, E536).

New Criticism tended to reify the literary text as a source of meaning. Bloom combats such reification by exposing meaning as a dynamic of intertextural relations. Other critics are busy performing similar deconstructions of the reified text. In *Kabbalah and Criticism* Bloom turns for a moment to assess the French writers who "are at least as guilty of reifying their own metaphors as any American bourgeois formalist has been. To say that the thinking subject is a fiction, and that the manipulation of language by that subject merely extends a fiction, is no more enlightening in itself that it would be to say 'language' is the thinking subject, and the human psyche the object of discourse" (105).

One might object that Bloom has reified the processes of misprision as a rhetoric of revisionism. In this he follows his Gnostic predecessors, both Hellenistic and Romantic. Thus, the *Hypostasis of the Archons* attempts to establish the *reality* of the archontic rulers: "By starting from the invisible world the visible world was invented" (153). Similarly, Blake's human mental processes, the Zoas, give rise to the material world of objective forms. So too, Bloom's ratios of revision are responsible for creating both the individual work of art and the poet who produces that work. Because every poetic object exists only in its readings, each reader partakes of the process of poetic creation. He partakes in the act of creation in his every reading of a poem.

What misprision then might we apply to Bloom? It is most fitting to see his ratios of revision as a synecdoche for Blakean revisionism: the part (the ontological interdependence of poems) standing for the whole (the interdependence of all objects of thought). In this sense Blake, Shelley, Coleridge, Wordsworth, and to a lesser extent the other figures of the English Romantic movement revived the vision of integrated experience that they found in the forebodings, the hauntings, and the myths of tradition. Blake particularly revitalizes the ancient questions by putting Gnostic myth in the service of a critique of Enlightenment reason. As Karl Jaspers says: "Since the basic questions of philosophy grow, as practical activity, from life, their form is at any given moment in keeping with the *historical* situation; but this situation is part of the continuity of tradition. The questions put earlier in history are still ours; in part identical with present ones, word for word, after thousands of years, in part more distant and strange, so that we make them our own only by translation."[28] Harold Bloom's misprision of Blake reenacts many of these basic questions in terms of contemporary problems of textuality.

The Gnostic, Blakean, and Bloomian attempts to discuss the problem of reification reveal the peculiar blindnesses of contemporary critical thought. For Blake and the Gnostics, the error of object creation included more than textuality. Moreover, these mythographers held out a faith in a humanity, a divine spark, or innate human nature that even accounted for the error of appearances. For Bloom, the human is replaced by a ratio, a form or rhetoric through which poems and poets are created. And here Bloom approaches the mechanical, following closely those contemporaries whom he criticizes in *Agon:* "Deconstructive and other post-Heideggerian paradigms tend to the so-called linguistic model, which reduces to the very odd trope of a demiurgical entity named 'Language' acting like a Univac, and endlessly doing our writing for us" (43). The Harold Bloom of the seventies appears to have fallen into this same trap. His revisionary ratios speak not of humanity, but of a single abstracted principle similar to Blake's concept of jealousy. His critical space is narrowly confined to the dynamics of ego insecurity. Poetry is stripped of all connection to life; only the isolated poetic ego remains.

Problems in Bloom's revisionism typify Gnosticism, which in its strength narrates the cognitive structure of experience and in its weakness separates large parts of that experience in order to deny it. The process has much in common with Freud's theory of infant ego formation: "A tendency arises to separate from the ego everything that can become a source of unpleasure."[29] In this we find a dangerous side of Gnostic thinking, which reduces the world to abstract entities with the human sometimes appearing as the most abstract, remote, and impotent of the abstractions. We can say in favor of Gnostic attempts to describe the human element in experience that the myths are terribly self-conscious about the dangers of reifying a single cognitive function and supposing it the whole. Moreover, this hidden tradition with its implicit critique of reification can provide a valuable tool for examining the machinelike constructions of much postmodern thought.

In light of the Gnostic critique, we begin to read Bloom's poetic ego as a Gnostic Ialdabaoth supposing that he is the only God, or as Milton's Satan pretending to be a creator, or as Urizen presuming that he can reduce all to a mechanistic ratio, or as a Freudian id stripped of somatic origins. But the myth is fundamentally a critique of such mechanism, so that there arises in *Agon* a new Bloom who talks of pragmatism in searching for a theory based on the human subject. Paradoxically enough, the strength of Gnosticism, Gnostic Kabbalism, and Blake's revision of arcane tradition come to Bloom's aid, for such myth is predicated on a vision of humanity. Depending on the metaphor employed, this humanity lies within, or beyond, or above, or beneath, or innate to, or hidden in ordinary human experience. And such experience may be present or absent or an error in cognition or an ignorance of origins, or a lack of origins, but it is always constitutive of what we are.

Literal
Tiriel
Material

Nelson Hilton

Art no longer can prevayl
When the materialls all are gone
Swift, "Progress of Beauty"

"Literal imagination," so to term one method of and goal for performing Blake, attends particularly to the play of words, combining semantics with a semiotics of verbal sound and graphics. Literal imagination
discovers different connections between individual words, connections
that sometimes collectively become a level of meaning, which in turn
can connect to traditional interpretations. The literal imagination might
image the text as a game board—consisting of a grid of piers raised
in relief, say—and a given reading as an attempt to lay down a continuous path or line of interpretation from one side to the other across
those material supports. "Intentionality" or "meaning" is then to be
found more in the form of the field of play than in favorite crossing
configurations. Every successful path crosses the text (advanced play
begins by double-crossing the text), but the number of different possibilities being large (though finite) and the distinctions often excessively subtle, literal imagination contents itself with rewording different
kinds of connections. Such "content" (pleasure *and* material) is the
messy reward of literal imagination, and this orientation toward its
own message identifies literal imagination (to use Roman Jakobson's
model of communication[1]) as a potentially poetic, self-conscious, self-
reflexive activity ("criticism") playing with its constituent components
of context, contact, and code. The article of faith or Urizenic(-ally)
"assum'd power" (*U*2:1, E70) is that this activity connects with activity coded in the Blakean text. Such faith, with its implicit assumption that literal imagination is finally both addresser and addressee
appears to succumb to the wildest dreams of the reader's recapturing
the place of the author—except that this faith also assumes (the cor-

ollary of self-consciousness and self-reflexivity) the self-annihilating awareness of its own perceptual incompleteness (especially after working through some standard bibliography).[2] As per the parable of the printing house (in *The Marriage of Heaven and Hell*) we are (in the midst of) a paradoxical transmission from generator to generator: Blake writes our reading that we may write Blake's reading.

Literal imagination (as I imagine it) returns to the concept of allusion its original pleasures. Traditional criticism sees allusion as "reference, explicit or indirect, to a person, place, or event, or to another literary work or passage,"[3] but for literal imagination allusion is an invitation to play (*ad-ludere*): it is all-ludic, as in the early uses of the term recorded by the *OED* before such play was condemned as illusory and reified into reference and, implicitly, authorial intention. Such play is inescapably temporal; the allusion exists at a given moment of contact between the text and the player-reader. In the same player-reader with the same bit of text, allusions can appear, confirm themselves, and disappear over the course of readings (contextualizations). But as in sports or music, there are great plays and memorable performances, inspired conjunctions of player and structure that show each to advantage. Or, as in the different field of the courtroom, there are at times powerfully marshaled arguments that carry the day for new interpretations and deeply mark the legal text. Or, as Harold Bloom puts it, there are strong (mis-)readings. Successful plays, performances, arguments, and readings finally reflect the values of the surrounding social order. Should literal imagination prove anything more than just an Alexandrian enterprise carried on even as the library burns, its acceptance will reflect the culture's increasing concern with cognition (or, rather, "cognition technology") and with the possibility that cognition and, in particular, reading entail apparently nonlinear, counterlogical processes. As for the irrepressible allusiveness of the Blakean text, one finds the tip of the iceberg in critical dealings with its curious names, like *Tiriel*'s Har. Is it Har, the Hebrew word for mountain, with the accompanying biblical and moral associations? Is it Har, the High or Lofty One who answers many of King Gulfi's questions in *The Prose Edda?* Is it Har with the engraver's sense of its reversibility into the Pharaoh's "Rah"? Is it Har, the first syllable of the neoclassical ideal of Harmony? Can all these be thought together, with space for what one doesn't know has been left out?

Because *Tiriel* is the longest of Blake's early prophecies,[4] it is no surprise that some words appear in it more frequently than they do in any other Blakean work. Still, like that haunting abstract of Blake's *oeuvre* made of the ten most frequently appearing words in the *Blake Concordance* ("All o upon Los like as Albion man death over"), the words most frequently appearing in *Tiriel,* especially when seen in light of their other contexts (their Blakean semantic field), present a suggestive index of the main concerns of *Tiriel.* The defining quality of an indexical sign, according to C. S. Peirce, is its "real connection" to the object it denotes,[5] and the signs we will highlight as indexes of the concerns of *Tiriel* are really connected to that work by their appearing in it.

One dramatic instance of such indexical vocabulary is the first adjective in the manuscript, "aged," which in *Tiriel* accounts for nearly half (twenty-three) of the word's fifty-two appearances in Blake's verse. Though Tiriel is aged and "wrinkled" (that description appears only twice outside of *Tiriel*), Har can tell him "Thou art a very old old man but I am older than thou" (3:2). And "old" also occupies *Tiriel* (fourteen separate lines) to an extent unapproached elsewhere (11 instances altogether in the 100 plates of *Jerusalem,* for example). In Blake's lexicon, "aged" is a particular attribute of "time" and of "ignorance." "Time" offers a revealing association in view of *Tiriel*'s corner on the description "bald & aged." Erroneous though he feels it to be, Blake writes in *A Vision of The Last Judgment* that he has "accomodated my Figure of Time to < the > Common opinion as I myself am also infected with it & my Visions also infected & I see Time Aged alas too much so" (E563).

The association of "ignorance" with "aged" figures in the term "blind"; *Tiriel* accounts for fully one-third of Blake's total uses (seventeen of forty-eight) and far more than any other individual work. And it is, of course, Tiriel himself who is "blind & old" (4:60). The syntagm "Blind Stupid Ignorant and Incapable," which appears in a letter (to Butts, 22 November 1802) points to the word's semantic relations. Indeed, Tiriel's blindness is introduced, almost with him, in the poem's third line: "But now his eyes were darkned." And the deleted half-line was even more emphatic: "But dark were his once piercing eyes." Evidently we are to recognize that Tiriel once could see, once had vision— yet even there Blake edits out the possibility that Tiriel was at all "visionary." Blinding ourselves to associations of Tiresias and Oedipus, Tiriel's condition, together with some evocations of style in the text, can remind us of the two blind bards, the eighteenth century's *ne plus ultra* of inspiration, originality, genius, and vision, Homer and Milton.

Homer first floats up in a general way amid the Greek associations of the guardian Mnetha.[6] Then, wonderfully reflecting a kind of Homeric epithetizing, Tiriel arrives in the vales of Har and casts away "my staff the kind companion of my travel" (2:27). Still more obviously, when he returns the second time, led by Hela, Mnetha greets him with words evoking the delicacies of Pope's Homer: "Stand still or from my bow recieve a sharp & winged death" (8:2).[7] Allusions to ancient Greek mythology and literature (in neoclassical translation) extend far beyond these lines, and we will return to them. As for Milton, Alicia Ostriker hears in Tiriel's observation "This is the right & ready way" an echo of *The Ready and Easy Way to Establish a Free Commonwealth*.[8] And the lines that follow that remark, as Tiriel and Hela head back to the vales of Har, are planted with other echos: "be obedient to thy father for the curse is taken off thee," Tiriel commands, for "all the time of grace is past." The Homeric-Miltonic echos seem to coalesce at the work's conclusion, where Tiriel identifies himself as one become "subtil as a serpent in a paradise": "And now my paradise is falln & a drear sandy plain / Returns my thirsty hissings in a curse on thee O Har" (8:26–27).

An evocation of *Paradise Lost* and the Satanic forces transformed to serpents is clear enough, but "the drear sandy plain" missing in Milton turns us again to Pope's Homer.[9] Har then, to play at embodying some allusions, suggests not only God the Father, but also the Father of the Gods, Zeus/Jupiter, or perhaps, father before him, the castrated Chronos—Father Time himself. And in this connection one might dwell on the recently recognized correspondence between the drawing for *Tiriel* called "Har & Heva Bathing: Mnetha looking on"—which does not relate to any description in the text—and the striking painting by Blake's acquaintance James Barry, *Jupiter and Juno on Mount Ida*.[10] It is the named subject of Barry's painting, rather than the borrowed pose, that makes the correspondence especially suggestive; and here one might note as well the possible "r" for "v" interchange in Blake's handwriting, such that one literally can see "Heva" as "Hera" at some places in the manuscript.

Tiriel's parting action leaves the reader with a term that pervades his story and appears in it far more than in any other of Blake's works: "curse." As a performative, "curse" offers one of those exceptional verbal actions that fulfill themselves in the uttering: to curse makes a curse. Similarly, one might say, a curser is one cursed and "Such was Tiriel" (8:22). Though all the curses are Tiriel's—and all are thoroughly effective—it seems that the practice is not his invention. The lineage of cursing is sketched out in the curious transitions of section 6. Threatened by "a terrible fathers curse" (terrible father, terrible curse), the Cordelia-like *cum* Norse Death Goddess[11] Hela agrees to lead Tiriel to Har and Heva, adding

> . . . would that they would curse
> Then would they curse as thou hast cursed but they are not like
>   thee
> O *they are holy. & forgiving* filld with loving mercy
> Forgetting the offences of their most rebellious children
> Or else thou wouldest not have livd to curse thy helpless children
> (6:24–28, emphasis added)

In the stanza following this, Tiriel reiterates the threatened curse "Unless thou lead me to the tent of *Har child of the curse*" (6:34, emphasis added). The reading that sees Tiriel now identifying Har (the nearest antecedent) as an earlier "child of the curse" perhaps best accounts for the total reversal of assumptions that Hela immediately expresses:

> I lead thee to the tent of Har not that I mind thy curse
> But that I feel *they will curse* thee & hang upon thy bones
> Fell shaking agonies.
> (6:36–38, emphasis added)

Given this new genealogy, Har's "mother Mnetha" (2:21, 25) ought literally to be "anathema" ("I am Mnetha" [2:17] moves close to the anagram). It begins to seem that the world and story *Tiriel* communicates has its origin, like its end, in the great curse of excommunication.

One may easily see how the three terms detailed thus far can function as counters in the kind of artificial mythology imagined by Roland Barthes: "Truth to tell, the best weapon against myth is perhaps to mythify it in its turn, and to produce an *artificial myth:* and this reconstituted myth will in fact be a mythology. Since myth robs language of something, why not rob myth?"[12] Or, since criticism robs the text of something, why not rob criticism? And why not begin with criticism's notion of "allusion," stolen away from "a play upon words, a word play" (*OED*) by Bacon, Newton, Locke, and their epigones. Each term—"aged," "blind," "curse"—in itself connects to a variety of myths; each in itself is a kind of mytheme, an intertextual bit to be whirled in this particular kaleidoscope. None of the components making up "aged blind curse" immediately presupposes the others, yet together they begin to select a context. Because it is "aged," it seems ready to die; because it is "blind," one wonders what it once could see; and because it is a curse, it urges the question of how to respond otherwise.

Our exercise in counting (on) words can supply other data. Two locales stressed in *Tiriel* are the "palace" (*The French Revolution*'s eight uses exceed those in *Tiriel* only by one) and the "wood"—and everywhere is "desolate." The poem opens with Tiriel "before the Gates of his beautiful palace," yet owing to his curses the "once delightful palace" (1:1, 4) is overthrown. The "palace" is an imperial residence, of course (metonym of the source of patronage for the Royal Academy, *inter alia*), but the confusion registered by commentators who compare the poem's descriptions and the Greco-Egyptian elements of *Tiriel*'s illustrated buildings suggests there is more here than meets the eye. One has only to think of the "palace of wisdom" or "Satans inmost Palace of his nervous fine wrought Brain" (*M*12:41, E106), or even *America*'s "ancient palace, archetype of mighty Emperies" (*A*10:8, E55) to see this palace in other places (in the youthful Tennyson, for instance, dilating on the "Palace of Art"). As for the palace "gates," which Kathleen Raine strains to make the seven gates of Thebes as per Aeschylus, one can also recall *America* and the "gates of sense" (c:22, E59), "the five gates of their law-built heaven" (16:19, E58). The "wood" as well, whose four appearances in *Tiriel* far outstrip an at most single occurrence in other texts, offers some suggestive connections. When Tiriel leaves he identifies himself as "The wanderer who seeks the woods," and Har and Heva watch him "till he enterd the wood" (3:32, 35). Another elemental mytheme, "wood," riots in associations with the subjunctive of "will" (entering the "would" is leaving the "will"), with madness ("to run wood," "to be wood"), and with matter (following from the Greek *hyle:* wood, hence, conventionally, matter). So when Tiriel claims "No matter who I am" and Har responds by labeling him as "the King of rotten wood & of the bones of death" (2:20, 23), we may imagine an identification of Tiriel as one presiding over decaying material with infirm intentions. The real madness of the king through the autumn of 1788 and winter of 1789 with its accompanying political crisis suggests one intertext for *Tiriel;* George III's dislike of and dismay over his sons was notorious, though his daughters he considered "all Cordelias."[13]

And the matter with *Tiriel* would be the madness on realizing the exhaustion of artistic material. Here, perhaps, we can think of Blake starting out in a culture of used-up mythologies and the already old reign of Reynolds, as social dislocations made ridiculous the invocation of epic art and heroic ideal. David Irwin studies the concerns of late-eighteenth-century English art and comments, "Looking through exhibition catalogues of the Royal Academy, the Society of Artists and the Free Society of Artists, one is confronted by a bewildering array of subjects drawn from classical history and mythology."[14] Ijim, in one construction, says that the world of "Tiriels house" (see illustration 1), is "as false [as] Matha," that is, learning (Greek *mathe;* but perhaps Ijim falsely remembers "Mnetha") and—weird image—"as dark as vacant Orcus."[15]

The idea that *Tiriel* in some way comments on the state (cant or curse) of the arts circa 1789 first appears with S. Foster Damon's sense that "Har represents degenerate poetry" and Heva "is degenerate painting"; more recently, Robert N. Essick closely considers the *Tiriel* designs and finds them "a pictorial commentary on eighteenth-century aesthestics."[16] The tip-off image for this approach is "the cage of Har" (3:12) in which Tiriel is to help Har and Heva "catch birds. & gather them ripe cherries" (the "warbling birds" of 8:25). It is emphasized as "the great cage" (3:21; see again illustration 1) where Har goes to sing.[17] Perhaps the most revealing gloss on *Tiriel*'s plurality of Blakean cages is "How Sweet I Roamed" in the earlier *Poetical Sketches,* where the speaker reports how "Phoebus fir'd my vocal rage; . . . And shut me in his golden cage" (E413). Damon finds that the symbolism of the great cage "obtrudes a little too much!" and concludes patly: "Har in his cage represents, of course, poetry in the conventional metres which Blake was now casting off."[18]

But if we credit this insight, which has struck many subsequent critics, we might begin to look for supporting associations. And, indeed, one can start by recalling the heavy neoclassical formulations à la Pope's Homer cited above, not to mention the gamut of mythologi-

1. H. Ramberg and P. S. Martini, *The Exhibition of the Royal Academy, 1787*, British Museum.

cal, biblical, and Miltonic references. In this context Tiriel's closing lament takes on new resonance, especially his next-to-closing description of the weak infant with "all youthful fancies" (8:18) scourged off,

> . . . compelld to number footsteps
> Upon the sand. &c
> And when the drone has reachd his crawling length
> Black berries appear that poison all around him. Such was Tiriel.
> (8:19–22)

Already in the second half of the eighteenth century "drone" denoted "a monotonous tone of speech" and a "monotonous speaker." Here Blake distinguishes the drone from his poem's loose fourteeners by setting it in rigid iambic pentameter. "Foot" has been the name for a division of verse for centuries, and in this context of numbering them in the vales of Har one might place Dryden's definition (quoted in Johnson's *Dictionary*) that "poetry is the harmony of words, harmony of numbers" (for *Tiriel*, the drone of Har monotones in the cage).[19]

Because the death of Tiriel ends the poem, it is easy enough to say that, on one immediate level, Tiriel is the poetic "material," the material for art or myth or narrative such as it exists here. This sound allusion can be pressed in other ways. Much has been made, for instance, of the name's appearance in Cornelius Agrippa's *Occult Philosophy*, where "Tiriel is called the Intelligence of Mercury" (see Damon 306). But Mercury, we can recall, is also alchemical "prima materia";[20] ergo, Tiriel is the intelligence of prima materia: the logic perhaps, in the material itself, which now "returns . . . in a curse"—even, perhaps most simply, the curse of being old. Tiriel's disintegration evidently follows from the decay and death of his wife, Myratana, who has for this reason been equated with "Tiriel's Inspiration" (Damon 306). Myratana has, through her name, been associated with Myrina, queen of the Mauretanian Amazons in Jacob Bryant's *A New System, or, An Analysis of Ancient Mythology* (1774–76).[21] If this makes for a creditable allusion, what then of the enigmatic "Anathema Maranatha" of 1 Corinthians 16:22? According to the *OED* the phrase was (erroneously) interpreted to signify a great curse; suggestive for our discussion is its citation of Miles Coverdale's 1535 version, "Anathema Maharan Matha"—a corruption of Luther's fictitious Hebrew phrase meaning "devoted to death." What the devoted Tiriel has to say as his wife dies can point literally to a different kind of allusive association:

> What Myratana. What my wife. O Soul O Spirit O fire
> What Myratana. art thou dead. . . .
> (1:29–30)

As the "Soul-Spirit-fire" wedded to Tiriel, Myratana in effect kept him alive and, perhaps one may infer, able to see. We might then hear the apostrophe to "my wife" as the address of a two-bit Prospero to "my art," with the growing realization that now, "art thou dead." Art dead, what remains is the emphatic response "dig a grave" (1:33, 34, 35, 41), even the engraving this work of art never achieved—its author being perhaps too busy in the graving of others (R. Cosway's *Venus Dissuades Adonis* [1787] or G. Morland's *The Idle Laundress* [1788], for instance).

As for Tiriel, without "Soul-Spirit-fire" Myratana he drifts back into the vales of Har, claiming (as noted above) "No matter who I am" (2:20). This claim to spiritlike existence can be read as seconded by Har, who says Tiriel "passes thro thick walls & doors" (2:24). But Heva nonetheless takes him in a maternal embrace ("her mothers arms")[22] and identifies him as a material relative, "the old father of Tiriel / Thou *art my Tiriels* old father" (2:37–38, emphasis added; alas no Stephen Dedalus's "old father, old artificier" to stand us and our "art materials" ever in good stead here!).

"The logic of language subverts the order of consciousness," writes the Lacanian Stuart Schneiderman,[23] and we face just such a proposition here, hearing "art material" in the heart of *Tiriel*'s *literal* being. "Art" appears twelve times in *Tiriel* as the second-person singular form of "to be"—a number not particularly surprising since Blake uses the form frequently and *Tiriel* involves a considerable amount of dialogue. We have already drawn on two instances (the first and fourth) for their allusive possibilities, and we may as well lift the remaining ten occurrences from our artist's context and complete syntax: "art thou poor blind man. that takest the name of Tiriel" (2:16); "Tiriel is king . . . who art thou" (2:17); "art a very old old man" (3:1); "thou art Tiriel" (3:6); "art so like Tiriel" (3:22); "art thou Eyeless wretch" (4:5); "art discovered I will use thee like a slave" (4:24); "art thou Pestilence" (5:8); "from my blind orbs art" (6:31); and, finally, "art the daughter of Tiriel" (6:40). The appositeness of these almost subliminal snippets can be intensified if one looks, as Blake probably did, into Junius's *The Painting of the Ancients*: "Art can doe nothing without the materiall; whereas the materiall without Art hath her own worthiness."[24] But with its mishmash of old myths and illusions of allusion, *Tiriel* calls that classical relation of art and material into question. Material without art is meaningless ("Where man is not nature is barren" [E38]). Tiriel is "material" because, as he says, he was "Compelld . . . to humble the immortal spirit" (8:23 [Bentley reads "handle"])—though the immense question of who or what did the compelling appears only to pass away. For the end and last word on such humbling art material, however that came about, is death—from old age, exhaustion, dessication, alienation, or sterility: "He ceast outstretchd at Har & Hevas feet in awful death" (finis).

By the time of *Europe*, perhaps four years later, the security of *Tiriel*'s conclusion has dissipated, and the speaker of *Europe*, plate 3, is eager to know "what is the material world, and is it dead?" Achieving an answer there depends on "love-thoughts" and "sparkling poetic fancies"—turning away, that is, from the material of the past. So Tiriel's last line announces to Har a new Torah: "Mistaken father of a lawless race my voice is past." William F. Halloran notes this as an ironic allusion to Christ's accepting the task of redeeming mankind in *Paradise Lost*, "Father, thy word is past, man shall find grace" (3:227—a "grace beyond the reach of art," no doubt). According to Tiriel, however, "all the time of grace is past / You see the parents curse" (6:11–12). We might rather emphasize "the Voice / Of aged Tiriel" (1:4–5) that first appears saying "accursed race of Tiriel. behold your father" (1.6), "his silver voice" (4:63), "his awful voice" (7:6) *as itself the* (mistaken) *father*, now literally performing itself into the past. "The father," to invoke Lacan, "is present only through his law, which is speech"[25] (literal imagination reads further than this law extends). But in suggesting that the past is dead and "false Matha," *Tiriel* can be seen as a material return on Quid's spirited claim in *An Island in the Moon*, "that Homer is bombast & Shakespeare is too wild & Milton has no feelings they might be easily outdone" (E455). The first step, as per the later vision of the printing house in Hell, is to clear away some of the rubbish.

Outdoing the ancients requires new material and new forms, material and forms we are still only beginning to understand in Blake. One enjoyable road of excess leads into Blake's use of language (that material *and* form) and I have tried here to illustrate a few steps toward proceeding, with *Tiriel*, along that pathless way. The driving force is a

kind of allusive, associative, anagrammatic madness or *jouissance*—
literal imagination—that can only try to stabilize itself with strictures
of context, concordance, and lexicon. If a successful or powerful or
even useful reading reflects the consensus of the interpretative community, then the mad career of literal imagination may no doubt be
safely indulged by all in the secure knowledge that the community will
suffer nothing useless. Like the "pitiable foolish young man" of "A
Memorable Fancy" we can "commit ourselves to this void, and see
whether providence is here also" (E41). But literal imaginers, like
other aspiring players of the Blakean text, bring a seasoned historical
awareness to their consideration of the judgments of any particular
"interpretative community" ("What is now proved was once. only
imagin'd" [E36, emended]). Given the status of our present knowledge of textual operations, to inventory effects, as we have begun to do
here, can come close to inventing them. Such an invent-ory is the present stage of an emerging effort to formulate a semiotic of (formulate
forms for) the Blakean text, a semiotic that in its plethora of referential possibilities and crazing paths of associations should have significant bearing on our considerations of all writing and reading. Emerson
reminds "The American Scholar" that "one must be an inventor to
read well."[26]

Blake's De-Formation of Neo-Aristotelianism

Donald Ault

A Genealogy of This Inquiry

This essay has emerged out of two significantly different ideological impulses and two very different historical moments. I first developed the "calculus of perspectives" for *The Book of Urizen* in 1971 in an attempt to make intelligible what I felt was a significant dimension of the poem's subversive power—by mapping a highly formal system that contains the seeds of its own internal structural crisis. I was relatively unfamiliar with structuralism or semiotics at that time, but my previous training in advanced mathematics and my practical work in engineering design and drawing pulled me toward strategies that became more familiar—though through the emergence of poststructuralism they have now been (in their formal obsession) pushed out of critical fashion. In fact, the excessive formalism of the perspective calculus at the time I conceived it seemed so compulsively antiliterary that I was repeatedly encouraged by my colleagues at Berkeley to put it aside, which I have done until now.

I wrote the perspective "calculus" portion only five years after being a student in R. S. Crane's final seminar on literary criticism and method at the University of Chicago. As much as I resisted the substance of Crane's methodological tactics when he was my teacher, his insistence on "adequacy" of textual explanation and the rigor with which he pursued his own (often lonely) intellectual beliefs had a deep, and I suspect irradicable, effect on my sense of moral commitment to follow my own imaginative demons, wherever they may lead. In retrospect I can see that the calculus of perspectives originated in part as an attempt to think through possibilities of form and structure that would never have occurred to Crane and that I believed might expose the imaginative bankruptcy of the "Chicago Neo-Aristotelian" approach to literature (which, to the extent it actually existed was more an intellectual atmosphere dominated by the shadow of Richard McKeon than a critical dogma). Yet, like Stephen Dedalus's rejection of the Church or Blake's response to Newton, my calculus of perspectives was scarred ideologically by the methodological impulses against which it was reacting.

What has emerged in this attempt to explore the ways my fourteen-year-old unpublished essay on *The Book of Urizen* could have been influenced by my training under Crane resembles a psychoanalytic narrative reenactment in which my present awareness of the intervening history of criticism is the analyst and my prior critical struggle with *The Book of Urizen* is the analysand. As with all such reenactments, however, the participants have contaminated each other. What follows is consequently more like a fictional, meta-methodological fantasia that imitates (in all the Neo-Aristotelian complexity of that term) the rigorous and responsible argumentation that marked all of Crane's writing and teaching. The essay is marked by the gap in time and critical intentions between its various sections, and by the drastic compression of the original, detailed analysis of *The Book of Urizen,* which seemed inappropriate for an exercise in method such as this.

Preliminary Considerations

The essential character of the method of inquiry that informs the Chicago school of Neo-Aristotelian criticism reveals itself in Wayne Booth's paraphrase of a typical assignment his mentor R. S. Crane gave his class: "in what ways would Aristotle have been forced to revise or extend the *Poetics* if he had known *Macbeth?*"[1] If this faith in the rewritability of Aristotle to accommodate anything that can be called literature is to be tested against the disruptive texts of Blake, Crane's assignment would have to be rephrased: "How would Chicago Neo-Aristotelian critical method be forced to revise its rewriting of Aristotle in order to account for the characteristics of Blake's poetry?" Perhaps the more pressing question is, "Does Blake's poetry present a clear and present danger to the faith in Aristotle's adaptability to all literary productions?" The dogmatic (and decidedly non-Chicago) formulation of this question would be: "Does the extent to which Neo-Aristotelian methods fail to account for Blake's texts rule out Blake's texts as authentic poetic productions?"

Answering these questions requires pressing to their limits two different sets of assumptions inherent in the Chicago rewriting of Aristotle. One of these sets of assumptions involves the "how" of criticism, the supposedly repeatable procedures of empirical testing and falsification of hypotheses and the criteria of "adequate" explanation to be invoked in the interrogation of literary texts. In this exploration it is important to note crucial differences between R. S. Crane's and Richard McKeon's treatment of the "how" of method. The other set of assumptions concerns the "why" of literary production and experience (or reception). It is convenient to call these assumptions "theoretical" rather than "hypothetical" because (as the etymology of "theory" indicates) these assumptions constitute a comprehensive "view" or "sight," a model of fictitious entities or across-the-board first principles that may require vastly different testing procedures than those appropriate to hypotheses (in the sense of conjectural suppositions within a theory).[2] These theoretical dimensions of Neo-Aristotelian method include the analytical separation of aspects of concrete artistic production and reception into Aristotle's four causes (formal, efficient, material, and final) and the emphasis on a distinction between "mimetic" and "didactic" literary texts. In exploring these theoretical assumptions it will be informative to contrast Crane's treatment of literary mimesis and causality with that of Wayne Booth. Though the insistence on rigorous procedures of testing hypotheses is an attempt by Crane to align his method with "progressive" scientific canons of empirical proof, the theoretical (causal, mimetic) dimensions of Neo-Aristotelian method have often seemed old-fashioned—significantly out of touch with twentieth-century criticism—in part because of their misuse by sympathetic and unsympathetic critics alike, as Booth clearly points out (104), but in part because of the apparent conceptual and ideological remoteness of their concerns (and the theoretical entities they entail) from the emphases of virtually every dominant critical fashion in recent years.[3]

In order to determine what (if anything) can be salvaged from this cumbersome, categorical critical apparatus in the service of opening up fields of inquiry into Blake's poetry, it is necessary not only to examine these dimensions of Neo-Aristotelian critical method but to explore imaginatively to what extent these presuppositions are flexible enough to be restructured to accommodate Blake. Since Blake's poetry is so unlike those works upon which the Neo-Aristotelians found it most comfortable to work their methods, we should expect that, once the fundamental strategic moves of their method(s) are exposed, at the very least a drastic transposition and rearrangement of the internal structural relationships within the theory itself will have to take place in order to account for Blake's poetry's peculiar "working or power" (Crane's privileged terms for the distinguishing feature of mimetic, as opposed to didactic, works).

The "How" of Chicago Method: Techniques of Permissible Inference

R. S. Crane was obsessed with the responsibility he felt to make literary criticism as scientifically respectable in its procedures of proof and inference as the subject allowed. He was powerfully influenced by T. C. Chamberline's "Method of Multiple Working Hypotheses" and the falsification procedures of Karl Popper.[4] For Crane this testing of hypotheses involves two contrary movements: "treat[ing] any alternative hypotheses as if they were of our own devising, and marshal[ing] as much evidence as we can find in support of each of them"; and "treat[ing] our own hypothesis as if it had been provoked by someone else and do[ing] our best to refute or qualify it by looking for relevant facts with which it is inconsistent in whole or in part" (245). Crane relentlessly strikes out against what he considers to be the fallacy of "the sufficiency of positive corroboration," borrowed from the practice of law (241). Crane invokes these self-deflating strategies of inference to check what he sees as the excesses of those practitioners of New Critical, archetypal, psychoanalytic, symbolic, and other "a priori" methods who invariably find support in every text for precisely what they are seeking because they look only for evidence to confirm, rather than to refute, their paradigms of literary meaning and value.

In place of the exaggerated concern for a priori paradigms that predetermine what a critic should look for in a literary text (verbal technique, archetypal pattern, dialectical oppositions, unconscious drives, etc.) Crane substitutes an equally exaggerated concern for "adequacy" and "economy" of explanation of literary "facts," which, for him, must exist independent of interpretation. Crane's tests of adequacy include: asking what important aspects of the literary objects under examination a particular critical method or procedure "force[s] us to leave out of account";[5] employing the "minimum number of unanalyzed terms" in an explanation;[6] insisting that an explanation provide both necessary and sufficient conditions for its probable accuracy (the critic should be responsible for showing that *"only* if his hypothesis is true, would the work or passage in all probability have been written as it is, by the writer who wrote it, at the time when it was written").[7]

In terms of economy, Crane assumes that the simplest explanation is always the best. He argues, for example, that the most obvious and unambiguous meaning of a word in a text should be assumed to be its adequate meaning unless a critic is able to prove that an adequate explanation of the presence of a word in a literary text *requires* the enumeration of a variety of the meanings it *potentially* had at the time the work was written (as verified by the *OED*), by reference to the author's probable "intentions." The compulsion to presume the opposite—that words in literary texts tend to express as many meanings as they possibly have at a given time—is, for Crane, a symptom of the a priori method of approaching works with preconceived models of literary meaning.[8]

By contrast, the equally Aristotelian (but more comprehensive) analysis of methods and principles by Richard McKeon, in what must be considered an ur-document of Neo-Aristotelian philosophical criticism, the massive "Philosophy and Method,"[9] provides a technology by which to situate the limitations of Crane's method by surveying the *range* of methods and principles whose differences have the power to transform the "subject matter" they attempt to treat. In McKeon's analysis, the history of philosophy has been tormented by the failure of philosophers to recognize that when considered from the perspective of one of the three primary methods (dialectic, logistic, and inquiry),[10] each of which can put to use three fundamental types of principles (comprehensive, simple, and reflexive),[11] alternative methods (and their use of principles) can easily be reduced to absurdity. Thus falsification procedures of the sort Crane insists on as tests of hypotheses are relevant only to the method he is employing (inquiry or the analysis of problems) and the kind of principles he is invoking (simple). In significant ways, McKeon's essay implicitly anticipates P. K. Feyerabend's more recent critique of Popper's method as founded on "the naive-falsificationist attitude,"[12] which assumes (as Crane himself assumes) that "objective facts" exist independent of interpretation or speculation.[13] McKeon's insistence that shifts in methods and/or principles produce shifts in what is considered to be subject matter (that is, what constitutes a fact) is a milder and decidedly more categorical version of Feyerabend's doctrines of "incommensurable" frameworks of explanation.[14] McKeon says: "The methods of dialectic, of logistic, and of inquiry are processes which differ so radically that they completely transform the contents, forms, and purposes of philosophy. Yet they are so closely related that the same statements can be repeated and seem to refer to the same subject-matter and problems and yet have meanings so different in dialectic, in logistic, and in inquiry that a vast portion of philosophical literature is devoted to pointing out the absurdities which no one could fail to recognize in what philosophers have said" (664–65). Or again, "There is no unique determination even of methods and principles which might permit a formal comparison of the structures of philosophical systems or analyses; but instead, the patterns are multidimensional and can be made to coincide only for limited areas"(673). Accordingly, applying McKeon to Crane exposes an implicit vulnerability in Crane's methodological rigor: his doctrines of adequacy, economy, necessary and sufficient explanatory conditions, falsification, etc., are relevant only within the methodological parameters of inquiry that he assumes to be "common sense" and therefore beyond further question. The insight, for example, that a dialectical detour might be infinitely richer in its human meaning than a straight road to a fixed destination cannot occur (at least not with ease) within the pure analytic of Crane's method of inquiry.

The "Why" of Chicago Method: Hierarchical Causality and Mimesis

The four "causes" central to any Aristotelian analysis of a text are not treated in precisely the same way by all Chicago Neo-Aristotelians. To Wayne Booth, for instance, the four causes are unambiguously distinct, clear-cut, and nonproblematic: there are no complicating crossovers or interferences between the causes, though they are hierarchically interdependent. In one especially succinct account, Booth defines them as follows: the "formal cause" is the "structure" of the work and corresponds to the "object imitated" (rendered, represented); the "final cause" is the "end" or "purpose" of a work, the "effect" it has on readers "of good judgment and normal sensitivity"; the "efficient cause" is the manner or technique of imitation; and the "material cause" is language (105–12). By emphasizing that the object imitated is formal or structural, Booth tries to avoid an easy source of misunderstanding of the Neo-Aristotelian concept of mimesis. The object imitated does not in some simple sense exist independent of and prior to the act of imitation but comes into existence through its operation. It is after the fact of the completed work that the formal cause or structure of the work is analytically separable. It is because of this paradoxical relation between the final cause and the formal cause or object imitated that the characteristic move of Chicago criticism is to place the critic hypothetically in the position of deciphering after-the-fact authorial decision making. These four causes are usually stratified in a way somewhat like the following: the material cause exists for the sake of the efficient, the efficient for the sake of the formal, and the formal for the sake of the final.

Crane, on the other hand, in his nearly definitive essay on "plot"[15] refrains from labeling the causes of a mimetic work so neatly. Crane's strategic treatment of the elements that constitute different senses or aspects of plot (which differs in emphasis from Booth's account) sets in motion a tension within his theory that begins to make it relevant to the study of Blake, whose works do not appear to be mimetic in either Booth's or Crane's sense of the term. Though Crane posits features in mimetic works that correspond to those outlined by Booth, his deployment of critical terms is strategically different. Rather than emphasizing the four causes as such, Crane identifies what he calls "three elements" of mimetic works, supervened upon by a fourth "synthesizing principle." These three elements are language (as "the linguistic medium," not explicitly called the "material cause"), the manner or technique of imitation (not explicitly characterized as the "efficient cause"), and the things imitated (referred to by Booth as the "formal cause," but called by Crane "the *matter* of [the writer's] invention" [my italics]). The fourth or "final cause" in Booth's treatment appears (unnamed as such) in Crane's account as the "working or power" (conditioned by the "synthesizing principle") of the plot to affect the reader in specific ways.[16]

That which Booth labeled as the final cause is what Crane calls both a "formal principle" and a "first principle of construction" but never the "final cause" per se in his essay on plot. This synthesizing principle can come only from the third element of the plot (the object of imitation—the structure or formal cause in Booth's treatment), because, for Crane, the working or power is itself "the form of the plot" (622). Crane restricts the objects legitimately capable of being imitated or rendered in mimetic plots to actions, characters, and thoughts (or states of mind) and identifies these three features (rather than the formal, efficient, and material causes per se) as the "causal ingredients" of plot as "structure," one of which must always be the synthesizing principle that formally organizes the plot and makes possible its working or power (620–22 and 631–32). Crane's terminological strategy in situating action, character, and thought (which might easily be seen as elements of plot) at the level of causes, and situating (what Booth identifies as) the formal, efficient, and material causes at the level of elements eliminates the possibility that plots could have material or efficient causes as their synthesizing principle. Thus Crane's analysis allows for mimetic plots "of" (that is, formally synthesized by) action, character, or thought but not plots "of" technique or language.[17]

This interconstitution of the object imitated and the working or power of the plot is further complicated in Crane's theory when he defines the structure of incidents being imitated (or rendered) as the *"matter or content"* of the plot, a *"necessary substrate* of unified and probable action . . . the *material system of happenings"* (631; my italics) as distinct from the "plot proper" or "constructive first principle," the working or power that arises from the successive decisions a writer makes in response to the series of artistic problems that the precise rendering of the plot's events forces upon the writer (631–32). Both the plot (as structure or substrate of action) and the plot proper (arising from the series of artistic decisions in the face of unfolding artistic problems) are by nature irreducibly sequential. Although sequence plays a decisive role in each sense of plot, thus ruling out plot or *mythos* as "simultaneous unity" as it appears in Northrop Frye's own rewriting of Aristotle,[18] the two kinds of sequences do not coincide, since the plot proper involves a formal synthesizing principle over and above the sequence of the plot as a structure of events or incidents. Crane's emphasis on sequence and, especially, on the analytic separability of plot as structure of sequential incidents from plot proper as source of producing sequential effects in a reader[19] is central to any rewriting of Neo-Aristotelianism that tries to take into account the ontological priority of Blake's subversive manipulation of plot sequence to reorganize his readers' perceptions.

Crane's Shaping Principle and the Rewriting of Plot in Terms of McKeon's Analysis of Methods and Principles

We have just seen that the synthesizing principle, which for Crane is a prerequisite of the working or power of the plot, is simultaneously "formal" in one sense and "final" in another (just as the formal structure is also in one sense the "matter of invention" or the "material system of happenings"). In his pivotal *Tom Jones* essay, Crane says that the "power, which constitutes the form of the plot" (what Booth calls the final cause), "most sharply distinguishes works of imitation from all other kinds of literary productions" (622). In another, equally fundamental essay, however, Crane extends the legitimate operation of such a shaping principle (or "form" in the "constructive sense of the word") to intellectual (critical) as well as mimetic productions in language.[20] He consequently argues that if form is a constructive first principle for mimetic writers it can become a first principle in criticism of their works as well (143). The necessary presence, for Crane, of shaping principles that exert "a kind of impersonal and objective power, which is at once compulsive and suggestive" over all "organic" linguistic compositions (142–43) opens up an ontological indeterminacy in the formal/final cause in that the shaping principle exists prior to linguistic production (in its compulsive power) yet comes into existence only through the act of production: a writer "can know what he can do, in fact, only after he has done it" (144). This ontological opening in Crane's "shaping principle" makes possible an inductive leap that begins to unlock the subversive possibilities inherent in the Neo-Aristotelian method.

Taken in conjunction with the subtle discrepancies that exist between Crane's, Booth's, and McKeon's treatments of causes, methods, and principles, Crane's extension of the operation of shaping principles to intellectual productions as well as fictional works opens the possibility that what Crane called the "plot of thought" may exceed the "states of mind" experienced by characters engaged in actions. If the operation of shaping principles can be legitimately extended to critical writing, the plot of thought may also be extended to embrace, as the things "imitated" or "rendered" in it, the philosophical methods of dialectic, logistic, and inquiry delineated by McKeon. Such an expanded plot of thought would formally imitate a plot synthesized by technique (or efficient cause) and would necessarily undermine, if not erase, the roles occupied by action and character in conventional plots, effecting their drastic migration from the region of objects of imitation (the place of the formal cause) into the arena opened up in the efficient cause by virtue of the expansion of thought to include the constitutive power of philosophical method as simultaneously a form of thought and a technique of rendering thought.

This redistribution of the role of elements in the Neo-Aristotelian causal hierarchy entails an even more radical methodological shift. If a fictional plot can have for its object of imitation (or rendering) one or more of the philosophical methods McKeon defines (dialectic, logistic and/or inquiry), then its synthesizing principle can itself be selected from among McKeon's inventory of comprehensive, simple, or reflexive principles that are used by those methods. A plot in which a philosophical principle in McKeon's sense acts as the formal synthesizing principle to produce the working or power of the plot by fictionally operating on philosophical methods as the objects of imitation inverts the philosophical use of principles by methods. Action, character, and thought (in its conventional sense) would operate in such a plot as pretexts (techniques or efficient causes) in the fictional rendering of philosophical methods by means of a comprehensive, simple, or reflexive principle.

How *The Book of Urizen* Rewrites Neo-Aristotelianism

The title of Blake's *The Book of Urizen* suggests not only that it is a poem about forms or processes of ur-reason, but that it enacts fictionally a critique of the primordial types of philosophical method. In Blake's own time two dominant types of philosophical reasoning were what McKeon calls logistic and dialectic. Blake's plot of ur-reason can be seen as a rendering through characters and actions of the fundamental conflict between these methodological strategies. According to McKeon, "the logistic method is adapted to trace knowledge back to the elements of which it is composed and the processes by which they are related. . . . All forms of the logistic method implicate, whatever the basic elements and processes employed, the necessity of univocal definitions based on indivisible particles, simple ideas, or arbitrary signs, and of simple processes and relations which govern their organization into systems" (662–63).

If the object imitated or rendered by *The Book of Urizen* is the logistic method itself, it can be expressed through a structural algebra that maps the actions of the poem in terms of increasingly complex analyses of primitive or undefined (as if axiomatic) terms or elements. Blake's rendering of this logistic object or process of imitation is designed to expose the fatal weakness of logistic method: Blake drives this method toward an ontological crisis by rendering or representing it by means of characters and actions (as its efficient cause) that obey the laws of dialectical method as defined by McKeon: "All forms of the dialectical method implicate in some fashion the impossibility of independent finite substances, of clear and distinct ideas, and of fixed univocal definitions, since all things, all thoughts, and all processes and statements are influenced by the organic wholes of which they are dependent parts and in which they are distinguishable only momentarily and as a consequence of analysis"(662).

Rendering this interaction between such mutually incommensurable methodological drives through a fictional plot would be impossible without a "synthesizing principle" or "starting-point" (665) that turns in on itself and is capable of rendering conscious the way it anatomizes its own potentially totalizing drives. McKeon's name for such a principle is "reflexive," and it is particularly characteristic of the method of "inquiry" (or "problematic") because it functions to make intelligible the "transition from analysis to action and operation" (668). Reflexive principles act "by affording knowledge of the form of knowledge required, by indicating actions affecting the action in question, by providing analyses of the process of analysis, or by undertaking inquiry into the modes of inquiry"(667). Reflexive principles thus fundamentally apply to their own logic of operation in such a way that, when allowed to function, for example, in logistic method they become especially subversive and "constitute a major problem in the vicious circle fallacy, since when propositions are allowed to apply to themselves, a proposition which asserts its own falsity is false if it is true and true if it is false"(676).

What I propose to do in the following re-visionary (and, from the point of view of methodological purists, perhaps misappropriated) Neo-Aristotelian reading of Blake's *The Book of Urizen* is trace out some of the consequences of considering the poem as mimetic—with "mimesis" expanded to include philosophical method (in this case "logistic") as its object of imitation. This reconceived mimesis would involve a rendering of the logistic method dialectically through actions, characters, and states of mind functioning as the technique or efficient cause, synthesized (Crane's term, though ultimately misleading in this context) under a reflexive principle of "perspective transformation."[21] Although in this analysis language continues to function as material cause of *The Book of Urizen*'s plot, as it does in traditional Neo-Aristotelian analyses (such as Booth's), its role as material is thrust into the foreground by the working or power of the poem's reflexive principle, and calls attention to its subversive materiality. As self-asserting marks on the page, written language serves to desubstantialize the illusion that the actions, characters, and thoughts (in the conventional sense of states of mind) of the plot are the authentic objects of imitation. In the process, the foregrounding of linguistic materiality undermines language as merely the medium of imitation, thereby dispersing the drives of logistic method (or formal cause) and dialectical method (or efficient cause) toward constituting a totalizing form by invoking the potentially disintegrative power of the controlling reflexive principle (final cause). Considered under this hypothesis, the peculiar working or power of the plot of *The Book of Urizen* would "de-form" the fundamental presupposition of Neo-Aristotelian method that unity of total form/affect is the primary end of aesthetic construction: this de-formation would derive from the specific way the synthesizing/disintegrating reflexive principle operates both to undermine its own functioning and to expose the fatal limitations of the drives toward totalizing form which both the logistic and dialectical methods have as their end or purpose.

The Logistic Structure, the Dialectical Technique, and the Reflexive Synthesizing/ Disintegrating Principle of *The Book of Urizen*

From the perspective of the hypothesized formal cause or object imitated (the logistic method), each successive action, character, and thought functions to decompose or analyze the primary undefined simple elements into their constituent parts. In this logistic sense each new perspective contains a greater number of simple elements and is therefore more limited in that more explicit relational laws enter into it and place constraints on the things perceivable within its framework. From the perspective of the hypothesized efficient cause, however (the actions, characters, and states of mind functioning as dialectical operators), each successive perspective is a synthetic derivative composite perspective, more complex and comprehensive than the ones preceding it, that exposes what was hidden by prior perspectives. The reflexive principle of perspective transformation that guides the interference between these logistic and dialectical dimensions of *The Book of Urizen* creates an inverse relation between the reader's perception and that of the characters. The progressively more restricted perspectives (from the point of view of the multiplying characters) allow the reader to perceive reflexively the larger network of relations in which the prior actions were embedded. The degree of limitation of a character's perspective is in inverse relation to the degree of analysis possible under that perspective. As the plot unfolds, this working or power of the reflexive principle becomes increasingly clear by means of inversion, division, and substitution, so that by the end of the poem, the initial primitive (ostensibly simple) logistic elements have been totally replaced by multitudes of derivative characters and events.

The logistic structure (or object of imitation) of the plot demands that the poem begin by appearing to invoke simple principles, which are created "by decomposing wholes into indivisible elements and simple relations. . . . [They] are first principles; they are not subject to proof; and they are prior to the conclusions which depend on them" (McKeon 666–67). Indeed, *The Book of Urizen* initially seems to provide such primitive, undefined terms with a vengeance—the "Eternals" and "Urizen," whose apparent originary power and monolithic identities invite us to map them in terms of algebraic structures. (The algebra through which the constantly decomposing logistic structure of the poem can be most efficiently presented in the argument of this essay requires only the most superficial grasp of composite mathematical functions, that is, functions that act on other functions, though the actual content of the unraveling functions will eventually become somewhat convoluted.)

In the first two chapters of the poem (and even more subversively in the "Preludium")[22] Blake immediately uses the material cause of the poem (the linguistic medium) reflexively to complicate the apparently indivisible and primordially distinct logistic narrative particles named Urizen and the Eternals: he renders them dialectically as opposing aspects of the narrative context in which they initially appear:

1. the aspect of Urizen under the perspective of the Eternals as "obscure, shadowy, void, solitary" (2:4), a "dark power" (3:7), a "petrific abominable chaos" (3:26), a power which is "hidden" (3:7 and 4:8), and "secret" (3:7), "unknown" (3:10), etc.; designated by

$Et[U]$ or U_1

2. the aspect of Urizen under the perspective of Urizen as victor over "monsters Sin-bred" (4:28), creator of "a solid without fluctuation" (4:11) and a world of "Law" (4:40), dwelling in a "void" (4:16), etc.; designated by

$U[U]$ or U_2

3. the aspect of the Eternals under the perspective of the Eternals (projected as the problematic unified term "Immortal"),[23] as expanding and contracting sense perception, by dialectical implication as light or definite knowability or "eternal life" (3:39), a perceptual/ontological organization in relation to which they perceive U_1 as "chaos" (3:26), etc.; designated by

$Et[Et]$ or E_1

4. the aspect of the Eternals under the perspective of Urizen, as living in "unquenchable burnings" (4:13) and in a state of "fluctuation" (4:11), forces or beings that "die" (4:12), etc.; designated by

$U[Et]$ or E_2

The Eternals' perception of Urizen as shadowy, chaotic, obscure, and unknowable dialectically opposes Urizen's account of his own world as lawlike and knowable (his secrets written down and his visions unfolded). Similarly, Urizen's account of the Eternals as living in pain and unquenchable burnings dialectically opposes the indirect glimpses of the Eternals as the sensually expansive Immortal[24] or as horrified by the inexplicably emergent "shadow" (3:1) and "soul-shudd'ring vacuum" (3:5), just as Urizen's reference to the Eternals' dying opposes the narrator's assertion at the beginning of chapter 2 that "Death was not." The perspective the Eternals have of Urizen in chapter 1 (U_1) reveals as much about the Eternals as it does about Urizen; likewise Urizen's perspective on the Eternals in chapter 2 (E_2) reflects a fundamental meaning of Urizen himself as a narrative pretext of the efficient cause of the plot. On the other hand, the perspectives U_2 and E_1 reveal how these character-pretexts perceive themselves, in contrast to the complementary perspectives U_1 and E_2, which reveal things about these narrative beings or forces that their own perspectives suppress (or that do not exist from their own perspectives).

Thus the terms that comprise the primary elements in the logistic algebra are themselves cognitive acts of perception that function as modes of ontological power relations. Though the logistic object of imitation is based on an illusion or pretext that these elements are independent entities (or characters) that enter into and are partially distorted by the limited perspectives U_1, U_2, E_1, and E_2, the term Urizen exists as separate from the term Eternals only by virtue of these dialectical perspectives. There is, then, a precise sense in which the Urizen that enters into the Eternals' perception as a shadowy, dark, unknowable activity (U_1) is reflexively Urizen's act of perceiving the Eternals as fiery, fluctuating, pain-dwelling, and dying (E_2). By the same token, the Eternals that enter into Urizen's perception as fiery, tormented beings (E_2) are reflexively the Eternals' act of perceiving Urizen as a shadowy chaos (U_1). U_1 and E_2 are thus dialectical inversions of each other, which can be designated in the logistic calculus as

$$U_2 = \frac{1}{E_2} \text{ and } E_2 = \frac{1}{U_1}$$

Mapped in such a blatant form, Blake's strategy in the beginning of *The Book of Urizen* becomes transparent. He is constructing a plot that enacts in the narrative and in the reader's response nearly unbearable tensions between being, power, and knowability and between the drives of consciousness toward logistic univocality and toward dialectical opposition. Blake refuses, however, to allow either the characters (as pretexts) or the reader (as an agent in the dialectical process) to find a place of security or a vantage from which a comprehensive principle (in McKeon's sense) could be rigorously constructed and that would dialectically reconcile the conflicts of the plot, thereby becoming the true synthesizing principle of the plot's working or power: "The function of a comprehensive principle is to bring into relation, and thereby render intelligible, things, ideas, and statements which would otherwise be irreconcilable, and to exhibit thus the organic and dynamic interdependence of all things" (McKeon 666). By contrast, the adventures of the initial aspects U_1, U_2, E_1, and E_2 in succeeding chapters of *The Book of Urizen* force into narrative consciousness the specific ways in which these initial (apparently) dialectically opposed perspectives are shadowy abstractions from incommensurable perspective fields in which the initial (apparently) primary logistic elements are embedded. The reader's desire to resolve these perspectival conflicts dialectically is progressively undermined by the operation of the plot's authentic working or power, the reflexive perspective transformation that increasingly foregrounds the incommensurability (the retroactive revisability) of these aspects or perspectives through maximizing the subversive material functions of language.

The plot of chapters 1 and 2 of *The Book of Urizen* can be mapped logistically in the following way:

Chapter 1: U_1
Chapter 2: $E_1 + (E_2 \longrightarrow U_2)$

The first composite of the poem's primitive logistic elements emerges in chapter 3 when what was represented in chapters 1 and 2 as a conflict between simultaneously opposing and mutually exclusive perspectives (the components of Urizen and the Eternals) is reflexively reelaborated in chapter 3 as a series of causal interactions between those opposed aspects. The arising of the "shadow of horror" (3:1), the emergence of the "vacuum" (3:5), the hiding "dark power" (3:7), etc., at the outset of chapter 1 seems to the Eternals to be a sudden unexplainable appearance, a primordial given of the plot, just as Urizen's sudden decision to set himself "apart" seems to be an equally inexplicable given, since the reasons he gives to justify his revolutionary withdrawal specify conditions in Eternity (such as pain, fluctuation, unquenchable burnings) that conflict with the narrative glimpses of Eternity prior to his speech. His attribution of death to the Eternals (4:12) especially conflicts with the narrator's explicit exclusion of Death from Eternity (3:39).

Though these and many other fundamental aspects of the primary elements of the plot in chapters 1 and 2 dialectically oppose one another, the "void" is common to both U_1 and U_2, and sensual flexibility or fiery energy is common to both E_1 and E_2. This overlapping of aspects allows the logistic analysis of perspectives in chapter 3 to take place, and the provisionally dialectical aspects make possible a more radically composite reflexive incommensurability to emerge in the plot than existed before.

Throughout chapters 1 and 2, Urizen is engaged in various "battles" that do not seem to involve the Eternals but rather generate from his self-closure and self-begetting. Urizen (as U_2) sees one of his most heroic acts as the battle in which he reduces fire to solid in the void ("Natures wide womb") in which he has found himself (4:14–23). He restates this victory as the defeat of the "Seven deadly Sins of the soul" (4:30). This battle and victory, which, from the perspective of U_2, lies in the past, is reenacted through the expanded perspective of chapter 3. The fiery, painful energy Urizen attributed to the Eternals bursts forth as "the seven deadly sins of the soul" (4:49) "in the flames of eternal fury" (5:2), creating in the plot the conditions against which Urizen previously strove and yet created from his "inward" turning (4:15). The emergence of the Eternals into the plot in the fiery form (E_2) created by Urizen's perception of them (and which the Eternals have up to this point repressed) tears Eternity itself apart, thus creating the void with which the poem so inexplicably began (4:45–5:11) and leaving the chaotic vision of U_1 in the gaping void. What in chapter 1 was a mysterious, threatening "hiding" of Urizen as a "dark power" (3:7) is now treated in this derivative perspective as Urizen's "hiding" in flight (5:20–22) from the "flames of eternal fury" that "pour thro' the void on all sides / On Urizens self-begotten armies" (5:2, 15–16). This logistic composite of chapter 3 can be mapped as

$$E_2[U_1]$$

That is, the plot causally connects the dialectically opposing and reciprocal perspectives E_2 and U_1; the chaotic darkness and hidden form of Urizen in chapter 1 (U_1) is here rendered as caused by the perspective of the Eternals Urizen presented in chapter 2 (E_2). Ironically, Urizen's retreat brings into existence, from the Eternals' point of view, the very thing Urizen wished to avoid—death. His avoidance of the fires takes the form of a "roof" (which is like a "womb," a "globe," and a "heart," [5:28–37], all associated with life) but the labor this construction requires yields a Urizen who is "hoary, and age-broke, and aged, / In despair and the shadows of death" (5:26–27). "The vast world of Urizen" that appears at this point (5:37) reflexively elaborates the "wide world of solid obstruction" (4:23) he created in the perspective of U_2, embedded in the fiery activity of E_2. Thus the primary perspective transformation in the plot of chapter 3 is:

$$E_2[U_1] \longrightarrow E_2[U_2]$$

The first derivative composite perspective of the poem ($E_2[U_1]$) objectifies U_1 in E_2 under the fiction of a causal reflex, which retroactively seems to have been presupposed by the mutually exclusive existence of E_2 and U_1 in the first place. After we have passed through the second composite perspective ($E_2[U_2]$), U_2 no longer exists in its simple form of unfluctuating solid, but is transformed into the pulsating roof/womb/globe/heart, making Urizen's previous "solid" appear to have been an abstraction from the larger network (embedded in fiery E_2).

To recapitulate: this dialectical interplay of compounding logistic perspectives is rendered as three causal reflexes: (1) Urizen's transformation of E_2 into $U_2 = $ law/solid; (2) the Eternals' embedding of U_1 in E_2 or $E_2[U_1]$ = fiery/void; (3) Urizen's transformation of $E_2[U_1]$ into $E_2[U_2]$ = roof/womb/globe/heart. In this set of transformations the initial polarized logistic elements E_2 and U_2 become interlocked into the fabric of the composite globular image in such a way that their initial projections as isolated E_2 and U_2 are seen as abstractions from the emergent set of plot relationships in which they are now embedded.

Although the development of the perspectives outlined above introduces projections of prior aspects in such a form that they appear to be genuinely novel elements, this same development pushes into subordinate function the whole stretch of actions of chapters 1 and 2. Although chapter 3 unfolds a more complex set of relationships, which are reflexively presupposed by the perspectives of chapters 1 and 2, the actions of chapters 1 and 2 come prior in the plot because (1) from the perspective of the plot's working or power, they generate a more direct sense of mystery, horror, and alienation (because of the radical disjunction of perspectives) in an abstract and undefined context than can occur in later phases of the plot; (2) from the perspective of the object imitated (the logistic method), the simple (or primitive, undefined) elements of chapters 1 and 2 are fictionally rendered as cognitively prior in the sense that we cannot perceive the analytical perspectives of chapter 3 until we have passed through and assimilated the simpler perspectives of chapters 1 and 2; and (3) from the perspective of the efficient cause (the rendering of character, action, and thought through dialectical technique), the emergent composite network attempts to imitate a synthesizing comprehensive principle that resolves prior conflicts into a unified whole. Thus the four primitive elements (U_1, U_2, E_1, and E_2) analytically generate the later derivative perspectives and are at the same time the *most complex* because *least analyzed* elements in the poem.

The first composite perspective $E_2[U_1]$ suddenly reenters the plot consolidated in the guise of a new character-pretext named Los (5:38–6:6). Los participates in Urizen's view of the Eternals by dwelling in "intense fires" (6:6) and in pain; Los reenacts Urizen's "howlings" (5:24) earlier in chapter 3 when the fires poured through his world; and Los perceives Urizen (who literally separates from Los in this action) as the Eternals initially did—as separated by a void space, as being a "dark Demon" (6:2), "obscure" (5:40), and "unorganiz'd" (6:8). The moment of Los's emergence thus reenacts the beginning of the poem, now projected through a composite perspective:

$$Los_1 = E_2[U_1]$$

If the working or power of the poem were a "comprehensive" principle, Los_1 would function as a dialectical synthesis of opposing perspectives, but instead his appearance reflexively undermines (or falsifies) the possibility of the new incommensurable account of the Eternals' and Urizen's perspectives as mutually excluding each other. As such, Los_1's task is strategically problematic: keeping "watch for Eternals to confine, / The obscure separation alone" (5:39–40) (embedded in dislocating syntax and interrupted by the intrusive comma) signifies that Los_1 confines the Eternals as much as he "confine[s] / The obscure separation." Los_1 can confine a separation only if the separation is itself the act of confining, just as the avoidance of Urizen's chaos by "all" in chapter 1 (3:25–26) is the inversion of Urizen's being hidden. Further, the Eternals' perception of "Death" as an aspect of Urizen's world is the reciprocal reflection of Urizen's perception of the Eternals as dying (4:12): "The Eternals said: What is this? Death / Urizen is a clod of clay" (6:9–10). Thus the "Earth" that "was not" and the "Death" that "was not" (3:36, 39) from the perspective of E_1 in chapter 1 now both clearly exist in the Eternals' perspective, but, like Urizen originally did, they perceive death not as an aspect of their own world but as constitutive of an external being they name "Urizen."

Los_1 is not the more derivative perspective of the pulsating globe ($E_2[U_2]$), which anticipates the emergent body of chapter 4(b), but the prior perspective of $E_2[U_1]$ of Urizen as a dark, unorganized chaos embedded in a fiery context. The action of chapters 4(a) and 4(b), which depicts the emergence of the human body from inside out in successive phases that parody the logistic calculus of the plot, requires a new composite (Los_2) whose actions reflexively analyze Urizen's framing a roof/globe around himself in response to E_2. The appearance of Los_2 is marked by the rousing of "his" fires after "the wrenching apart" of Urizen and Los is healed (7:1–9). Los_1 initially served as a transition between the Eternals and Urizen; now Los_2 is connected to Urizen and brings "fires" (derived from his E_2 component) into the chaotic world of U_1. Los_2 can be mapped as the embedding of Los_1 in U_1 or

$$Los_2 = U_1[Los_1]$$

Blake treats the emergence of the new relationship between Urizen and Los under Los_2 as the action of melting Urizen's rocky form into the fluid raging form of the "Immortal" in chapter 4(a). Los_2's reflex to bind the changes of Urizen (8:10–11) is a derivative form of U_2 and anticipates the transformation of Los_2 by the end of chapter 4(b) into Los_3. Whereas the action of chapter 3 could be mapped as

$$E_2[U_1] \longrightarrow E_2[U_2]$$

the action of chapters 4(a) and 4(b) can be mapped as

$$U_1[Los_1] \text{ (or } Los_2) \longrightarrow U_2[Los_1] \text{ (or } Los_3)$$

The perspective of Los_2 is flexible enough to allow Blake to reveal the subtle reflexive transfer of logistic qualities from Urizen to Los. Los_2 is structurally surrounded by U_1—there is a U_1 component in the composition of Los_1, and Los_1 is now structurally embedded in U_1. The subtle takeover of Los_1 by U_2 in the process of chapter 4(b) allows Los to remain a separate named character while virtually becoming indistinguishable from Urizen as an agent-pretext in the plot for a while; following line 10:28 ("Los beat on his fetters of iron"), the pronouns "he" and "his" equally refer to Urizen and Los. The U_2 component begins to dominate the plot of chapter 4(b) at the point at which the "name" "Urizen" becomes officially "eternal" (10:11): "His prolific delight obscurd more & more / In dark secresy hiding in surgeing / Sulphureous fluid his phantasies" (10:12–14). This action simultaneously expands and restricts the initial context of the plot in which the Eternals perceived Urizen as a hiding and secret power. The prolific delight that Urizen obscures inverts the Eternals' perception of him as "unprolific" (3:2) and is thus a projection of the Eternal "unquenchable burnings" (4:13) as covert sexual energy under the perspective of Los_2. The prolific delight Urizen is obscuring in chapter 4(b) is reflexively that aspect of himself he originally projected onto the Eternals (E_2).

Because Los_1 entered chapter 3 as a technique of the dialectical efficient cause of the plot for compounding perspectives under the guise of the fiction of causal connection and derivation, it is appropriate that the emergence of causality should itself be objectified in Los_2's construction of the links of time as a projection of Urizen's obscuring his prolific delight, which in turn reenacts Urizen's reduction of fluctuation to solid in chapter 2. Los_1 transformed into Los_2 at the point in chapter 3 at which "Los rouz'd his fires" (7:8) by incorporating the E_2 component of Los_1 into U_1; prior to that point Urizen was in a *"dreamless* night" (7:7, my italics). Los_2 transforms into Los_3 at 10:29 when Los heats his furnaces (which analytically reenacts Los's rousing of his fires at 7:8). After Los heats his furnaces at 10:29, the U_2 power begins to reassert itself and a "roof" again forms as Urizen enters "a horrible *dreamful* slumber" (10:33–35, my italics), marking his appropriation of Los_2 to his unconscious U_2 power fantasies.

The imagery of the developing body in chapter 4(b) parallels the branching network of perspectives in the plot in that each new "Age" makes the body more complex, and each new complexity renders the body more limited. In the process, the phases of the body's development sequentially analyze out the "roof" and the "globe" (now treated as a "globe of blood" or heart) of the composite perspective $E_2[U_2]$ of chapter 3. Only the womb aspect of that composite perspective remains unanalyzed in the formation of the body, and it will emerge as a sexual analysis of the "globe of blood" of chapter 4(b) into the first separate female character (Enitharmon) in chapter 5 (13:58–18:15).

The evasion and implication that take place within the linguistic medium of the poem mirror the evasive and submerged actions of the characters who dialectically function as the technique by which the logistic substructure of the plot is undermined. As the poem moves from phase to phase of emerging analytical and composite perspectives, the techniques the characters employ are less subtle, more externalized and obvious, so that the relationships of the plot become less implicit. As the poem continues, more and more characters and actions are needed to embody the increasingly complex and limiting aspects of the plot's relationships.

At the opening of chapter 5, Los's fires, which signaled the emergence of Los_2 in chapter 3 (7:8), now *"hid[e]* their strong limbs in smoke" (13:23, my italics), inverting Urizen's hiding from the fires in chapter 3 (5:19–21). As a logistic analogue under Los_1 of the fires of E_2, Los_3's fire's act of hiding reveals that Urizen's prior hiding from the fires simultaneously entailed the Eternals' hiding from Urizen's chaotic/chained form, a reciprocal relationship that was avoided in earlier perspectives but will emerge explicitly in chapter 5.

The verbal texture of the dialectical action-pretext near the beginning of chapter 5 resurrects the primordial situation of chapter 1 now viewed through the sequence of composite perspectives of the unfolding plot:

> 4. Shudd'ring, the Eternal Prophet smote
> With a stroke, from his north to south region
> The bellows & hammer are silent now
> A nerveless silence, his prophetic voice
> Siez'd; a cold solitude & dark void
> The Eternal Prophet & Urizen clos'd
> (*U*13:35–40)

The "Shudd'ring" reflex of Los to his situation produces and is produced by the "cold solitude & dark void" the Eternals grasped at the outset as "this abominable void / This soul-shudd'ring vacuum" (3:4–5) wrapped in silence and cold (3:18, 27). Though the surface details of the plot in chapter 5 closely approximate U_1, the perspective is dominated by U_2. In this way Blake reveals the complex connection, through Los_3, between Urizen's lawlike form and his shadowy secret form as it is about to manifest itself in the actions of the Eternals themselves.

Because the form of Los_3 is composed of elements of U_1 and U_2, Los's pitying Urizen (13:50ff.) divides Los from his own constituents, a division that is depicted as a recapitulation of the separation of the "globe of blood" in chapter 4(b). The emergence of the "globe of blood / Trembling upon the Void" (13:58–59) analyzes the perspective of the circulatory system in chapter 4(b) as well as the composite perspective of the roof/globe/womb/heart of chapter 3 (5:28–37).

Blake originally introduced this image-complex into the plot of chapter 3 both in order to analyze its aspects sequentially and to reveal (retroactively in chapter 5) that this separation is to a great extent a product of the Eternals' own action. Thus the emergence of the globe of blood as a dialectical connection between U_1 and U_2 reintroduces the Eternals, who dropped out of the plot at the emergence of Urizen's world in the shape of a throbbing heart/womb, perceived by the Eternals as "Death" (6:9).

The perspective of Los_3 radically alters the meaning of the Eternals. In terms of the logistic calculus, the Eternals now embody the following composite structure:

$$E_3 = E_1[Los_3]$$

In this form they perceive the "Void" (now the "Abyss of Los" [15:5]) not "in Eternity" as at the beginning of the poem (3:2) but rather at a great distance:

> The Abyss of Los stretch'd immense:
> And now seen, now obscur'd, to the eyes
> Of Eternals, the visions remote
> Of the dark seperation appear'd.
> ($U$15:5–8)

The Eternals now perceive by means of "eyes," which emerged during the creation of the body in chapter 4(b). Their ability to expand their perception resurrects the term "Immortal" in a now plural form (15:11), associated with the expanded perception of E_1 in chapter 2. The expansion of their seeing is now limited to an analogy to the scientific magnifying "glasses" (or telescopes) (15:9). When, at the end of chapter 5, they erect a "Tent" called "Science," it closes out precisely those visions their "expanding" eyes make available to them (19:2–9).

At the point in the plot at which the Immortals (E_3) perceive Los's abyss, the globe branches out into an explicitly "female form" (18:7)— the heart image being connected to the womb image by a covert reference to the menstrual cycle. The emergence of a "female form" out of the globe of blood requires the mediation of E_3, for this aspect reflexively analyzes the Eternals' full implication in the logistic structure of the plot.

9. All Eternity shudderd at sight
Of the first female now separate
Pale as a cloud of snow
Waving before the face of Los

10. Wonder, awe, fear, astonishment,
Petrify the eternal myriads;
At the first female form now separate
(*U*18:9–15)

In chapter 1, the Eternals could not grasp their implication in the creation of the "soul-shudd'ring vacuum" (3:5), the "void" (3:4), and "chaos" (3:26) or its female womblike nature (4:17), which they "all" created by avoiding. Though implicit in "Natures wide womb" (4:17) in which Urizen condensed his solid and in the womb-aspect of the roof/globe he constructed, the explicit female nature of the "obscure separation" (5:40) does not become conscious in the plot until the Eternals appear in their most restricted and derivative form (E_3).

The separation of the female from Los analyzes out the U_1 component from Los_3. If we break Los_3 into his component parts we find that

$$Los_3 = U_2[E_2(U_1)]$$

If the U_1 component is separated out, under the aspect of E_3, we find that the perspectives of the plot have reached a logistic crisis toward which Blake has been building. The separation out of the U_1 component leaves Los in the precarious state of yoking the most dialectically opposed logistic elements of the plot, U_2 and E_2: this partially accounts for his desire to reunite with the female. At the same time it explains the division of Los into the functions of Orc (a projection of E_2) and Urizen (a projection of U_2) in subsequent chapters. Yet the U_1 component cannot be simply pulled out of that interlocked relationship in its original form. The U_1 that is separated not only assumes an explicitly female form but leaves its traces in the remaining Los character-pretext by the mediation of E_3, which, we must recall, retains the fullness of Los_3 as a component of its makeup. Further, the petrification of the Eternals is clearly the objectification of U_2, the petrific Urizenic solid, in Eternity itself. As such, an equivalence of perspectives exposes another aspect of this central crisis of the plot.

We have seen that

$$E_3 = E_1[Los_3]$$

As before, Blake treats the reflex of the Eternals, E_3, to the separated female form, the U_1 aspect embedded in Los_3, as a causal reflex, the takeover of the Eternals' world by Urizenic solidity. Thus, the emergent Eternals, E_4, can be mapped logistically as two equivalent functions:

$$E_4 = E_3[U_1] \quad \text{and} \quad E_4 = \frac{1}{U_2}$$

This critical event reveals the complexity of Blake's use of a reflexive principle of perspective transformation to enact the interference between the logistic method (as formal cause) and the dialectical method (as efficient cause). The Eternals, as E_1 and E_2, were initially polarized from the Urizenic aspects U_1 and U_2. Now they are revealed to be abstractions from an interlocked network of incommensurable perspectives. The petrifying reflex of the Eternals is externalized in an image that is the inverse of Urizen's roof/globe in chapter 3: whereas Urizen formed the globe around himself to shut the Eternals out, the Eternals form the tent around the void to close the Los complex inside. Urizen's forming of the roof and the Eternals' forming of the tent are the same act projected reflexively through two vastly different perspective transformations.

Orc's gestation and birth are simultaneous with the emergence of the tent in chapter 6 (19:17–20 and 19:37–40), revealing that, just as U_1 and U_2 were the simultaneous incommensurable aspects of Urizen in chapters 1 and 2, the tent and Orc are complementary aspects of the Eternals:

$$Orc = \frac{1}{U_1}[Los_3]$$

and

$$Tent = \frac{1}{U_2}[Los_3]$$

This inverse relationship further emphasizes the interlocked relationships between Urizen and the Eternals that were suppressed by earlier perspectives. The situation in chapter 6 nearly reverses the primordial logistic relationships. The Eternals are solidifying, closing off, excluding sexual activity in a manner appropriate of U_2 of chapter 2. Thus the "fire" Urizen initially perceived as bound up with eternal life is transferred to the center of Urizen's world under the precarious aspect of Los_3. The birth of the fiery Orc petrifies and paralyzes the Eternals: "A shriek ran thro' Eternity: / And a paralytic stroke; / At the birth of the Human shadow" (19:41–43). Orc is thus simultaneously the remnant of Eternal fire, a parody of E_2, and a new version of the "shadow of horror" (U_1) of the first line of the poem. When the Eternals close the tent (19:47), they are totally transformed into U_2 and disappear from the poem as separate characters, as Orc assumes the "fierce flames" of the earlier E_2 and substitutes for the Eternals in the plot.

The plot of the remainder of the poem is effected by techniques of logistic inversion, division, and replacement that become increasingly complex. I provide below merely the schematic form of key logistic moves in the rest of the plot: after the Eternals are analyzed out of the poem, Urizen (U_2) returns as Orc is bound down by Los_4 or the Chain of Jealousy, followed by the disappearance of Los, Enitharmon, Orc, and finally Urizen—all of whom are replaced by multiple character-pretexts who reenact prior events under increasingly derivative (composite) and limited (analyzed) perspectives. By the end of the poem none of the original elements remain, and the plot seems to approach the historical world of conventional mimesis in which action, character, and thought are the proper objects of imitation. Only by means of the sequence of perspective transformations in the guise of a plot involving characters and actions could Blake produce the working or power of this interlocked network's subversiveness in its full concreteness.

Abstract of Some Key Remaining Logistic Structures in *The Book of Urizen*

Chapter 7

$$\text{Chain of Jealousy} = Los_4 = U_2[\text{Orc}]$$
$$U_3 = Los_4 = U_2[\text{Orc}]$$

Chapter 8

$$\text{Fuzon} = U_2 \left[\frac{1}{E_2} \right]$$

$$\text{Net} = U_2 \left[\frac{1}{\text{Tent}} \right]$$

Chapter 9

E_2 is replaced by Fuzon
U_2 is replaced by Inhabitants

Note: all first-, second-, and third-generation character-pretexts have been replaced by derivative plot elements.

Ideological Conclusion

This essay has attempted to consider what was left unthought in the Neo-Aristotelian relentless and rigorous rewriting of Aristotle. Crane's exaggerated concern for adequacy of explanation—in his commitment to ratifying his critical explanations of effective intention by primary recourse to textual facts (which he assumes exist independent of inter-pretation) and to falsifying his own hypotheses—would threaten to fetishize the material text in his theory, if the ideological dimension of this unconscious fetishization of textual fact had not been short-cir-cuited by his recourse to the invisible hierarchy of Aristotelian causes. The materiality of the text—especially in its physical existence as writ-ing (which is virtually ignored by the Neo-Aristotelians in their con-sideration of language as material cause)—is subordinated to the other three causes, for the sake of which the material text exists.

In this transgressive rewriting of Neo-Aristotelianism I have at-tempted to demonstrate how *The Book of Urizen* can be construed as a fictional rendering of formal methodological techniques in such a way that they undermine their own operations and reveal their inherent power to co-opt the human imagination and the material power of lan-guage. In the process of considering the plot of *The Book of Urizen* I have found it necessary to abandon decisively the authoritarian for-mal/final cause, Crane's shaping principle that compels the material elements to cohere into an organic unity or wholeness that produces satisfying emotional effects in ordinary readers. Blake's de-formation of Neo-Aristotelianism through fictional techniques drastically rear-ranges the Neo-Aristotelian causal hierarchy and reveals the extent to which this formal compulsion is a deeply sedimented patriarchal bias that betrays a yearning for a godlike shaping principle manifested in human productivity. This working or power of organic wholeness is analytically available most directly in Chicago criticism through the methodological strategy of placing the critic in the role of justifying

(after the fact) why an author made such-and-such a decision in response to a hypothesized artistic problem-situation (which is then
tested against the supposed independent facts of the text). Such an
attempt to recapture the effective intention of the author more than
resembles the attempt to "justify the ways of God to man" (after the
fact). In this essay I have employed this strategy pretty much as Neo-
Aristotelians would: but the working or power I have been attempting
to justify is dispersive, disintegrative, and reflexive in a way that suggests the compatibility of the working or power of my own essay with
that of Marxist or feminist criticism, even though its material concerns
and procedures of inference by no means resemble those explicitly
ideological techniques of accounting for human production and reception.

Finally, McKeon's attempt to formalize all possible philosophical
moves into a network of finite methods, principles, and subject matters
appears in this de-forming rewriting to be the outcome of a compulsion
to reenact on Western civilization the drive toward a totalizing reassur-
ance that there is rest, finally, in a democratic world of irreducible
pluralism, treated as if this goal itself were not already thoroughly
ideological. Consequently, this rewriting of Neo-Aristotelianism through
The Book of Urizen's fictional enactment of the subversive interference
between McKeon's primary methods and principles urges us to replace
McKeon's democratic ideal with Feyerabend's anarchistic incommensurability.

Blake and the Deconstructive Interlude

Dan Miller

Now that more than twenty years have passed since Derrida's first publication, talk about something called "deconstruction" would appear to make little sense. The introductions, surveys, and critiques have proliferated to the point that we all now know, it seems, what deconstruction is and what it does. Much of the Derridean vocabulary has made its way into common critical parlance, and at least one version of deconstruction has attained the status of an institutionally accepted and approved mode of interpretation. The polemics between Meyer Abrams and J. Hillis Miller already appear dated.[1] Though deconstruction is still able to spark controversy, the focus of debate has shifted. Deconstruction itself is no longer at issue; instead discussion has to do with its limits and effects. Recent attacks come not from traditionalists but from the political left as such critics as Edward Said, Frank Lentricchia, and Terry Eagleton question the political implications of deconstruction and its ability to deal with the historical and social dimensions of literary texts.[2] Some think that critical theory is on the verge of moving beyond deconstruction, and if that is indeed the case, there is little need to rehearse yet again what deconstruction is or what it does.

For Blake also the issue seems to have been settled long ago. The old disputes about the coherence of Blake's poetic vision, the intelligibility of the prophecies, and his place in the literary canon have been resolved, all of them in Blake's favor. He now occupies a secure and even central place in the tradition: he is a name to be invoked, a figure by which to define English Romanticism and, after Northrop Frye, the totality of literature. Thanks to Blake's great interpreters—S. Foster Damon, Frye, David Erdman, Harold Bloom—and the legions of exegetes who followed, the once-obscure prophecies come close to making "amazing good sense."[3] And we know Blake's value, for Frye has given us the prophet of transcendental imagination, and Erdman has celebrated the moral and political visionary. When both Blake and deconstruction are this well known, a deconstructive reading of Blake would be, at best, a perfunctory exercise in applied method.

There are some grounds, however, for believing that, in both cases, the issue is still very much alive. The critical receptions of Blake and Derrida have followed the usual pattern for insurgent, extracanonical figures: proclamation by a small circle of devotees, challenge to the prevailing discourse and its norms, counterattack by traditionalists, public debate that forces each side to caricatured extremes, and finally incorporation of the heterodox, properly adjusted, into orthodoxy. It is a familiar story. Blake recounts it several times in the Lambeth prophecies as Orc and Urizen fight battles in which all victories must be indecisive. And Derrida repeatedly meditates on the means by which dominant philosophies contain and control, yet all the while secretly depend upon, foreign elements. The lesson told by both writers—one of the few things that the two in fact do share—is that very familiar narratives such as this are inevitably misleading. The fact that the case appears to be closed, for both Blake and deconstruction, may be the strongest indication that something has been missed and that real issues remain.

A deconstructive reading of Blake, even a preliminary look at how such a reading might proceed, requires an initial detour. To locate what the institutionalization of Derrida might have overlooked, we need to return to the matter of deconstruction itself and to some of Derrida's texts that are, by now, old works, well read and understood. Though there are compelling reasons, many of them advanced by Derrida himself, for abandoning the vocabulary and much of the identifiable procedure of deconstruction, we will learn shortly why the critic has no other point of departure than what the historical moment offers. Even at the risk of producing yet another primer, we have to talk about deconstruction one more time exactly because of "Derrida," the figure described so confidently by contemporary theory. A step backward to early works may make it possible to move, not necessarily forward, but on a trajectory slightly different from the one that has been officially mapped out for deconstruction. At issue here is deconstruction as critical method: the nature of its interpretive tactics, the grounds it claims as a "valid" technique of reading, its ends and limits. These are exactly the issues that appear to have been resolved, but in most cases they have been resolved much too simply and quickly. What all the attention to deconstruction as method has obscured is the change Derrida's argument forces in the concept of method itself. In one sense—in a very strictly limited but important sense—deconstruction is *not* a critical method.

The *locus classicus* for definitions of deconstructive reading is the 1971 interview published in *Promesse,* later issued and translated as *Positions,* in which Derrida sets out the *"general strategy of deconstruction."*[4] That deconstruction involves the double gesture of reversal followed by displacement is well known. Less often recognized is the paradoxical character of the two-handed operation:

> On the one hand, we must traverse a phase of *overturning* [*renversement*]. To do justice to this necessity is to recognize that in a classical philosophical opposition we are not dealing with the peaceful coexistence of a *vis-à-vis,* but rather with a violent hierarchy. One of the two terms governs [*commande*] the other (axiologically, logically, etc.), or has the upper hand. To deconstruct the opposition, first of all, is to overturn [*renverser*] the hierarchy at a given moment. To overlook this phase of overturning is to forget the conflictual and subordinating structure of the opposition. Therefore one might proceed too quickly to a *neutralization* that *in practice* would leave the field untouched, leaving one no hold on the previous opposition, thereby preventing any means of *intervening* in the field effectively. (41, *56–57*)

Even this opening phase of deconstructive reading has proved, as Derrida foresaw, hard to hold on to. (The translator omits a sentence that, in the original, comes after the first sentence quoted: "J'insiste beaucoup et sans cesse sur la nécessité de cette phase de renversement qu'on a peut-être trop vite cherché à discréditer." ["I must emphasize the necessity of the phase of overturning, which, perhaps, will be too quickly discredited."]) Many have in fact sought to discredit this aspect of deconstruction, charging it with being an arbitrary act of textual violence. The operation does involve a degree of violence, but it is not arbitrary: the violent nature of the opposition justifies the forcefulness of the reversal. Inversion is methodological violence; it intentionally misdescribes a discourse (or, perhaps more accurately, a discourse as it has been traditionally understood), but it violates the apparent truth of the text to demonstrate that this truth is not free of its own violence. This inaugural gesture is diagnostic; the force required to effect the reversal measures the force sustaining the hierarchy. If literary and philosophic texts are univocal discourses, overturning their founding oppositions would be an unjustified interpretive act. But if texts are fields of conflict, however much they present themselves as unified, then *renversement* is necessary to reveal that fact.

This phase is unavoidable, for without it criticism is governed by the same conceptual and metaphoric paradigms that dominate the text and is therefore limited to "the effaced and respectful doubling of commentary."[5] Yet, though necessary, this procedure never succeeds. In fact, it succeeds as diagnosis exactly to the degree that it always fails. "It is not a question of a chronological phase" that can be completed at "a given moment"; rather the "necessity of this phase is structural; it is the necessity of an interminable analysis: the hierarchy of dual oppositions always reconstitutes itself" (41–42, 57). Though inversion reveals the inherent violence of the hierarchy, the opposed terms and the relation itself remain intact. Merely to invert the hierarchies that, for example, subordinate writing to speech, representation to direct presentation, or the word to the concept, and then to assert the superior value of writing, representation, and the word accomplishes little. Nothing been done to alter the relations of subordination and superior value, and the concepts themselves are unchanged. Writing is still the record of speech; representation, a derivation from presentation; and the word, a medium for the concept. Though reversed, the opposition remains metaphysical and still obscures the conflict that constitutes it. Deconstructive *renversement* is less a decisive act of overturning than a permanent (or "interminable") revolution, always necessary because continually failing.

The inversion performed by one hand only prepares for a more dextrous action by the other, and in this sense is a purely tactical movement. Once the textual conflict has been demonstrated, analysis can begin to draw out its logic:

> That being said—and on the other hand—to remain in this phase is still to operate on the terrain of and from within the deconstructed system. By means of this double, and precisely stratified, dislodged and dislodging [*décalée et décalant*], writing, we must also mark the interval [*l'écart*] between inversion, which brings

low what was high, and the irruptive emergence of a new "concept," a concept that can no longer be, and never could be, included in this previous regime. If this interval, this biface or
biphase, can be inscribed only in a bifurcated writing (and this
holds first of all for a new concept of writing, that *simultaneously*
provokes the overturning of the hierarchy speech/writing, and the
entire system attached to it, *and* releases the dissonance of a writing within speech, thereby disorganizing the entire inherited order
and invading the entire field), then it can only be marked in what
I would call a *grouped* textual field: in the last analysis it is impossible to *point* it out [*d'y faire le point*], for a unilinear text,
or a punctual *position*, an operation signed by a single author, are
all by definition incapable of practicing this interval [*de pratiquer
cet écart*]. (42, 57–58)

Derrida's metaphors are precise: *décaler* means to shift, to stagger, to
offset (as one line of rivets against another), to establish a time lag;
and *écart* indicates a swerve, a step aside, a deviation or variation or
difference ("pratiquer cet écart" could be rendered "practicing this
difference"). While the first gesture inverts the system of oppositions,
the second offsets the two levels, subjecting the whole order to a displacement that reveals the unacknowledged principles organizing the
text. Dislodging the dominant hierarchy aims at producing the logic
or, as Derrida often phrases it, the "law" governing the discourse. In
this sense, deconstruction is no different from any other mode of analysis. Its goal is to describe regularities within the object and to formulate the rules that govern them. Deconstruction departs from traditional
methods in its assertion that the logic of the text becomes visible only
as a result of active critical intervention, one that must produce what
Derrida calls, in quotation marks, a "concept" that has been suppressed by the text. The classical case is that of the opposition between
speech and writing, analyzed in detail in *Speech and Phenomena, Of
Grammatology*, and *Dissemination*.[6] Why has Western metaphysics and
aesthetics consistently subordinated writing to speech? Reversing the
hierarchy shows that the opposition has been designed to safeguard
the values of being, presence, and self-identity against the threat posed
by a force that, as displacement shows, inhabits both speech and writing, yet has been consigned to and concealed within the idea of writing.
What is that threat? There is no name for it outside the traditional

system of names, no concept for it apart from the inherited order of concepts, so the given name and concept, "writing," must be used. But by staggering the opposition to show that writing is not the simple opposite of speech, that writing as the interplay of presence and absence is at once the foundation of speech and its inescapable contrary, the critic can use the term with a difference. To describe the system of the text using its own language, analysis must be bifurcated, employing traditional terms but somehow marking them (by quotation marks or other typographical means, by word play, or, most importantly, by style and argumentative strategy) so that they will designate both the orthodox concepts and that which those concepts function to contain and conceal.

This second gesture may seem as arbitrary as the first, but the work of this hand, applying force from a different direction, actually corrects the excesses of the other. Though deconstructive reversal always fails to escape metaphysical paradigms, the succeeding act of displacement shows that those paradigms also inevitably reach their limits. Through deconstructive analysis, the text reveals what it was meant to hide; the text itself supplies the term—words, concepts, images, or tropes—that are already doubly marked:

> Henceforth, in order to better mark this interval [*marquer cet écart*] . . . it has been necessary to analyze, to set to work, *within* the text of the history of philosophy, as well as *within* the so-called literary text . . . certain marks, shall we say . . . , that *by analogy* (I underline) I have called undecidables, that is, unities of simulacrum, "false" verbal properties (nominal or semantic) that can no longer be included within philosophical (binary) opposition, but which, however, inhabit philosophical opposition, resisting and disorganizing it, *without ever* constituting a third term, without ever leaving room for a solution in the form of speculative dialectics (the *pharmakon* is neither remedy nor poison, neither good nor evil, neither inside nor outside, neither speech nor writing; the *supplement* is neither a plus nor a minus, neither an outside nor the complement of an inside, neither accident nor essence, etc.; the *hymen* is neither confusion nor distinction, neither identity nor difference, neither consummation nor virginity, nether the veil nor unveiling, neither the inside nor the outside . . .). (42–43, *58–59*)

The analytic vocabulary is not imported: Plato's text offers *pharmakon;* Rousseau's offers *supplement;* Mallarmé's offers *hymen.* The texts themselves supply both the language and the concepts used in analysis. Were this not the case, deconstruction could stand charged with being mere method in the most reductive sense, a technique applied to an object with which it has no real connection. The art of deconstructive reading consists in locating those terms that mark both what the discourse includes and what it attempts to exclude. Any deconstructive reading that develops an independent vocabulary (or that directly imports Derridean vocabulary) runs the risk of mystification, for the terms in themselves can designate metaphysical concepts only. It is only in the use of the terms that analysis succeeds or fails in articulating the limits of metaphysics. These "marks," which Derrida calls undecidables only *"by analogy,"* occupy places within the traditional hierarchies yet also disrupt the system; they are apparent anomalies that prove to be the most lawful elements of all as they articulate the underlying logic of the discourse.

The second deconstructive operation thus corrects the methodological error of the first, but what justifies the act of displacement? What, if anything, has deconstruction actually done to the text? Derrida speaks of "intervening effectively," but the question of what the intervention does is not easily answered. Classically, interpretive methods find their justification in the nature of their objects; a valid method is one best suited to its object, one that respects the nature of the object, one that does not violate the integrity of the object. An allegorical reading, for example, asserts its validity on the grounds that the text is informed by allegorical intentions or that a larger order of significances, which is the true object of allegoresis, has shaped the work. Deconstructive claims to validity are the same. The method is justified by the nature of its object, which is, as Derrida defines the term, a text: "A text is not a text unless it hides from the first comer, from the first glance, the law of its composition and the rules of its game. A text remains, moreover, forever imperceptible. Its laws and its rules are not, however, harbored in the inaccessibility of a secret; it is simply that they can never be booked [*elles ne se livrent jamais*], in the *present,* into anything that could be called a perception."[7] A discourse is a "text" to the degree that the factors organizing it cannot be immediately seen, cannot be presented conceptually in the way that the discourse presents its own concepts. Rousseau's or Plato's discourses do not—and in fact cannot—make explicit that which governs the treatment of speech and writing; the law that subordinates writing to speech, concealed by the opposition itself, emerges only as the displaced "concept" of writing as *différance*, spacing, and trace. More than simply a conflict of forces, the text is an arena in which the function of some elements is exactly *not* to appear, not to make themselves evident to reading. This paradoxical character of the object justifies all the paradoxes of deconstructive method. The text is that which always holds something more, something beyond yet within itself, and the method of inversion-displacement simply applies the leverage necessary to make the text show what it was constructed to hide.

If we understand the text in this way, and if we keep in mind the contradiction involved in perceiving the text as a discourse whose logic is necessarily imperceptible, then deconstruction has *done* nothing at all *to* the text. The method achieves validity in a classical sense: it is the analysis most appropriate to its object and therefore best constructed to describe the object as it is. If by "text," we mean both the discourse as it presents itself to reading and the "illegible" elements that order the discourse, then deconstruction does little aside from bringing the text into view. Hence, in the section devoted to the "Question of Method" in *Of Grammatology*, Derrida asserts that his is an immanent reading: "Although it is not commentary, our reading must be intrinsic and remain within the text" (159, *228*). An "intrinsic" reading is one that does not look beyond the text "toward something other than it, toward a referent (a reality that is metaphysical, historical, psychological, etc.) or toward a signified outside the text whose content could take place, could have taken place outside of language, that is to say, in the sense that we have given to the word, outside writing in general" (158, *227*). Deconstructive reading remains focused on its object, the text, and refuses to search for grounds beyond it. To this extent, the claims for validity made by deconstruction differ not at all from those made by more traditional methods, and Derrida can avow, in good faith, "I believe in the necessity of scientific work in the classical sense."[8]

Of course, the special object of deconstruction, the text that is at once legible and illegible, has forced method to unorthodox extremes. Shortly after the definition of text in *Dissemination* quoted above, Derrida warns that the object is such that no method in itself guarantees success: "There is always a surprise in store for . . . any criticism that might think it has mastered the game, surveyed all the threads [of the "web" or "woven texture" of the text] at once, deluded itself, too, into wanting to look at the text without touching it, without laying a hand on the 'object,' without risking—which is the only chance of entering into the game, by getting a few fingers caught—the addition of some new thread. Adding, here, is nothing other than giving to read" (63, 71). The two-handed procedure of deconstruction risks getting its fingers caught in the very textuality it attempts to describe; the uncertain "object" guarantees that an "objective" view will miss it and that the more active operations of deconstruction will find themselves entangled in the very thing they seek to analyze. Within a deconstructive reading, there can be no absolute distinction between object and procedure of the kind that holds for classical methods. The acts by which deconstruction produces the unthought laws of the text are themselves caught up in textuality.[9]

Yet this does not mean that deconstructive reading achieves semiotic freedom or autonomy. It means, in fact, the opposite. Reading must be as lawful as the text: "One must manage to think this out: that it is not a question of embroidering upon a text, unless one considers that to know how to embroider still means to have the ability to follow the given thread. That is, if you follow me, the hidden thread" (63, 71–72). Criticism must be both reading and writing, an account of the text and a text in its own right, but this only increases the requirement of methodological rigor:

> One must then, in a single gesture, but doubled, read and write. And that person would have understood nothing of the game who . . . would feel himself authorized to merely add on; that is, to add on any old thing. He would add nothing: the seam wouldn't hold. Reciprocally, he who through "methodological prudence," "norms of objectivity," or "safeguards of knowledge" would refrain from committing anything of himself, would not read at all. . . . The reading or writing supplement must be rigorously prescribed, but by the necessities of a *game*, by the logic of *play*, signs to which the system of all textual powers must be accorded and attuned [*signe auquel il faut accorder le système de tous ses pouvoirs*]. (64, 72)

"Game" and "play" here emphasized the rule-governed nature of textuality, not freedom from constraints. To be more than commentary and to determine the imperceptible laws of the text, reading must actively manipulate the work at hand, but that treatment is as strictly governed as any traditional method. Hence, if reading must be *"exorbitant,"* as Derrida puts it in *Of Grammatology*, in order to chart the "orbit" of the text, and if this exorbitance "cannot be given methodological or logical intraorbitary assurances" (161–62, *231–32*), it still must meet all the requirements of method, including the possibility of failure.[10]

Deconstruction is, then, an exorbitant method, one that exceeds both the manifest sense of the text and the logical requirements of normal methodology. Yet—and this is the paradox that deconstructive practice must embrace—this exorbitance is strictly regulated; even as the search for the hidden thread forces interpretation to adopt unusual strategies, it must closely and carefully follow laws laid down by the thread's path. Far from licensing interpretive freedom, deconstruction intensifies the constraints on critical practice. When reading detours beyond the perceptible bounds of textual meaning, the possibilities of failure increase dramatically. More than any other method, deconstruction makes the critical text accountable. It must attend to the form and mode of its own assertions, careful to avoid duplicating the metaphysical claims of prior criticism—or the simple converses of those claims—in its own prose. More so now than before, criticism requires an answerable style.[11]

As interpretive method, deconstruction is a risky business. Though it makes the traditional claims of valid methods, it lacks their traditional assurances. It provides discrete steps to be performed in an invariable order, but the object that mandates those steps and that order is never simply *there*, in full view, given directly to perception—or to reading. Consequently, deconstruction resorts to arts of indirection that easily go astray. Second, deconstruction is fundamentally provisional in the sense that neither step has any inherent justification. The methodological absurdity of inverting oppositions has a diagnostic purpose, but its main function is to prepare for displacement. That second operation is equally illicit; it rearranges the hierarchical system not because rearrangement is of any value in itself but only to make possible an account of the concealed textual logic. Third, these steps are so provisional as to be, in effect, self-canceling. Displacement corrects the errors of inversion but then becomes itself dispensable once the law of the text emerges. Finally, each step accomplishes its goal by failing. Inversion demonstrates but does not escape or even blunt the force of metaphysical oppositions, and displacement, though it marks what lies outside those oppositions, discovers the law that mandates metaphysics.

Exactly because these deconstructive operations never succeed, they must be interminable. There can be no moment at which the work of deconstruction is finished, no time when the analysis is complete. Derrida has spoken of an interminable analysis, and this holds true even given the provisional, self-canceling character of the procedure. In effect, this is a permanently provisional analysis. It has no choice but to continue indefinitely for, in the attempt to describe the founding assumptions of literary and philosophic practices, it has available to it only the means supplied by those practices. Deconstruction seeks to present that which traditional modes of representation—and their corresponding modes of analysis—have necessarily elided, yet its resources can come only from those modes. Deconstruction is resolutely methodological because the only field in which it can operate, Western metaphysics and aesthetics, requires and defines method. The deconstructive critic must labor to show, by careful method, the foundations and limits of inherited methodology. At some point, the method of deconstruction must involve a reflection on method, a critique of method defined as a procedure with set rules for attaining a definite object (such as a correct or true description of a literary text). But, once again, this reflection leads to an interminable analysis, not to the destruction of method, for the analytic tools must be drawn from method and the goal of analysis is to understand the necessity as well as the limits of methodology.

The provisions and planned failures and strategies of deconstruction have a relatively simple justification. To describe the suppressed logic of a philosophic or literary discourse using the terms supplied by that discourse, deconstruction must make use of whatever lies close at hand. As Derrida says in *Of Grammatology*, "We must begin *wherever we are* . . . [since we cannot] justify a point of departure absolutely. *Wherever we are*: in a text where we already believe ourselves to be [*Quelque part où nous sommes: en un texte déjà où nous croyons être*]" (162, 233). This means not simply that reading begins with the text at hand, but that it has only the concepts and methods supplied by existing traditions of interpretation, among which are the norms of referential meaning, authorial intention, and the unity of the text. To begin to read differently can therefore be only a violation of the text as we know it—as we have no choice but to know it. Deconstruction aims at disturbing the received readings of texts, and its larger goal is to alter those paradigms of understanding that constitute metaphysics and govern all reading, but its point of departure is simply what the historical moment offers. It begins with the texts and the reading that history supplies. In this sense, the beginning is always arbitrary: the exigencies of the interpretive situation determine where and how analysis opens. The interpreter confronts a text, the choice of which is not fortuitous since it has been shaped by a very specific history of prior readings. Though the deconstructive critic attempts to trace what those prior readings have elided, those readings constitute the only available avenue to the text. Only after deconstruction is complete would the critic be able to know what the logical, theoretically justifiable, truly methodological beginning should have been, but that moment is one that can never arrive. "Therefore, I am starting," Derrida writes, "strategically, from the time and place in which 'we' are, even though in the last analysis my opening [*overture*] is not justifiable, since it is only on the basis of *différance* and its 'history' that we can allegedly know [*que nous pouvons prétendre savoir*] who and where 'we' are."[12] Quotation marks multiply as Derrida insists on the historicity of interpretation while at the same time acknowledging that history is an interpretive construct and that the established historical text also requires new reading, one that would follow the workings of those elements—here designated by the neologism *"différance"*—that have fallen outside the stories we tell about our past.

Finally, deconstruction moves critical reading from the assurances of method to something much closer to strategy. Method fixes a procedure, while strategy describes only possible moves, responses to situations that may arise, frequently successful maneuvers, advantageous dispositions of forces. "In the delineation of *différance* everything is strategic and adventurous" (7, 7). Method demands an object, both in the sense of an object of study (the determinate text, the identifiable author, the literary or social context) and in the sense of a goal or end (a valid reading of the text, an accurate depiction of the author, a correct relation between text and context). The objects of deconstruction are less easily defined and require much more analytic flexibility. The unity of the text, the identity of the author, the explanatory power of context, validity, accuracy, correctness—all these are central concepts within the discourses whose unacknowledged limits deconstruction sets out to map. Put much too simply, deconstruction attempts to be a method of analyzing methods and, as such, must put method to use yet cannot finally ground itself on method. Hence, analysis turns from set procedure to strategy "because no transcendent truth outside the field of writing can govern theologically the totality of the field" (7, 7). All methodological constraints, among them the norm of truth beyond method, apply to deconstruction—but only to a certain point; they are to be carefully respected yet ultimately figure only as moves within a larger game.

Even the notion of strategy proves inadequate, for it suggests a fixed goal and an end: this term also must be doubly marked. Strategy is an adventure because ultimately (though this ultimate, again, never comes into being) it has no aim:

> Adventurous because this strategy is not a simple strategy in the sense that strategy orients tactics according to a final goal, a *telos* or theme of domination, a mastery and ultimate reappropriation of the development of the field. Finally, a strategy without finality [*Stratégie finalement sans finalité*], what might be called blind tactics, or empirical wandering [*tactique aveugle, errance empirique*] if the value of empiricism did not itself acquire its entire meaning in its opposition to philosophic responsibility. If there is a certain wandering in the tracing of *différance*, it no more follows the lines of philosophical-logical discourse than that of its symmetrical and integral inverse, empirical-logical discourse. The concept of *play* keeps itself beyond this opposition, announcing, on the eve of philosophy and beyond it, the unity of chance and necessity in calculations without end. (7, 7)

Taking advantage of whatever is at hand, deconstruction may seem to operate empirically. Its legible-illegible object makes impossible the orderly, fully grounded procedures of classical philosophy. Yet empiricism has been defined by metaphysics, so the term is used here to suggest only a similarity: the adventures of deconstruction are not those of the empiricist. Moreover, Derrida's account of the general strategy of deconstruction in *Positions* (and recapitulated in the "Hors Livre" to *Dissemination*) is itself strategic. That procedure, which confessed to being chancy, provisional, and self-canceling, now should be understood as a tactic required by the situation where we are. Beyond the two-stage operation, deconstruction is some other process, closer to strategy than to method, and closer still to continual improvisation than

to strategy. This is a strategy so absolute that it encompasses all traditional strategic goals as part of its repertoire of maneuvers. Derrida's
own practice in his treatments of Mallarmé in *Dissemination*, Genet and
Hegel in *Glas*, Francis Ponge in *Singéponge*, and Freud in *La Carte
postale: de Socrate à Freud et au-delà* quickly leaves behind the schema
of inversion and displacement.[13] The analysis of Rousseau in *Of Grammatology* bases itself on "what [the writer] commands and what he
does not command of the patterns of language that he uses" (158, 227),
but after that, deconstruction moves toward more subtle handlings of
texts. Ideally, reversal and displacement should be practiced simultaneously, but when that happens, the distinction between the steps begins
to blur. In Derrida's hands, deconstruction proves to be more fluid and
complex than most accounts of the method suggest.

When deconstruction was new to the American academy in the seventies, the time and place asked for proof that literary and philosophic
works did have, in Derrida's terms, "textual" or, in de Man's phrase,
"figural" bases. However, now that deconstruction has come to be identified with the liberties of misreading and the indeterminacy of meaning, it is time to show how strict are the constraints on interpretation
and how little, not how much, freedom reading merits.[14] In "Différance," an essay among the earliest translated (1973) and one of
those by which Derrida was known in the seventies, he traces the motif
of "difference" through Saussure, Hegel, Nietzsche, and Freud. The
entire argument cannot be summarized here, but its concluding statements are important, for they insist on the coexistence of meaning won
and meaning lost, of secure reading and errant interpretation:

Here we are touching upon the point of greatest obscurity, on the
very enigma of *différance*, on precisely that which divides its very
concept by a strange cleavage. We must not hasten to decide. How
are we to think *simultaneously*, on the one hand, *différance* as the
economic detour which, in the element of the same, always aims at
coming back to the pleasure or the presence that have been deferred by (conscious or unconscious) calculation [*le plaisir ou la
présence différée par calcul*], and, on the other hand, *différance*
as the relation to an impossible presence, as expenditure without
reserve, as the irreparable loss of presence, the irreversible usage
[*usure*] of energy, that is, as the death instinct, as the entirely
other relationship [*raport au tout-autre*] that apparently interrupts

every economy? It is evident . . . that the economical and the noneconomical, the same and the entirely other, etc., cannot be thought *together*. (*Margins of Philosophy* 19, 20)

By "the economical," Derrida indicates any system of production, exchange, and consumption—textual or psychic—in which the means lead to an end that, in principle, reproduces the beginning. Through the detours of sublimation, the psyche wins the pleasure originally desired but denied by reality; by means of the detours of word, image, figure, character, and plot, the text gives to reading the meaning originally intended but not immediately presentable. By "the noneconomical," Derrida designates a system in which there is necessary loss, in which the end eludes the means, and in which the beginning shows itself an unrecoverable illusion. Here the *pulsion de mort* intervenes in the circuitous route to pleasure and disrupts satisfaction; the differential character of *écriture* so interferes with progress toward meaning that meaningful identity, *le même*, fails as the goal of the journey.

"We must not hasten to decide," Derrida warns, which of these inflections of *différance* to embrace. Though the two of them cannot be "thought *together*," there can be no decision between them, for a choice of either would be mystification, open to deconstructive attack. To conceive *différance* as the successful detour from intention to achievement would be to affirm all the classical models of reading. To think of *différance* solely as loss would be to elevate that loss itself to the status of *telos* and meaning, thereby falling back into traditional interpretation. To read for meaning and to read for the failure of meaning are variants of the same procedure; they are the exegetical analogues of positive and negative theology. The only alternative is to refuse the choice and to accept the inconceivable simultaneity of both "differences." What forms the text is the commerce between the two economies:

Elsewhere, in a reading of Bataille, I have attempted to indicate what might come of a rigorous and, in a new sense, "scientific" *relating* of the "restricted economy" that takes no part in expenditure without reserve [*la dépense sans réserve*], death, opening itself to non-meaning [*l'exposition au non-sense*], etc., to a general economy that *takes into account* [*tenant compte*] the nonreserve, that keeps in reserve the nonreserve, if it can be put thus. I am speaking of a relationship between a *différance* that can

> make a profit on its investment and a *différance* that misses its
> profit, the investiture of a presence that is pure and without loss
> here being confused with absolute loss, with death. Through such
> a relating of a restricted and a general economy the very project
> of philosophy . . . is displaced and reinscribed.[15]

It is a question not of realizing the profit to be gained by reading, nor
of figuring the losses in what escapes understanding, but of calculating
the simultaneity of gain and loss. Deconstruction does not just subvert
textual meaning; it does not merely demonstrate that meaning depends
on the play of meaning and non-meaning that Derrida terms *écriture*
or *différance*. Rather, it seeks to show how the law of meaning and the
law of that which escapes meaning together legislate the text. Deconstruction thus "reinscribes" philosophy, which is not to abolish it, but
to replace it within new boundaries. And the same holds true for criticism. Again we have a twofold analysis, but the paradoxes have been
exacerbated. The two hands must do their work simultaneously, with
deft coordination, to show how these two inconceivably simultaneous
economies constitute textuality.

Consider deconstruction an extended, in fact indefinite, interlude,
the interval of game between the acts of a play. The interlude is not
strictly a part of the drama; its relation to the events on stage may be
only tenuous. But it is necessary to maintain the proper timing of the
action, particularly for an audience that requires a strong mixture of
entertainment in its instruction. Of course, the interlude may contain a
key to the heart of the drama, and this idle entertainment may prove
more than palliative. The interlude is the extrinsic period that, by the
logic of the supplement that Derrida repeatedly expounds, must be
there; it is the necessary accident. And its presence changes the show.
Deconstruction is not a universal hermeneutic: the method will not
produce the specific truth of the text's message or its particular effect
on the reader or its place in history or the character of its author.
Neither will it discover within the text themes upon which the critic
can meditate, nor forms that the reader can contemplate. Deconstruction is exactly *not* what Fredric Jameson claims Marxist analysis is,
"the absolute horizon of all reading and all interpretation" that orders
and encompasses other methods.[16] Deconstruction is instead the discipline that any method oriented toward positive content needs to undergo. Deconstruction makes a difference in all readings and writings,

but that difference will be registered in the altered practices of other methods. The interlude, however long, plays on the play around it.

Since, with deconstruction, the chances of failure increase, a full reading of Blake would require careful preparation and certainly more time and space than are available here. The best we can do is roughly chart one itinerary that a deconstructive analysis might follow. The critical path to avoid is that which finds deconstructive motifs in Blake's poetry or shows how Blake anticipates Derrida, or how Derrida fulfills Blake, or how the two complement each other. Such correspondences are easily discovered, or manufactured, and a reading of this sort would only relapse into thematism, which is exactly not the purpose of deconstruction. Critical gestures of this order reduce both texts—Derrida's as well as Blake's—to univocal discourse and thereby avoid the textual complexity that deconstruction is designed to investigate.

Ideally, a rereading of Blake begins with full justification of the choice of Blake. For deconstruction, the choice of texts cannot be fortuitous or random. We need to examine carefully the status of Blake within the canon as well as the degree and kind of authority attributed to Blake by his most influential critics. Such an investigation might well reveal strains of idealism consistently governing the appropriation of Blake: the Neoplatonic idealism of Kathleen Raine and George Mills Harper, the quasi-mystical idealism of S. Foster Damon, an idealism of the author in both early and late Harold Bloom, and the purely literary idealism of Northrop Frye.[17] In *Positions*, Derrida speaks of his own choice of "certain texts classed as 'literary' " that "organize a structure of resistance to the philosophic conceptuality that allegedly dominated or comprehended them" (69), and, in this light, Blake may well serve as the strongest counterargument to idealist definitions of Romanticism. Deconstruction turns to Blake, then, because of the "Blake" that has already been given to us as an exemplary figure within Romantic and post-Romantic literature.

A rereading of Blake must begin "wherever we are," and the Blake we now have is the prophet of eternal vision and transcendent imagination. We can start, then, with the frequently quoted passages in *A Vision of the Last Judgment* that assert the absolute nature of a series of parallel oppositions—the eternal and the temporal, truth and appearance, inspiration and memory, the enduring and the transient, the true art of imagination and the debased art of allegory: "The Last Judg-

ment is not Fable or Allegory but Vision   Fable or Allegory are a totally distinct & inferior kind of Poetry. Vision or Imagination is a Representation of what Eternally Exists. Really & Unchangeably. Fable or
Allegory is Formd by the Daughters of Memory. Imagination is Surrounded by the daughters of Inspiration who in the aggregate are
calld Jerusalem. . . .   The Hebrew Bible & the Gospel of Jesus are
not Allegory but Eternal Vision or Imagination of All that Exists. . . .
⟨Allegory & Vision⟩ [⟨& *Visions of Imagination*⟩] ought to be known
as Two Distinct Things & so calld for the Sake of Eternal Life" (*VLJ*68,
E554). The issue here is not the value of imagination nor the subordinate place assigned to allegory. Rather, the critical task is to determine
what the concept of vision includes, what it denies, how it operates
within Blake's argument, and what principles govern the distinction between vision and allegory. In this discourse, vision actually designates
two functions, one representational and the other ontological: "Vision
or Imagination is a *Representation* of what Eternally Exists," yet there
is also, exemplified by Scripture, an "Eternal Vision or Imagination *of*
All that Exists" (my italics). At one moment, vision is the representation of an eternal object; at the next moment, it indicates the direct disclosure of that object or, more radically, becomes the object itself:
"This world of Imagination is the World of Eternity. . . .   This World
⟨of Imagination⟩ is Infinite & Eternal whereas the world of Generation
or Vegetation is Finite & [*for a small moment*] Temporal There Exist in that Eternal World the Permanent Realities of Every Thing which
we see reflected in this Vegetable Glass of Nature" (*VLJ*69, E555).
Subtly but significantly, conceptual relations slide and Blake's language
wavers—the "Vision" of eternal existence becomes "Eternal Vision"
and then the self-reflexive "Visions of Imagination"—as it attempts to
unite representation and substance in one concept.

The difficulty Blake's text encounters cannot be resolved by appeal
to the idealist maxim *esse est percipi*, though this is the route taken by
Frye and most of Blake's critics.[18] Idealism does pervade *A Vision of
the Last Judgment* and the rest of the corpus, but Blake's idealism is
far from coherent or consistent. In his annotations to Reynolds's *Discourses* he makes the traditional claim of Platonic idealism that "Knowledge of Ideal Beauty. is Not to be Acquired It is Born with us Innate
Ideas. are in Every Man Born with him. they are ⟨truly⟩ Himself"
(E648). And as good idealist, he sees the visible world reflecting and
repeating the eternal "Permanent Realities." He also holds that a mode

of intellect superior to mundane rationality produces ideal knowledge, though in a letter to Trusler he calls it "the Imagination which is Spiritual Sensation" (E703). The term "Spiritual Sensation"—almost an oxymoron—should complicate any strictly idealist reading. In his annotations to Berkeley's *Siris* Blake asserts that "Knowledge is not by deduction but Immediate by Perception or Sense" (E664), and the idealist eternal archetypes lose some of their transcendent status. Critics have taken pains to render Blake's argument consistent, but diverse philosophic strains struggle throughout the writings. Blake's discourse interweaves, often within single passages, a radical idealism of active perception (and enduring form) with an equally radical naturalism of active sensation (and perceived objects). And this tension continues from the early works, most notably *The Marriage of Heaven and Hell*, all the way to *Jerusalem*.

This is exactly the case in *A Vision of the Last Judgment*. Blake tries again to define the imagination and maintain its substantiality distinct from natural perception. But his argument is forced to intricate extremes and finally proves circular: "The Nature of Visionary Fancy or Imagination is very little Known & the Eternal nature & permanence of its ever Existent Images is considerd as less permanent than the things of Vegetative & Generative Nature yet the Oak dies as well as the Lettuce but Its Eternal Image & Individuality never dies. but renews by its seed. just [*as*]⟨so⟩ the Imaginative Image returns [*according to*]⟨by⟩ the seed of Contemplative Thought the Writings of the Prophets illustrate these conceptions of the Visionary Fancy by their various sublime & Divine Images as seen in the Worlds of Vision" (*VLJ*69, E555). The passage begins with the claim that the image itself is eternal existence ("the Eternal nature" of the imagination's "ever Existent Images") and with the contrast between this true eternality and the merely apparent permanence of natural regeneration ("the Oak dies as well as the Lettuce"). Yet, the argument continues, "Its Eternal Image and Individuality never dies. but renews by its seed," and the question a deconstructive critic will ask here is simple: what renews or supports or sustains what? "Its Eternal Image" is clearly the image of the oak, but is "its seed" the acorn that grows into the oak, or is it something else, a germinal element that somehow regenerates the image itself? If this seed is an acorn, then Blake is saying that the image of the oak is eternal because though one tree may die, acorns will always give rise to other oaks. The eternality of the image would then depend upon "Generative Nature," the natural recurrence of the physical object. The two orders that the argument intends to distinguish—nature and imagination—have crossed within the seed, which seems itself uncertainly natural and eternal. And because the distinction between nature and eternity reflects that between allegory and vision, we have to consider the status of this particular image. Is the seed itself allegory or vision—or something else?

As the passage unfolds, the seed, which is either trope or logical absurdity, gives rise to a second analogy: "just [as]⟨so⟩ the Imaginative Image returns [according to]⟨by⟩ the seed of Contemplative Thought." Blake's emendations indicate some difficulty in ordering the terms of the comparison. At the cost of distorting syntax, we could reduce all this to a simple analogy: as the acorn is to the oak, so "the seed of Contemplative Thought" is to "the Imaginative Image." This would keep the two orders separate, but the uncertain syntax deserves respect, because the analogical problem will not disappear. There seems little point in analogizing eternity and nature when the passage means to insist on their absolute distinctness. The eternal image can hardly require even a "Contemplative" seed. The analogy suggests that the image is eternal simply because it is repeatedly conceived in human minds, but what then occasions the recurrence of the image in contemplation? If a truly Platonic archetype does so, then *that* image would be truly transcendent and without "seed." But if natural oaks cause the oak image to recur in contemplation, then the seed of "Thought" is once again the acorn, and the analogy collapses. Blake has encountered a problem in imaging the imaginative image. That which proves the image eternal and substantive is finally just the "seed," an image that pertains to both worlds, nature as well as eternity. The metaphor connects the two realms that Blake had intended to separate. And with this term, repetition and representation enter the domain of imagination. So Blake's paragraph closes with the highly involved sentence in which prophecies "illustrate these conceptions" (or, represent these representations) of the imagination by "various" images "as seen in" (as imaged or represented in) the "Worlds of Vision." The language of vision is double, at once a discourse of substance, in which the only enduring objects are eternal images, and a discourse of representation, in which images endure because they are sustained by permanent objects. The vision-allegory hierarchy rests ultimately on a seed, which may be either a visionary image or an allegorical figure—or something that cannot be classed conveniently as either. We begin to see the emergence, by way of a discursive uncertainty (or undecidability), of a "concept" that eludes the system of allegory-vision and nature-eternity.

A Vision of the Last Judgment offers a genetic account of the imagination along with the logical definition, but what appears to have been a history of poetic vision has been cut away by a later owner of the notebook. We can substitute plate 11 of *The Marriage of Heaven and Hell,* which contains a mythic history of the origins and fall of poetic vision. With this text, we can also shift from argument to narrative and suggest some of the paths that fuller analysis of Blake's prophecies could take:

> The ancient Poets animated all sensible objects with Gods or Geniuses, calling them by the names and adorning them with the properties of woods, rivers, mountains, lakes, cities, nations, and whatever their enlarged & numerous senses could percieve.
>
> And particularly they studied the genius of each city & country. placing it under its mental deity.
>
> Till a system was formed, which some took advantage of & enslav'd the vulgar by attempting to realize or abstract the mental dieties from their objects: thus began Priesthood.
>
> Choosing forms of worship from poetic tales.
>
> And at length they pronounced that the Gods had orderd such things.
>
> Thus men forgot that All deities reside in the human breast.
> (*MHH*11:E38)

On first reading, this brief myth falls into the familiar pattern: originally subject and object were one, but by a disastrous act of abstraction, the divine splits off from the human, which in turn is alienated from its own creations. A second, more critical reading reveals that this story, which seems to tell of the original human condition, has no real beginning. From the outset, "sensible objects" and "mental dieties" are distinct and enmeshed in that circular relation described in *A Vision of the Last Judgment.* Formally, the story asserts the extreme opposition between this world, in which the gods have fled from objects and human minds for a tyrannical existence of their own, and that prelapsarian time when objects and images were intimately, creatively linked. But, from the first, the relation between object and image is that of animating (which assumes some degree of difference), naming (which implies representation), and ornamenting (which suggests an aesthetic rather different from Romantic organicism).

This myth has been put to strong use. For example, the first quotation in Hazard Adams's *Philosophy of the Literary Symbolic* is this plate of *The Marriage of Heaven and Hell*,[19] and Adams returns to the story a number of times in order to argue that "man . . . is not only a devourer of language but is also a constant creator of forms in language in the manner of Blake's 'ancient Poets,' whom Blake declares to have confronted a potentiality and set about making (by naming) the world of culture" (343). Much hinges on the reading of plate 11, for Adams uses it to ground his survey of post-Kantian language theory and "to rehabilitate the symbolic by insisting on a notion of it as the creator . . . of culture" (23) in order to combat the "danger in structuralism" (25) and the aridity of poststructuralism. Adams's attack on the newer criticism is more theoretically sophisticated than most, yet here is his comment on plate 11: "Given Blake's emphasis on creativity, the statement about this at the beginning is put rather curiously, however: 'The ancient Poets animated all sensible objects with Gods or Geniuses. . . .' Were the 'sensible objects' existent previous to their animation by the poets? Only, I think, as potential possibilties of vision. Blake did not intend us to imagine men, at that critical moment of the invention of language, originally confronting real inanimate sensible objects. Rather, he intended the poets by the constitutive power of language—namely metaphor—to have *created* those objects . . . by anthropomorphizing them" (105). The critic helps Blake say what he meant to say even if his statement was "curiously" otherwise. Myths of originary naming and Adamic language are common, but if Blake's story is at all part of this genre, it departs significantly from the norm.

On a second, closer reading, plate 11 tells a more complicated story. Blake's syntax makes pronoun reference ambiguous, much as it does in *A Vision of the Last Judgment* and important parts of the prophetic works. Does "them" in the first sentence refer to "sensible objects" or to "Gods or Geniuses"? Do the divine images name and adorn natural objects, or do those objects contribute their names and qualities to deities? The problem is priority: which term is the source of poetic perception, the "seed" of the eternal image? Did "Echo" first name a property of mountains and only later a nymph? Was Narcissus a mythical figure first, endowed afterwards with the name and properties of a specific flower? Blake's second sentence, with its equally ambiguous pronouns, does not decide the matter. Either the poets begin with an object, "each city & country," then subsume it under a god, or they start with a mythic image, the "genius," which they then realize as a "mental deity." The syntax of the narrative consistently prevents the reader from assigning priority to either term. Objects may be "animated" by images and, in this sense, be secondary, but it also may be the case that objects, poetically apprehended, give rise to the sense of an indwelling "genius" and then to the image of a deity.

This ambivalent, circular relation between image and object makes it impossible to fix the cause, agency, or moment of the fall. The overthrow of poetry by abstraction has at least two sources. It is precipitated by an unspecified, external act of exploitation: "some took advantage . . . & enslav'd the vulgar." The crisis enters from the outside; corruption comes from "some" who are already corrupted. Yet this fall into priesthood is made possible by a previous lapse into system. Blake does not specify the agents of systematization, but the only available candidates are the ancient Poets. "Till a system was formed" is grammatically a dependent clause within the previous sentence, "And particularly they studied the genius of each city & country. placing it under its mental deity." Blake has disrupted the sentence to give the impression of a discontinuity where none, either grammatical or narrative, actually exists. The poets studied the images of objects and placed objects under images until they formed a system. What in the poets' activity results in system? Here again, the narrative refuses to specify, but the only possible source for system is the animation of objects by deities. Narcissus and Echo give form to natural phenomena and derive their character from physical objects, yet they also contribute to a larger mythology that can split itself off from the world and exist independently. The poets themselves have made the fall possible and perhaps inevitable. Blake's myth remains a crisis narrative, but the crisis announced in the third paragraph is only apparent and masks the real exigency, which is continual and unresolved.

With the elaboration of a system of images, whose relation to objects is not immediately or intuitively certain, plate 11 returns us to the theme of allegory and the general problem of representation. The passages from *A Vision of the Last Judgment* and *The Marriage of Heaven and Hell* are consistent in their inconsistencies. In both cases, analysis discovers an element that seems not to fit the discourse—"representation" within vision, a "seed" that is neither natural nor eternal, the narrative crux of a fall from poetry caused by poetry. There is no proper name for this factor that disrupts yet organizes the governing oppositions within Blake's texts, but a convenient and strategically useful term can be found in a word condemned by Blake and most Blake critics. For the sake of analysis, and with suitable double marking, we can call it "allegory." The double marking is, of course, necessary to distinguish this sense of allegory from the allegory that Blake rejects as the creation of memory and natural experience. But the term deserves this use because, within Blake's text, it marks the place of all that vision seeks to transcend but cannot leave behind—the inevitability of some mode of representation within all perception, the figural component of the imagination. Allegory, therefore, can serve to suggest that moment when the argument on "vision" and "allegory" reaches its limits and finds the distinctions untenable, or when the exposition culminates in the image of a seed that is neither imaginative nor natural, or when the story of the Fall loses narrative coherence and becomes the emblem of a permanent, unnarratable crisis. One line of deconstructive analysis would then trace the progress of the word itself through Blake's prophecies. That reading would find allegory consistently denigrated as a fallen mode of representation and perception, yet as consistently rehabilitated as a limit upon the Fall and a potential means of regeneration. Though Blake tends to discount allegory in his prose, the poetry treats it with strict equivocation. Another line of analysis, however, might look to Blake's poetic practice and gauge the differences between what the discourse asserts and what it practices. In a very abbreviated way, we pursue that course here.

Finally, then, deconstruction turns to the image itself. Once more, the text has already been selected by prior Blake criticism. It is almost a critical commonplace to end readings with quotations from plate 98 of *Jerusalem,* the most uncompromisingly apocalyptic passage in the prophetic books. If we hope to find the imaginative image in its purest, most transcendent form, it should be here, when the nightmare of history has come to a close and the false garment of nature has fallen away to reveal the true image of humanity and the human world. An apocalypse of vision, a revelation of eternal images, an imaging of the imagination itself—this climactic moment is as ambitious as Dante's celebration of divine light or Milton's description of the Son emerging to battle Satan:

And they conversed together in Visionary forms dramatic which
    bright
Redounded from their Tongues in thunderous majesty, in Visions
In new Expanses, creating exemplars of Memory and of Intellect
Creating Space, Creating Time according to the wonders Divine
Of Human Imagination, throughout all the Three Regions immense
Of Childhood, Manhood & Old Age[;] & the all tremendous un-
    fathomable Non Ens
Of Death was seen in regenerations terrific or complacent varying
According to the subject of discourse & every Word & Every
    Character
Was Human according to the Expansion or Contraction, the Trans-
    lucence or
Opakeness of Nervous fibres such was the variation of Time &
    Space
Which vary according as the Organs of Perception vary & they
    walked
To & fro in Eternity as One Man reflecting each in each & clearly
    seen
And seeing: according to fitness & order. And I heard Jehovah
    speak
Terrific from his Holy Place & saw the Words of the Mutual Cov-
    enant Divine
On Chariots of gold & jewels with Living Creatures starry & flaming
With every Colour, Lion, Tyger, Horse, Elephant, Eagle Dove,
    Fly, Worm,
And the all wondrous Serpent clothed in gems & rich array Hu-
    manize
In the Forgiveness of Sins according to the Covenant of Jehovah.
    (*J*98:28–45, E257–58)

The speakers in this final and eternal human conversation are, of
course, Blake's four Zoas, described a few lines earlier as "Chariots
of Humanity Divine Incomprehensible" (98:24, E257).

Readings of the passage have been remarkably consistent. Adams
finds here "the making of reality in the language of man" (114). Harold Bloom observes, "Word and vision are one here . . . The mind
so directly creating space and time, regenerates even the nonexistence
of death, inverting or creating it at will."[20] Minna Doskow finds that

here the "original division [between "man" and the "natural world"] based on the subject-object distinction is thus overthrown in imaginative unity" and that Blake's apocalypse transcends "any separation between self and other, or perceiving subject and objective universe."[21] For most critics, this revelation is a consummation of idealism: everything attains utmost clarity as the creative, originary imagination overcomes all divisions and distinctions. The real merges with the ideal.

Much in the passage does support such a reading, but here also the idealist vision reaches its boundaries and betrays the continuing presence of allegory. Plate 98 celebrates an absolute; it is a song of praise to the originary and final human imagination. Within this vision of infinitely productive imagination, everything is activity and unrestricted circulation. The multiplicity of "every Word" and "Living Creatures" passes into and out of the singularity of "One Man." Images and words emerge from the "Tongues" of humanity and from Jehovah's "Holy Place," but their paths are strictly ruled by the source. Blake intones "according to" and "according as" no less than six times, and all creations return to their point of origin, either in actuality (through the responses of conversation and the process of "reflecting each in each") or in principle (by following the rule of "according to" and by never failing to "Humanize"). Cause and effect chase each other in circles: perception varies "According to the subject of discourse," while the discursive word shapes itself "according to" the state of perceptual "Nervous fibres." This eternal conversation creates even its own speakers, for the "they" of line 27 are the "Visionary forms dramatic" that spring from "their Tongues." Imagination is not simply a human faculty, for it shapes even the divine humanity that possesses it. Blake has articulated on a massive scale the traditional concept of imagination as access to the infinite, unlimited freedom, and pure creativity, as escape from causality, condition, and contingency. Blake's imagination achieves this by elevating all objects to the status of the word. Language reclaims the natural world figured by the "all wondrous Serpent" and restores its human meaning. As the world becomes word, discourse restores significance even to death, the most extreme possible loss of meaning. Toward the end of the passage, "Living Creatures" accompany divine "Words," creation and discourse in parallel, as if Adamic language had in fact returned.

The vision of the great reunification, however, does not erase all conceptual relations. While the imagination seeks to overcome the differences and distinctions of fallen perception, a system of oppositions still governs Blake's discourse. The lawfulness implicit in "according to" balances the freedom of absolute creativity; a principle of "fitness & order" coexists with the desire for "New Expanses"; and the particularity of "Lion, Tyger, Horse, Elephant" continues alongside the unity of "One Man." Blake's epithets for the imagination tend toward oxymoron: "*Visionary* forms *dramatic*" created by "the wonders *Divine* / Of *Human* Imagination." All these relations are summed up in the contrast between speech and sight that pervades the passage. Plate 98 is at once a discourse on vision and a vision of discourse. The poet *hears* Jehovah speak and then *sees* the words spoken. Freedom, creation, and unity are consistently linked to speech, and all that is ordered, particular, and lawful pertains to sight. Speech is dramatic; vision, formal; and apocalypse weaves back and forth between the two. Blake does not subordinate the visual to the verbal or sight to speech, but he does attempt to maintain both dimensions equally throughout the passage. In this revelation, there are no limits to creation, yet the creations are all bounded and particular; and though vision perceives determinate forms, these do not constrain eternally productive speech. Plate 98 joins together concepts that, though not antithetical, coexist only with some tension.

The critic who looks to other things than "good sense" will note a shift in the tenor and language of the passage. Blake's catalogue of wonders rises from an overview of the apocalyptic, but still fully human conversation (*J*98:28–33), through the series of "regenerations" (*J*98:33–40), to a sudden allegory of the divine (*J*98:40–45). A sentence ends and a new one begins with an allegorical progress or triumph: words on chariots with attendant "Living Creatures" emerge in procession from Jehovah's mouth—an image almost baroque in its exorbitance. The verbal and visual dimensions come together in an extreme figure. The word is now both visual and verbal, at once the free creation of speech and the lawful term of a "Covenant." A third term again enters the system of oppositions: between the visible world of "Lion, Tyger, Horse, Elephant" and the spoken words intervene "Chariots of gold & jewels," vehicles of visible speech. Blake's language for the imagination has become markedly theological as the bond between unity and particularity (and the object of Blake's sixth and final "according to") takes the form of a "covenant." Though this is a "Mutual" covenant ordained for freedom, the opposite of the unequal and enslaving "Covenant of Priam" described soon after (J98:46–54), it is still a compact or contract, a lawful binding of parties, and the legal character of the trope is important. When the world becomes word, metaphors cannot be mere metaphors. Further, the covenant itself passes from Jehovah to the world by figural displacement: words on chariots are metaphor for divine speech; "Living Creatures" are scriptural metonyms for the chariot; and the natural variety of "Lion, Tyger, Horse, Elephant" is a synecdochic extension of the four "Living Creatures." This covenant moves from the divine source of words to the world by means of verbal tropes.

Chariots carry the covenant and bind the free word to the ordered image. But, like the figure of the seed, the image (or word) of the chariot is an intransigent element: it bonds together the two dimensions of Blake's vision but fails to take a proper place in either the argument of infinitude and freedom or the motif of order and form. At the heart of Blake's apocalypse, the reunification of the human and the natural, is this image of an artificial object, ornamented "with gold & jewels," carrying visible words, and attended by "Living Creatures." Here, where humanity is "clearly seen / And seeing," emerges an image that does not deliver clarity, an obscure spot within revelation. We are confronted with a complex image whose meaning is far from immediately evident. Apocalypse culminates in difficult allegory.

What does the chariot signify? Why is it necessary to the covenant, and why does a legal term, even metaphorically, intrude in the final vision? Revelation, it seems, has given way to interpretation, for an understanding of the chariot image can come only at the end of a long investigation. The passage itself will not decide the sense of the image; it sends the reader elsewhere. The central images of Blake's prophecies are highly allusive as well as allegorical, and an unfolding of this particular image involves tracing a long series of allusions. The chariot is extensively elaborated in the closing plates of *Jerusalem* but also has a long history in the prophecy as a whole, both in the poetic text and the designs (the enigmatic picture on plate 41 is a notable case), and in Blake's prophecies generally. A reading of the entire corpus would not be enough, for each instance of the image leads still other places. At the very least, an adequate reading would have to consider the divine chariot in books 6 and 7 of *Paradise Lost*, Beatrice's car in the late cantos of *Purgatorio* (which appears in Blake's Dante illustrations with features similar to his chariot images), the theme of the *merkabah* in Jewish mysticism and similar motifs in Neo-platonism, the vision of the throne in Revelation 12, the archetypal *merkabah* in Ezekiel 1 (and in Blake's watercolor *The Whirlwind: Eze-kiel's Vision of the Eyed Wheels*), and related passages in Isaiah 6 and Daniel 7. Particularly in the scriptural antecedents, the chariot-throne is associated with a covenant and the physical word, a book that Eze-kiel and John must consume.

We cannot follow through with this kind of intertextual reading here, and though mandated by the image itself, this analysis would still not resolve the issue. We would encounter similar problems in Ezekiel and Revelation: a vehicle where there seems to be no need for one, a highly ornamented artifact that bridges the distance between the divine and the human, a complex and spatially involuted image appearing at the moment when final clarity has been promised. What Blake's revelation reveals, more than anything else, is the intransigence of allegorical representation and the interminable analysis that allegory provokes. Deconstruction may be described as the kind of reading that, at the apocalyptic moment, finds itself forced back into the text, into Blake's other texts, and into all the surrounding texts. Blake's revelation, for idealist critics, asserts free creation and determinate form, yet it practices difficult interpretation and problematic images. A full deconstructive reading shows the logic that mandates this disparity.

Conclusive statements are out of place. We have only anticipated, not performed, a full reading, and our finally antimethodical method will never guarantee results beforehand. We need to do much more before we can arrive at even provisional conclusions, and then deconstruction will insist that all conclusions be permanently provisional. Interludes in the exegetical drama will have to multiply before we see how the play itself changes. But we have ventured the "concept" of allegory and, through that intervention, opened Blake's argument, narrative, and images to reading and its risks. We are at the verge of seeing how, for example, the allegory of the chariot sustains Blake's apocalypse even as it also blocks revelation.

Rouzing the Faculties: Lacanian Psychoanalysis and the Marriage of Heaven and Hell in the Reader

Mark Bracher

Readers of Blake have long recognized that the poet has designs on them. In fact, Blake himself says so quite explicitly, speaking, for instance, of his desire to cleanse the "doors of perception" (*MHH*14) and to "rouz[e] the faculties to act" (E702) so that his readers might cast off the "mind-forg'd manacles" (*SE*46:9, E27) to which they are all subject. To this end, Blake employed an impressive array of philosophical, theological, and political subjects and themes as well as some striking stylistic and narrative techniques. In the past half century Blakeans have made considerable progress in comprehending these difficult and often intractable elements, but relatively few attempts have been made to understand how these elements might work to effect that psychological transformation of the reader that Blake so expressly desired. Though many commentators refer to "the reader" in discussing Blake's poetry, their attention tends to focus on the reader's immediate (and transient) response, rather than on more substantial and permanent transformations that the poetry might promote. The only long-term changes that are even considered are alterations of the reader's philosophical ideas—i.e., the reader's "sacred code" (*MHH*4),—and even here, little is said about how such alteration is elicited, or about its significance for the reader's total psychic economy.[1] This omission is of course easily explained by the fact that criticism has until recently lacked the tools to carry out such an investigation: it has had no clear notion of how literature might promote psychological transformation. Now, however, although a comprehensive theory of such transformation has still not been developed, advances in our understanding of the role language plays in the psychic economy make it possible to begin to analyze and assess Blake's poetry in the terms in which he himself clearly viewed it: as a force capable of promoting change in the reader.

In what follows I will attempt to develop some key elements of such an analysis by focusing on *The Marriage of Heaven and Hell,* which contains some of Blake's most programmatic statements on the force of poetry, and which exerts this force on the reader in a number of definite and readily observable ways. I will concentrate on three effects that both Blake and his readers see his poetry as producing. These include evocation of desire, elicitation of interpretation, and construction of a new linguistic code. To help explain how these effects occur and, more important, what their significance is for the reader's total psychic economy, I will employ the psychoanalytic model of mental functioning developed by Jacques Lacan—a model in which image, desire, interpretation, and code are key elements.[2]

Image and Desire

The first thing a reader of *The Marriage* encounters is a picture: the poem's title page (see illustration 2). One can approach the pictorial element of Blake's composite art in at least two significantly different ways. The method that has predominated in Blake criticism is to attempt to "read" the images by translating particular visual forms into (verbal) concepts. This approach, which takes the picture as a message to be deciphered by the viewer, has incontestably produced valuable results. But Blake himself advocated a somewhat different response, suggesting a method that, he believed, could promote transformation in the viewer. In *A Vision of the Last Judgment* he declared of his pictures: "If the Spectator could Enter into these Images in his Imagination approaching them on the Fiery Chariot of his Contemplative Thought if he could Enter into Noahs Rainbow or into his bosom or could make a Friend & Companion of one of these Images of wonder which always intreats him to leave mortal things as he must know then would he arise from his Grave then would he meet the Lord in the Air & then he would be happy" (*VLJ*82, E560). We can distinguish two different movements here, although Blake's syntax works to conflate them and thus problematize any attempt at absolute separation: the movement of entering the images, via the Imagination, and the movement of approaching them, in Contemplative Thought. The first movement can be seen as an affective and even identificatory movement, the second, one of interpretation.

We can see how the first process works by allowing ourselves simply to gaze at the title page of *The Marriage,* attempting not to interpret

2. *The Marriage of Heaven and Hell* (copy H), pl. 1, Fitzwilliam Museum, Cambridge.

or understand it but rather to "Enter into these Images in [our] Imagination," by allowing our gaze to travel where it will and respond with free association. When I approach the title page in this manner, my gaze is drawn first to the two figures embracing at the bottom of the page. As it lingers there, I feel a disturbance or frustration, which, when I focus attention on it, seems to be because the two figures are not embracing fully: there is no genital contact. In fact, some force seems to be pulling at the figures' feet, drawing them apart. Their heads and arms seem to be slipping from each other's grasp. I feel a kinesthetic sensation; my arms want to reach and grasp more firmly.

Disturbed and unfulfilled, my gaze moves upward to the figures in the flames, scanning the bodies for one in which it can find repose. Here, too, I am frustrated. All of the figures seem off balance, out of control. Some, moreover, seem incomplete, obscured, or even devoured by the flames. My gaze moves on to the couple standing (or strolling) beneath the trees. Here I encounter a different sort of disappointment: the figures seem static, insubstantial, even lifeless. And although they are close together and seem not to be in danger of being separated, there seems to be no real union between them: the figure on the left seems to be walking or holding the arm of the right-hand figure, which seems to be either standing still or drawing away from its mate. The figures, in fact, do not even seem to be in precisely the same plane: the left-hand figure seems to be either behind or to one side of the other. My focus then shifts to the right, where a figure whose position I immediately enter into seems to be kneeling and lamenting over his (I assign my own gender to this figure) mate. Here, however, the frustration, the separation, the sense of loss are more immediate than in my response to any of the other couples, for I imagine the supine figure to be dead.

Frustrated by all the human forms, my gaze moves to the trees, whose gracefully curved branches seem to offer a type of repose and satisfaction. My gaze is drawn to the trees on the left because of their greater mass and intricacy and also (I suspect, once I focus on them) because they seem to embody inverted human figures. These figures, too, create a certain uneasiness in me: I somehow feel distorted, bloated, disfigured, devoured, and obliterated through residing in them. The dynamics of these images—heads pointed downward—sends my gaze down along the left-hand margin of the plate to the origin of the flames. No figure here stops my gaze, so it follows the movement of the flames upward toward the right-hand tree. It continues to move up through the foot, trunk, and limbs of the tree and into the sky, where it seizes a brown inkblot that appears immediately to be a bird, and I experience the kind of release I feel when I dream that I am flying. Eventually my gaze is drawn out and away from the bird by the branches of the trees that reach into my field of vision, and I now become aware of the larger patterns and movements in the design. I notice what seems to be a counterclockwise motion following the route I have just traveled: down from the left-hand tree into the fire, up through the flames to the tree on the right, and from there up through the branches and over to the top of the other tree.

But I am still frustrated; I have found no image or gestalt that makes me feel fulfilled. This frustration leads me to reflection and interpretation. Why am I frustrated? What would make me feel fulfilled? The question implicit here is: what ideal or desire underlies and motivates my gaze? Two central features of my ideal image would seem to be perfect equilibrium and perfect union with another body, qualities that manifest the desire to recover the symbiotic union of the neonate with the mother. In my response to Blake's images, I can be seen to seek such gratification in two ways: first, by wanting to unite (through identification) with another figure, and second, by wanting that figure itself to be united with another figure. My search for repose, balance, and control, as well as for union, can be interpreted as a manifestation of fear of change, imagined as dismemberment or death. This interpretation is reinforced by the fact that my disappointment was particularly acute when I imaginatively entered into forms that were off balance, inhibited, or disfigured in some way. What is at stake for me, ultimately, is my own sense of well-being, conceived of (implicitly) as permanence and as union or sameness with others.

Having recognized through the interpretation of my responses both the particular fantasies and the more general desire that informed my gaze, I immediately want to look for a different sort of image in order to see if there is an alternative, more accessible way to fulfill my desire for well-being. I return to the image of the circular process. Perhaps the happiness Blake said his readers would find by entering his images can be attained through identificatory participation not in a single body-image but in all of them successively, and in the process as a whole— entering into one state and leaving it, moving into another. I recall particular passages from *The Marriage* and *Milton* that explicitly advocate this processual mode of being. Approaching Blake's picture now on these "Contemplative Thoughts," I reenter the flames. This time I feel myself swimming/flying in them with abandon, rising upward. My movement is arrested momentarily by the inert form of the tree and the mourning/supine couple, but then resumes when my gaze encounters the figure of the bird. It strikes me now that yielding to the flames has resulted in my recovering the one state that I found fulfilling in my earlier tour of this plate's images: that of the bird. The autonomy and self-affirmation that I originally experienced in the image of flying are available even more intensely in immersion in the flames/waves of process—a state of disorientation, disfiguration, and even dismemberment and dissolution. This image of continuous process and change that supersedes all static states is fundamentally different from the state of balance and union that I first sought. I now feel drawn to discover this new image everywhere. I feel myself attracted to the words "Marriage" and "and," which appear much more fluid and processual than "Heaven" and "Hell," whose rigid letters strike me as substantial, unyielding, lifeless. Multiplicity and transformation attract me; monolithic, substantial identity repels me. I now recognize a contradiction in my earlier search for permanence: while searching for images of stasis, balance, and control, I also found the most static figures the most disappointing. Before, I sought self-affirmation in stasis; now, I react to stasis as to death. And, conversely, I now respond positively to images of dismemberment and dissolution of the body—images that previously made me uncomfortable.

Such are the workings of my Imagination and Contemplative Thought when I approach the images in the manner suggested by Blake. When we inquire what effects this sort of response might have on a reader-viewer's psychic economy, a number of Lacan's observations prove helpful. First, there is the significance of the fact that my response focused on body images. According to Lacan, the image of the body is the most fundamental category or matrix of all perception and experience. Like Freud's body ego, it is the basis of one's feeling of self, or self-awareness, and as such it constitutes the unity of the subject*

---

* Abbreviations used for Lacan's works are as follows:

SJL—Le séminaire de Jacques Lacan, ed. Jacques-Alain Miller (Paris: Éditions du Seuil); vol. 1, *Les écrits techniques de Freud, 1953–54* (1975); *Le moi dans la théorie de Freud et dans la technique de la psychanalyse, 1954–*

(*SJL*1:144). In addition, it underlies all our experience of the external world: "the fundamental, central structure of our experience is properly of the imaginary order" (*SJL*2:50), which "is made around the specular image of one's own body, or the body of the other" (*SJL*2:119). Thus "it is the image of one's body that is the principle of all unity that one perceives in objects" (*SJL*2:198). Moreover, "perception is a total relation with a given tableau where man always recognizes himself somewhere. . . . [That is,] the object [of perception] is always more or less structured like the image of the body of the subject. The reflection of the subject, his specular image, is always found somewhere in every perceptual tableau, and it is that which gives it a quality, a special inertia" (*SJL*2:199)—i.e., a (subjectively experienced) significance or emotional weight. The image of the body thus makes possible "the humanization of the world: perception in function of images linked to the structuration of the body" (*SJL*1:162). As such, it "permits the organization of the ensemble of reality" (*SJL*1:144).

Like perception, desire too depends fundamentally on the image of the body. For desire emerges only in relation to a body image perceived in the external world: "the subject originally marks and recognizes desire by the intermediary not only of his own image but of the body of his *semblable*" (*SJL*1:169). "The first *élan* of appetite and

---

55 (1978); vol. 3, *Les psychoses, 1955–56* (1981); vol. 11, *Les quatre concepts fondamentaux de la psychanalyse, 1964* (1973) (English edition: *The Four Fundamental Concepts of Psycho-Analysis*, trans. Alan Sheridan [New York: W. W. Norton, 1977]. All references are to the English edition); vol. 20, *Encore, 1972–73* (1975).

DI—Lacan, "Le désir et son interpretation," *Bulletin de psychologie* 13 (1959–60), 263–72. Summary by J.-B. Pontalis of portions of Lacan's 1958–59 seminar.

EC—Lacan, *Écrits* (Paris: Éditions du Seuil, 1966).

ES—Lacan, *Écrits: A Selection*, trans. Alan Sheridan (New York: W. W. Norton, 1977).

FI—Lacan, "Les formations de l'inconscient," *Bulletin de psychologie* 11 (1957–58), 293–96. Summary by J.-B. Pontalis of portions of Lacan's 1957–58 seminar.

H—Lacan, "Desire and the Interpretation of Desire in *Hamlet*," trans. James Hulbert, in *Literature and Psychoanalysis: The Question of Reading: Otherwise*, ed. Shoshana Felman (Baltimore: Johns Hopkins University Press, 1982), 11–52.

PL—Lacan, "Seminar on 'The Purloined Letter,'" trans. Jeffrey Mehlman, *Yale French Studies* 48 (1972), 38–72.

desire passes in the human subject by the mediation of a form that he sees at first projected, exterior to him" (*SJL*1:198). "To the projection of the image, follows constantly that of desire. Correlatively, there is reintrojection of the image and reintrojection of desire. . . . And in the course of this cycle, the desires are reintegrated, reassumed by the child" (*SJL*1:202).

These observations clearly suggest that one of the most striking features of Blake's pictorial art—his integration of body images into virtually all elements of his perceptual tableaux—evokes a recapitulation in the viewer of the constitutive movement of his or her perception and desire. By making us literally see the human body in everything, Blake's designs prompt us to reenact, and thus perhaps rework, those originary perceptual acts by which we constituted our worlds. As we scan Blake's pictures, we automatically (unconsciously) search for the form of the human body or body parts. And when we discover such an image, it evokes one of two basic responses—identification or aggression—according to whether or not the image coincides with the image of our own ideal ego. "If the other saturates, fills, the ideal image," Lacan observes, "[the other] becomes the object of a narcissistic investment. . . .   If, on the other hand, the other frustrates the image, it engenders the maximum destructive tension" (*SJL*1:311).

In light of these observations it becomes clear that my response to Blake's title page involved activation of fundamental, constitutive elements of my psychic economy. In fact, it involved those very processes by which the therapeutic action of psychoanalysis occurs: first, the projection of desire; second, its recognition as projected desire; and third, its articulation/integration into the public symbolic order of language (see *SJL*1:205–9; 1:223; 3:267). We will later have occasion to elaborate on the therapeutic process of psychoanalysis. For the moment, however, this sketch should be sufficient to suggest a parallel movement between the psychoanalytic process and my response to Blake's pictures. First was the projection of desire: my search for an image I was comfortable with. Second was the recognition that my visual response involved projected desire. And finally came my articulation of this desire, my relating it to larger themes, such as process versus substance, change versus permanence, union versus separation. It is only through this sort of interpretation that desire becomes fully integrated. In fact, Lacan suggests, it may be that this interpretation should be carried through to one's most fundamental assumptions and values. "Should we," Lacan asks, "push the analytic intervention until the fundamental dialogues on justice and courage, in the great dialectical tradition?" (*SJL*1:223). Blake's composite art does push us this far, and in doing so, it offers us the opportunity to integrate our desire with the symbolic, linguistic order of public values and knowledge. Blake calls this integration a marriage of heaven and hell. And it is in such a marriage, according to Lacan, that the efficacy of psychoanalysis resides: "the entire analytic experience," he declares, "is developed at the joint of the imaginary and the symbolic" (*SJL*1:157; see also 2:297).[3]

Such a marriage involves an alteration of both partners: desire (hell) acquires new modes and aims that offer it fuller expression, and the public symbolic system or code (heaven) is altered so as more fully to accommodate desire. Seen from the perspective of Blake's reader, this means that the speech act that is the text of *The Marriage* uses the symbolic—the code of language—both to pressure the reader's desire and to oppose and revise the categories of the code itself.

Interpellation

The first of these effects, which (following Althusser[4]) I will refer to as "interpellation," is a relatively common phenomenon that can be most easily observed in statements that address an auditor or reader directly. As Lacan explains, when we are told, "You are this," or "You are that," "this 'you are this,' when I receive it, makes me in that speech-act other than I am; [it] pins, tufts [*capitonne*] the subject" (*SJL*3:315). The "you" of the "you are this" is "a manner of trapping the other, of trapping him in the discourse, of hooking signification to him" (*SJL*3:337). This trapping occurs because the subject is forced "to inscribe [the message] as an element of his interior discourse, to which he has, whether he wants to or not, to respond in order not to follow it" (*SJL*3:340).

Though the clearest form of interpellation occurs in direct address, interpellation is present in some form in all discourse. "Starting with a speech act," Lacan observes, "a game is instituted, in everything comparable to what occurs in *Alice in Wonderland*, when the servants and other persons of the queen's court begin to play cards by dressing themselves as these cards, and becoming themselves the king of hearts, the queen of spades, and the jack of clubs. A speech act engages you to sustain it with your discourse, or to repudiate it, . . . but even more, to yield to many things that are in the rules of the game. . . . Once introduced into the game of symbols, you are always forced to conduct yourself according to a rule" (*SJL*3:63). Lacan finds a prime example of such interpellation in Poe's "The Purloined Letter," where the action of each character derives from—and changes according to—his or her position in the triadic "game" of hide-and-seek being played with the letter. The subjects are here seen to *"model their very being on the moment of the signifying chain that traverses them"* (*PL*60; emphasis added).

We experience such interpellation, then, in all acts of reading (and listening). Poetry, however, differs from most speech acts in that it often interpellates us to a position that is significantly different from our habitual position. *The Marriage of Heaven and Hell* dramatizes this power of discourse quite clearly. In the fourth memorable fancy, for example, both Blake's persona and the angel are said to impose on each other in presenting their visions: the angel "took" (*MHH*17) Blake's speaker through the stable, etc., and the speaker catches the angel "by force" (*MHH*19) and carries him away. The interpellative power is also manifested by the final memorable fancy, when "the angel hearing the [devil's words] became almost blue" and then, after a direct engagement with the devil's discourse, "stretched out his arms embracing the flame of fire & he was consumed and arose as Elijah," utterly transformed by the devil's utterance (*MHH*23–24).

Blake, then, could not have failed to recognize the interpellative power that his own poem exercises on the reader, and we ourselves can recognize it throughout *The Marriage*. One particularly powerful instance occurs in the opening "Argument," which calls on us to question right and wrong, and in such a way that we are forced, in order to be able to interpret the passage, to assume a relativist perspective. As John Howard points out, the Argument uses an allusion to Isaiah to evoke several conflicting interpretations of who is the "just man" and who is the "villain."[5] What is crucial here is not the allusion to Isaiah or the opportunity for several different interpretations; most utterances offer such opportunity, after all. Rather, the decisive factor is the manner in which the poem pressures us to construct and assume a single perspective that is in itself relativist. The narrative achieves this effect by declaring that the demeanor and action ("path") that once characterized the just man now typify the villain. We are thus made to conceive of a single path that characterizes at one time a just man and at another time a villain—a conception that is by definition relativistic. Although we remain free to make whatever specific interpretation we like, we are forced by the terms of the narrative to assume a relativist rather than absolutist moral perspective. The effect is somewhat like that of a complex question (e.g., "When did you stop beating your wife?"), whose terms force one to answer affirmatively one or more implicit, prior questions ("Have you beaten your wife?" "Have you stopped beating your wife?") before one can begin to answer the present question. Blake's Argument asks the reader, in effect, "Who are this 'just man' and this 'villain' who can at different times walk the same path (take the same action), and what is the nature of their common path?" No matter what answer we give to this question, we are forced to answer affirmatively the implicit prior questions: "Can a just man and a villain engage in the same course of action (while maintaining their respective identities as just and villainous)?" And "can a single path (course of action) sometimes be just and other times villainous?" In Lacanian terms, we are forced to inscribe the message as an element of our interior discourse: in order to interpret the Argument, we must tacitly accept—provisionally, at least—the notion implied there that right and wrong are problematic and that no code is universally and eternally valid. After we have interpreted the Argument, we are of course free to reject this notion. But to the extent that we succeed in interpreting the passage, we will also have succeeded (whether we realize it or not) in seeing certain actions, at least, as morally ambiguous: we will have become, for the moment, moral relativists.

The interpellative force of the Argument thus reinforces in the cognitive, conceptual register, the movement away from monolithic meaning and identity—single vision—that is elicited by the visual images of the title page. The following plate (*MHH*3) opens by evoking our desire for full being with the fantasy of a new heaven and a return to paradise. This lure is followed with directions on how to progress to this desired state: first we must accept contraries, for they are "necessary to Human existence." This proposition is made to seem acceptable by means of several compelling examples: "Attraction and Repulsion, Reason and Energy, Love and Hate." From the pre-Socratics on, these oppositions have been recognized as fundamental, and so we comfortably embrace them. But as soon as we swallow this proposition, we are hooked into the position that "evil" itself is somehow necessary—and therefore good: "From these contraries" that we have just embraced as necessary, "spring what the religious call Good & Evil. Good is the passive that obeys Reason[.] Evil is the active springing from Energy." We are here interpellated into a position from which "good" and "evil" have no clear, unambiguous significance. Even if we reject the proposition here advanced—and we cannot be certain whether we should—we once again have to inscribe the message as an element of our interior discourse, as Lacan observed, and respond to it in order not to follow it. That is, we are forced to identify evil with activity and energy, which, because of their close ties with vitality and life, we equate with good. Evil is thus implicitly good. Similarly, by being forced to conceive of good in terms of passivity, we are coerced into an ambivalent feeling toward good. Though we may agree or disagree with the assertion—or reserve judgment— the assertion determines the terms of our reflection, thus radically limiting our possible moves.

The interpellation exercised by the following plate (*MHH4*) compounds our task without loosening the restrictions on our moves. And the fact that the statements made here are said to issue from "the voice of the Devil" only exacerbates our helplessness. Can the voice of the Devil be trusted? If so, we must accept the Devil's contention that "All Bibles or sacred codes. have been the causes of the following Errors." If not, we are forced to refute the Devil's position. Any attempt at refutation, however, must tacitly accept the terms of the Devil's assertion. That is, we must think of good and evil in terms of reason, energy, body, and soul, as the Devil has done; all we can do is attempt to alter the distribution or significance of these terms. But because the Devil himself defines these terms, we must first find some ground for refuting his definitions—an attempt that will be futile, because the ultimate ground of all our values and assumptions, our "sacred code," is precisely what is being challenged.

Code

Interpellation, then, not only pressures us to assume certain perspectives or conclusions, it can also work to unsettle and reconstitute the fundamental symbolic code that underlies all of our values and assumptions. In fact, *The Marriage* quite obviously—apart from its interpellative forces—constitutes an alternative system or code. Readers have been struck by this fact from the beginning. Originally seen by some commentators (most notably, T. S. Eliot) as a symptom of Blake's supposed intellectual isolation, the uniqueness of Blake's code is now acknowledged to be the result of the poet's recognition that, as his protagonist Los puts it in *Jerusalem*, "I must Create a System, or be enslav'd by another Mans" (*J*10:20, E153). In *The Marriage* we have Blake's most accessible and explicitly self-reflective presentation of an alternative system or code. Blake here challenges the orthodox code, which positions body apart from soul, human apart from God, and desire beneath reason, and he offers an opposing code that radically alters the positions of and relations among these and other crucial signifiers. This much is obvious and widely acknowledged,[6] but we need to inquire further into the ultimate effect and significance of the new code.

Specifically, what role does the symbolic system or linguistic code play in an individual's psychic economy, and what difference can a new code make in that economy? According to Lacan, the human subject is largely constituted "by its place in the symbolic world" (*SJL*1:95). The individual's internalized linguistic code functions much like the rules of chess, marking out in advance, through the equivalences and oppositions it establishes among signifiers, all the possible moves and combinations of a person's perceptions, thoughts, demands, and even desires. In short, it is the ground from which the subject attributes and experiences meaning (*ES*285).

This power of the internalized code is centered in what Lacan calls "*points de capiton*," key signifiers that, like buzzwords, are subjectively compelling, capable of moving a subject. Without them, all language would have the effect of a foreign tongue that one cannot understand (which, Lacan says, is precisely the situation with psychotics, for whom certain *points de capiton* are absent [*SJL*3:304–5]). Like the upholstery buttons that anchor the fabric and padding to the frame of a sofa, *points de capiton* anchor subjective experience to the common, externally existing linguistic code. As such, they are "a schema for taking into account the dominance of the letter in the dramatic transformation that dialogue can effect in the subject" (*ES*154).

Points de capiton thus play a key role in defining the subject's sense of being. This is because the ultimate function of language is to give us a sense of our own being: "The pure function of language,"

Lacan says, "is to assure us that we are, and nothing more" (*SJL* 1:180). Language holds the key to this assurance because it defines what it means to be: being is constituted by language. "Being, the logos [*verbe*] itself, only exists in the register of speech. Speech introduces the hollow of being into the texture of the real. . . . Before speech, nothing is or is not" (*SJL*1:254). Because being is thus a construct of the linguistic code, it is in relation to this code, internalized as what Lacan calls "the Other," that "being finds its status" (*ES*251). As the constitutor of being in general, this Other is thus also "the locus from which the subject's question of his existence is presented to him" (*ES*193)—a question that, Lacan says, "bathes the subject, supports him, invades him, tears him apart even" (*ES*194). By defining what it means to *be*, this internalized code constitutes the standard against which each subject implicitly (unconsciously) judges his or her fullness of being, or fulfillment. The definition of being that is given by the code is thus the ground of the various strategies and institutions through which individuals and societies seek fulfillment (see *SJL*1:16). All purposive behavior (and as we shall see, ultimately all desire) is thus a quest for *being*, as defined by the code, and the direction taken by such behavior is ultimately determined by the *points de capiton*—by the way in which they situate being, and by the paths that they provide to being.

The symbolic code of the Other is thus constitutive of the human subject at the most fundamental level, and this fact suggests one reason for poetry's transformative potential: poetry can create a new code and thus redefine what it means for a person to be. "Poetry," Lacan says, "is the creation of a subject assuming a new order of symbolic relation to the world" (*SJL*3:91). Such change can have great significance. "The slightest alteration in the relation between man and the signifier," Lacan declares," changes the whole course of history, by modifying the moorings that anchor his being" (*ES*174).[7] Given this understanding of the constitutive role played by language in the psychic economy, and the capacity of poetry to transform language, it follows that poetry has considerable transformative potential. Insofar as a poem such as *The Marriage of Heaven and Hell* offers the reader a new code, in which the positions of certain key signifiers—*points de capiton*—are significantly altered, it has the potential to promote significant changes in the reader's psychic economy. *The Marriage* itself indicates the significance of such alterations, telling us that codes can be the cause of error (*MHH*4) and that one's subjection to a code constitutes the greatest subjection possible (*MHH*13).

The new code embodied in *The Marriage* significantly alters the positions of a number of key terms constituting the definition of being. The most crucial alteration of the traditional, sacred code occurs in the position occupied by "God" in relation to other signifiers. By altering the position of "God"—which, as the name of Being itself, is perhaps the most significant *point de capiton* for most people—the poem provisionally redefines what it means to be, and thus has the potential to alter, for the moment, at least, the ground that regulates our speech and desire. In general, the poem systematically dismantles the traditional signification of God as a transcendental being that is the source of all other being. Such alteration is most obvious in propositional statements in which the signifier "God" is severed from its normal attributes and linked with properties not normally associated with it. The signifier receives its greatest dislocation in the assertion, "God only Acts & Is, in existing beings or Men" (*MHH*16). Here, and in statements like, "The worship of God is. Honouring his gifts in other men" (*MHH*22), "those who envy or calumniate great men hate God, for there is no other God" (*MHH*23), and "All deities reside in the human breast" (*MHH*11), the position of God, or Being itself, in relation to human being is changed from one of separation and domination to one of virtual identity.

This relocation of God in relation to individual existing beings is reinforced by a parallel relocation of particular attributes of this Being; thus the "glory," "bounty," "wisdom," and "work of God" are disconnected from transcendent Being and inserted into actually existing beings as, respectively, "the pride of the peacock," "the lust of the goat," "the wrath of the lion," and "the nakedness of woman" (*MHH*8). The traditional relation of God to Jesus is likewise radically altered: in place of a God who is "One," and "visible in Jesus Christ," Blake presents a "Jesus Christ [who] is the greatest man" and who "mock[s] the sabbaths God" (*MHH*23). Here the traditional relation of identity between God and Jesus Christ is replaced by a relation of separation and even opposition. Thus wherever we encounter "God" in *The Marriage*, we experience a fundamental reversal that, along with a similar displacement of related signifiers like "body," "soul," "angel," and "devil," works to redefine being in the Other, which regulates our thought and desire.

An analysis of the proverbs alone also reveals a correlative displacement in the positions of a host of corollary terms. A large number of proverbs, for instance, embody alterations of the human essence or ideal—i.e., of the definition of human being. Many deal with the significance of the wise man and the fool (18, 19, 32, 37, 47, 52). Many promote the value of individual uniqueness (39, 44, 50, 62, 65) and of flexibility or versatility (41, 48, 61). Others work to establish the corollary values of excess (2, 13, 14, 15, 26, 46), exuberance (64), delight (53), genius (54, 66), and desire (4, 67). Still others establish new positions for truth and vision (33, 34, 38, 69). It is also significant that the proverbs offer multiple and even contrary perspectives on the same phenomena, thus implicitly locating certain key signifiers in several different (sometimes contradictory) positions, an effect that forces the reader to engage in an active attempt to position these terms, i.e., to interpret them.

The diabolical code that Blake presents in *The Marriage* thus has the capacity to produce significant transformations in a reader's psychic economy. But for this potential to be realized, the reader must first internalize the new code, at least in part. That is, this code must alter the reader's Other, that "pure subject of modern game theory" (*ES*304) that establishes all the possible moves of the subject who is reading the poem. Without such internalization, the poetry has no more impact than a philosophical argument that the reader rejects.[8] One factor promoting internalization is interpellation, whose force we have already observed. But for interpellation to elicit profound and significant internalization, it must work in conjunction with the reader's desire.

Desire, Interpretation, and Psychological Transformation

To understand this process of transformation, we must consider the role of desire and its relation to language in the psychic economy—particularly in interpretation. Desire, in Lacan's view, is a manifestation of the general quest for being, directed toward particular objects. More specifically, desire is the result of lack of being, in two senses. The "real, earlier lack" (*SJL*11:205) is the lack of immortality, the fact of finitude. In addition, there is the lack of the symbolic system fully and adequately to express biological need. These deficiencies of the real and the symbolic produce a situation in which the demand for being becomes inscribed in particular objects that respond to need. Desire, directed toward particular objects that were articulated in response to biological needs, pursues those objects not as means of satisfying the needs but as partial representatives of that which is lacking: the subject's immortality or full being. Thus it is that "desire is the metonymy of the lack of being" (*ES*259; translation modified), and every object of desire is a part of being that represents the whole of being.

The "being" that any particular object represents, however, is not always identical with "being" as it is implicitly defined by the symbolic system internalized in the Other. In fact, several different, nonconcentric codes could be said to operate within the psychic economy, and their mutual ex-centricity is what underlies metonymy, the perpetual displacement of desire from one object to another. This metonymy is "rendered necessary by the lack of being" (*ES*,259; translation modified), which is due not only to the finitude of all objects, but also (and more fundamentally) to the absence in the symbolic system of an absolute signifier, a univocal definition of being—the absence of a single, absolute Other. (As Lacan puts it, there is no Other for the Other [*ES*316].) Because the whole (full being, immortality) cannot be possessed or even fully and coherently articulated, a partial representative must suffice. Hence the displacement from (a never-present, nonexistent) whole to a part. And hence also the displacement from part to part: because no part can ever equal the whole and completely fill the lack, desire is always unsatisfied, always moving to another part. That is, the failure of the Other to provide an absolute signifier—one that would reveal the meaning of being, or the truth about truth—is compensated for by fantasy; an image fills in for this impossible signifier (*H*15–16).

The primary object to fill in for being is the phallus, which, in Western culture at least, symbolizes the highest potency or being that an individual can attain. Seen ontogenetically, the phallus is what the mother lacks, and what the child cannot give to the mother—what the mother desires but what the child neither is nor has. This phallus, this being that is lacking, comes to be associated with the image of the penis, because the father seems to fill the mother's lack, and the penis is the most tangible object that the mother lacks and the father possesses. But the phallus is not the penis. The phallus, as an imaginary substitute for the (nonexistent) absolute signifier of being, is itself lacking: no object or state can ever fill the lack of being. Hence other objects, or images, arise and assume the place of the phallus (*H*38), the most prominent being the breast, feces, the gaze, and the voice— objects, respectively, of the oral, anal, scopic, and invocatory drives (*SJL*11:103). All such objects—designated by Lacan as the *objet a*— are representatives of that fundamental something that is lacking: the phallus (*SJL*11:103), or immortal life (*SJL*11:197)—i.e., full being.

These objects and their corresponding fantasies make their presence felt not only as conscious desire but also as unconscious desire—i.e., as symptoms, including physical and behavioral dysfunctions and (more important, for our purposes) slips of the tongue, jokes, and witticisms. Now the symptom, in all forms, Lacan says, is essentially metaphor (*ES*166, 175), a substitution of one signifier for another. Metaphor can be explained as the eruption of unconscious demand for being, as articulated in particular unconscious fantasies and objects of desire, into the subject's speech, which is multiply determined by articulated need, conscious attention, and unconscious signifiers, de- sires, and fantasies. This substitution of a conscious signifier for an unconscious one is subtly present in all speech as the difference between the *énonciation* and the *énoncé*. The *énonciation*, or act of speaking, is always grounded in unconscious desire and fantasy (and, hence, a chain of signifiers), which, however, are usually latent rather than manifest in the *énoncé*, the statement that is spoken. At times, though, as a result of gaps, ambiguities, or other features of the consciously modulated statement, the desire or fantasy forces its way into this sig- nifying chain. The result is a metaphor, which, if not allied with con- scious intention, is also a symptom. Lacan gives an example of such a metaphor-symptom in a slip of the tongue related by Heine and cited by Freud (see *FI*294ff.). Asked how he was treated by a millionaire, a man of moderate means replied, "He treated me entirely as an equal, in a fashion totally famillionaire" (*"de façon toute famillionaire"*). Lacan explains that the condensation of the two words *familière* and *millionaire* occurred because *"millionaire"* was for the speaker the object of a strong fantasy which forced its way into the conscious dis- course.

Hence it is that metaphor, Lacan says, is the source of the *point de capiton* (*ES*303), the connection between subject and system. In meta- phor a signification residing in the unconscious as desire and fantasy "inflects, commands the usage of the signifier, to the point that any sort of preestablished . . . lexical connection is untied" (*SJL*3:248). More specifically, metaphor involves a reallocation of attributes among signifiers, and in this way unconscious, unsymbolized elements, residing at the level of the *énonciation* and struggling for being, force their way into the consciously directed *énoncé* in the form of a newly appointed signifier. Metaphor is thus "a certain passage of the subject to the meaning of desire" (*ES*258, translation modified; see *EC*622). It provides a closer approximation of *what* is desired—i.e., being—and thus is linked to the question of being (*ES*175), the unending quest for the absolute signifier.

Metaphor and metonymy, as Lacan defines them, are thus "the two aspects of language that generate the signified" and hence also are "determining effects for the institution of the subject" (*ES*285). As such, they are central factors of the psychoanalytic process itself, where metaphor figures as symptom, as we have seen, and metonymy as interpretation of the symptom. Neurosis occurs when, by repression, "speech is driven out of the concrete discourse [*énoncé*] of the subject and finds its support either in the natural functions of the subject"—as a symptom—or in the images that constitute the imaginary (*ES*69), the objects of fantasy and desire. Repression is thus simply the fact that there are "internal limits on what one can say" (*SJL*1:295), that "there is among the elements of the repression something that participates in the ineffable—essential relations that no discourse can express sufficiently, except . . . between the lines" (*SJL*1:269). This ineffable, repressed element is a subjectively intense experience (trauma) that needs articulation in the universal, common language [*énoncé*] in order to be integrated into the subject. The return of the repressed is thus a quest for being, which, we recall, is a status that can only be conferred by language. The repressed, Lacan declares, "insists, and demands to be" (*SJL*2:354). Hence "neurosis is a question that being poses for the subject 'from before the subject came into the world' " (*ES*168); and "the subject's want-to-be [is] the heart of the analytic experience, . . . the very field in which the neurotic's passion is deployed" (*ES*251).

Psychoanalysis works its transforming effect by integrating the particular subject's want-to-be—the unconscious, unsymbolized experience and desire—into the common symbolic system of the *énoncé*. This integration is achieved through verbalization: "Speech," Lacan declares, "is the all powerful instrument in the treatment" (*ES*275); it "is the mill wheel by which human desire is constantly mediated in reentering into the system of language" (*SJL*1:203). For "[t]hat which insists on being can only be satisfied in recognition [which occurs in language]. The end of the symbolic process is that non-being comes to be, that it is because it spoke" (*SJL*2:354).

More particularly, this coming-to-be occurs because "psychoanalysis manipulates the *poetic function* to give to a person's desire its symbolic mediation" (*SJL*1:106, emphasis added). This involves, first, the moment of metaphor, the eruption of desire into the chain of spoken discourse. Such eruption is promoted in the psychoanalytic session by loosening the subject's speech (in the practice of free association) from restraints of propriety, courtesy, and coherence (*SJL*1:204). In the absence of such restraints, the subject's speech is more susceptible to interference from the unconscious, and the subject's relation to the analyst becomes characterized by projection of the unconscious desire and fantasy. In fact, the first step of analysis is precisely to evoke a maximum projection of these fantasies (*SJL*2:204).

The value of such projection is that it reveals to the subject "the captivating images that are at the foundation of the constitution of his ego" (*SJL*1:204), i.e., those metonymic objects that are the cause of the interference in the subject's speech. Once this projection (the transference) occurs, the analyst works to bring the subject to recognize these captivating images as constituting the subject's ego. The analyst does this by first forcing these projections into the verbal medium: sitting out of the analysand's field of vision, and passively refusing all interaction with the subject except speech, the analyst produces a situation in which the only means of expression left for the unconscious fantasy is speech. Once the unconscious fantasies are verbalized, interpretation can occur, which has the function of integrating the fantasy into the common system of symbols (*SJL*1:223).

The moment of interpretation is closely connected with metonymy (*SJL*11:176), which, as we have seen, is the ground of desire. In fact, Lacan says, "As it draws to its end, interpretation is directed towards desire, with which, in a certain sense, it is identical. Desire, in fact, is interpretation itself" (*SJL*11:176). Extrapolating from these suggestions, we can say that interpretation, like the metonymic movement of desire itself, is the quest for a more adequate, less partial object. The difference between desire and interpretation would seem to be one of emphasis: in interpretation, the focus of conscious attention is on the metonymic relations of different objects, and the possession of the object is not of explicit concern; in desire the reverse is true. Interpretation, then, involves the step-by-step construction of metonymic (often part/whole, or synecdochic) relationships whereby the object of a particular fantasy is established as a partial representative of being itself (or, at least, a partial representative of a less partial representative of being itself), as defined by the Other. For example, a particular object of fantasy such as the desire for caviar (*ES*258–59) is shown through interpretation—metonymic displacement—really to be a desire for something larger, less partial, more whole and fundamental. Apparently irrational feelings and behavior are thus shown to be metonyms, partial representations and embodiments, of the fundamental, universal quest for being, a quest that often manifests itself in relation to sex (the hysteric) or death (the obsessional). By recognizing how his or her real quest is for being, rather than for a particular object per se, the neurotic is able to emerge from a desire that is localized and fixed on particular objects (see *ES*321) and accept other metonymic objects of being that are more accessible or less conflictual with being as defined by the Other.

Even the movement from part to part is valuable in this regard. For in this metonymic displacement from one part to another, "the common denominator is produced, namely the little meaning . . . that proves to lie at the basis of desire" (*ES*259). The being that is lacking (which lies at the basis of desire) is here at least attained in the form of meaning—which subsists precisely in the connections among, or movement between, signifiers. The common denominator, the meaning, that emerges in the movement from one part (signifier) to another constitutes a whole in relation to these parts, and even though it is itself irredeemably partial in relation to being as such, it is less partial than the parts of which it is the common denominator. This is precisely the value of interpretation: to arrive at common denominators that are less partial parts and thus less deficient in the being that is lacking.

Psychoanalysis, then, is successful "to the extent that the subjective drama [the unconscious fantasy] is integrated into a myth having extensive, indeed universal human value" (*SJL*1:215). This involves "letting the subject understand in what round of discourse he is caught [i.e., his unconscious fantasy], and at the same time in what other round he has to enter [i.e., the *énoncé* of conscious demand]" (*SJL*2: 123). In thus bringing the subject's desire to speech and integrating the unconscious fantasy with the discourse of the common code, which is the matrix of conscious demand, psychoanalysis accords being to an element previously excluded from being (*SJL*1:298), establishing it as part of a larger whole. As we have seen, it is in relation to the Other that being finds its status: only by having our own desires articulated in terms of being, as it is implicitly defined by the common symbolic system we inhabit, do we experience ourselves truly to *be*. Whenever our subjective being is linked linguistically, by *points de capiton*—even in the most indirect fashion—to what the common code defines as being, then our desire is recognized, our particular being is affirmed: "the contingent falls—the accidental, traumatism, the impediments of [personal] history—and it is *being* which then comes to be constituted" (*SJL*1:258; emphasis added).

On the basis of this understanding of the psychoanalytic process, we can see how a similar alteration of the psychic economy might be promoted by reading and interpreting literature. In the first place, literature—particularly poetry—often releases us in part from the normal ties of speech. As we have already seen in our analysis of *The Marriage*, poetry can present us with a discourse that, in order to be understood, forces us to loosen our normal ties of speech and take up residence (provisionally, at least) in a new code. This effect is similar in important ways to the loosening that Lacan describes in the analytic process: it opens a path for our desire to express itself. All literature thus elicits the reader's desire, and in Blake's case this effect is clearly intentional, as we can see from the prefaces of his two major prophecies. In his address "To the Public" at the beginning of *Jerusalem*, he calls his readers' attention to the "Thunder of Thought, & flames of fierce desire" (*J*3:6, E145) that are present in his poem, and at the beginning of *Milton* he asks for his "Arrows of Desire," essential weapons in the "Mental Fight" for the establishment of freedom and justice (*M*1:10, 13, E95). The role of desire is even more explicit in *The Marriage*. As critics have noted, *The Marriage of Heaven and Hell* is in many ways a celebration of desire. But the most important role of desire in the poem lies not in its function as a central theme, but rather in its presence in the reader—in service of that psychic transformation that Blake wanted to produce.

In addition to evoking desire in a manner similar to that of psychoanalysis, literature elicits interpretation, which also bears significant resemblance to that of psychoanalysis. If we consider that, as Fredric

Jameson notes, all literary interpretation is essentially the translation of the text's narrative into a master code,[9] then it becomes evident that both literary and psychoanalytic interpretation essentially involve the integration of a particular, idiosyncratic discourse into a discourse having universal value. The activity of interpreting a metaphor, which can be taken as paradigmatic of all interpretation, shows the effects of this process of integration in greater detail. When we encounter a metaphor for the first time—a "live" metaphor—we are alerted to its metaphoric nature by its incongruity with the established code: it doesn't "make sense." Like a joke or witticism, metaphor forces us, in order to make sense of it, to assume a perspective or code different from our dominant, habitual code. Consider what happens when we encounter one of Lacan's examples of metaphor, "Love is a pebble laughing in the sunlight" (*ES*158). To make sense of this statement, we have to find a perspective from which "love" and "pebble laughing in the sunlight" coincide. The way we attempt to do so is by matching attributes. When attributes are found that are shared by the two sides of the equation—in this case, perhaps, qualities like self-sufficiency, invulnerability, or (alternatively) relative insignificance or transience— these qualities assume, for the time being, at least, the status of primary attributes for the signifier ("love"). In this way the positions of the attributes as well as of the original signifiers undergo a significant shift, thus constituting a new perspective or code, which, if internalized, constitutes an alteration of our Other, the ground from which we speak, desire, and act.

It is at this point that our desire and fantasy reenter the field of play, at least in literary interpretation, which unlike getting a joke, usually allows a plurality of precise Others to be actualized. But whatever particular desire or fantasy informs, motivates, and directs the interpretation, it is translated into the terms of the text, a translation that involves the same metonymic movement as psychoanalysis: interpretation integrates a fantasy—for example, the fantasy of self-sufficiency or of insignificance—by establishing a metonymic (usually part/whole) relationship between the fantasy and the terms of the metaphor. In the example we are using, love and the pebble are seen as particular instances of the larger, more general condition (e.g., of self-sufficiency or of insignificance).

This process of evocation of desire and its subsequent integration through interpretation occurs throughout *The Marriage*, most noticeably in our response to the proverbs. That the proverbs evoke desire (in the form of emotion) is clear. In proverb 57 Blake explicitly calls attention to the affective impact of language, declaring, "Damn braces: Bless relaxes." Here in encapsulated form is the foundation of affective stylistics: words elicit emotional responses from the hearer or reader. Because of this, reading the proverbs provides a sort of inventory of desire and fantasy, like that which Lacan says analysis is designed to produce, and which we have seen the pictures produce. Blake himself was well aware of this result, as he indicated when he followed the advice given by Lavater in *Aphorisms on Man:* "If you mean to know yourself, interline such of these aphorisms as affected you agreeably in reading, and set a mark to such as left a sense of uneasiness with you" (E583).

In addition to evoking projection of desire, the proverbs also promote its integration and transformation, by interpellating us into interpretation. Such interpretation involves first of all the attempt to find common denominators among the multiple signifiers of the proverbs. These common denominators are determined not merely by the signifiers in the text, but also by our desire: we seek to interpret the text in terms that are meaningful (as determined by our Other) and to structure these terms to accord with our desire (as determined by our unconscious fantasies). The text and the fantasies aroused by it are thus displaced into the consciously modulated discourse governed by a new code, and the partial objects of our desire are replaced by a common denominator—a less partial object—more adequate, we hope, to our want-to-be. In interpreting the proverbs, we are forced tacitly to conceive of the fantasies they embody as metonyms of a larger desire, and the objects of these fantasies as parts of a larger whole, which is ultimately being itself. In this way, a path is opened for desire to become displaced or sublimated to more accessible, less conflictual objects. Moreover, in eliciting this interpretive movement of integration into greater wholes, the proverbs and the alternative code they embody promote restructuring of our Other that involves, finally, a reconstitution of the meaning of being. The proverbs call on us to alter the positions of and establish new relations among various key signifiers—an alteration that ultimately constitutes a new definition of being, which, as Lacan observes, is "the fundamental reference of all discourse" (*SJL*3:155–56).[10]

Both effects—the elicitation of desire and the alteration of the

Other—can be seen to operate in the proverbs. The first proverb, "In seed time learn, in harvest teach, in winter enjoy," feeds desires of self-aggrandizement based upon the fantasy of phallic potency: the possession of the seed, the capacity to create, and the ability to reap the benefits of such creation. But though the images of the proverb call forth fantasies of phallic potency, the positions of these images in relation to the other signifiers in the utterance create incongruities that demand interpretation. The incongruities involve the pairing of seed time with learning, harvest with teaching, and winter with enjoyment, couplings that run counter to the linkages provided by the common code of our habitual Other, which associates seed time with putting forth (for which teaching rather than learning is a metonym), harvest with taking in (for which learning rather than teaching is a metonym), and winter with the antithesis of enjoyment. The effect of these incongruities is to pressure us, as we interpret the proverb by matching attributes (as described above) of the paired terms (the metaphors), to relinquish the male, phallic position of possessor and giver of the seed and to assume the female position of receiver of the seed. For in order to make learning accord with seed time, we must interpret them both as metonyms of receptivity, and seed time is a moment of receptivity only from the female perspective. The second admonition—"in harvest teach"—also demands the female position, for in order for harvest and teaching to accord with each other, each must be seen as a metonym of generosity and giving forth. And if this is the case, then harvesting must be grasped not from the scythe-wielding, phallic perspective of the harvester—the active, potent position—but from the scythe-receiving position of the wheat, the self-sacrificing donor. Finally, in order for winter and enjoyment to be coordinated, we must see them both as metonyms of passivity and dormancy, a perspective that deprives enjoyment of the active, dominating phallic quality with which it tends to be associated in our Other. Interpreted in this way, the proverb arouses phallic fantasies only to cut them off in the interpretation.

In addition to thus drawing us into a new position with regard to our phallic fantasies, the proverb also interpellates us into a new position in relation to death, the other major theme (along with sex) by which being is defined, according to Lacan (see *EC*451–53). The presence of death is more subtle here than that of sex, but it is significant nonetheless: the image of winter habitually carries with it the sense of decline and loss of vitality, and harvest in this instance—especially to the extent that interpretation forces us to assume the position of the harvested wheat—carries with it a distinct sense of loss of power and life. But in both cases these metonyms of death are linked with images of fulfillment, so that as a result, death is subtly displaced from its usual position as the opposite or negation of being and is drawn closer to the realm of being itself. This realignment constitutes an alteration by the poem's code of the definition of being implicit in the code of our Other, and it summons us through interpretation to an Other that can accommodate the alteration.

Interpretation of this first proverb, then, involves a provisional moving of "the moorings that anchor our being"—those *points de capiton* such as giving/taking, activity/passivity, male/female, and life/death that determine the meaning of being as constituted in our Other. Specifically, the connection of being with active, phallic potency—and even life—is loosened, while that with generosity and receptivity—and even death—is strengthened. And this (provisional) alteration of the Other displaces the phallic fantasy, directing desire away from this particular metonym of being and toward the metonym of the female position.

The second proverb, "Drive your cart and your plow over the bones of the dead," also evokes sexuality and mortality in a powerful manner—here in the context of the Oedipal fantasy. But though the first proverb worked to subvert the phallic fantasy, the present one seems designed to reinforce it. Such, at least, is the effect of the admonition to "drive . . . your plow," plow being an obvious metonym for phallus not only in the vulgarly Freudian sense but also in the sense of power, particularly the power to plant and cultivate new life. This phallic fantasy, moreover, is here expressed in its primal and most powerful form, that of the Oedipal desire:[11] we are told to push our phallus-plow "over the bones of the dead," uprooting the fathers as we possess and penetrate the universal mother, earth. As in the first proverb, however, we are called to move beyond mere indulgence of this Oedipal fantasy and interpret it, the pressure to interpret coming from the triviality of the terms of the proverb (it is very unlikely that Blake is talking merely about farming here). To understand what the proverb is really talking about, we must see the described activity as a symbol—a metonym or part—of a larger, more important reality. The cart and plow, implements of agricultural activity, thus appear as metonyms of implements of cultural activity in general, and "the bones of the dead" as metonyms for the result or remains of past life, or the past in general. The proverb as a whole is thus a metonymic admonishment for individuals and society at large not to remain subservient to the past but to use the remains of the past as a road to the future, or as material to be broken up and assimilated into the soil that nourishes new growth. The Oedipal fantasy thus becomes sublimated into a less particular and partial desire and thereby loses much of its specifically phallic and Oedipal character—by the very fact of being seen as a metonym rather than as itself the ultimate or absolute term.

Through this interpretation, the Oedipal fantasy is enlisted in the cause of breaking free of the limitations of the past—particularly of those paternal dicta and interdictions that form the core of the values and beliefs that, as Freud pointed out, civilization is founded on. By activating the fantasy of ultimate transgression—the Oedipal fantasy— and then metonymically displacing our desire to different objects through the interpretation it elicits, the proverb subtly redirects the energies attached to the primal fantasy toward the less restrictive, more productive ends of restructuring the code of the Other that underlies all our desire and action. In fact, interpretation of this fantasy moves toward a provisional restructuring of the Other similar to that promoted by the first proverb. By urging the use and transformation rather than veneration of the dead, the proverb subverts the opposition between life and death and allows us to rise up "over the bones of the dead" in a much more substantial way than that imagined by the original Oedipal fantasy: it offers a way to rise above the power that death possesses when it is identified with non-being. Death is inevitable, but if death is part of life, then it loses its power to deprive us of being. This is one of the most fundamental alterations of the Other that is possible, and it continued to occupy Blake long after *The Marriage*, becoming what is in many ways the central purpose of *Milton*.[12]

The third proverb continues the fantasy of transgression: "The road of excess leads to the palace of wisdom." This proverb appears to encourage transgression in general: any exceeding of boundaries will lead to the desideratum, the palace. Here it is helpful to be attentive to the metonymic nature not only of words, but of syllables and phonemes as well, recalling how unconscious fantasies can be carried by parts of words—such as "on" in the example "famillionaire." Thus it may be that the road of ex-cess gives metonymic, displaced expression to the way of in-cest, the primal transgression and ultimate excess and success, and that it promises to lead us to the p(h)allus of wisdom. But if (unconscious) fantasy can travel on syllables and phonemes, so can conscious thought, as Nelson Hilton's practice has demonstrated.[13] If, following Hilton's method, we move to interpret the phonemes of this proverb, we may wonder whether the road of excess/incest is the road traveled by Oedipus (where he encountered and murdered his father), whether the palace to which it leads is that of his mother, and whether the wisdom is that of Silenus (repeated by the chorus in *Oedipus at Colonus*), that it is best never to have been born. Or is the palace/phallus to which this road of excess leads the Pallas of Wisdom that opposes excess: the phallic (motherless, fully armed) Pallas Athena—Virgin Wisdom, avoidance of excess, the classical Greek wisdom of the golden mean? In either case, the palace/phallus that one excessively seeks may actually be the p(h)allus of wise-doom, wise-dumb, or wish-dumb. Instead of possession of the p(h)allus, excess gets one deprived of it.

In this way, our Oedipal fantasy is engaged to carry us down the road of ultimate power (prevailing over the father) to the possession of the phallus (that which satisfies the mother's desire and thus fills all lack of being), only to arrive at castration—utter deprivation, the impossibility of possessing the all-potent signifier-object that can fill all lacks. But in such deprivation one comes, perhaps, as close as is possible to possessing this absolute signifier of being. Through such phonemic, metonymic erring, we can arrive at the recognition that the palace/phallus is always inescapably lacking. We thus accede to what may be the only true wisdom—that attained as a result of suffering, or lack of being—and acquire the only palace/phallus there is: that which is absent. We approach the recognition that the absolute truth about being is that there is no absolute truth, and that the absolute signifier of being is that which signifies the lack of such a signifier.

If we have not arrived at the position of castration through interpretation of the third proverb, the fourth brings us there immediately: "Prudence is a rich ugly old maid courted by Incapacity." The fact that the incapacity (a form of castration) is said to be the state of anyone who courts Prudence makes us shy away from embracing this particular type of wisdom. Prudence has a certain value—she is rich—but as an ugly old maid she offers us not the phallus (active desire, and the accompanying sense of full potency, or being), but merely the fecal substitute, money. Prudence is thus established not only as a poor substitute but also as something that involves deprivation of the very means of fulfillment. Moreover, in being identified as an ugly old maid—an object of repulsion to desire—rather than a severe, castrating father (an external restriction on desire), prudence and the concomitant castration are established as intrinsic to the subject rather than extrinsic: a function of the subject's own incapacity rather than of an external force of deprivation. The proverb thus evokes a certain repulsion and negative judgment toward that prudential aspect of ourselves that governs desire: the internalized castrating father, the superego. And insofar as the proverb calls upon us to determine whether it is the incapacity or the courting of Prudence that comes first—i.e., whether it is the (negative) desire or the prudential judgment against prudence that is decisive—we are called upon to reflect (prudentially, perhaps) that each implies the other, and that both are inescapable: not having full being (the phallus) makes it necessary to be prudent, and being prudent results in never having full being. Once again, we are forced to accept the inescapability of castration, whether we pursue prudence or the road of excess.

This dialectic between desire and castration forms the dynamic of the fifth proverb as well: "He who desires but acts not, breeds pestilence." The message that this proverb offers to our fantasy is that not acting on our desires brings about that very state—pestilence, a metonym for defilement, sin, less than full being (hence, castration)—that we are trying to avoid by not acting. We refrain from acting on desire because we feel that to act on it will reduce us to the level of beasts (another, displaced form of castration), but such restraint, the proverb declares, itself "breeds"—an image of phallic potency, but a potency that enacts the very castration (bestiality, loss of being) from which we are fleeing. Here again, the terms of the proverb interpellate us into a position where we are forced to submit to castration: either we accept castration at the outset by giving in to desire and thus relinquishing the will's potency of self-determination, or we attempt to possess this phallic potency of the superego and thus put up a resistance to desire that only increases desire's force. The act of renouncing the phallus (desire) is thus revealed to be a surreptitiously phallic act (it "breeds"), which, in secretly trying to possess the phallus (self-potency), winds up losing it (in "pestilence").

This simultaneous inescapability of the phallic urge to omni-potence (or full being) and its impossibility are also central to the sixth proverb, which, like the fifth, offers indulgence of our phallic fantasy, only to undermine it in the very terms of proposing it. When we encounter the statement, "The cut worm forgives the plow," we tend to take it as an endorsement of the same phallic self-assertion that the second proverb seemed to support in telling us to drive our cart and our plow over the bones of the dead. We tend to identify with the position of the plow rather than with that of the worm—partly because we have already been interpellated to such an identification by the second proverb, partly because humans literally plow but aren't literally worms, but mostly because the action of the plow accords with that of our phallic fantasy. When we pause to interpret the proverb, however, to integrate it into the common code, we have to recognize that the worm, too, is a phallic symbol—perhaps even more overtly than the plow. We have avoided identifying with the position of the worm because as a creature of weakness the worm represents the phallus as lacking—a signifier of castration that is made all too obvious by the fact that the worm is cut. Here our phallic fantasy, aroused by the proverb with its image of plowing, is abruptly cut off by our interpretation, which once again, as in the previous proverbs, forces us to accept castration in the realization that the very act of phallic assertion (plowing) results in deprivation of the phallus (the worm is cut). Stated conceptually, the act of attempting to possess full being results in its loss. The proverb thus interpellates us into a position of accepting castration, the lack of full potency and being, i.e., into the position of the worm rather than that of the plow. This is also the function of the emphasis on forgiveness, for forgiveness is the opposite of the phallic urge: rather than asserting its own rights and pursuing omnipotence, forgiveness yields to the phallic urges of others.

But if passages such as these can work to cut off or reroute fantasies of phallic dominance, other parts of the poem work more directly to sublimate the phallic urge or displace the quest for being onto more accessible objects. Two of the immediately following proverbs, in fact, leave the explicitly phallic urge and turn to the scopic drive. The proverb, "A fool sees not the same tree that a wise man sees," implies not just that different people see things differently but that some seeing is better than others—specifically, the wise man's is better than the fool's. Seeing properly is thus a way of having full being, while not seeing properly amounts to a lack of being, or castration (as Oedipus's act of blinding himself suggests). This evocation of our desire to see more adequately is reinforced by the ninth proverb, which first of all evokes the equally primal fantasy of being seen (recognized, admired): "He whose face gives no light, shall never become a star." Being seen or recognized is, like possession of the phallus, a metonym for having full being. Someone whom others take note of—particularly someone who elicits the desire of others—achieves a greater sense of being. This is what motivates the infant's desire to be the object of the mother's attention, as well as the desire of adults to achieve as much recognition as possible. Such recognition also helps overcome the non-being that is associated with death, as the image of the star in the present proverb implies. In this image, the proverb unites the scopic drive (here, the desire to be seen) with the desire for immortality, or becoming a star in the heavens: one achieves immortality or full being by being seen, achieving recognition.

The tenth proverb, "Eternity is in love with the productions of time," reinforces this fantasy of recognition and immortality. Here, where the productions of time, of which human existence is a part, are recognized and even desired (loved) by Eternity, the fantasy of recognition is indulged on a cosmic scale. Eternity—that metonym of being which, as the opposite of temporal limitation and death, comes the closest to equaling the whole of being—subsumes all the particular others from which humans desire recognition and love, and thus induces us to embrace the productions of time, precisely so that we may escape time in achieving recognition by Eternity. Thus, instead of viewing time as the opposite of being and the metonym of death, we are here interpellated to embrace it as that part of being through which we can be embraced by Eternity and achieve full being. In this way the significance of Eternity itself is altered, distanced from its usual tight association with the unmoving, unchanging, and becoming more closely linked to change and transformation ("productions")—attributes normally considered antithetical to Eternity. Once again, the meaning of being itself undergoes a shift, and new routes are opened up for our thought and desire.

Insofar as our desire for being, in the form of the fantasy of recognition and immortality, has been sufficiently aroused, we will pursue this object by seeking in these proverbs more specific indications as to how it can be attained. The first indication is that in order to be seen, one's face must give light. And because a radiant glow of this sort is often associated with wisdom, we may recall the eighth proverb and, remembering that wisdom is there identified with proper seeing, conclude that our face gives light when we see properly. Because being is gained by being seen, and being seen is a result of superior seeing, being thus becomes displaced from phallic assertion to vision. Vision, of course, is largely a function of language, the most significant object to which desire is redirected. Language occupies a central position in *The Marriage* and is represented as a sublimated form of both the phallus and the instrument of castration. The castrating aspect of language is presented on plate 11 (E38), in the account of how language as an alien, preestablished system (what Lacan calls the "Law of the Father") works to alienate individuals from their subjectivity. Language is presented as a system of metaphors that repress the signified (subjective meaning) under the signifier—"calling ['Gods or Geniuses'—i.e., subjective reality] by the names and adorning them with the properties of woods, rivers, mountains, lakes, cities, nations," and other external objects, "till a system was formed." The acceptance of this system as the ultimate authority (i.e., as one's Other) results in a primal repression: "Thus men forgot, that All deities reside in the human breast." The linguistic system, that is, denies the primacy of subjective experience (the residing of deities in the human breast).

But though this discourse on the ancient poets interpellates us into the position of castration and alienation, the next two plates (*MHH* 12–13, which constitute the second memorable fancy) allow us to participate in the phallic potency of language—the position of the interpellater rather than the interpellated. For Ezekiel, whose position we share, language as system is the servant rather than the master of subjectivity: "firm perswasion" (subjective conviction) produces "the voice of honest indignation," which is equated with "the voice of God." This combination—"firm perswasion" plus the metaphoric utterance it produces (i.e., one that cannot be understood literally, in terms of "a finite organical perception")—is the "Poetic Genius," which is "the first principle," of which all other Gods are tributaries, and by which one "conquers enemies & governs kingdoms." The phallic potency of language is here unmistakable. Language, particularly in its metaphoric capacity, has the power not only to alienate us from ourselves but also to express our desire, our subjectivity—the deities that reside in our breast. As Lacan observed, language can be made, through metaphor, to mean something else than what is says (*ES*155).

The following plates interpellate us into a series of positions in which we are forced to accept the castrating dimension of language and work through the castration to regain a position of phallic potency. On plate 14 we confront "the cherub with his flaming sword," an antagonist whose possession of the phallic sword clearly signifies our own castration and alienation, or separation from paradise. The cherub's "guard at the tree of life"—i.e., his denial of immortality, or full being, to the subject—indicates the paternal interdiction (what Lacan calls *"le nom/non du pere"*) that characterizes the child's entry into the symbolic system. This is the repressive force that sustains "the whole creation," without which things would "appear infinite. and holy." But we are also shown how to recover from our castration. Recovery, we are told, "will come to pass by an improvement of sensual enjoyment," i.e., an enhancement of subjective experience. Such an enhancement of the subjective is possible only on the basis of a prior alteration of the symbolic, specifically, by the obliteration of those *points de capiton* that constitute "the notion that man has a body distinct from his soul." And this alteration of the symbolic system (the code of our Other) involves a "melting away" of "apparent surfaces" (signifiers) "and displaying the infinite which was hid" (the signified that had been forced beneath [and obscured by] the signifier). We are thus offered the fantasy that such poetic intervention effectively neutralizes the castrating power of language-as-system—dismisses the cherub with his flaming sword and appropriates the castrating/phallic power of language for itself.

The imagery of the following plate (*MHH*15), elaborating on this infernal printing, makes the phallic power of language-as-utterance (*parole*) explicit, but in such a way as to make possession of the phallus inseparable from castration. Each of the first four "chambers" of the printing house of hell is inhabited by a phallic form of some sort: "a Dragon-Man," "Dragons," "a Viper," "precious stones," "an Eagle with wings" (i.e., a winged phallus), and "living fluids" (seminal fluid). The result of all this phallic activity—penetrating the cave's mouth, hollowing the cave, adorning it, causing it to be infinite, and "melting the metals into living fluids," which are then "reciev'd by Men"—is the establishment of alternative symbolic codes with new signifiers ("Unnam'd forms"), which emerge from a less restrictive episteme (the Platonic "cave") and thus liberate humans from the restrictive cavern of the old code-episteme with its "narrow chinks." But the phallic potency of producing a new code entails a type of castration as well, which we here experience affectively as well as intellectually. In order to occupy the position of phallic potency, that is, we must identify with the somewhat threatening (castrating) bestial forms rather than the narcissistically satisfying "Men," who occupy the position of passivity, receptivity, submission to the code produced by the other creatures. To become the producer of a new code, the possessor of phallic potency, requires that we give up our present identity as "Men" (i.e., give up being as it is defined by the code of our Other) and embrace the new being as defined by the new code, a being that, from the perspective of the habitual code, appears monstrous and destructive.

Our fantasies of phallic potency and our anxiety of castration in relation to language receive powerful recognition and validation from plate 16. This occurs through the anchoring of the phallic and castrating aspects of language in that ultimate reference of all discourse, "being": "Thus one portion of being, is the Prolific. the other, the Devouring." The Prolific and Devouring aspects of being clearly bear a metonymic (whole/part) relationship to the phallic and castrating aspects, respectively, of language. In particular, the identification of the restrictive power as "chains," which are said to be "the cunning of weak and tame minds," allows an easy connection between the restrictive power and the metonymic chains (logic, syntax) of the sacred code, or language. In assuming this metonymic relationship between language and being, we integrate our phallic fantasy into a (new) code having universal value: our fantasies—of phallic potency and of castration—come to be inscribed in the code as instances of the fundamental nature of being itself, thus achieving that recognition, that integration of imaginary and symbolic, that is essential to psychological integrity. The legitimation of the phallic fantasy occurs through its metonymic relation to "the causes of [the world's] life & the sources of all activity," and by the pejorative characterization of the resistance to this phallic potency as a position that we can recognize as neurotic: one that "takes portions of existence and fancies that the whole" (see the account of neurosis given above).

But though this discourse defends and promotes fantasies of phallic potency, it also interpellates us to an acceptance of castration, by asserting the dependence of potency's metonym on castration's metonym: "the Prolific would cease to be Prolific unless the Devourer as a sea recieved the excess of his delights." We accept the discourse as a whole because it legitimizes our sublimated phallic desire and frees it through an identification with being itself; but in accepting the discourse, we also accept the necessity of castration and its participation in being. We are thus forced to accept that language, like being itself, cuts both ways. Like Jesus, the word made flesh, it brings "not . . . Peace but a Sword"—a dual phallic and castrating power. Language is both a "Messiah"—a way to freedom, atonement, and fulfillment—and a "Satan or Tempter," agent of seduction and self-alienation.

Such, at least, is one path our interpretation can take through the discourse of the Prolific and the Devouring. In the memorable fancy that follows (*MHH*17–20), we have little choice: we are thrust upon this path by a powerful interpellation. Here we are forced to experience, with the speaker, the power of language from both sides: that of being interpellated, imposed upon, castrated by it, and that of using it to express one's own subjective realities and force others to recognize them. In the first episode of the fancy, we see the "eternal lot" of the speaker as that lot is determined by the angel's orthodox code. We are made to experience a series of repulsive images, which, however, disappear as soon as the angel leaves, to be replaced by a pleasant scene. What we thus experience is the fact that any given code automatically interpellates a hearer into a particular position that entails a proximity with certain specific images and fantasies, together with their attendant anxieties and desires. This is stated quite explicitly when the speaker declares to the angel: "All that we saw was owing to your metaphysics"—i.e., to the fundamental signifying chains of the angel's code. In the second episode of the fancy, we experience the same fact, only this time from the other position, that of phallic potency, as the speaker, with whom we have identified, shows the angel the angel's lot. In this fancy we thus experience in both the imaginary and the symbolic registers the power of the symbolic code to determine imaginary, subjective experience—i.e., the code's phallic/castrating power.

After a condemnation of logic and systematic reasoning—of remaining within a particular symbolic system, not conversing with devils (desire) and thus opening up the symbolic to the imaginary—we encounter the poem's final memorable fancy, in which we are led through an experience of how our desire can express itself even when we are within an alienating code that denies recognition to our desire. This phallic potency resides in interpretation, and we experience interpretation here in what is perhaps its most potent form—a proto-deconstructive reading. One key term of the orthodox code, "Jesus," is interpreted in

such a way as to contradict another key term, the "ten commandments," which the orthodox code places in concord with "Jesus" (as
the angel puts it, "Has not Jesus Christ given his sanction to the law of
ten commandments?"). In this way, "Jesus," the supreme *point de
capiton* of the sacred code, is placed in opposition to other *points
de capiton* and, in fact, to codes as such: "Jesus was all virtue, and
acted from impulse: not from rules." This interpretation allows recognition not only for particular desires forbidden by the ten commandments, but for all desire whatsoever. Desire, the antithesis of system, is
thus inscribed as a radically self-deconstructing element of the symbolic system itself, and desire as such thus acquires being.

Hence, through this final fancy, we experience two ways of over-
coming the castrating power of language and regaining phallic potency: we can accept the code but interpret it in such a way that it
accommodates our desire (the speaker's strategy), or we can refuse to
accept the given code (Jesus' strategy) and thus (implicitly or explicitly) subscribe to an alternative code. Our desire, that is, can gain
recognition either through (strong) reading or (strong, poetic) writing. As Blake's speaker indicates at the first ending of *The Marriage,*
we can either "read the Bible," the given code, "in its infernal or diabolical sense," or we can write a "Bible of Hell," a new code in which
our desires are explicitly recognized, legitimized.

As we have seen, it is in such recognition of desire—such a marriage
of heaven (the sacred code) and hell (desire)—that Lacanian psychoanalysis locates the efficacy of the psychoanalytic process. By evoking
our repressed desires, by providing us with a new code that offers fuller
recognition to our desire, and by interpellating us to a position where
we must either accept such a code or construct it through interpretation, Blake's poem arouses our faculties to act in such a way as to enact
a marriage that constitutes psychological transformation. This process
constitutes a marriage of heaven and hell in another sense as well: by
eliciting deep fantasies of phallic potency and castration within a metaphysical context, the poem allows our desire to assume more coherent,
less conflicting forms, in which a (displaced and sublimated) fulfillment (heaven) is possible even in face of the inescapable reality of castration, or human finitude (hell).

Blake, Women, and Sexuality

Brenda S. Webster

One eighteenth-century contemporary of Blake's described him as an "insane and erratic genius."[1] In their efforts to normalize Blake and to find shared historical and religious meanings later critics not only shy away from the bizarre or disturbing elements of his work but generally ignore its personal emotional components, its combat with "The torments of Love & Jealousy" (*FZ* title, E300).

In particular, Blake's attitude toward sexuality creates a variety of problems for critics. Liberated sexuality seems a source of high value for Blake—he links it with vision and art—but sexuality also elicits his most hostile, negative, and regressive images. Critics take several approaches to Blake's contradictions. Early critics like S. Foster Damon, who sees Blake as a pure mystic, simply deny the importance of his preoccupation with sex and fantasies of sexual freedom. Damon urges the reader not to take seriously Blake's apparent justification of "illicit ways" and assures us that Blake didn't follow his teachings himself, citing as evidence his ideal marriage to a submissive wife (99). Other critics are reluctant to think about Blake's bizarre or explicit sexual illustrations and what these imply about his personality or his attitudes toward women. They see him as portraying degradations of erotic life only so that error may be clarified and redemption achieved.[2]

More recently, commentators instead see Blake as celebrating unrepressed sexuality. But here, too, the full force of Blake's sexuality creates problems, and some critics deny its emotional implications. Forty years after his classic book, Damon now remarks, as though it is an emotionally neutral issue, that Blake, like Shelley, thinks incest is innocent and "the very root of marriage."[3] Even such a sophisticated critic as Diana Hume George praises Blake for articulating a nonselfish, nonaggressive sexuality. She regards him in this respect as freer and more advanced than Freud but does not see that Freud is simply more self-aware.[4] Blake's rhetoric often serves as a cloak or defense that distracts the reader, and Blake himself, from seeing the aggressive or selfish nature of the sexual fantasies he is portraying.

Idealization isn't the only way of dealing with Blake's emotional dynamite. Some critics do not have to mobilize defenses to avoid perceiving Blake's negative attitudes. They may consciously agree with them. Before it was taboo to say such things, a male critic—I don't think it is an accident that most of the Blake critics until recently have been male—could admit satisfaction with Blake's views of women.[5] Bernard Blackstone's misogynistic remarks are embarrassing in their forthrightness but I think he has correctly caught Blake's anger at women's power and his wish that they be properly subservient. Male critics who are consciously more benign toward women may still respond to Blake's underlying fantasies without being quite aware of it. This creates a subtler kind of distortion—a not seeing what might be uncomfortable. One critic, Jean Hagstrum, misreads the line "In Beulah every female delights to give her maiden to her husband," noting that "maiden" means maidenhead.[6] The point of the line is that Blake's ideal female freely provides her husband with other women like Oothoon in *Visions* (*VDA*7:26, E50). At the end of his essay, Hagstrum's funny tone of mixed apology and male congratulation suggests that at some level he understands very well what Blake is talking about. He concludes that "some modern women may have much to object to in Blake's latest thought about the relation of the sexes. But it's hard to believe that *l'homme moyen sensual* would reject the hearty bread and full bodied wine the late Blake is offering him" (118). Erdman, as I will show later, similarly fails to see the male sexual fantasy in *Visions*.

Women critics have parallel difficulties with Blake's sexuality. Early feminist critics generally see Blake as much more favorable to women than he actually is.[7] These writers respond positively to Blake's struggle against the patriarchal system and its paternal oppressors, which suggests that he wishes to free women to be equal partners of men. Also seductive to feminists is Blake's deemphasis of the penis in favor of a total body sensuality, seemingly more in tune with, and more accepting of, woman's sexuality. Unfortunately, as a poet-prophet Blake is not any more interested in redefining sexuality to give a more equal place to women than as a husband he was interested in giving equal status to his wife. In his own marriage, when his wife offended his brother, he made her kneel down and beg his forgiveness, or, he told her, she would never see his face more.

In general, earlier critics ignore Blake's radical sexual ideas and fantasies; and later critics, while acknowledging them, ignore their regressive and aggressive content and Blake's guilt over them. The limitation of conventional criticism, including feminist criticism, is that it tends either to ignore these fantasies (or this fantasy world) or to recast them in terms of official theologies or ideologies and so misses the special energy of the fantasies and their unconscious origins. The power in Blake's work derives from his recognition and description of demonic forces (the eighteenth-century equivalent of unconscious drives) that influence every aspect of human relationships, but most particularly sexuality.

Critics who ignore Blake's radical sexual ideas and fantasies do so partly because of a feeling that to acknowledge them would be to diminish or interfere with his religious or moral authority and return him to the status of eccentric genius. Because Blake's work embodies religious values that point to transcendence, it seems particularly offensive to relate his cosmic speculations to his fantasies or to his personal biography. One critic argues, for instance, that to accept a biographical interpretation of a major prophecy (*Milton*) would be to see Blake as "mad Blake indeed."[8] This feeling of incompatibility between any kind of cherished meaning and the fantasies or personal motives of the poet is one of the main blocks to understanding between psychoanalytic critics and other sorts. Conversely, if one values Blake as a prophet of sexual revolution, pointing out his guilt and conflict diminishes him as a type of Übermensch just as much as pointing out his underlying sexual fantasies diminishes his visionary claims. But to understand Blake adequately, both sides (sexuality and guilt) have to be recognized. The history of desire frozen in his images and dramatic situations has to be connected with his transcendent vision, and his conflicts of conscience with his expressions of sexuality. When this is done, we see a radically different Blake.

If we accept at least as a working assumption the importance of psychosexual issues in Blake's work, and if we are to go beyond impressionism or commonsense psychology, we need a theory of mental functioning to serve both as a framework for clarifying our responses to Blake and as a technique for exploring his psychic preoccupations and the ways in which they, paradoxically, both energize and limit his poetry.

Of the available psychologies, Freudian psychoanalysis is most productive for studying Blake. The psychoanalytic emphasis on Oedipal conflict and motives of "Love & Jealousy" is in many ways similar to Blake's own. Freudianism is unique in its emphasis on the problems caused by man's long dependency and the psychic cost involved in the taming of his sexual and aggressive impulses. The early stages of development are crucial to Freud because the fantasies and modes of experience associated with them are outgrown only imperfectly. Stress in the adult can awaken them. Blake's diffusive narratives are given what coherence they have by a linked series of fantasies made familiar by psychoanalysis. Particularly in his late work, Blake's manifest emphasis begs to be described as Freudian. In works like *Vala*, he not only deals exhaustively with the mutual entanglements of parents and children but he literally depicts the staples of the Freudian view of the psyche: he illustrates acts of incest, he shows children watching adults copulate and he presents a woman with a penis (the Freudian phallic woman) and a man without one. It is not surprising then, that a psychoanalytic approach can reveal aspects of Blake's attitudes toward women and sexuality that are not available to other methods. This in turn opens up other important related topics for investigation; for instance, his development toward a male-centered creative world and his growing sympathy with paternal figures makes sense as part of a reaction against the female.

As Paul Ricoeur has argued, psychoanalysis need not be considered as the enemy of religious meaning[9] (or of other meanings); instead it should be considered a useful tool for clarifying religious values. Blake himself performs this kind of analysis on traditional religious structures, values, and on the concept of an authoritarian God (old Nobodaddy). Blake's most brilliant analysis goes into the repressed and repressive character of Urizen. Blake acutely observes the distortions induced by Urizen's anxiety—his need for sadistic and total control, his terror of sexuality. This kind of insight into the role of anxiety or suppressed sexuality is essential to evaluating the religious vision. But Blake's insight into Urizenic values and personality doesn't necessarily mean that he himself is free of similar anxiety-caused distortions.

Fantasies in a text offer the literary critic a way into unconscious preoccupations. They give him an opportunity to see elements from the past reexperienced (much as the analyst observes the past reenacted in the transference). The artist replays the early patterns of conflict and desire through character and image rather than by projecting them onto the person of the therapist. Through creative reorganization similar to the reorganization of the self that takes place in therapy, the artist integrates fantasy material into a meaningful world.[10] If integration of fantasy, dream, or childhood memories is successful the work elaborates them in ways that illuminate their meaning.

Though the artist is not necessarily conscious of his fantasies as he integrates them into his larger design, he has to let them come near enough to the surface to allow their expression without being too threatened by them. His success may have something to do with being able to allow the fantasies to proliferate freely and then to elaborate or play with them in different textual contexts without being overcome. If he fails to balance the relative claims of his conscious design and the fantasy material (with its own logic and unity), his failure should be clear in a text that doesn't work aesthetically—is confused, dull or highly contradictory. The fantasies, instead of adding intensity and depth to the text, may be narrowed down to a single repetitious form, or if themes are being used primarily as a defense to control fantasies that are too frightening, then these fantasies may subvert or undercut the writer's conscious concerns (as in Blake's late prophecies). There are as many varieties of failure as there are of success. Analyzing the fantasy content in its relation to the text helps isolate the areas in which integration has succeeded or where it has failed and unconscious motives overwhelmed the text.

In Blake perhaps more than in most writers the fantasies are not difficult to spot. The difficulty is in knowing what to do with them when we do see them. Perhaps the first task is to determine the extent of the fantasy in the body of the text and also its degree of primitiveness. (Like a disease in the body, it may change forms, move around, have different patterns in different places.) Fantasies are not such simple entities as has been assumed (Frederick Crews ironically comments on the monotony of certain standard ones);[11] they are elusive in that they perpetually shift, expressing first wish, then fear, first from one person's viewpoint, then another, changing who does what to whom with no regard for ordinary logic. A fantasy is not just an idea or wish; it reflects a totally different, archaic way of seeing and experiencing things that has its own kind of logic, expressing a wholly different way of perceiving and experiencing the world. Depending on what stage of development it derives from, it can be extremely primitive or very far removed from its archaic sources, perhaps no more than a faint verbal echo. Seeing evidence of a fantasy is only a first step. Only a full reading of the text can tell us the dimensions of the fantasy and its effect on this particular text.

For instance, in *Tiriel* a father accuses his sons of causing their mother's death. Tiriel could have made his accusation in a variety of ways. He could have said "she died gnawed by grief." The verb gnawed here has a nuance that Freudians would relate to the oral stage but any orality in the statement as I have formulated it is far removed from primitive fantasy; it is only a verbal echo, a half-dead metaphor. But Tiriel instead accuses his sons of devouring their parents' flesh and draining their mother dry. Later Tiriel reverses the situation and asks Pestilence to poison his sons (*T*5:8–10, E282). This is slightly less literal; he doesn't threaten to eat them as does the witch in Hansel and Gretel, but his acts still have the extreme and reversible quality characteristic of early fantasies. We don't need Freud to relate this to oral needs. Blake does it himself when he has Tiriel explain his own murderous greed as due to maternal deprivation and a harsh weaning (*T*8:14–23, E285). The point is, again, not labeling the fantasy but experiencing through it the issues that are vital in the text—questions of love, separation, and conflict. Once these issues are experienced, it is possible to see the ways in which the fantasy is given special resonance in the text. Does the fantasy enrich or limit? Is it integrated or invasive?

In order to explore these issues more fully, I am going to consider Blake's attitudes toward sexuality and women. To follow Blake's development, I divide his attitude toward women into two stages with a transition. In the first, roughly the stage of the revolutionary prophecies, he sees women (and sexuality) as a source of salvation and continually imagines his heroes liberating females from paternal tyrants. But even in the early work where he has a more positive use for women there is a strong undercurrent of hostility and fear, which is important to recognize if you want to understand his later attitudes. In mid-life during the decade-long writing of *Vala* he goes through a transitional stage during which he becomes increasingly negative toward sexuality. As he Christianizes the work in rewriting, he comes to see woman as responsible for the Fall. What he is coming to think of as the "Female

Will" is blamed for war and all the world's evils (*J*30:30, E176). His negative images of women become ever more extreme and bizarre. The only positive images of women are totally weak females sequestered in a separate realm called Beulah. Finally, in his late Christian prophecies, *Milton* and *Jerusalem*, he suggests that the female should cease even to exist independently and become reabsorbed into the body of man where she belongs.

One of the main reasons for Blake's increasing negativity is that he isn't talking about adult love at all. Instead he constantly recreates Oedipal dramas in which his heroes experience the emotions—rage, deprivation, desire—of an adolescent or younger boy caught in dreams of competition with his father for his mother's love. In the early work you have to interpret to see this, but one need not worry about reading it dogmatically into Blake's material, because in his late work he makes it perfectly clear in the illustrations and the text—showing us, for instance, a naked adolescent first embracing his mother then chained to a rock by his jealous and fearful father.

Blake's obsession with incest has an unfortunate effect on his attitude toward women. Because he is obsessed with the overthrow of paternal rivals, he feels guilty and begins to blame women for causing trouble between fathers and sons. Another reason for Blake's increasingly negative attitude is that his demands on women as nurturers and lovers are so total—it wouldn't be unfair to call them infantile—that he can't help imagining them as being enraged and wanting revenge. So his ambivalence toward women is inherent in his harboring these kinds of pre-Oedipal and Oedipal fantasies.

Blake's attitudes are expressed in various ways in his poems. His early poems *Thel* and *Visions of the Daughters of Albion* suggest the absolutism of his ideal of the totally giving woman and how it brings with it even in his early work a countering image of woman as murderous. For ease of understanding the layers of Blake's fantasy, I present his views of women developmentally, starting with what he expected and feared from woman as nurturer, then moving on to what he hoped from her at a later stage as sexual gratifier.

In *Thel*, an early lyric, Blake presents what at first seems simply a benign model of a good nurturing mother. In a pastoral setting, he creates fairy-tale creatures—a Lily, a Cloud, and a Clod of dirt who instruct the reluctant heroine Thel how to care for others. However, when looked at more closely what Blake is expressing is the wish for a mother's unlimited giving, even if it means her death. Both Lily and Clod give their lives in the act of nourishment. A lamb crops the Lily's blossoms; the Clod exhales her life in "milky fondness" over the infant worm (*Th*4:9, E5). The heroine is enjoined to think with satisfaction that at her death her own body will be food for worms. "If thou art the food of worms. O virgin of the skies, / How great thy use. how great thy blessing" (*Th*3:25–26, E5). Critics preach at Thel and criticize her for her selfishness. They do not appreciate that the prospect of being eaten by worms—death as being devoured—might be terrifying, nor do they perceive behind Blake's moral tone the implicit degradation and forced submission of the woman. The implications of the imagery are much clearer in a poem by another poet. In Andrew Marvell's famous "To his Coy Mistress," the speaker reminds the woman he is trying to seduce that she can be as coy as she likes to him but eventually worms shall try her "long-preserved virginity"—there the threat is plain enough.

At the end of *Thel* after describing the ideal of maternal sacrifice, Blake goes on in a coda, seemingly out of keeping with the mood of the piece, to describe the dangers of sexuality and the hatred between men and women. The language of courtly love evokes the deadly woman with "poison" smile who will be prominent in Blake's later work. In *Tiriel*, a narrative poem written just before *Thel*, there is another such image. She is called Pestilence (and is here clearly imagined as a punishment for infant greed). She is invoked by the tyrant Tiriel to punish his sons who he says have killed their mother by greedily draining her life ("Nourishd with milk ye serpents. nourishd with mothers tears & cares / . . . [you] have draind her dry as this" [*T*1:26–31, E277]). It is striking that the invocation of Pestilence contrasts line by line with the Lily in *Thel*. This is Tiriel's invocation of Pestilence:

Where art thou Pestilence that bathest in fogs & standing lakes
Rise up thy sluggish limbs. & let the loathsomest of poisons
Drop from thy garments as thou walkest. wrapt in yellow clouds
Here take thy seat. in this wide court. Let it be strown with dead
And sit & smile upon these cursed sons of Tiriel
(*T*5:8–12, E282)

And here is the Lily:

Thy breath doth nourish the innocent lamb, he smells thy milky
　　garments,
He crops thy flowers. while thou sittest smiling in his face,
Wiping his mild and meekin mouth from all contagious taints.
(*Th*2:4–7, E4)

In each line the Lily replaces Pestilence's noxious qualities with
beneficent ones. Even the Lily's beauty, whiteness, and perfume are
prized not for themselves but for the pleasure they give the infant lamb
who smells her "milky garments" before he crops her blossoms. Most
important is the Lily's relation to the lamb as contrasted with Pestilence's to the sons. The Lily welcomes the lamb's greedy feeding with
a loving smile even though it means her death. In what constitutes a
final contrast between the two figures, the cropped Lily wipes the
lamb's mouth of all contagious taints.

The contrasting images of Pestilence and Lily are perhaps Blake's
earliest portrayal of the two types of feminine nature that became so
important in his myth. We can see now that the ambivalent double
image is self-perpetuating. Guilt over greed creates the punishing image of Pestilence, so Blake creates an ideal image to cancel out or com-
pensate for imagined murderousness: his Lily reverses Pestilence's
attributes. But then new guilt over the idea of devouring the mother
creates the idea expressed in Thel's coda that woman is sexually threatening. In fact, Blake's efforts to create an ideally satisfying figure have
to be continually renewed. The paradoxically smiling Pestilence develops in later poems into a series of wicked females whose smiles promise
love but proffer death.

Going back even further in the self-perpetuating cycle of crime and
punishments, Blake gives psychological reasons for the extreme greed
of his characters. They feel deprived. He imagines them as so needy
that they become either monstrous or depressed if the ideal mother
doesn't offer herself.

Another important aspect of the ideal woman is her aspect as sexual
gratifier. *Visions of the Daughters of Albion* presents a nurturing woman
who unlike the Lily offers not food but total sexual gratification to
the male hero who is seen as quite helpless and hopeless without her.
The poem is particularly interesting to feminists because the chief
woman character, Oothoon, is very strong and preaches what appears
to be a doctrine of reciprocally free love to the male character. How-

ever, what is really involved is a male fantasy of having a harem of beautiful women. Oothoon in one of her final speeches offers to net girls of "mild silver" and "furious gold" for her lover and watch him while he enjoys them "In lovely copulation bliss on bliss" (*VDA*7:26, E50). There is no reciprocity. Theotormon, the semiimpotent hero, is furiously jealous and rages at Oothoon abusively after she has been raped. Generosity is all on one side: hers.

Still critics persist in seeing the poem as somehow in favor of women's rights. David Erdman suggests, following Schorer, that it is a versification of Mary Wollstonecraft's *The Rights of Women*.[12] This is oddly off the mark. Blake pictures Oothoon as totally benevolent and totally available. Wollstonecraft feels that woman's first duty is to develop her mind and particularly her reason. Far from seeing woman as devoted to "Happy, happy love," she wants to substitute equality based on reason for women's sexual character as gratifier of man.

Blake's fantasy of sexual gratification in *Visions* has another level that is vital to understanding his attitude toward women. On this level, the sexually gratifying woman is imagined as a sexually permissive mother. This is important not in order to prove a Freudian point but because Blake's attitude toward women is so saturated with his conflicting feelings toward the mother. He is interested in his female characters primarily insofar as they can be placed in triangular situations that remind him of the Oedipal triangle of mother, father, and son. In *Visions'* triangle, the heroine Oothoon is raped by an older man named Bromion while she is on her way to give herself to her young lover, Theotormon, who then spends the rest of the poem lamenting. Though she is not literally Theotormon's mother or sister, Blake suggests that this is a mother-son relationship in several ways. One of the clearest of these is his opening illustrations.

The opening illustration of Oothoon (see illustration 3) is developed from an engraving by Vien showing a procuress holding onto a small cupid by his wings. Blake adapts the figures but gives them an opposite meaning. His naked woman lifting full breasts and kissing a small male figure leaping from a flower suggests both the maternal nature and the special nonpossessive quality of Oothoon's love, which combines generosity and lack of restraint. The next illustrations replace the idealized view of mother and child with sexual fantasies. The mother-son theme continues in the image of a small naked male angel standing in the lap of a woman riding a cloud horse (see illustration 4). The sexual nature

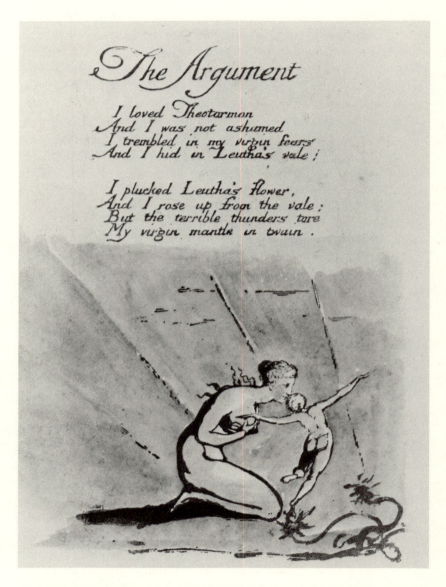

3. *Visions of the Daughters of Albion* (copy J), pl. iii, detail, Lessing J. Rosenwald Collection, Library of Congress.

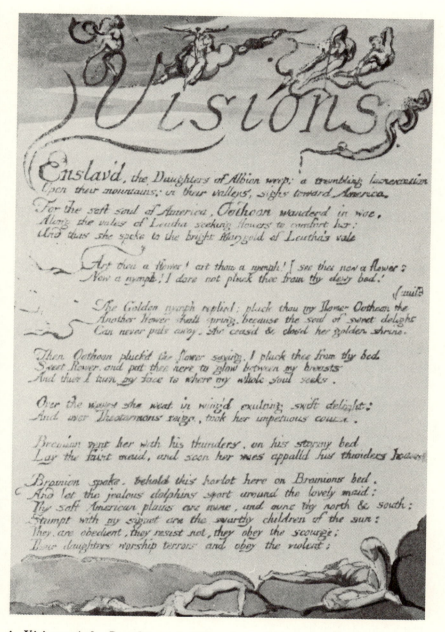

4. *Visions of the Daughters of Albion* (copy J), pl. 1, detail, Lessing J. Rosenwald Collection, Library of Congress.

of the embrace between woman and small angel is clearly shown by the penis and testicles Blake has drawn emerging between the woman's legs where we should expect the neck and head of her cloud mount. In some versions, Blake has added a beak or bill to the penis, which seems equivalent to biting teeth in its potential to injure the maternal body.

In the illustration Blake's images of mother and child are untroubled by any hint of a rival. The fantasy is of undisputed possession of the mother. Blake's description of Oothoon raped by a paternal tyrant fits such a fantasy's assumption of the mother's resistance to the father— her loyalty to the child. However, what Theotormon struggles with in the poem is that Oothoon doesn't regret the rape. Moreover, she is aroused by it. Her arousal represents the side of parental lovemaking that the child denies because it signifies the mother's unfaithfulness to him. This idea of unfaithfulness makes emotional sense of Theotormon's extreme jealousy and his angry wish to punish Oothoon which is expressed in sexualized imagery. Blake makes Oothoon collaborate in Theotormon's ambivalent wish to punish and possess her by having her writhe naked calling on his eagles to penetrate her flesh.

Blake doesn't use just visual imagery to suggest the young boy's fantasies about his mother and sexuality. In presenting Theotormon's reaction to the rape, Blake uses imagery that evokes a young child's possible reaction to a situation that arouses impotent rage. Theotormon's first act is to surround Oothoon and Bromion with "black jealous waters" (*VDA* 2:4, E46). If the image isn't quite clear in context, it becomes clearer when we remember a previous character of Blake's, the serpent Envy, who expresses its jealousy by discharging a river of filth ("then She bore Pale desire" [E446]). Using feces as a weapon is characteristic of very young children. Melanie Klein, for example, cites cases of children who react to observations of parental intercourse with angry soiling.[13] From Blake's imagery one might infer his own repressed memory of such a reaction, but whatever the source of his insight, as artist Blake is able to connect Theotormon's childishly ineffectual rage with the body imagery that best expresses it.

Blake's imagery not only evokes a young child's reactions to parental sex at a time when his only weapon is his own excrement, but he also connects this reaction with other psychological themes typical of the child's perceptions. For instance, the rape's violent sadism suggests a child's perception of intercourse. Blake depicts Theotormon as being caught in the emotions of this stage (hating the sadistic Bromion) but unable to fight back successfully, Theotormon turns his anger against himself (in one illustration he whips himself) and against Oothoon. In another illustration his eagles approach Oothoon to rip her naked body—an image of sexualized violence (illustration 5). Oothoon urges Theotormon to give up his anger and his masochism and enjoy her. She reminds him that she, like a mother choosing her son's wife, would gladly supply other women for his pleasure. In a series of monologues, she acts like a psychoanalyst encouraging him to dredge up his forbidden sexual desires—the forbidden "joys of old" (*VDA*4:4, E48); here again the imagery turns to childhood as she reminds him of "Infancy, . . . lustful, happy! nestling for delight / In laps of pleasure" (*VDA*6:4–5, E49). But unlike a psychoanalyst, instead of helping him give up his incestuous wishes, she urges him to act on them and free himself from his sense of failure.

What Blake seems to be doing is evoking a set of early experiences of despair and rivalry and then imagining the woman—in the past, the mother—who could by her total generosity make up for what he had suffered. When this is understood, it is easy to see how far Blake is from portraying equality between the sexes. His male characters are no more capable of mature love than a man jealously fixated on his mother is in real life.

Subsequent prophecies reinforce the interpretation of Oedipal drama in *Visions* and show what a pervasive and haunting theme it was for Blake. In the next prophecy, *America*, the hero Orc, furious about earlier deprivation, rapes his sister—committing the incest that Theotormon failed to do—while the young patriots overthrow the paternal tyrant.

In still later prophecies, we read in more detail how Orc was originally chained to a rock by his father, Los, who was furiously jealous of the boy's closeness to his mother, Enitharmon.

> But when fourteen summers & winters had revolved over
> Their solemn habitation Los beheld the ruddy boy
> Embracing his bright mother & beheld malignant fires
> In his young eyes discerning plain that Orc plotted his death
> Grief rose upon his ruddy brows. a tightening girdle grew
> Around his bosom like a bloody cord. . . . [He]
> Calld it the chain of Jealousy.
> (*FZ*60:6–22, E340–41)

And none but Bromion can hear my lamentations.

With what sense is it that the chicken shuns the ravenous hawk
With what sense does the tame pigeon measure out the expanse?
With what sense does the bee form cells? have not the mouse & frog
Eyes and ears and sense of touch? yet are their habitations.
And their pursuits, as different as their forms and as their joys:
Ask the wild ass why he refuses burdens: and the meek camel
Why he loves man: is it because of eye ear mouth or skin
Or breathing nostrils? No. for these the wolf and tyger have.
Ask the blind worm the secrets of the grave, and why her spires
Love to curl round the bones of death? and ask the ravnous snake
Where she gets poison: & the winged eagle why he loves the sun
And then tell me the thoughts of man, that have been hid of old.

Silent I hover all the night, and all day could be silent.
If Theotormon once would turn his loved eyes upon me;
How can I be defild when I reflect thy image pure?   (woe
Sweetest the fruit that the worm feeds on. & the soul prey'd on by
The new washd lamb ting'd with the village smoke & the bright swan
By the red earth of our immortal river: I bathe my wings.
And I am white and pure to hover round Theotormons breast.

Then Theotormon broke his silence. and he answered.

Tell me what is the night or day to one oerflowd with woe?)
Tell me what is a thought? & of what substance is it made?)
Tell me what is a joy? & in what gardens do joys grow?
And in what rivers swim the sorrows? and upon what mountains

5. *Visions of the Daughters of Albion* (copy J), pl. 3, detail, Lessing J. Rosenwald Collection, Library of Congress.

In an illustration Blake pictures Orc as a naked adolescent embracing his mother while his father watches angrily, a red chain of jealousy around his neck. Throughout this whole series of poems Blake is depicting Oedipal dramas in which father and son are alternately dominant.

In discussing Blake's gratifying females, the Lily in *Thel* and Oothoon, it is important to realize that imagining them and their satisfaction of his most forbidden desires was uphill work against guilt. Not only are they mother figures and so taboo, but there is also guilt in imagining the death of paternal rivals. Coping with this guilt is apparently too much for Blake. Even in *America* the hero's triumph doesn't last long. The poem ends with the father god's vengeful cold mists descending on the rebels. The dangers of woman's retaliatory anger for the incestuous and greedy impulses are even more severe. In thinking himself further and further back into the experiences of childhood, Blake becomes more angry and fearful.

By the time he finishes *Vala*, a transitional work of his middle years that he worked on for over a decade, Blake's images of women have taken on a preponderantly negative tone. Though he still keeps a formal split between good and bad women, the good ones never again capture his imagination, but his fantasies about what bad women do to males get more and more violent and bizarre. *Vala* is fascinating because it shows his changing attitude toward women as well as how the change is connected with his shift from revolutionary to Christian. In its early drafts we see him giving way totally to negative fantasies: women destroy men's bodies, unweave them on their looms, drain them in sex, appropriate their penises—these are just a few of the horrors he expresses. Blake becomes increasingly certain that any attempt to satisfy basic needs for food and sex is bound to have horrible consequences. Rather than being satisfied, the characters receive a destructive version of the need itself: if they want food, they are eaten; if they want sex, they are castrated. Blake views essential needs as dangerous not only because they leave the individual vulnerable to painful deprivation, but also because they are too excessive and too mixed with aggression, thus damaging those chosen to satisfy them.

An episode at the beginning of *Vala* exemplifies the mutually destructive activities of male and female. Enion, a type of earth mother, initiates the pattern by destroying Tharmas in retaliation for his jealous possessiveness. Enion literally takes him apart. She draws out and manipulates his nerves, "every vein & lacteal" (*FZ*5:17, E302). She then gives birth to him again by reweaving him on her loom. Her woven child soon becomes a self-glorying, righteous bully who addresses her as "my slave" and revenges himself for her earlier treatment of him by raping her.

Tharmas's body fuses with Enion's during intercourse, creating a monstrous woman-serpent. This is a variation of an earlier fragment describing the even more bizarre mating of a woman with a penis and a man without one. Here, though, Blake seems to be suggesting that sexuality is horribly dangerous because the woman appropriates or absorbs the man's penis in intercourse. She also seems to appropriate the creativity that Blake associates with male sexuality. She acquires a poetic voice. Enion's first act after the rape is to sing. In a later revision, Blake gives her a serpent's voice whose complaints suggest that the absorbed male is protesting within her.

Having imagined himself into a corner where the male is threatened with either feminization or death or both, Blake tries through revisions to lessen the female's power or to transfer it to the male. His most successful strategy is his concept of an outside will, Christ, directing events. This seems to be a strong internal reason for his shift from revolutionary to radical Christian. He needs Christ to help him control his imagined women and his impulses. With Christ there, retaliatory acts become a necessary if painful part of a benign pattern of redemption. Within the protection of a Christian framework, Blake is able to reintroduce his idea of the totally giving woman to counter his fears of the murderous mother. In extensive additions to *Vala* he works up the concept of a realm called Beulah, the married land, inhabited by benign females. He first introduces them right after the Enion-Tharmas episode, and their self-abnegating actions soften or deny woman's power to mutilate or kill men. Blake contrasts Enion's cruel treatment of Tharmas with an ideal state where Beulah's "Females sleep the winter in soft silken veils / Woven by their own hands to hide them in the darksom grave / But Males immortal live renewd by female deaths" (*FZ*5:1–3, E302). Although the males do not actually kill these females who reportedly delight in self-immolation, this Eden seems created out of fear, not love.

Blake continues to build up his countering idea of Beulah. In *Milton*, Beulians nourish the sleeping hero feeding "His lips with food of Eden" (*M*15:14–15, E109). In addition, in *Milton* Blake imagines the poet Los totally recreating time so that the satisfaction of basic needs will be central. Los's time is defined by satisfaction of hunger. In between each moment of time stands a daughter of Beulah "To feed the Sleepers on their Couches with maternal care (*M*28:49, E126). This conceptualization literally insists that there is no time in which one experiences the maternal figure's absence. In making creation take place in the space-time where the mother nurtures, Blake also suggests that creativity depends on the maternal environment. Blake amplifies his description of Beulah's loving responsiveness: "Beulah to its Inhabitants appears within each district / As the beloved infant in his mothers bosom" (*M*30:10–11, E129). In his fiction of males resting in Beulah, Blake gratifies the wish for nurture while simultaneously denying infantile dependence. Beulah's women are correspondingly weak and fearful of the creative and inspired males. The female world of obedience, where they are taught how to die smiling each winter, is carefully separated from the male world of creation—a second realm Blake names "Eden." Man drops into Beulah only temporarily for a rest cure before continuing his virile forward progress: "thro' / The Bosom of the Father" (*M*31:4–5, E130). Beulah is not only the world of self-abnegating nurture—that of Thel's Lily—but also the world of sexual gratification. In Beulah, the female ransacks sea and land for gratifications to the male genius who in return will clothe her in gems. Blake lectures the recalcitrant bride of the Divine Voice in *Milton*, urging her to "give / Her maidens to her husband: delighting in his delight / . . . As it is done in Beulah" (*M*33:17–20, E133). This is the fantasy of the sexually generous mother-wife we saw in *Visions*. But Blake has become much more righteous, using biblical language and thought to bolster his ideas. He continues, "& thou O Virgin Babylon Mother of Whoredoms / Shalt bring Jerusalem . . . / Shalt give her into the arms of God your Lord & Husband" (*M*33:20–24, E133).

All in all, Blake's concept of Beulah, which isolates and weakens women, doesn't really solve anything. It seems impossible for Blake to imagine real men and women coexisting in a state of peace. Outside of Beulah, Blake's portrayals of women's murderousness go on. His evil women characters increasingly split off, doubling and tripling as though he can't control their rampant proliferation. Their acts too are increasingly horrible. In *Jerusalem*, for example, he has them dancing in the flayed skins of their victims waving the men's severed organs.

From this it is clear that though Blake valiantly tries to control the fantasy of the destructive mother and give it redemptive meaning, woman's independent presence is still threatening. In his prophecies *Milton* and *Jerusalem*, he moves toward what might be called his final solution to the woman problem. At the end of *Milton* he suggests for the first time that if the conflict between men is to cease, woman must stop existing. Sexual organization, which, using a phrase from Ezekiel, he now calls "the Abomination of Desolation," must disappear "Till Generation is swallowd up in Regeneration" (*M*41:25–28, E142–43). But although Blake announces the end of sexual organization, male sexuality continues to stand as a model for the human, while the female is either incorporated or isolated restrictively in Beulah. In *Jerusalem* he repeats his ideas about the Beulians as gratifiers of male genius. It is clear the female has no independent existence except as gratifier and she must accept the male's "Fibres of dominion" (*J*88:13, E246).

Finally, during the writing of *Jerusalem*, Blake begins to feel that female sexuality can be dispensed with altogether. He considers female sexuality inferior to the total body sensuality of the child, for the loss of which he holds women responsible. Blake makes Christ sanction his views by reinstating this total body sensuality. When Christ does this, he effectively breaks the female's power over the male.

Sexual organization is permitted in order for Christ to be born, but once born, his Maternal Humanity must be put off lest the sexual generation swallow up regeneration. At *Jerusalem*'s climactic moment, Enitharmon, who has been resisting giving up her independence, suddenly caves in under the weight of Blake's rhetoric and announces her disappearance: "My Looms will be no more & I annihilate vanish for ever" (*J*92:11, E252). Her husband and brother Los reaches the final insight that "Sexes must vanish & cease / To be" (*J*92:13–14, E252).

Blake's view of male-female relationships hasn't been clear to readers partly because it is at first to be contradicted by his enormous sensitivity to feminine traits such as tenderness and maternal care. Blake views these traits in two ways. On the one hand, they belong to the ideal Female and help her to care for the Male Genius; on the other hand, the poet can incorporate and use them in creation and in drawing close to other men. In this latter view Blake anticipates the modern recognition of bisexuality and its importance for creativity, which arises as a dialogue between the male and female parts of the self. But Blake did not extend the right to express traits of the opposite sex to his females. When they do express them, they become threatening Female Wills and, as we have seen, must be destroyed.

Jerusalem makes it clear that Blake's obsession with sex and women is stronger in his late prophecies than in the early ones. But his emphasis and the structure of his defenses have changed. Sexual liberation has been replaced by forgiveness of sins. In the early work, when he fights on the side of impulse, he is fairly conscious of his incestuous and other wishes. (This is a positive fact. His dramatizations of the conflict between impulse and guilt or conscience have an immediacy and power lacking in the late work.) In his middle and late work, he fights his impulses with all his power. He repudiates the incestuous act at the heart of his concept of liberated sex and describes it as the original sin and cause of the Fall. This seems at first a plausible solution—certainly it is a traditional one—to the problem of what to do with one's forbidden impulses, but it doesn't succeed artistically or humanly. Blake can't really transcend his incestuous wishes though he sincerely wants to. He just splits them off from his consciousness. He has to fight very hard to keep them from his awareness though they come out in various ways in the poems. This not only weakens the poetry where the avowed Christian purpose is opposed by subterranean fantasies but it is an additional reason for his misogyny. Women are now the temptresses and whores who pander to his suppressed wishes.

Having given you an idea of Blake's real attitude toward women and sketched its development, I'd like to describe briefly my own involvement with Blake and with a psychoanalytic approach to him on the way to making a few concluding remarks about the difference between his early and late work. When I read the early revolutionary prophecies, as an adolescent, the overthrow of tyrants and freeing of sexuality was deeply appealing. Later, I found a whole other side—the objective religious and political meanings laid out by the critics. It took years of learning about his cosmologies and myth, his cycles, his system, before I was ready to go back and look at what first attracted me—his sensitivity to the emotions of the child and the outcast, his defense of free sexuality. Like many feminist critics, I expected to find a man in favor of a truly liberated sexuality and equality. But though Blake does make a strong defense of sexual freedom in his early work, it is one-sided and ultimately regressive, a freedom for the male to enact fantasies of total gratification. Still what is remarkable is the degree to which Blake is in touch with these unconscious fantasies and the translucence with which he is able to mirror them in his work—a translucence unparalleled in other artists.

Blake had varying degrees of consciousness about what he was doing. On one level, he projects unconscious material seemingly without much awareness. In the case of his attitudes toward women, he is largely dramatizing or reenacting early experiences and is too caught up in them to be critical. The more seriously one takes Blake, the more crucial it is to find the places in his poetry where anxiety interferes with genuine insight or vision. Mature sexual love needs the same integration and transcendence of the infantile past as morality and moral judgments. A psychoanalytic approach is helpful in drawing attention to the places where submerged feelings distort the subject, the poet's handling of it, or our own responses. A psychoanalytic approach provides insights not only to sweeping topics like sexuality, but also to particular literary problems. For example, Blake often combines things for psychological reasons—in *Island* he mixes scatological filth and pure lyrics for defensive purposes and he adds a discordant coda to *Thel* under the pressure of fearful fantasies. In both cases a psychoanalytic method exposes his underlying preoccupations and helps clarify our response to them.

On a second level, when the subject is less frightening or emotion laden for him, Blake is aware of just the things that Freud saw and describes them with the insight of a master psychologist. For instance, when he consciously describes a certain type of rational and moralistic man struggling against impulse, his observations about the Urizenic character—the symbolic connections he makes between anality (in his images), cruelty, rationality and morality—are in many ways similar to Freud's descriptions of the compulsive or anal personality. But it is important to keep the two levels of awareness separate. One cannot praise Blake for going way beyond Freud, but ignore the conflicts at the heart of his concept of liberated sexuality, which ultimately lead to his misogyny.[14] Blake provides special revelations of the way the mind works and, especially, of the obduracy with which it clings to wishes and fantasies that keep us, men and women, from living together in a way that satisfies our desire for equality and love.

Blake's Feminist Revision of Literary Tradition in "The SICK ROSE"

Elizabeth Langland

This essay weds feminist and formal-thematic methodologies to analyze Blake's "The SICK ROSE." The process exposes a range of assumptions inherent in each method, assumptions that bear critical investigation.

The feminist method is, of course, not one thing only. As Carolyn Heilbrun notes: "It is important . . . that we recognize feminist criticism as moving with enormous speed through many stages of development and essential that we do not shoot down those who are not yet at what we may consider the 'cutting edge' of our discipline."[1] Elaine Showalter defines two distinct modes of feminist criticism: (1) the *feminist reading* or *feminist critique,* "an historically grounded inquiry which probes the ideological assumptions of literary phenomena,"[2] and (2) *gynocriticism,* whose "subjects are the history, styles, themes, and genres and structures of writing by women; the psychodynamics of female creativity; the trajectory of the individual or collective female career; and the evolution and laws of a female literary tradition."[3]

Showalter prefers gynocriticism because it is capable of a "theoretical consensus" (183) that eludes the feminist critique. The basis for this consensus lies in gynocriticism's emphasis on difference: the distinct quality of women's literature. The feminist critique, on the other hand, which stresses woman as reader and the text as historically grounded, focuses on interpretation rather than difference—even when it takes women writers as its subject—and thus it remains inevitably pluralistic. For many feminist critics that pluralism is a cause for celebration. Annette Kolodny speaks forcefully for this "playful pluralism": "[the feminist] claims neither definitiveness nor structural completeness for her different readings and reading systems, but only their usefulness in recognizing the particular achievements of woman-as-author and their applicability in conscientiously decoding woman-as-sign."[4] Showalter, however, worries that as long as the feminist critique remains pluralistic—offering yet one more competing interpretation of a work—it seems not to accomplish the goal of feminist criticism: to make itself essential (183–84). Further, to the extent that feminist critique remains dependent on male-oriented methodologies for its results, this methodological dependency formally affirms patriarchy even as the content of feminist critique seeks to undercut it. These are valid concerns. They underline the pervasive problem for both gynocriticism and the feminist critique—that is, how to bring feminist discourse from the periphery to an authoritative center.

Any feminist article on a male writer, such as this one on Blake, belongs to the feminist critique. Though Showalter finds theoretical consensus impossible in feminist critique, such a consensus in fact manifests itself in the tendency of feminist critique, as it has evolved, not merely to interpret but to question the very grounds of interpretation (183–84). Because the feminist critique has the power to uncover the politics of interpretation, it reaches a theoretical consensus in pointing to the radical contingency of value and meaning, to the ideological content of supposedly value-free productions. As such, it shows an ever-increasing methodological sophistication, and its discourse provides an ever-more central and trenchant critique.

Exploring contingencies of meaning is, of course, the agenda of other current methodologies, like deconstruction; and decoding ideological dimensions of texts is also performed by historicist methods such as Marxism. Feminist critique, however, insists on dismantling both patriarchal calcification of meaning and fixed categories of ideological analysis: it simultaneously operates in the arenas of deconstruction and Marxism while submitting these methodologies themselves to radical critique by uncovering their own contingent and ideological biases. Though openly ideological, feminist critique is not committed to any particular ideology or science (which usually finds its roots in patriarchy). Further, precisely because feminist critique is openly ideological and commits itself to exploring the historical determinants and effects of a work's production and reception, its conclusions more directly challenge assumptions concerning how we go about reading and writing than do those of gynocriticism, which addresses the ideological question only obliquely by focusing on texts by women.

This feminist critique of Blake uses a formal-thematic methodology, which at first glance seems to be a marriage of two approaches inherently at odds with each other. Unlike feminist critique, the formal-thematic method privileges the text and its autonomous integrity, presuming that the text raises the questions appropriate to be asked of it. It is appreciative criticism, not openly ideological. In this sense, the formal-thematic method shares the attitude of gynocriticism. Myra Jehlen astutely notes that gynocriticism attracts women because it allows the critic to remain sympathetic and appreciative toward the text. Gynocritics shares this stance of appreciating the text with the formal-thematic method, but ironically this is gynocriticism's inherent weakness. Because it makes no direct attack, but erects an alternative tradition, gynocriticism is frequently ignored or made marginal by the academy. Gynocriticism's theoretical consensus will not easily accomplish, then, feminism's central agenda of transforming the canon. The practitioner of the feminist critique, dealing with the ideological questions explicitly, faces two possibilities. On the one hand, the practitioner may try to remain appreciative by simply claiming to have discovered what had been obscured in the text by previous criticism. On the other hand, if the ideology of the feminist seems "to bring questions to the text that the text itself does not raise,"[5] the feminist critic may more actively establish a new sense of the poem.

Jehlen suggests that one way out of this contradiction is to engage it more directly. She remarks that "the critical issues manifest themselves precisely at the points of contradiction. . . . to focus on points of contradiction as the places where we can see the whole structure of our world most clearly implies the immanent relativity of all perception and knowledge" (600). The contradiction that concerns us here, the contradiction between discovering new meanings and establishing new meanings, can be confronted by making the poem itself an allegory of interpretation. Though this move may seem to finesse this radical difference between discovery and establishing meaning, it puts us in the position of saying that feminist criticism works, that it generates new meanings, because all literature is more an allegory of its own reading than we have suspected. Certainly analyzing a writer like Blake, whose own tendencies are strongly subversive—indeed have long been recognized to criticize consciously patriarchal assumptions through the creation of negative father figures such as Urizen—leads us naturally to such provocative conclusions.

This essay presents, then, a feminist critique of Blake's "The SICK

ROSE" through the formal-thematic method, culminating not only in an interpretation of this specific poem but in some questions about the basis for reading, interpretation, and knowledge in general. The analysis is segmented into successive "moments," signaling the way that feminist critique has already evolved and making contributions to its further evolution.[6]

We shall first examine the critical tradition in which readings of the poem have evolved; second, explore contextual questions, such as the way in which postulating a "speaker" or point of view for this poem expands the interpretive field; and third, investigate the ways language, syntax, punctuation, revisions, and illuminations work to establish new readings. The formal-thematic approach provides the methodology, and the feminist perspective raises the relevant, new, and illuminating questions.

The first moment of this feminist critique invites us to look at the poem's traditional associations.

> O Rose thou art sick.
> The invisible worm,
> That flies in the night
> In the howling storm:
>
> Has found out thy bed
> Of crimson joy:
> And his dark secret love
> Does thy life destroy.
> (*SE*39, E23)

The "rose" and the "worm" function in literary traditions, traditions to which Blake belongs and that he also treats ironically, traditions from which readers often draw very directly, oversimplifying the poem. Within this tradition, readers automatically identify the rose as feminine or female—more, as possessing qualities desirable in a woman, such as unspoiled beauty, innocence, and freshness—and the worm as a phallic force destroying purity, bloom, freshness, and innocence. Reading within a literary tradition, readers supply these associations, invited, too, by the sexual suggestiveness of such images as "bed of crimson joy." E. D. Hirsch, for example, summarizes one theme based on these associations seeing the poem as an "account of Beauty destroyed by Evil . . . the fatal attraction felt by evil for the innocent, passive, helpless, and beautiful."[7] I choose this interpretation as a starting point because it is the interpretation of glosses provided in high school and college anthologies. Feminist critique recomplicates the terms by pinpointing the patriarchal bias in these assumptions. From a feminist perspective two points in Hirsch's commentary are notable. First, Hirsch assumes an explicit sexual or gender character to the beauty and the Evil. Within the parameters of the poem, they could, theoretically, be male Beauty and female Evil, but the assumption that Beauty is female and Evil is male is so thoroughly taken for granted by Hirsch as to be beyond argument. Indeed, when Hirsch knocks down the straw man of his own simple interpretation—"such a reading for all its attractiveness is not entirely accurate"—he simply refers to the rose with feminine pronouns without justifying the attribution: "part of the rose's sickness is her ignorance of her disease" (234).

Second, for Hirsch, as for many commentators on Blake's poem, there is as logical a connection between "female" and "corrupt" as there is between "rose" and "female." The assumption is that the rose is already corrupt and therefore participates in its further corruption by the worm. Hirsch remarks, "The rose is the type of female who, enjoying the outward show of modesty (the rose and the sheep in 'The Lilly'), promotes the repression and hypocritical customs of the 'Father of Jealousy' " (234).

Harold Bloom's analysis anticipates Hirsch's, elevating the rose's guilt even above that of the worm: "Yet the worm is scarcely at fault; by his nature he is the negative, not the contrary of the rose. The rose is less innocent; she enjoys the self-enjoyings of self-denial, an enclosed bower of self-gratification, for her bed is already 'of crimson joy,' before it is found out."[8] Both Hirsch and Bloom depend largely on the association of female with nature and on other poems within the *Songs of Experience*—particularly "THE LILLY" and "My Pretty ROSE TREE"—to develop this thesis. Only in the latter poem is the rose identified explicitly as female:

Then I went to my Pretty Rose-tree;
To tend her by day and by night.
But my Rose turnd away with jealousy:
And her thorns were my only delight.
(*SE*43:5–8, E25)

The female gender of the rose is then imported to "THE LILLY"—
"The modest Rose puts forth a thorn"—so the thorn can be glossed as
a female's false modesty that will "stain her beauty bright." All of
these associations, then, become a subtext for "The SICK ROSE."

The issue of context for "The SICK ROSE" is an important one to
which we shall return more fully later in the second moment of this
feminist critique. For now, we note that the thesis developed from the
above associations answers very nicely to men's deep suspicion that
women's beauty is deceptive and their fear that what that beauty con-
ceals is corruption and death. In some sense, then, the worm is not an
independent agent; it is simply a manifestation of the rose's inner sickness—hence, its "invisibility."

A first moment of this formal-feminist analysis, then, profitably exposes the suspicion and possible hostility present in certain kinds of
interpretations of the poem, hostility toward a certain kind of woman,
one who hypocritically pretends to modesty and whose hypocrisy becomes a disease infecting *"Love! sweet Love!"* ("A Little GIRL
Lost"). So the Lilly is celebrated for delighting in Love without the
false modesty (thorn) of the rose and the threat (false humility) of
the sheep.

Building on these interpretations, Brenda Webster pursues a Freudian biographical analysis of "Blake" to locate the frustrations and hos-
tilities within Blake himself where, beneath a superficial celebration of
free love for all, Blake actually indulges in "a masculine fantasy of
incestuous gratification."[9] Webster illuminates her analysis by questioning what two other Blake critics, Mark Schorer and David Erdman,
have accepted uncritically, that "Blake's picture of 'free love' here was
supposedly influenced by Mary Wollstonecraft's *Vindication of the
Rights of Woman*" (Webster 107). Webster points out that "the emotional forces of the two works are entirely different." Wollstonecraft
felt that " 'the end, the grand end, of [women's] exertions should be
to unfold their own faculties.' Far from seeing woman as devoted to
'happy, happy Love,' [as Blake does] she wanted to substitute equality
based on reason for woman's 'sexual character' as a gratifier of man"
(Webster 107).

Webster's Freudian and feminist analysis of Blake suggests an interpretation of "The SICK ROSE" within this same framework, that is,
the poem is a product of a "masculine fantasy" (Webster 107), where
the female is lauded for her receptivity and criticized for her false

modesty and secrecy, or, more chauvinistically, for any withholding of herself from the male.

In this first moment of our analysis, we see that all of the critics, including Webster, are reading Blake's "The SICK ROSE" in the context of the critical tradition that has grown up around Blake and some of Blake's supposed doctrinal statements. Webster's assumptions and associations rely as heavily on that tradition as do the interpretations it criticizes. Her feminist perspective functions mainly to expose a biographical Blake, not to complicate our reading. But our formal-feminist critique can take us further, to a second moment focusing on contexts.

In a second moment of this feminist critique, we turn from reading in the context of language as generator of images and associative symbols to reading in the context of speakers and perspectives. This second moment of feminist critique incorporates insights from reader-response criticism because we are reading the critics as well as Blake's text. The existence of one context for reading implies the possibility of other contexts. The feminist critic recontextualizes, accepting that the determination of context is a function of ideological perspective of the critic as well as author. The notion of perspectival vision, of things appearing differently depending on the viewpoints from which they are seen, has had a long history in Blake criticism. The *Proverbs of Hell* are filled with statements of this idea. A feminist perspective demonstrates that although critics have not called attention to the speaker of "The SICK ROSE," they have read the poem in the context of a patriarchal speaker. When Blake creates a speaker who closely mirrors readers' own patriarchal attitudes, readers do not ask questions about distortions in perspective—not, that is, until feminism changes the lights.

The value of a feminist perspective does not depend simply on the insight that the speaker may be reading sickness into the rose. Other critics have reached a similar conclusion.[10] That insight is central, but the feminist perspective is more prominently present here in a habit of mind and procedure—questioning the ways meaning has been foreclosed within a certain reading tradition, and remaining receptive to alternative possible readings that expose patriarchal bias or imposition.

The feminist critique foregrounds the large range of assumptions and personal biases reader-critics import to a text by observing what reader-response critics have documented, the extent to which a text is produced by a reader. In this second moment of the feminist critique, we grow sensitive to biases in interpretation, to the ways in which certain interpretations, as well as texts, have been canonized to support patriarchy. By placing Blake's "The SICK ROSE" within the literary tradition that it is seen to echo rather than revise, critics have effectively prescribed how the poem is read. Harold Bloom's reading, for example, inadvertently exposes the gender-specific biases in his interpretation. Bloom hears "the shock of terrible pity" in the first sentence: "O Rose thou art sick." But "pity" is not fully consonant with the reading Bloom provides in which the "rose is not blameless, and has an inner sickness" and in which, ultimately, the worm is "scarcely at fault" (Bloom 135). Indeed, "condemnation" would better express the tone of the opening line to a poem about a rose whose inner sickness and concealment corrupt an apparently innocent worm. Why then does Bloom speak of "terrible pity"? I suggest he does so to emphasize his own compassion for the state of things, particularly the corruption of the rose, a corruption to which he, as authoritative reader of the poem, is superior and (apparently) immune. Condemnation suggests that the rose might remedy her condition. Pity implies condescension and suggests the rose's inability to redeem her nature. She is both fallen and helpless. But just as Bloom explicitly focuses on condescension, the implicit message in Bloom's insistence on pity coupled with blame is a contempt for the female's fallen nature.

The tone of the opening line to "The SICK ROSE"—a function of point of view—is a crux here. Is the rose—or her situation—being condemned? Or is it pitied? Where does guilt lie? Whose agency confers the sickness and guilt: the rose's, the worm's, or the speaker-viewer's?

The general assumption among critics is that Blake is to be identified with the speaker of this poem, which leads either to a patriarchal blindness to the poem's possibilities or to a feminist condemnation of Blake as chauvinist. Both cut off possibilities of reading. From the perspective of the second moment of feminist critique, however, much in the poem argues against such ready identification. Indeed we might ask whether the speaker is necessarily male. Although the poem's attitudes are patriarchal, the speaker could be female. The opening line reveals the attitudes and the problems. The speaker seems distanced from corruption and absolved from all guilt and responsibility for the implied sexual situation "he" perceives precisely because he invokes all the feminine associations of the rose. The opening line, then, according to a Bloomian patriarchal reading, which collapses reader, "Blake," and speaker, presupposes a protective, even chivalrous attitude toward helpless feminine beauty: "O Rose thou art sick." But reading as a feminist, reading outside the patriarchal imprimatur, necessarily produces a different response colored by identification with the rose instead of the speaker.[11] In the traditional patriarchal reading, the author/ speaker/reader identifies the rose as female, and the masculinist reader has the immediate advantage of decoding the symbols from a comfortable position above guilt. This position is unavailable to the feminist reader who is caught in the tension between the object being judged and the judge.

Again, we must ask, whose agency is it that confers corruption? The rose's, the worm's, or the speaker's? In the other rose poems, the speaker credits the rose with agency: "The modest Rose *puts forth a thorn*" [my italics] ("THE LILLY," *SE*43:1, E25), or "my Rose *turnd away with jealousy*" [my italics] ("My Pretty ROSE TREE," *SE*43:7, E25). In "The SICK ROSE" the ostensible agency belongs to the worm: "Has *found out* thy bed / Of crimson joy: / And his dark secret love / *Does thy life destroy*" [my italics]. Yet critics, encouraged by the speaker's attitudes, ignore differences between Blake's perspective here and in other *Songs;* they are only too willing to credit a prior agency to the rose who has practiced concealment so her bed must be "found out" by the worm. The poem itself supports no such agency on the rose's part. Indeed, we discover a reading into or imposition of bias onto the rose—a projection of guilt onto her—because the "found out" is a product of the speaker's sighting the invisible worm and its actions.

Of course, we may logically respond that there is no necessary guilt in the rose, rather that the "invisible worm" with "his dark, secret love" is the source of corruption; the rose is innocent victim. But the interaction between rose and worm is complicated. Do the worm's attitude and his corruption corrupt the rose? If so, why do they? Actions themselves aren't usually a source of corruption in Blake's *Songs.* If we look at another encounter with a worm, in *The Book of Thel,* the girl's refusal to enter her grave plot, to encounter the sexuality and death implicit in the naked worm, defines her failure.

In *Visions of the Daughters of Albion,* the speaker states, "Sweetest the fruit that the worm feeds on," lines cited by critics in support of embracing one's sexual experience. Morton Paley argues that the heroine of the *Visions of the Daughters of Albion* "has the courage to confront Experience." Though raped and rejected she "can yet declare the sanctity of bodily love."[12] Critics apply these attitudes to the *Songs of Experience* as well. Mark Schorer states, "The bulk of the poems in *Songs of Experience* are directed against the conventional restraints imposed upon sexuality . . . mistaken attitudes toward sexual love are made the root of all errors in experience."[13] But in "The SICK ROSE," the rose is never seen from this more generous perspective, although she easily could be. A feminist ideology reveals that the two perspectives are related, opposite sides of the same coin that accounts women's value in male terms: either she must be unviolated—an uncontaminated vessel for male procreation of legitimate heirs—or, if violated and impure, she should become an ardent vessel for male lust. These dual, seemingly opposed concepts are related by Blake specifically in chapter 1 of *Jerusalem* where he presents the concept of the "virgin harlot," or the Madonna and whore. In a third moment of the feminist critique, I shall establish that Blake's techniques reveal an effort to unseat the conventions and evade the categorizations that have nonetheless characterized Blake criticism.

All of these traditional associations critics have brought to Blake studies—associations of nature and woman, of the body with the female (part of a Christian hierarchy)—surely could bear reexamination in light of the issues we are raising in our three, interrelated moments of feminist critique. The specific kinds of questions we are asking may cause us to rethink the whole issue of conventional associations for the female in Blake. In this second moment of feminist critique of "The SICK ROSE," however, we continue to explore the ways in which categories or contexts shape interpretations.

Clearly, interpretations of the rose of Blake's song, "The SICK ROSE," have "embedded" her in the tradition of the pure virgin. We may consider the phrase that has been a focus of interpretations of the rose as negative—"bed of crimson joy"—a phrase that Harold Bloom glossed as "an enclosed bower of self-gratification." However, from a second moment of feminist critique, we may easily reread "bed of crimson joy" in a positive light. A bed provides an image for all life experience, from conception to death. Blake is playing on this rich range of associations: nuptial bed, childbed, sick bed, death bed, narrow bed, as well as the more obvious flower bed, a locus of growth. Bloom's "bower" is a constriction of the text's "bed," a constriction that allows the speaker and fellow interpreters to hold the rose culpable for her experience. Such contradictions authorize us to try another perspective and to look more closely at the speaker whose attitude is subtly problematic when put in the context of the other *Songs*.

The speaker of "The SICK ROSE" is explicitly marked by strong sexual biases common to the Nurse in "The NURSES Song," the priests in "The GARDEN of LOVE," and the father in "A Little GIRL Lost." All of these "perceivers" create the guilt by their attitude toward the situations they evaluate. The guilt, in short, is a product of their minds, not inherent in the situations that seem, if anything, innocent and pure.

The nurse, speaker of "The NURSES Song," hears the children's whisperings with their sexual overtones, and her own repressed and disguised longings stimulate her jealousy and her projection of corruption onto the children: "The days of my youth rise fresh in my mind, / My face turns green and pale" (*SE*38:3–4, E23). Like the nurse in secretive and guilty temperament, the priests in "The GARDEN of LOVE" are "binding with briars, my joys & desires" (*SE*44:12, E26). These are the words of a speaker who has "turn'd to the Garden of Love, / That so many sweet flowers bore" (*SE*44:7–8, E26)—sweet flowers reminiscent of the innocent rose—but graves and tombstones now replace these flowers. Significantly, too, the speaker partially implicates himself in the transformation from flowers to graves in the Garden of Love; he claims that he "saw what I never had seen: / A Chapel was built in the midst, / Where I used to play on the green" (*SE*44:2–3, E26). This statement suggests either that the Chapel did not previously exist and has been built (its presence with its institutional associations now contaminating the Garden of Love) or that the speaker could not previously *see* it. In "The SICK ROSE," we find the same insistence on changes in perception or changed perception that characterizes other poems. The speaker himself underscores here that central procedure in Blake's *Songs of Experience*: an experienced viewer looks back on things innocent or value neutral and either discloses the discoloring envy in another's viewpoint or reveals it in his own.

Similarly, in "A Little GIRL Lost," the father blights and corrupts the girl's innocent experience: "But his loving look, / Like the holy book, / All her tender limbs with terror shook" (*SE*51:27–29, E29). Although the prophetic voice opening the poem anticipates a "*future*

Age" when it will seem impossible that *"Love! sweet Love! was thought a crime"* (*SE*51:1, 4, E29) the rest of the poem does not bear out this hopeful promise.

Strategies in these other songs support an interpretation of the rose as a function of the speaker, who, ironically, is identical with yet distanced from the worm in point of knowledge. They have both "found out" the rose. There is, however, a difference between speaker and worm in the discovery: the worm has found out her sexual passion or "bed of crimson joy"; the speaker has discovered her sickness, a difference that favors the worm who discovers a normal instinct, not a perversion. The burden of interpretation of sickness rests with the speaker. The sick rose is like the poison tree and the "dismal shade / Of Mystery"—the tree that grows "in the Human Brain" and is sought in vain through all of nature in "The Human Abstract" (*SE*47:13–14, 24, E27). It is a production of a mind. Appropriately, the drafts of "The Human Abstract" and "The SICK ROSE" occur on the same page of the notebook.

We note, too, that the speaker has revealed that the worm is invisible. The agent of affliction is no more visible than the Tree in "The Human Abstract." How does the speaker spot it so readily? We must at least consider if it, too, is in the speaker's mind.

Subsequent lines—"That flies in the night / In the howling storm"— adumbrate the worm's journey and suggest his origins. E. D. Hirsch has argued, "Just as there is no tree of mystery in nature ('The Human Abstract'), so there is no invisible worm. He is an invention of the 'human brain.' What brings him to the rose is the howling storm—the setting for man's perversion of the natural order in this poem as in *Lear*. The perverted human order is contrasted with the open, natural order; dark secrecy with crimson joy, sickness with health."[14] This argument resembles mine superficially; it makes the same identification of the invisible worm with the Tree of Mystery. But the argument is curiously truncated in not seeking to identify *which* "human brain" has invented the worm.

I have called Hirsch's logic "curious" because he seems to identify the evil of invention and perception with the rose: "The rose existed in her natural paradise of crimson joy before the advent of the corrupting worm, . . . but that paradise was not abstemious; it was crimson. . . . In this case the evil is within the rose as much as in external forces, and Blake satirizes her as much as he regrets her fatal sickness." Hirsch's logic depends on Miltonic associations: " 'Worm' is traditional for 'serpent' and before Milton's serpent perverted Eve he flew through the howling storm of chaos and old night" (235). For Hirsch, the rose is subtly linked with Eve and hence perverse, otherwise it is hard to see why he insists on the rose's sickness. This logic and discussion return us to views we earlier characterized as belonging to a first moment of this feminist critique in which we examined the literary traditions informing critical readings of the poem. But, in this second moment of the feminist critique, we might pursue other implications to the night and chaos that are also Miltonic and that relate more directly to our arguments about interpretation and context. In *Paradise Lost* Satan claims first, "The mind is its own place, and in itself / Can make a heav'n of hell, a hell of heav'n" (1:254–55), and later, "Which way I fly is hell; myself am hell" (4:75), statements demonstrating Milton's fundamental belief that pandemonium is a quality of mind, not a place. Blake's "howling storm" and the "night" are likewise the chaos and darkness in a mind that obscures and corrupts all it perceives; the worm is simply a projection of the speaker's vicious perspectives that will spoil what they have "found out" and render evil the innocent.

This tension between innocent experience and corruption is characteristic of the *Songs of Experience,* and it suggests an alternative perspective on "The SICK ROSE." The secrecy and corruption may be a product not of the rose, but of the speaker. This is an interpretation more generous to Blake. The first feminist moment concludes that Blake is a thoroughgoing chauvinist, even a misogynist, who sees the rose (traditional literary symbol of female perfection) as corrupt in itself, whereas nothing else in Blake's *Songs* is quite so innately corrupt. The second critical moment, exploring the subversive qualities within the poem itself, shows us Blake experimenting with literary tradition and its patriarchal assumptions.

A third moment of feminist critique focuses on notebook contexts; revisions; the written, printed text; and the illuminations to establish the formal legitimacy of this feminist rereading of Blake's lyric. I have already remarked that the drafts of "The Human Abstract" and "The SICK ROSE" occur on the same page of the notebook. Equally significant, "The NURSES Song" immediately precedes "The SICK ROSE" in the published *Songs,* as well as in the notebook, and underscores

Blake's exploration of attitudes toward and perspectives on experience. When the nurse hears the children's whispers, her own repression makes her jealous: "The days of my youth rise fresh in my mind, / My face turns green and pale" (*SE*38:3–4, E23). "Days of my youth" originally read "desires of youth," revised to "days of youth" before its final revision. The changes support the nurse's corruption. In the final revision, Blake has inserted the personal pronoun "my" underlining the particularity of recall: her concealment, her loss. He has also changed the more particular "desires" to the rather general "days," a revision that underlines the innocence of the youth by distancing us from the nurse; it removes her projected, embittered interpretation already sufficiently suggested by "green and pale." In the end we see the nurse's own thwarted desires and her sexual jealousy, which do not allow her to participate in the joys of youth's days, represented by the "voices of children . . . heard on the green" (*SE*38: 1, E23). Blake's use of "green" ("on the green" and "green and pale") as noun and as adjective within four lines only confirms that he thoroughly understood the determinative power of context in creating both sense and significance in his poetry.

It is also provocative that the only other title in the *Songs of Experience* that duplicates the pattern of "The SICK ROSE" is "A POISON TREE." Both use—and among the *Songs* are distinctive in their use—an adjective with strong negative connotations: "sick" and "poison." Both capitalize the noun and its descriptive adjective. The capitalization emphasizes both the condition and the object infected. Both predicate a condition at the outset by announcing it in the title. But though readers can readily locate the source of poison in the speaker's mind in "A POISON TREE," because the speaker himself does, they resist locating the sickness in the speaker's mind in "The SICK ROSE." Yet "The SICK ROSE" offers another, potentially classic, instance of warped perspective.

Because the speaker of Blake's "LONDON" is often identified with the speaker of "The SICK ROSE," and the speaker of "LONDON" unequivocally identifies with Blake, it is illuminating to compare the strategies and tones of the two poems.[15] It is in the strongly ironic and bitter tone of "LONDON" that readers hear Blake himself as speaker. But the wide-ranging sensibility exhibited there is not present in "The SICK ROSE." The speaker in "LONDON" recognizes the "mind-forg'd manacles" even as the victims he perceives "cry," "sigh," "curse" (*SE*46: 5–9, E27) and thereby blacken, appall, bloody, blast, and blight the landscape. There is outrage in every line of the poem.

"The SICK ROSE," in contrast, seems almost complacent. The speaker is so far distant from, so little anguished by the sickness he relates: "And his dark secret love / Does thy life destroy." However, in Blake's first version of the poem in the manuscripts, lines 7 and 8 read: "O dark secret love / Does life destroy." That version reveals a more immediate anguish in the speaker, who appears there to mark the significance of the sick rose in his own life. Blake's final revision—"And his dark secret love / Does thy life destroy"—by adding personal pronouns preserves, even emphasizes, the distance between speaker and subject established early in the poem. And that preserved distance asks that we turn our attention to the speaker, the heart of the poem's meaning.

These concluding lines to the poem underwent yet another distinctive change before being restored to the version published in the *Songs of Experience*. Blake revised "And his dark secret love / Does thy life destroy" to "And *her* dark secret love / Does thy life destroy" [my italics]. This intermediate revision is provocative because it draws on an alternative tradition of female as snake, as part of a diversion of Satan in the Garden of Eden. The revision shows Blake to be keenly aware of gender in the poem—not identifying the rose but rather the worm as female—which unseats traditional literary assumptions. We can only speculate on why he experimented with the line and change of pronoun by considering how the change affects the poem's meaning. The lines continue to emphasize sexuality, now homosexuality—a lesbian encounter—which the speaker regards with fear and horror as destructive, perhaps because threatening to male sexuality. The change in pronoun suggests, too, an infection of the mind, not only of the body. "Dark secret love" becomes a form of knowledge—and not merely carnal knowledge and physical penetration—but an appropriation of the rose's meaning through interpretation.

Blake's punctuation in the illuminations also supports this reading of the poem. Blake's second line, "The invisible worm," is followed by a period in both the Keynes facsimile (Z copy) and the Erdman *Illuminated Blake* (I copy). Most of Blake's editors emend the punctuation to a comma, but it is interesting to speculate what Blake's intention might have been in following his sentence fragment of article, adjective, noun with a period. In doing so, he gives his second line an equivalent declarative weight to his first—"O Rose thou art sick. / The invisible worm."—and makes "invisible worm" an appositive to the sick rose, an immediate linking of sexuality and disease. He also calls attention to the worm's invisibility, but only the words used to invoke invisibility are visible, not, apparently, the worm itself. Only the interpretation is visible, not the experience on which it is purportedly based.

Finally, Blake's illumination of "The SICK ROSE" supports a new reading. First, the illumination is quite complicated and highly suggestive. Second, there are significant variants in the hand coloring of the design. David Erdman's *Illuminated Blake* uses the I copy but also summarizes variants in the A, B, V, and Y copies. The Keynes facsimile is based on the Z copy. The mere fact of multiple variant finishings feeds my thesis that Blake was experimenting with changing contexts as a part of his meaning.

In both the I and Z copies, the rose is bent down to the ground, but in I it appears opened, in Z closed. The unopened rose of Z is a fully developed bud ready to burst into bloom—the fact that it hasn't bloomed suggests prepubescent innocence. Critics have, however, interpreted this closed flower in another way to support readings that fault the female rose. W. H. Stevenson, for example, states that "the design shows a rose, fully blown yet closed, drooping over, round and beneath the text,"[16] a conclusion that emphasizes the rose's mature and secretive sexuality. It seems a bias on Stevenson's part to be able to decide so confidently from the illustration that the rose is "fully blown yet closed." If we accept the blooming rose of the I copy, which to Erdman confirms the rose's sickness because the rose's "crimson globe is fallen to the ground,"[17] then the sickness visited upon her appears to be what has bowed her, not an inherent aspect of her blooming beauty.

We need not search far for an agent of sickness, because a very visible worm penetrates this rose in both the I and Z copies. In A and B, copies where the worm is not visible, Erdman notes that "it is only our acceptance of the speaker's view that compels this [perception of the 'dark secret love' as vermiform]." The relationship of the speaker and worm in both variations—invisible and visible worm—supports the interpretation above. If the worm is invisible in the illumination, we must question its reality; the rose's sickness, if it in fact exists, has been given an agent by the speaker who, we may argue, projects his own sexual ambivalence onto the rose. If, in contrast, the worm is visible in the illumination, then the speaker's insistence on its invisibility suggests another form of psychological disturbance opposite to projection: an internalizing of the wormlike action and guilt born of so thorough a sympathetic recognition of the worm that the worm actually disappears to the speaker's eyes.

Both the I and Z copies of the illustration depict not only a worm entering the rose but a caterpillar feeding on its leaves and a pensive figure, of ambiguous gender, whose garments wind about the rose so as to be iconographically reminiscent of the serpent. Erdman interprets this figure as a female in a scroll skirt "tangled almost worm-like down the main stem." But the figure could also be male; the ambiguity of this figure's gender supports the ambiguity of the worm's gender as revealed in Blake's textual revisions. Erdman suggests that this prostrate figure has been ravished by the worm "on his way to the open blossom," but that seems a readerly imposition comparable to Stevenson's above. How are we to decide where the worm has been or what is the cause of prostration? Indeed, the illumination at such points is working to make the reader become an increasingly active agent of interpretation, increasingly implicated, like the speaker, in a particular set of patriarchal values.

The caterpillar feeding on the leaf is, Geoffrey Keynes notes, a creature who for Blake "as for the Bible and the Elizabethan poets [is] the symbol of the 'pillager' or despoiler. Elsewhere Blake denoted the 'catterpiller' as the chief enemy of the rose, equating it with the priesthood, who lay their curses on the fairest joys."[18]

The caterpillar's feeding, like the priesthood's in other poems we have mentioned ("The GARDEN of LOVE," "The Human Abstract"), suggests the way in which perspective or interpretation per se destroys or creates evil. The caterpillar, in terms of the second moment of feminist critique, is the speaker's representative in an illustration that circumscribes the rose in phallic assaults, assaults from which her thorns (much mentioned by critics and seemingly so threatening) offer no defense whatsoever. But a physical defense is nothing against the power of the mind. However, lest we circumscribe the caterpillar too narrowly, Erdman opens up this interpretation, suggesting that "caterpillars are also emblems of eternity, reminding us that a worm hidden in secret may be reborn as a boy or girl found," and reminding us that we remain always in an ambiguous realm of interpretation. The only fixity is of fluidity, unstable meanings for the Blakean symbols.

Finally, another figure, ostensibly female, weeps while a female figure, the spirit of the rose or of joy, flees from the rose as the worm penetrates it. Erdman interprets this escaping figure as "the human form of Rose . . . who stretches out her arms possibly in joy, probably in terror: her face usually an enigma." Erdman notes further that "in Y there is no enigma. . . . Her face registers desperation, and we see the sharp proboscis of the worm turning out from below her dress as if about to attack her." This Y variant clearly resolves certain ambiguities of the other hand colorings, and it resolves them in expected ways: the rose feels terror at the worm's assault. Ultimately, Blake found these ambiguities rich enough to preserve in the other copies, refusing the obvious interpretation and opening up others.

The possibility that joy may be escaping, that the face expresses joy, is an image that illustrates another of Blake's notebook lyrics, "Eternity":

> He who binds to himself a joy
> Does the winged life destroy
> But he who kisses the joy as it flies
> Lives in eternity's sun rise.[19]

Blake's rhyme here—joy/destroy—is replicated in "The SICK ROSE." The notebook lyric speaks of two ways of responding to joy—one that is death dealing, the other that is life affirming. For the speaker of "The SICK ROSE" the rose is diseased: "Does thy life destroy." The speaker does not perceive the winged figure of joy escaping. He looks only at the rose and, circumscribing and binding it in his own mind, sees it as diseased; he has, in fact, destroyed it. But the reader, who stands outside the speaker, may see the *"joy as it flies"* and live *"in eternity's sun rise,"* in direct contrast to the speaker's vision, syntactically parallel, of the "invisible *worm* / That *flies in the night* / *In the howling storm"* [my italics].

Harold Bloom describes "The SICK ROSE" as "one of Blake's gnomic triumphs."[20] The triumph, feminist readers conclude, is far more gnomic than Bloom imagines. It is nothing less than a subversion of traditional literary imagery to implicate readers themselves in the speaker's blighting and blasting process. The "mind-forg'd manacles" grip more tightly and more terrifyingly than we are prepared to imagine, and they are not easy to release.

We return, by way of conclusion, to some of the questions raised by yoking the formal method and the feminist perspective. In the third moment, I provide textual evidence for Blake's distance from his speaker and follow this logic to its conclusion. But critics have made the opposite argument, and I face the accusation of having created just another competing argument. But I can make a stronger claim. My conclusion focuses on interpretation—the power of the mind to create and destroy. My formal-feminist critique raises significant questions about the contexts and preconditions for interpretation. The exercise of interpreting one poem has led me to explore grounds for interpretation and to arrive at a new subject: the nature of critical knowledge itself. That is an important end of feminist reading, to raise questions about how and what we know and to keep those questions grounded in a material reality that recognizes the ideological bias of all literature as a source of its artistic power and greatness, an ideological bias that pervades a work's inception, its production, and its critical reception.

Representations of Revolution:
From *The French Revolution*
to *The Four Zoas*

David Aers

This essay offers a critical account of the ways in which Blake represents the processes of radical social transformation in the prophetic books up to and including *The Four Zoas*. Although it draws attention to serious problems and even contradictions in Blake's writing about revolution, the essay meets the poems on grounds they themselves have chosen, sharing their view that the issues involved are fundamental to all projects of human emancipation.

However my reading of Blake differs from Leopold Damrosch's, his recent book voices the kind of involvement Blake's longer poems seek: "As a prophet Blake claims to announce the truth" and it is "important to consider how his poems might be perceived as true by modern readers." "Blake's prodigious genius is evident in the daring with which he attacks the most fundamental problems, and we read him only half-heartedly if we do not respond as human beings to his prophetic demands."[1] Increasingly uncommon as such moral and metaphysical language is in advanced academic criticism, it is appropriate to the claims made by Blake's writings. Their seriousness calls for a critical dialogue; their range, depth, and scope continually raise issues with which many people are still struggling. The subject of the present essay is one of these issues.

My intention is to shift critical preoccupation and mode, a shift in terrain. My own preoccupations, however congruent with some of Blake's, inevitably set out the grounds of the present inquiry. Nevertheless I hope that this critical mode avoids that theoretical imperialism in which the very possibility of hearing the other is denied. In Bakhtin's terms, I hope that the commentary encourages a "dialogic" engagement with a writer whose own texts are so rarely "monologic" and whose work contributes a major critique of "monologism."[2] This is, of course, hardly an unproblematic hope. Even the seemingly anarchic poststructuralism favored in the United States, a display of gamesome signifiers always lacking an "original" or "transcendental signified," even this obsessive linguistic revel habitually manifests a narcissistic imperialism in which the historical moment of the text's production is simply dissolved, the specific questions that moment posed to different individuals, social groups, and ideological formations, solipsistically ignored. Of course, a critical method committed to such systematic amnesia concerning the history of social formations and their political culture is not without its own contemporary political and historical meanings.

Whatever the theoretical and practical difficulties involved in my own method, I would describe its aspirations in the following way, aspirations that are part of a recognizable if loosely defined tradition. It seeks to approach the literary text as a social text created in specific circumstances. These circumstances are not "background," a remote reference point comprising a separate domain of study that can be left to "historians." On the contrary, because these contexts are carried in language they are inscribed in the minute particulars of the texts: they permeate them. No static dualism of literature and "background" can help us understand this situation. Here Bakhtin / Vološinov offers us some relevant reflections as we try to press beyond such dualistic assumptions and the related dualistic construction of "individual" over against "society": "Each person's inner world and thought has its stabilized *social audience* that comprises the environment in which reasons, motives, values and so on are fashioned. . . . In point of fact, *word is a two-sided act.* It is determined equally by *whose* word it is and *for whom* it is meant. As word, it is precisely *the product of the reciprocal relationship between speaker and listener, addresser and addressee.* . . . I give myself verbal shape from another's point of view, ultimately from the point of view of the community to which I belong."[3] In this model language, the construction of social subjects, social experience and politics are indissolubly bound together: "The structure of experience is just as social as is the structure of outward objectification. The degree to which an experience is perceptible, distinct, and formulated is directly proportional to the degree to which it is socially oriented." (87)

The very generation of meaning is bound up with structures of power and control in the community. So is "literature," "criticism," and teaching. Bakhtin / Vološinov's approach transcends the misleading dualisms of literature and background, individual and society, public and private. In the writings we study, the world is mediated, prevalent perceptions reinforced or challenged, contemporary values and problems represented and worked over, a web of discourses engaged with.[4] They were made by actual people in living and complexly diversified relationships created within determinate circumstances and systems (of production, of political order, of sexual organization, of ideology). Any effort to understand a text should include an attempt to re-place it in the web of discourses and social practices where it was made. This helps us pick up the implications of its different voices and modes, helps us grasp what Bakhtin, in *The Dialogic Imagination*, calls their "socio-ideological meaning" in terms of a "knowledge of the social distribution and ordering of all the other ideological voices in the era" (417). A daunting ideal, certainly, but one we should, in my view, at least strive toward.

The method I pursue also seeks to encourage self-reflexivity: an awareness of the theoretical and political premises of our reading, teaching, and scholarly production; an awareness of the ways in which our own moment and the choices we make within it shape our perceptions. All attempts to recover a specific web of discourses and practices in the past take place within our own ideological horizons, which can never be that of the texts we read. We must try to include a reflexivity about our own horizons (not to say Urizen's) in our critical work, articulating as clearly as possible the evaluative criteria and premises of our approaches. In doing this we are less likely to foster a critical imperialism than if we naturalize our approaches. And if the aims of the method I have sketched can exist only in tension, it is an inescapable tension. All our knowing, whether of past or present others, is produced in contingent, social, political, and gender specific circumstances.

The fact that the talented community of Blake scholars have not spent much time worrying at the substantial problems considered in this essay is itself an example of how ideological and political paradigms shape the critical discourses cultivated in the institutions of higher education. Our institutions are privileged parts of capitalist social formations—ones so highly militarized and accustomed to such massive levels of aggression, violence, and fear that they live in perpetual readiness to launch weapons of mass slaughter across the globe. The daily threat of genocide, of holocaust, has become naturalized, celebrated, and multiplied, at unimaginable cost, as a sign of freedom and civilization's strength. Radical social transformation is hardly an issue in Britain and even less so in the United States—except when it rears its rebellious head in countries over which the metropolitan power has a proprietorial interest, economic and military (Nicaragua, Chile). The community of professional critics flourish within, not above, this situation. Our paradigms (selecting basic questions, fields, and methods of inquiry) are affected by their position in such a culture. Our reading of Blake will inevitably bear the mark of that culture, in what is ignored as well as in what is addressed. Recent works like those by Baldick and Lentricchia ought to increase awareness of just how politically and socially determined academic criticism has been, whether in its New Critical, archetypal, structuralist, or deconstructionist phases.[5] Blake's admirers might be especially open to such accounts, for his poetry brings out the political dimensions of writing and reading, of literature and hermeneutics. It encourages a self-reflexivity about the presence of institutional, gender, ideological, and class positions shaping our own outlook and discourse. And it cultivates this self-reflexivity within a revolutionary perspective, an overall commitment to the radical transformation of dominant forms of human social existence as Blake saw them.

In Blake's poetry the development of the human subject depends on a texture of interactions with others, a process quite alien to the dichotomizing categories "individual" and "society" normalized within our traditions of various individualisms. At their happiest, as in the *Songs of Innocence*, human interactions create the mutual trust and security essential to open and responsible people living in peaceful community. In an outstanding book, Heather Glen has recently shown how these *Songs* confront a grimly oppressive reality while simultaneously showing alternative possibilities of being "rooted in some of our actual experiences, yet threatened most immediately by much that we ourselves do."[6] Unless such trust and acknowledgment of mutual dependency can be maintained, we are likely to evolve versions of identity like those Blake figures in Urizen, "Where self sustaining I may view all things beneath my feet" (*FZ*VI:72:24, E349). The sad consequences of this domineering and individualistic form of autonomy Blake explored around Urizen in *The Four Zoas* and returned to in *Jerusalem*.[7]

But the prophetic books become increasingly preoccupied with a possibility not envisaged in the *Songs*. What if the relations within which the human being grows up are not only systematically exploitative but also ones where the ruling class's values have gained such control that they pervade all areas of being? If something like this were to happen then the existing social organization, its institutionalized violence, its cruel forms of work (so powerfully described by Blake), its massive inequalities in access to the resources of material and mental life, its legitimizing ideologies, all this might seem so "natural" as to preclude alternative possibilities of living. If such were the case, leading social groups would have attained a "hegemonic" control.[8] The very construction of subjectivity would be assimilated to this and the most intimate relations between even the exploited would be incorporated.[9] So the relations between chimney sweepers, marvelously described by Heather Glen, might be far more disastrously affected than the *Songs of Innocence* allow. No longer would they include prefigurations of an "alternative possibility" grounded in a "mutually satisfying actuality" within the exploitive violence Blake characterizes so memorably.[10] If, as Blake suggests in *Milton*, "Human Thought is crushd beneath the iron hand of Power" (*M*25:4, E121), and if this state seems pervasive, then Blake would be left with at least three massive problems. First, what relationships can offer the necessary prefigurations for the transformed world? Without such contemporary prefigurations a revolutionary must write the most abstract utopianism, a frivolous activity in itself but dangerous to self and others if it affects consciousness and practice. Second, how can the existing hegemony be dissolved or overthrown, and by whom? This is a crucial question about agency and resources. Third, what explains the revolutionary's genesis if such a hegemony really exists? I will now concentrate on Blake's engagement with these substantial issues in his representations of revolution up to *The Four Zoas*.[11]

In *The French Revolution* Blake projects a fairly simple two-class model. A neo-feudal aristocracy (with a liberal fraction) rules over "the Commons." The poem does refer to cities and villages, to plowmen, peasants, shepherds, husbandmen, soldiers, officers, and bourgeois leaders; it also refers to women and children who seem to constitute a separate domain of decorous passivity. Yet none of these references to people inhabiting thoroughly different situations in the social formation leads to any differentiation of the third estate. Blake settles for the homogenizing language of "the Commons," "the people," and "the Nation."[12] This language enforces the dual-class model and a perception of those in opposition to the traditional ruling class as united bearers of a universal liberation. In doing this Blake swallowed the ideology of one revolutionary group, the bourgeois Jacobins.[13] This encouraged a dissolution of the very different life experiences and politics of peasants, urban artisanate, casual laborers, rioting Parisian women, lawyers, and bureaucrats (key groups in the composition of Jacobinism) and merchants. The consequences were the risk that the text would present experience that no one ever lived, or could live, and ideas no one ever thought, even while it proclaims itself to be a meditation on historical processes and experience.[14]

Perhaps the most troubling difficulties for the revolutionary project the poem espouses can be seen in the oration from the spokesman of "the voice of the people" (*FR*11:206–12; 204, E295–96). Sieyès presents an unequivocally political version of the Fall. Most humans are apparently "bound" in the ruined world, "To wander inslav'd." They are thoroughly passivized: physically intimidated, they are also "deprest in dark ignorance" by their rulers. Such total control would seem fatal to any revolutionary project. The oppressed come "To worship terrors, bred from the blood of revenge and breath of desire," to worship "beastial forms" and "more terrible men." The very forms of desire are incorporated, the energies of the oppressed "madden'd with slavery" and bound into the dominating religious ideology and institutions (*FR*11:211–16, 12:227–28, E295–96). There seem to be no resources within present human relations from which alternative forms of social life might be created. But if this is so, there are no grounds for constructing revolutionary visions and peering beyond the fragments.

The French Revolution, however, moves swiftly from this dismal vision of an "inslav'd" humanity to one of gentle collaboration in which the vicious past is totally transcended (*FR*11:217–12:240, E295–97). Of course, the poem's sharp and witty critique of aristocratic power and religious ideology carries an energy that promises us the traditional state of affairs is not "natural," that things could, surely, be otherwise. But the crucial transition itself is negotiated simply by deploying images from the natural cycle of day succeeding night (*FR*11: 217–12:219, E295–96). "Then" comes the revolutionary transformation (*FR*13:220, 223, E296). But in the contexts Blake has evoked, if the army abandoned the rulers and "blood ran down the ancient pillars" (*FR*13:246, E297), one would have no reason to connect such events with the forms of human emancipation celebrated in Blake's work (as here, *FR*12:220–34, E296). Yet the poem does just this. It figures forth a human regeneration in which "the bottoms of the world were open'd, and the graves of the arch-angels unseal'd," while "the Senate in peace, sat beneath morning's beam" (*FR*16:300–306, E299–300). The use of the passive ("were open'd," "unseal'd") deletes the key agents and contributes to the text's evasion of profoundly troubling questions about revolution it has raised.

Visions of the Daughters of Albion engages with these unresolved issues. The poem opens and closes with the "Enslav'd" daughters totally passivized, their contexts unchanged by the revolutionary Oothoon.[15] In Blake's presentation there is no sign of interaction between the daughters. The slave-owning rapist's claim, picking up an idea noted in *The French Revolution* (*FR*11:215, E296), becomes plausible: the oppressed, "stampt with my signet . . . worship terrors and obey the violent" (*VDA*1:21–23, E46). Oothoon herself appears in peculiar isolation from any reciprocal, sustaining relationships, a version of consciousness that could only foster myths of independent autonomy whose inadequacies Blake's poems have already superseded.[16] It is hardly surprising that the poem offers no way out of the disastrous states it depicts—revolutionary rhetoric in such contexts is both inadequate and inexplicable.

But Blake does not abandon the problems set by the revolutionary social dimensions of his vision. In *America* he figures revolutionary forces in Orc. Those commentators who have emphasized the destructive and dehumanized aspects of Orc in his earliest appearances are certainly correct. He enters with an act of masculine violence that looks much like the rape opening the *Visions*, only now it is glossed with the all-too-familiar male cant that the female really "joy'd" in such violence (*A*2:4, E52). Nothing could be farther from the delicate images of mutuality and trust cultivated in the *Songs of Innocence*. Nor is this observation a naive failure to observe the difference between the world of innocence and experience: it points, rather, to the fact that the "end" is prefigured in the "means." Contrary to some scholars' impressions, it is not merely Urizen who sees Orc as a dehumanized terror. He describes himself as an "eagle screaming in the sky," "a lion / Stalking upon the mountains," a whale lashing the abyss, "a serpent folding" around the female's limbs while he "siez'd" her in his "fierce embrace"; the female sees him as a serpent, eagle, lion, whale, fire, and lightning ($A1$, 2). All these figure domineering, predatory, violently coercive action. They all exclude mutuality, care, and reciprocity, exhibiting a thoroughly macho version of revolutionary force such as Shelley criticized in *Laon and Cythna*. Out of such a process only disaster can emerge.

This the conclusion of *America* seeks to deny. Instead of using the vision of the *Songs* to explore the fatal limitations of the Orc mentality, its *un*revolutionary and very traditional devotion to "masculine" violence, the poem claims that at least the Orcian revolution achieves sexual liberation and gratification ($A15{:}19–26$, E57). In context, however, this is far from plausible. To proclaim that Orcian "fierce desire," echoing the "fierce embrace" of the early rape ($A1{:}10$, 2:1–3, E51–52), unproblematically frees the "desires" of females, leaving them "naked and glowing with the lusts of youth," would seem likely only to those enjoying the sexual fantasies analyzed in Andrea Dworkin's *Pornography: Men Possessing Women*.[17] The revolutionary (or revolutionized!) women have no voices. Although there is expression of pleasure in the body and sexuality, this is defined *for* women by revolutionary man: women exist solely in the domain of masculine (Orcian) sexual desire. Nor should we overlook another peculiarly male feature in this definition, namely, the tendency to treat sexual desire, masculine and feminine, as an autonomous force abstracted from the full human being and the matrix of relationships within which meaningful life can alone be sustained. The concomitant version of human freedom is similarly distorted. It lacks images of relationship, reciprocity, affection, mutual recognition. Others cannot be perceived as subjects or listened to as different voices with whom dialogue is possible. Such considerations help us see the folly of thinking that the violently masculine and traditional-enough forms of desire figured in Orc could contribute to human liberation and joy.[18] *America* actually figures an ominous collusion between Orc and Urizen, the values of masculine, violent revolutionary and masculine, violent conservative. Orc's "cloudy terrors," his "fierce flames" giving "heat but not light" converge with the Urizen depicted in fires, "But no light from the fires" ($U5{:}17$, E73). The flames burning round the thrones and abodes of men at the poem's conclusion cannot figure forth any transcendence of Urizenic forms of life. They can only confirm them.

In *Europe* Blake again concludes with "red" Orc in his "terrible" fury, now joined by the new figure Los who summons "all his sons to the strife of blood" (*Eur*14:37, 15:2, 11, E66). The scene is replete with the violence of war. The only interaction is that in which people reduce each other to threatening objects, things which must be destroyed (*Eur*14:32–15:12, E66). Coming from the writer of the *Songs* this is a peculiar version of radical human transformation, although we recognize its affinity with the end of *America*. It is worth pausing over the contexts of *Europe*'s conclusion, for they increase our understanding of the difficulties now overwhelming Blake's thinking about revolutionary transformations.

The poem offers a strikingly one-dimensional image of the social contexts of the desired revolution. The citizens' senses are "petrify'd against the infinite" (*Eur*10:15, E63). And their thought systematically "Shut up" within the categories of the present order. This generates a religion in which "man became an Angel; / Heaven a mighty circle turning; God a tyrant crown'd" (*Eur*10:1–23, E63). True enough, the youth of England curse the Urizenic order and the ideology of Kings and Priests (*Eur*11:1–5, E64). Nevertheless, they are educated, socialized into this order:

> The youth of England hid in gloom curse the paind heavens; compell'd
> Into the deadly night to see the form of Albions Angel
> Their parents brought them forth & aged ignorance preaches canting,
> On a vast rock, perciev'd by those senses that are clos'd from thought:
> (*Eur*12:5–8, E64)

The last phrase may imply other "senses," but the text shows us no alternatives among the citizens. On the contrary, even when "the flames of Orc" drive "The Guardian of secret codes" from Westminster the author writes this of the citizens:

> Every house a den, every man bound; the shadows are filld
> With spectres, and the windows wove over with curses of iron:
> Over the doors Thou shalt not; & over the chimneys Fear is written:

With bands of iron round their necks fasten'd into the walls
The citizens: in leaden gyves the inhabitants of suburbs
Walk heavy: soft and bent are bones of villagers
(*Eur*12:26–31, E64)

This completes a moving and particularized image of a desolately one-dimensional society in which Urizen's codes and practices dominate all domains of life. But once again it evokes the question emerging from *The French Revolution:* if this is anything like an adequate representation of people's experience, practices, and relations, then should not Blake abandon his vision of revolution and his model of humanity, which assumes possibilities of major transformation from the present reality? For the account leaves no spaces in which a counterculture can be created, no agents who might make alternative forms of relations and ideas, and certainly no prefigurations of the regenerate society. Without these it was perhaps inevitable that Blake's representations of revolutionary processes should become as undifferentiated and desocialized as those concluding *Europe* (*Eur*14:37–15:11, E66).

I will now move to *The Four Zoas,* a poem that opens by emphasizing the inseparability of human identity and fulfillment from community and active relationship (*FZ*I:3:4–6, E300–301). In such a perspective as that of the *Songs,* individual development and morality depend on human interdependence, the interplay of self and others, trust, cooperation. Yet the long poem concentrates on psychic fragmentation and the interlockings of many kinds of exploitation, mutual fear, and violence in a recognizably capitalist society dominated by Urizen's values. It focuses on the appalling "torments of Love & Jealousy" (E300), evoking a world in which sexual and family relations are a site of destructive conflict. Human cruelty and fiercely defended ideological delusions that encourage it are presented with great depth and connectedness. The resulting range of human suffering is sharply and compassionately realized. But the very power of this achievement and the nightmarishly totalizing effect of Blake's vision foregrounds fundamental problems we encountered in the earlier prophetic books.

To recapitulate the basic problem: if humans have produced a world such as Blake describes, where are the sources of radical transformation intrinsic to the projects of all reformers, let alone revolutionaries? No more do we meet the models of benevolent interaction generated in the *Songs* than we did in *America* and *Europe*. Indeed, echoes of those lyrics in *The Four Zoas* seem to yield up their vision as the product of "the shadows of Tharmas & of Enion in Valas world," as the compensatory, desocialized, and almost solipsistic fantasies of "sleepers entertaind upon the Couches of Beulah / When Luvah & Vala were closd up in their world of shadowy forms" (*FZIX*:131:19–22, E400).[19] As for Orc, Blake is now totally clear that the forms of life he figures do not offer any resources for breaking through the disastrous present.[20] On the contrary his energetic activity merely makes Babylon stronger (*FZVII*[a]:80:30, 44–48, E356). The poem now acknowledges explicitly that Orcian rebellion involves profound collusion with the dominant Urizenic reality, its assumptions, values, and practices.

Nor does the poem present the sphere of work as prefiguring human liberation, whether in development of material forces promising an end to the reign of scarcity over the majority of people or in the forms of organization working people might evolve in the face of their employers. Unlike many pre-Marxist and Marxist radical traditions, Blake's poem does not see the forces and relations of production as decisive areas in the desired transformation of the social formation and the forms of human life it makes possible.[21] Night II does, of course, concentrate on the labor processes with the kinds of pain and domination they incorporate. But they are represented in a way that denies the existence of significant working-class struggles and their potential for change. The "Human Imagination" is apparently turned to stone (*FZII*: 25:6, E314), while "Multitudes without number work incessant." The poetry evokes a state of dehumanizing labor under the "care & power & severity" of Urizen, "the great Work master" (*FZII*:28–32, E318–21).[22] As we are shown "many a net / Spread & many a Spirit caught, innumerable the nets / Innumerable the gins & traps," the poetry invites us to trace the weave of the nets (*FZII*:29:16–30:2, E319). We are led to connect the destructive processes of labor with the possessive individualism fostered in the capitalist society Blake inhabited, with the forms of education, with ruling scientific ideology, with militarism, with orthodox Christianity and the "moral" framework it supported. For the workers, the nets, gins, and traps seem to define existence. The famous passage on alienated labor, which Blake liked well enough to write into *Jerusalem* (plate 65), confirms the sense of how closed the system is, how lacking in the potential for emancipatory change:

They forgd the sword the chariot of war the battle ax
The trumpet fitted to the battle & the flute of summer
And all the arts of life they changd into the arts of death
The hour glass contemnd because its simple workmanship
Was as the workmanship of the plowman & the water wheel
That raises water into Cisterns broken & burnd in fire
Because its workmanship was like the workmanship of the
    Shepherd
And in their stead intricate wheels invented Wheel without wheel
To perplex youth in their outgoings & to bind to labours
Of day & night the myriads of Eternity. that they might file
And polish brass & iron hour after hour laborious workmanship
Kept ignorant of the use that they might spend the days of wisdom
In sorrowful drudgery to obtain a scanty pittance of bread
In ignorance to view a small portion & think that All
And call it Demonstration blind to all the simple rules of life
(*FZ*VII[b]:92:19–33, E364)

Characteristic of Blake's writing about labor in the prophetic books, this offers no grounds for cultivating ideas about a revolutionary working class, the privileged bearers of human emancipatory potential. Far from it, the vision here is of a working class assimilated to evolving capitalist production processes. The workers are represented as quietly accepting the degrading specialization imposed on them, accepting the new industrial discipline and its control of human time;[23] they accept the constitution of themselves and their labor power as a commodity for exchange on a market structured according to the employers' interests. The production processes become "arts of death" (foreshadowing our own industrial-military fusion), but such is the workers' assimilation that they can be persuaded to abandon all concern with the nature of the products they themselves make. Such incorporation in the system negates any possibility that the workers might grasp the totality within which they are exploited and that they actually construct. Even more starkly does it negate hope that the producers might create forms of association through which they can take control of the means, modes, and ends of production, reorganizing them to benefit the physical and mental life of all rather than of the privileged, powerful minority, Urizen's sons. Indeed, the working people are figured as not even offering *any* resistance.

Los too mostly internalizes the dominant practices and ideologies in the culture.[24] For example, in Night IV Blake reworks the *Book of Urizen* showing the attempts of the "Prophet of Eternity" to control Urizen:

> Pale terror siezd the Eyes of Los as he beat round
> The hurtling Demon. terrifid at the shapes
> Enslavd humanity put on he became what he beheld
> He became what he was doing he was himself transformd
> (*FZ*IV:55:20–24, E338)

As Blake had emphasized earlier in Night IV (*FZ*IV:53:23–24, E336), Los assimilates his Urizenic contexts and pays the penalty of fighting Urizen on his own ground, in his own modes. The defensive rage and fear, the frenetic attempt to bind down Urizen by force, involves a collusion with Urizen's fundamental assumptions. In this collusion Los's potential for creating alternative possibilities is "transformd," assimilated to the culture he would oppose and change. Aggressive practices, grounded in well-justified fear of the threatening other, transform consciousness and potential. We have seen how Orc's activity is represented within a similar configuration, one the poem continually repeats, fascinated at the way opposition to Babylon is so often mounted in forms that share much with its basic foundations and actually perpetuate it. We are pushed to agree with the narrator that the "fetters" of humans in Urizen's world "grew from the soul" (*FZ*VI:71:11, E348). Once more we encounter the citizens bound with mind-forged manacles in a manner that negates the qualifying dialectic of voices and interactions so movingly created in the *Songs*. Now, the text insists, Urizen gains "a New Dominion over all his sons & Daughters / & over the Sons & daughters of Luvah" (*FZ*VI:73:24–25, E350).

Perhaps this is what makes even Urizen a pitiful ruler. He too is seen as victim of the disastrous hegemony he has done so much to produce, a hegemony that joins rulers, would-be revolutionaries or prophets, and productive workers (*FZ*VI:70:39–45, E347; *FZ*VI:71:13–14, E348; *FZ*VI:72:22–39, E349). Urizen is himself subject to his own cruel web:

> Travelling thro darkness & whereever he traveld a dire Web
> Followd behind him as the Web of a Spider dusky & cold

> Shivering across from Vortex to Vortex drawn out from his
>   mantle of years
> A living Mantle adjoind to his life & growing from his Soul
> (*FZ*VI:73:31–34, E350)

Toward the end of *The Book of Urizen* this web is described as made of twisted cords, knotted meshes, "twisted like to the human brain," and it is called, "The Net of Religion" (*U*25:21–22, E82). The depiction in the later poem also makes clear that the web figures the way Urizen naturalizes the dominant practices and ideologies of the culture he rules: they take on an existence autonomous of his will and, like his workers, he becomes the victim of his own product (*FZ*VIII:100:30–34, E373). The web also symbolizes the disastrous transformation of human interconnectedness, interdependence, without which none can survive, into traps, a predatory world.

Once more we reach the impasse described earlier in my discussions of *The French Revolution* and *Europe*. If such a hegemonic order exists, if human work, imagination and relationships are as deformed as *The Four Zoas* suggests, then we have no hopes for the radical transformation of what is recognizably Blake's society and recognizably ours, one launched on a genocidal and suicidal path.[25] Blake's own revolutionary project, his continuing call to build Jerusalem, "called Liberty," now and "in hope," his prophetic and visionary stance, becomes a self-deceptive irrelevance (*J*54:5, E203; *J*12:43–44, E156).

The Four Zoas, however, does not acknowledge the corner into which humanity has painted itself, by the poem's own account. Instead, the long final Night reaffirms the revolutionary project of human liberation. It denies the consequences entailed by the poem's version of hegemonic order, the consequences of victims' propensity to internalize its values and become resigned, incorporated. In itself, Night IX has received great scholarly admiration. According to the immensely influential Northrop Frye, "There is nothing like the colossal explosion of creative power in the ninth night of *The Four Zoas* anywhere else in English poetry"; while to the almost as influential Harold Bloom, this Night is "the most poetically successful section of *The Four Zoas*, and taken by itself is one of Blake's most remarkable achievements."[26] High claims. Yet writers differ over the basic issue of what is being figured in Night IX. Some have claimed that it celebrates the "spiritual resurrection after death," a turning away from history to an "other-

worldly fulfilment."[27] More have more wisely attended to the "star-
tlingly literal . . . realistic scenes . . . in which the oppressed take
vengeance on their dethroned oppressor," although some of these, perhaps anticipating the emphasis of the later *Jerusalem*, have found the
vengeance "out of keeping with the theme of spiritual regeneration
predicated on forgiveness," or even as a mark of Blake's "sadistic
fantasy."[28] Most, however, have seen such features as inevitable revolutionary means to achieve the desired social transformation: "the whole
groaning Universe bursts its chains and explodes, releasing all the oppressed . . . Now is unchained the terrible democracy of Blake's apocalypse against Kings, Warriors, Priests and Merchants, . . . a brief
but violent dictatorship not only of the child-bearers (proletariat) but
the children themselves, the child laborers of street and mill" establishing a "thoroughgoing democracy."[29] Similarly, "the emphasis on work,
brotherhood and cooperation in Night IX links up with the rise of
utopian socialism during the period; and hence with more practical,
if no less utopian attempts at making such millenarian visions a reality."[30] Or, in a more psychologizing but congruent mode: "Night IX
shows us an expansion of consciousness beyond the limits of the self
and of orthodox reality, its commitment to the discovery and the building of a new age for all men, the restoration of its connections with
loins, emotions, what we would call the unconscious."[31] A grand vision,
certainly, but as one scans the scholarly industry on Blake it seems increasingly implausible to assert that "to anyone who has read through
the preceding Nights of this marvellous poem with sympathetic understanding, the events of the apocalypse will perhaps be clear enough."[32]
One of my aims here is to show how the different kinds of "clarity"
proposed by scholars involve critical oversight of problems in Blake's
poem, oversight that is, as so often, not without its ideological and political dimensions.

Night IX has several revolutionary surges, making use of the apocalyptic language traditionally deployed by Christians working and hoping
for radical change in their cultures. As much recent work has amply
illustrated, both in relation to the seventeenth century and to Blake's
period, this language is replete with political meanings in a culture
where religious discourse was pervasive.[33] In the first surge:

The thrones of Kings are shaken they have lost their robes &
    crowns

> The poor smite their opressors they awake up to the harvest
> The naked warriors rush together down to the sea shore
> Trembling before the multitudes of slaves now set at liberty
> They are become like wintry flocks like forests stripd of leaves
> The opressed pursue like the wind there is no room for escape
> (*FZ*IX:117:18–23, E387)

We earlier recalled that in the *Songs* Blake discloses how human fulfillment depends on mutual trust, security, and kind reciprocity. In *The Four Zoas* he substitutes an oppressively one-dimensional version of Urizenic hegemony for the possibilities found within the "fallen" world of the *Songs*. Now he represents the transcendence of this hegemony through the extremely violent collective action of the "oppressed." Only in such revolutionary practice will the "living flames winged with intellect," the "mental fire" and the "bright visions of Eternity" burst forth (*FZ*IX:119:19, E388):

> And all the while the trumpet sounds from the clotted gore & from
>   the hollow den
> Start forth the trembling millions into flames of mental fire
> Bathing their limbs in the bright visions of Eternity
> (*FZ*IX:118:17–19, E387)

Again the retributory violence is stressed: "Their opressors are falln they have Stricken them" (*FZ*IX:118:24, E387). The young Marx too thought that "The coincidence of the changing of circumstances and of human activity or self-changing can only be grasped and rationally understood as revolutionary *practice*," and classical Marxism argues that the ruling class apparatus of violent oppression means that, in the end, "revolutionary *practice*" entails armed struggle.[34]

Nevertheless the passages just quoted from Night IX raise more difficulties than Blake and his commentators acknowledge. Typical of approaches found in the latter is Northrop Frye's: "Suddenly revolution breaks out. When one is falling over an abyss in a nightmare, the body gives a self-protective jerk and the abyss vanishes as the mind wakes up. And when a revolution begins, whatever may happen to it eventually there is one breathless moment, just as the old tyranny comes crashing down, in which we become aware that we have bound ourselves to observe the rules of a foolish and evil game that we are not obliged to play."[35] In such commentary social, political, and economic processes are blandly ignored, the complex web of interlocking human agents and their diverse experiences dissolved. A comfortable "we" is posed as part of the "revolution" and yet in a peculiarly spectatorial, cozily aloof space. Such conventional-enough approaches ignore crucial issues in which literary and political dimensions are fused. How have the "poor" and "oppressed," the "trembling millions" achieved the collective consciousness and organization that enables them to "smite" and overthrow "their oppressors"? As I have shown, the poem's treatment of the oppressed, in and out of work, male and female, gives no hints of the potential that could lead to such an achievement. Quite the contrary. We have seen how laboring people of "wondrous power spent their lives" creating altars on which they are the victims (*FZII:30: 35–40, E320*). We have been shown states of anguished fragmentation, despair, and collusion in which the fetters imposed from without become the mind-forged manacles shaping every act of opposition by the fettered, making, I observed, Babylon stronger. Though the preceding Night does include attempts by Los and Enitharmon to deliver people from Urizen's webs, it too stresses the "warlike preparations" and organized violence of the ruler (*FZVII:101:26, E373, and see FZVII: 100, 102, E372–75*). Nor is this surprising, for like Night VII[b], Night VIII mediates European militarization and the effects of sustained war from 1792 up to 1815.[36] The poem's own representation of the "oppressed" undermines any attempt to imagine them initiating a revolutionary strike against the massed forces of Urizen. Are they not themselves part of his forces, assimilated? Are they not presented in a way that makes them more plainly part of the problem than its solution? Indeed, in the quotation above (*FZIX:117:21*), Blake's language seems to acknowledge his difficulties in this area. For as we found at a key point in *The French Revolution*, the poet uses the passive voice with a particular effect: in "the multitude of slaves now set at liberty," the verb concedes the helpless dependency of the supposedly revolutionary agents. It deletes the decisive, apparently liberating agent, and with this the vital processes of emancipation, while still asserting liberation and going on to treat "the multitude" as a self-organizing collective agent. This syntactic registering of a major problem is not, however, made a topic for reflection. But that is no good reason for criticism to uncritically pass over such crucial political and literary difficulties.

There is another substantial problem in the Night's representation of revolution that has also, I think, been ignored by scholars. It too we encountered in the much earlier *French Revolution*—namely, the homogeneity of the key social categories and the consequences of this choice. The main terms for those who smite the ruling classes are "the poor," "the opressed," and the "multitude" (e.g. *FZIX*:117:19, 23, E387; *FZIX*:123:8, E392). Such language fails to engage with the immense diversity of social situations and experience in Blake's England—let alone the "Universe," which the poet and his rather Eurocentric critics assume to be involved in this revolution. This diversity is of the greatest significance for those thinking, like Blake, of radical social change, its possibilities, forms and, perhaps, limits. Blake's categories serve only to obscure this. We need to try to recall something of what is being obscured, however briefly. The "opressed" in Blake's London endured very different forms of oppression to agrarian laborers or to the emerging industrial working class of the mills, iron works, and mines. Their culture and organizations were also very different.[37] It never was at all clear whether such sharp cultural and economic divisions could be overcome. Even within London there was massive and politically decisive diversity. Thanks to the relevant parts of E. P. Thompson's wonderful (but mistitled) *Making of the English Working Class,* we are not unfamiliar with the respectable London artisanate who created the London Corresponding Society (LCS), read Paine, and developed the radical religious and political traditions that flowered in Blake's milieu.[38] Are these among Blake's "poor," "opressed," "multitudes" smiting their "opressors"? Probably—although it is not easy to see Hardy and the LCS in this language. But London was also, as Blake's own poems often powerfully remind us, a city of unskilled workers dependent on a casual and seasonal labor market, a city of servants, beggars, and street sellers, Mayhew's London. The division between artisan culture and the poorer, really dispossessed working people was as sharp as that between the artisanate and the affluent bourgeoisie. Differences in life experience, values, expectations, and politics are, it needs stressing, of fundamental importance to those with projects like Blake's. They emerge plainly in studies of London.[39] Gareth Steadman Jones writes about the absence of political traditions among London's poorer citizens, the absence of artisanate concerns with increasing democracy and with Paineite reason. For them, key experiences were the overwhelming struggle to get enough to eat, their marginal hold on employment, the ever-pressing fear of starvation, sickness, age, the workhouse, the endless cycle of hardship. Among these groups a general hostility to the rich emerged in occasional outbursts when contexts they had not contributed to making allowed a brief attack on sections of the wealthy—Jones mentions the Gordon Riots, the 1795 Mobbing of the King, the 1816 Spa Field Riot, the Caroline Riots of 1820, the Reform Riots of 1832. And he writes persuasively of the "tangible and short-term" motivations of those dependent on the casual labor market:

> The ever-pressing demands of the stomach, the chronic uncertainty of employment, the ceaselessly shifting nature of the casual labour-market, the pitiful struggle of worker against worker . . . the arbitrary sentence of destitution and the equally arbitrary cascade of charity provided no focus for any lasting growth of collective loyalty. . . . Among such a population the new political philosophies forged by the French Revolution and the advent of industrial capitalism could find only the shallowest of roots.[40]

No one more powerfully than Blake himself fused pity and critical intelligence in writing about those engulfed in this social matrix, compelled to labor upon a crust of bread by soft mild arts, by manipulations of political economy and by more naked coercion (*FZVIII*:80: 9–21, E355; *L*6–7, E68–69). Despite this, his approach in Night IX manifests an abstractionism that makes serious attention to others impossible. The chosen categories tend to dissolve the diverse existence of others, drown their voices, substitute monologue for dialogue. The kind of imaginative, linguistic, and distinctively political failure here is recurrent in our radical traditions and deserves sustained historical examination into the present. It is a failure that disables Blake's attempt to represent collective human activity and revolutionary potentials.[41]

This judgment is reinforced as Night IX develops its representation of revolutionary action, action that is an integral part of the movement to the human fulfillment celebrated at the poem's close. There "Man walks forth from midst of the fires the evil is all consumd"; the Earth becomes a gamesome place where the seeds of life grow, the "war of swords" superseded by "intellectual War," the "dark Religions" superseded by "sweet Science" (*FZIX*:138:22–32, E406; *FZIX*:139:1–3, 7–9, E407). Though the quotations above from commentators show a consensus that the Night's movement to this exhilarating consummation is imaginatively satisfying and coherent, my own observations so far suggest that such a consensus rests on poor foundations. Nor does the poetry following the passages I have discussed do much to revise the kind of arguments I have made. In fact it *adds* to the problems. Perhaps a question quite in accord with Blake's own sense of his task can help focus on these. Are the kinds of human organization that might emerge from the actions figured in Night IX adequately represented by the Night's exuberant and consoling close? Addressing the question helps us attend to the imaginative modes of Night IX, their moral and political, their real human implications.

Passages already quoted (*FZIX*:117, 118) reflect the level of violence the Night envisages, and this aspect is remorselessly expanded. The "mighty multitude rage furious" and "rend limb from limb the Warrior & the tyrant" while the ghastly history of ruling class violence is paid in its own coin—"The Prisoner answers you scourgd my father to death. . . . So speaking he dashd him [the Judge] with his foot." Such violence, totally understandable, mirrors the mentality and practices of the "opressors." In Blake's terms it reflects Orc's assimilation to Urizen. The absence of any of the sustaining qualities celebrated in the *Songs of Innocence*, an absence fatal to any hopes of regeneration (as the *Songs of Experience* imply), should neither be ignored nor treated as inconsequential.[42] For the real meaning of the violence pervading the Night's representations of revolution is brilliantly grasped by a young Christian and communist contemporary of Blake: "We should be cautious how we indulge even the feelings of virtuous indignation. Indignation is the handsome brother of Anger and Hatred. . . . Let us beware that we continue not the evils of tyranny when the monster shall be driven from the earth. . . . Let us beware . . . lest when we erect the temple of Freedom we but vary the stile of architecture, not change the materials [of the temple of tyranny—i.e., "human skulls and cemented with human blood"].[43] Young Coleridge, for he is the writer, takes us toward a revolutionary perspective from which the exterminist course of Anglo-American culture becomes visible. This perspective is outside the world of Paineite Jacobinism and Burkean conservatism, a world where apparent oppositions conceal a shared set of fundamental assumptions—friendship.[44] Blake's own writing, like Shelley's, is often preoccupied with the insight Coleridge evokes, but this perspective is absent from the representation of revolution in Night IX.

Indeed, there are further aspects to the violence that scholars, perhaps deadened to their implications by our own culture, tend to over-look. It is surely rather bizarre to imagine a violent militaristic ruler (dominating psychic and social orders) being converted, made regenerate, by someone's "wrath" and threats of being cast out "into the indefinite / Where nothing lives." Yet so salvific is violence in Night IX that this is how the poem depicts Urizen's transformation (*FZIX*: 120:13–47, E389–90; *FZIX*:121–22, E390–92). And it pervades the ensuing mediation of revolutionary labor. We might expect the images of "rural work" (*FZIX*:124:6–21, E393) to represent the transcendence of the Urizenic labor processes described in Nights II and VII[b], to suggest some form of collaborative, mutually caring, and responsible production relations. What we get, however, is something far removed from this. The regenerate Urizen wields plow, seed, and harrow and his sons prepare the harvest (*FZIX*:124:6–125:25, E393–94). After the passage describing and placing the pastoral visions of "the sleepers who rested . . . closed up in their world of shadowy forms," Urizen begins harvesting.[45] The harvest, "the human harvest" (*FZIX*:131:39, 40, E400), is reaped by Urizen and his sons:

> The sickle Urizen took the scythe his sons embracd
> And went forth & began to reap & all his joyful sons
> Reapd the wide Universe & bound in Sheaves a wondrous harvest
> They took them into the wide barns with loud rejoicings & triumph
> (*FZIX*:132:5–8, E400)

The "multitudes," the agents of revolutionary practice, are now represented as utterly passive. Human interactions, dialogue and creativity are eliminated.[46] Instead we encounter an uncritical reproduction of coercive hierarchy and violence. Perhaps one reason why commentators pass by such features so blithely is that they identify themselves with the active, sickle-wielding males rather than with the mass of humanity homogenized into the figure of the harvest being reaped and bound up. In a fuller study it will be worth examining the factors that make it seem so natural to those of us within the privileged institutions of higher education in advanced capitalist and imperialist societies to read in this way. It is at least a topic worthy of reader reception theorists! Certainly there is no justification for readers to assume an identification with the active elite in texts like this.

In the present essay it must suffice to note how supposedly revolutionary practices have reproduced the earlier versions of collective passivization, in *The Four Zoas* and the prophetic books discussed earlier. Once more the absence of caring, responsive human interaction makes hopes for radical transformations both abstract and contradictory. Yet the poet continues to emphasize these disabling features, showing how "all Nations were threshed" and "Tossed . . . like Chaff" (*FZIX*:134:1–4, E402). Agency is extrinsic to the peoples supposedly involved in revolutionary transition. It is impossible to distinguish their situation and forms of life from the worst days of compulsory Urizenic labor. In both eras they are reduced to objects. No figuration could more successfully stifle our ability to imagine associating, interacting, positively interdependent human beings. The poet, however, insists that this process liberates both the "slave grinding at the mill" and "the inchaind soul," setting the "good of all the Land" before the formerly exploited and repressed (*FZIX*:134:18–135:3, E402–3). He even increases the violence with the vintage imagery from Revelation 14:

> Into the wine presses of Luvah howling fell the Clusters
> Of human families thro the deep. the wine presses were filld
> The blood of life flowd
> (*FZIX*:135:36–38, E404)

This adds another dimension. In the harvesting imagery there is no attempt to imagine the responses of the allegorical sheaves being sickled by Urizen and his sons; here Blake rectifies that silence by giving the allegorical grapes, the "human families," a voice. But the rectification makes it still harder to see how "human families" and their communities could possibly produce fuller and more loving lives through enduring such treatment: "in the Wine presses is wailing terror & despair" (*FZIX*:136:5, E404).

Not that this has bothered commentators who so often write about such passages in this idiom: "the vintage is at once a Dionysiac orgy of rebirth, the European war of Blake's age, and the self-immolation of the natural man."[47] Only the unexamined prejudices of those thriving in such a fundamentally violent culture as ours could explain how apparently sane people assume that the violence figured in Blake's poem and the destruction of "European war" could have anything to do with "rebirth." There is no difference between the "sharp hooks" used by the sons of Urizen in Night IX (*FZIX*:135:6, E403) and the "hooks" used in Urizen's "ranks of war" in Night VIII (*FZVIII*:102:16,

E374)—at least for the victims! Blake, like many commentators, seems for the moment to have forgotten the truth Anna Wickham recalled: "Of all pain, birth pains have an immediate justification. At the end of labour there is a child, but at the end of a crucifixion there is as likely to be a devil as a God."[48]

It is worth reemphasizing that Blake did not deny the pain inflicted on the human families in this revolution:

> But in the Wine Presses the Human Grapes Sing not nor dance
> They howl & writhe in shoals of torment in fierce flames consuming
> In chains of iron & in dungeons circled with ceaseless fires
> In pits & dens & shades of death in shapes of torment & woe
> The Plates the Screws and Racks & Saws & cords & fires & floods
> The cruel joy of Luvahs daughters lacerating with knives
> And whip[s] their Victims
> (*FZIX*:136:21–27, E404)

The links of this revolution to the violence of war in Night VIII are again clear. There Blake shows the violence as "Cruelty" in diverse forms that destroy bodies and "grate the soul into destruction" (*FZ* VIII:102, E374–75). Here the exaltation involves "cruel joy," and the "Human" experience is one of sheer "torment."[49] Plausibly enough, the forces of Luvah begin "to torment one another and to tread / The weak" (*FZIX*:137:20–21, E405). Urthona thrusts the human harvest into "his rumbling Mills":

> Terrible the distress
> Of all the Nations of Earth ground in the Mills of Urthona
>
> And Men are bound to sullen contemplations in the night
> Restless they turn on beds of sorrow. in their inmost brain
> Feeling the crushing Wheels they rise they write the bitter words
> Of Stern Philosophy & knead the bread of knowledge with tears
>   & groans
> (*FZIX*:138:2–15, E406)

This repeats patterns already described: a homogenous and passivized community, a violent regenerative agent acting from above, and acknowledgment that the supposedly revolutionary people are still victims enduring unbearable distress. Yet Blake refuses to represent the disastrous consequences all this entails for his revolutionary project, its fundamental categories and models of society. Instead he writes the beautiful and famous celebratory conclusion referred to earlier (*FZIX*: 138:20–139:10, E406–7).

Nothing, however, could be in sharper contradiction to the implications of Night IX than this lovely conclusion. The combination of massive violence with a total absence of affective human interactions, caring mutuality and kindness, can lead only to holocaust. The forms of life and practice Blake represents in Night IX can never be a model for the claimed regeneration beyond "evil" (*FZIX*:138:22, E406). On the contrary they collapse into those powerful myths about regeneration through violence, myths so brilliantly analyzed by Richard Slotkin and whose appalling effects in our culture have encouraged the most self-righteously genocidal action from the seventeenth century to the United States' recent wars in Asia and Central America, myths now threatening our survival as a species.[50]

I will conclude by suggesting that *The Four Zoas does* very briefly evoke possibilities of revolutionary transformation that break with these myths and evokes entirely different models to the ones found in Night IX. The pity is, however, these possibilities are not explored in the poem and are simply ignored in the final Night.[51] The location I have in mind is the conclusion to Night VII.[52] Here Blake concentrates on the antagonistic relations between Los, Enitharmon, and his Spectre. Despite the antagonisms, human experience is not represented as locked within a closed hegemonic order. In the torments of love, jealousy, delusory ideologies and the nightmare of past conflicts, Los comes to feel pity (*FZVII*:85:28, E367). This also involves accepting his Spectre, the "ravening devouring lust continually / Creating & devouring (*FZVII*:84:37–38, E360), as his own self, not a vicious other he can hold responsible for evil:

> Los embracd the Spectre first as a brother
> Then as another Self; astonishd humanizing & in tears
> In Self abasement Giving up his Domineering lust
> (*FZVII*:85:29–31, E367)

This is an extraordinarily moving moment and it challenges the very framework of the terrible conflicts and states (social and psychic) refracted in the poem. No longer colluding with Urizen and his methods, Los now feels "a World within / Opening its gates" and determines to "quell my fury & teach / Peace to the Soul of dark revenge & repentance to Cruelty" (*FZVII*:86:4–12, E368). The contrast with the supposedly revolutionary processes and assumptions informing Night IX could not be starker. Nor does Blake sentimentally pretend that Los's radical change of feeling and orientation guarantees anything. At first Enitharmon, not surprisingly, rejects his move as a delusory one in a Urizenic (Hobbesian) world where:

> Life lives upon Death & by devouring appetite
> All things subsist on one another thenceforth in Despair
> (*FZVII*:87:19–20, E369)

But Los, renouncing his earlier violence against her, perseveres, and Enitharmon joins in collaborative work, striving to "fabricate embodied semblances" that will suggest alternative possibilities of life for those in a world dominated by the collusion between Orc and Urizen.[53]

Blake's model here rejoins the vision of the *Songs of Innocence*: within Urizen's world even more affective, caring forms of life actually exist (and not only in fetishized textual play, self-referential linguistic revels) and it is these that hold the potential for the revolutionary transformations at the center of Blake's projects. Revolutionary values are grounded and cherished in the most intimate and trusting personal relations:

> But Los loved them & refusd to Sacrifice their infant limbs
> And Enitharmons smiles & tears prevaild over self protection
> They rather chose to meet Eternal death than to destroy
> The offspring of their Care & Pity
> (*FZVII*:90:50–54, E371)

Nothing could be farther from the representations of revolution in Night IX *or* from the representations of culture and society as closed one-dimensional systems that we encounter so often in the prophetic books of the 1790s. The parent-laborers bring the values and emotional experiences of the *Songs of Innocence* into the world of Urizenic experience as they evoke and enact an ethic of care and affection. Once again Blake stresses there is no guarantee that this will permeate and transform human reality. Los and Enitharmon have to abandon "self protection" to *risk* everything. Yet the risk is not taken at the dictate of some abstract moral system, not with an eye on the orders and re-

wards of the deity. Grounded on particular desires for nurturing relationships within Urizen's world, the activity is quite alien to the "impersonal" commandments of Urizenic law. Blake's hope here is that
through such practice the terrible destruction of human life, made inevitable by Urizenic assumptions (whether in their leftist or rightist
modalities), can be checked and superseded. He imagines an outcome
in which Los finds his enemy in his hands:

> he wonderd that he felt love & not hate
> His whole soul loved him he beheld him an infant
> Lovely breathd from Enitharmon he trembled within himself
> (*FZ*VII: 90:65–67, E371)

Blake writes not that Urizen becomes an infant, but that Los beheld
him so—perhaps sharing the vision that every criminal was once an
infant love,[54] the perception of potential in others cherished by the
Quakers in our culture, by Gandhian traditions in Hindu culture. The
forms of perception here are truly revolutionary: they avoid both
the profoundly misleading figuration of society as a one-dimensional
homogeneous mass, *and* they avoid the related contradictions of Night
IX traced in this essay, contradictions all too familiar within radical
politics.

The espousal of violence in Night IX is bound up with the despairing sense of Urizenic hegemony and mass passivization I have
outlined. It is part of an abstract utopianism that falsifies the diversity
of the problematic, dismal-enough present, and surrenders it to some
putative future to be won by the violent processes just described. This
utopianism participates in the mentality allegedly abandoned by the converted Urizen, a mentality that fails to grasp that the desired "futurity
is in this moment," or probably not at all (*FZ*IX:121:3–22, E390).
Perhaps another way of writing about the differences between the vision and assumptions at the close of Night VIII[a] and the representation of revolution in Night IX might be in the terms of Carol Gilligan's
wonderful study, *In a Different Voice*. Night IX, with the version of
society, power and relationships it assumes, lacks what Gilligan describes as "contextual particularity." This alone allows us: "the understanding of cause and consequence which engages the compassion
and tolerance repeatedly noted to distinguish the moral judgments of
women. Only when substance is given to the skeletal lives of hypothetical people is it possible to consider the social injustice that their moral

problems may reflect and to imagine the individual suffering their occurrence may signify or their resolution engender."[55]

The representation of revolution in Night IX, and the associated
contexts discussed in this essay, is characterized by an absence of such
"contextual particularity," such human "substance." This involves a
failure that is imaginative, moral, and, profoundly so, political. It contrasts with the achievement of the *Songs,* the close of Night VII and
much in Blake's writing,[56] writing that at its best helps us give "substance" and social scope to Gilligan's claim: "The truths of relationship, however, return in the rediscovery of connection, in the realization that self and other are interdependent and that life, however valuable in itself, can only be sustained by care and relationships" (127).
The dynamics she describes, fostered elsewhere in Blake, are crushed
in Night IX and the representations of revolution and society analyzed
above. Their crushing gives the lie to all claims that we are reading
a vision of revolutionary regeneration. It is the close of Night VII
that figures a radical transformation of subjectivity and social practice, a transformation without which the survival of our species is now
barely imaginable. There Blake figures an ethic of care, a commitment
to evolve a trust of the other, an abandonment of domination in the
quest for a community that will overcome destructive aggression, and
equally destructive passivization, by creating mutual security. This will
foster individuality in connection with others rather than in antagonistic competition and hostile separateness. It is there the revolution resides, not in the long representations of revolution in Night IX or its
antecedents.

ticipating in it through interpretive doublings that cannot help being like the text at many points, as they redeem Oothoon's rhetoric so that she will not be "perswading . . . in vain" (2:22). In what Leopold Damrosch calls "the accepted interpretation" it is Oothoon who is "accepted" by the reader and rejected by Theotormon.[2] "I am pure," she says (2:28), even though stamped with Bromion's "signet," raped, abused, chained, pregnant, ignored. "Yes, you are pure!" exclaims the critic, eager to perform with or on her the usual act of interpretation as if it had never been done before.

Looked at one way, the critic's role in this scene of interpretation is an active one as s/he ignores the stamp of Bromion's sign-net, the preinsemination of Oothoon within the text and of the text within the circuits of interpretation, to "legitimate" her orphan Truth. But does s/he not become remarkably like Oothoon in repeating her message of Truth—a message *about* (i.e., on the outside of) prophecy, vision, endless renewal, social transformation and freedom—a message that is itself composed of echoes and endlessly stuck repetitions? A message that claims everything for itself but is unable to do anything but repeat itself, seeming uncannily to proceed from whomever happens to be standing in its path: "Oothoon has learned / She knows / her own direct knowledge / She has learned / Oothoon has learned."[3]

Before continuing, it will be useful to articulate the outlines of this accepted interpretation. Even though it may sound like a caricature, Harold Bloom's version—suitably reduced in scale to serve as "authoritative annotation" for the Oxford Romantic anthology—provides an efficient example. For Bloom the poem "is a rapturous hymn to free love" in which "Oothoon is defeated because both her lovers are imaginatively inadequate": "Blake's insights here into the psychic origins of sexual jealousy have not been surpassed. Oothoon wishes to offer herself sexually to Theotormon, but is taken forcibly by Bromion. After a brief period in which she accepts the conventional morality which would condemn her as a harlot (for having enjoyed the sexual act, though it was a rape) she rises into an imaginative freedom that Theotormon can neither understand nor accept, and that Bromion understands but rejects out of natural fear."[4] A footnote identifies lines 11–13 of plate 2 (where Oothoon is "writhing her soft snowy limbs. / And calling Theotormons Eagles to prey upon her flesh.") as "the subtlest passage in the poem . . . the writhing of her limbs shows that Theotormon ought to save the situation by fulfilling her sexual desires, and ignoring the rape" (46). At first we might seem to find a contrast to this fleshy phallocratic message of "free love" in the spiritual "doctrine of the imagination" discovered by Kathleen Raine and others in what Frye dismisses as "the refined fantasies of spiritual eunuchs" (240). "Love [as Blake understood it] is of the soul. This love is so far from the promiscuity and license of the profane modern world as to be its direct opposite" (Raine 1:166). Yet in this case "direct opposites" exhibit remarkable similarities. "Oothoon . . . knows that bodily slavery enslaves the mind as well" and her tropes indeed keep collapsing the distinction as soon as it is made.[5] For Raine, Oothoon "sought her own rape" (1:166) while exercising "the freedom of every creature to follow its innate impulse of life" (2:128). G. M. Harper quotes Iamblichus as authority for "doctrine" that " 'the proper way of freeing ourselves from the passions is, first, to indulge them with moderation, by which means they become satisfied,' " and that "gratification, not repression, is the cure."[6] The transformation of sexual experience into "imaginative essence" for Raine, or the rise "into an imaginative freedom" for Bloom both follow the promiscuous lead of Oothoon's tropology in which either metaphysical or literal rape leads to mental or spiritual rapture.

Even those critics of late who have trouble with an unproblematic acceptance of Oothoon's Truth do not hesitate to take her as a transparent speaker of Blake's own beliefs and desires. Damrosch finds the message ambiguous, "torn by the same antinomies that we find everywhere in Blake. He hates sexual repression, but he is not sure what to replace it with" (198). Nevertheless the goal is still to find out what "Blake wants us to consider" (199) and "these considerations should not lead to a drastic revision of the accepted interpretation" (198).

David Aers seems much more critical, suggesting that Blake "may have slipped towards an optimistic, idealist illusion in his handling of Oothoon's consciousness. The illusion lies in assuming that revolutionary consciousness can ever be as uncontaminated by dominant structures and ideologies as Oothoon's appears to be."[7] For him Oothoon is represented as having "attained" a "clear revolutionary critique of sexual and social exploitation;" she has "reached" an "understanding of the psychological effects and perverted indulgences of repressed sexuality" (31). Blake's error is in assuming that "the female consciousness" can be suddenly and totally transformed, so that the Truth of what she says is the proof of her optimistic fictionality; Aers must first buy the correctness of her speech in order to reject her right to utter it—or Blake's right to have her utter it. "After Oothoon Blake's 'females'" are presented with a symbolism that "both discloses and affirms dominant male ideology," confirming "how traditional attitudes of male supremacism are very deeply rooted in our cultural heritage" (36–37). "Machismo rules," and "Los is his creator's mouthpiece" in a series of poems that "correctly" reflect Blake's entrapment in "the dominant male supremacist traditions" (40–41). Aers doesn't reveal how *he* escapes the dominant male ideology while Blake not only fails to do so, but actually reinforces the traditional culture that his poem "sets out to undermine" (38). Nor does he explain how he has such a clear and unqualified sense of what Blake "means" and what he "wants" (38).

Perhaps Aers should have considered the case of Susan Fox, whose transformation between 1976 and 1977 rivals that of Oothoon.[8] Less than a year after her formalist book, her *Critical Inquiry* article discovers that "it is one thing to despise oppression, and another to envision the means of the oppressed to end it" (513). Thus Blake's "doctrine of necessary equality" between the sexes is undermined by his pervasive use of "embarrassing stereotypes" (518) and his pejorative use of "femaleness" (516). In Blake's entire oeuvre Oothoon stands out for Fox as an exception, still "the single female character in all Blake's poetry who is both active and good" (512). The truth of her (and Blake's) Truth is unimpeached: "It is certainly true that Oothoon speaks for Blake in this poem, that she is as noble in its context as ever Los is in the final poems (more noble: she does not make mistakes), that she indicates a real and deep capacity in Blake for recognizing wisdom and courage and righteousness and strength in women. . . . Oothoon, whatever limitations her gender imposes on her power, is a complete woman, strong, willing, and wise. She is the first and last complete woman in Blake's poetry" (512).

Even Anne Mellor, who plows this field deeper than Fox, still sees Oothoon as the possessor of "liberated vision," though her creator reveals in his "consistently sexist portrayal of women" that he is himself unable "to escape the linguistic prisons of gender-identified metaphors inherent in the literary and religious culture in which he lived."[9] In the same issue of *Blake: An Illustrated Quarterly* Alicia Ostriker comes to Blake's defense by urging that he has an "antipatriarchal and proto-feminist sensibility" as well as a "homocentric gynophobia."[10] For her Oothoon is "a heroine unequalled in English poetry before or since. . . .   and not only attacks patriarchal ideology root and branch, but outflanks everyone in her poem for intellectuality and spirituality, and is intellectual and spiritual precisely because she is erotic" (158).

I have called my own entry into this ongoing conversation an "*un*-reading" for several reasons. First, because our access to the poem can be made at this stage only through or around the accepted reading; such is always the case. But more important, because the critical discourse on the poem and the discursive practices exhibited in it "reflect" each other in illuminating ways as they simultaneously participate in and presume to rise above the matrices of power and knowledge that influence the possibilities of discursive freedom. Together they constitute an arbitrary and repeatable system of order and belief, a system existing independent from any referential determination, which allows the meaning of the poem to be the truth of its own Truth. In my view the text can be more interestingly read as a text "about" the production of Truth than as a direct assertion of Truth; in this case, then, it is also a text "about" its own interpretations, which can come only from the same realm of curtural discursivity that is being staged in the poem.

This interpretive discourse is a production that the text provokes on the one hand but subverts on the other. Within the text Oothoon repeats her lesson endlessly without producing any discernible change in the status quo. The echoes in the text are then repeated in the interpretive text that constitutes our collective vision of the *VISIONS of the Daughters of Albion,* in the reading that is both accepted and accepting. In what follows I shall try to un-read some of these Truths by showing how the text both provokes and undermines them, trying the while to resist the satisfactions of a True(r) reading.

Background

Honour & Genius is all I ask
And I ask the Gods no more
—Blake, *An Island in the Moon*

Blake produced *VISIONS of the Daughters of Albion* during the period of high radical reaction and optimism following the outbreak of the French Revolution and Edmund Burke's provocative opening of debate in his *Reflections on the Revolution in France* (1790). The title page date of 1793 (as usual not definitive) and other evidence suggest that Blake might well have been working on it during the period beginning in February 1792 that has aptly been called "the *annus mirabilis* of eighteenth-century radicalism."[11] The debate was carried on at a high level of rhetorical passion, with an exaggerated and at times hysterical polarization of different positions into the rhetorical equivalents of Blake's "Angels" and "Devils" (*MHH*), with an urgency on both sides that presumed the political importance of public opinion and the power of Truth, properly conveyed, to influence that opinion. It has been tempting to identify the *VISIONS of the Daughters of Albion* as one of Blake's personal entries into the debate, and to relate it to some of the voices and issues in that debate as commentary and advocacy. In particular, Mary Wollstonecraft's *A Vindication of the Rights of Woman* (1792) has received special attention because of Blake's acquaintance with her and her circle, and because he makes his protagonist a woman who can be seen as a poetic counterpart of the historical author.[12]

Without invoking special knowledge of Blake's intentions, I will suggest several textual problems that should qualify our tendency to take this poem as Blake's personal entry into a controversy that had become a conspicuously collective enterprise, producing a series of works dependent on each other for their force and meaning, and on the specific historical situation that polarized potential readers. There are contextual problems too, reflected in Blake's careful "dialogical" attention to identifying voices and their interactions in a work like *The Marriage of Heaven and Hell*, where voices "impose" on each other without consummating the marriage anticipated by the title.

Blake's copy of Swedenborg's *Heaven and Hell* was inscribed with a quotation in pencil: "And as Imagination bodies forth y[e] forms of things unseen—turns them to shape & gives to airy Nothing a local habitation & a Name. Sh." Underneath this inscription Blake wrote his own comment in bold crayon: "Thus Fools quote Shakespeare The Above is Theseus's opinion Not Shakespeares You might as well quote Satans blasphemies from Milton & give them as Miltons Opinions" (E601). The Blake who wrote that comment had himself shown an early predilection for drama and a heightened sensitivity to the interrelationships between a poet and his personae and his audience.

From the earliest works we have, it is clear that the texts Blake writes are acutely sensitive to problems of voice, to the contingencies of public reception, and to the complex possibility of a "career" as both the source and result of a series of poetic gestures or acts. In his first poems to "meet the public eye," the conventionally introduced "productions of untutored youth" in *Poetical Sketches* (E846), we find sharply pointed parodies of public rhetoric. The morbidly exhortatory "War Song to Englishmen" is perhaps the most conspicuous of these, but there are others that display equal attention to conventional positions and rhetorical postures. In *King Edward the Third* the Bishop's eulogy of "Commerce" identifies his real interests, as the Duke's response ("O my good Lord, true wisdom drops like honey / From your tongue, as from a worship'd oak") does his (2:30, 36–37, E425–26). More witty, and more pertinent here, are the explicit parodies spoken by Dagworth:

> The tim'rous Stag starts from the thicket wild,
> The fearful Crane springs from the splashy fen,
> The shining Snake glides o'er the bending grass,
> The Stag turns head! and bays the crying Hounds;
> The Crane o'ertaken, sighteth with the Hawk;
> The Snake doth turn, and bite the padding foot
> (3:124–29, E430)

Which deserve comparison with Oothoon's:

> the village dog
> Barks at the breaking day. the nightingale has done lamenting.
> The lark does rustle in the ripe corn, and the Eagle returns
> From nightly prey, and lifts his golden beak to the pure east;
> Shaking the dust from his immortal pinions to awake
> The sun that sleeps too long.
> (2:23–28)

An Island in the Moon shows an amused eye for the histrionics of public preaching: "ah Mr Huffcap would kick the bottom of the Pulpit out, with Passion, would tear off the sleeve of his Gown, & set his wig on fire & throw it at the people hed cry & stamp & kick & sweat and all for the good of their souls" (E452). If Quid is the persona for Blake in that work, then his promise ("I will fall into such a passion Ill hollow and stamp & frighten all the People there & show them what truth is" [E465]) anticipates the curiosity about Isaiah and Ezekiel in *THE MARRIAGE of HEAVEN and HELL*. Were they self-conscious enough about their prophetic missions to worry "that they would be misunderstood, & so be the cause of imposition" (*MHH*12, E38)? Why did Ezekiel "eat dung, & lay so long on his right & left side?" (*MHH*13, E38). The Angel's concern about the place "to which thou art going in such career" (*MHH*17, E41) echoes the self-consciousness of a poet who identified the persona of his first work in illuminated printing as "The Voice of one crying in the Wilderness" (*ARO*, E1).

At a time when conflicting eternal truths were announcing themselves through the voices of Burke, Paine, Priestley, Wollstonecraft, Godwin and others, Blake had ample evidence that the same words and rhetorical tactics could be "adopted by both parties" (*MHH*5, E34) with the result of "imposing" rather than of "raising other men into a perception of the infinite" (*MHH*12, E39). To "Hear the voice of the Bard" (*SE*30, "Introduction," E18) adequately is not merely to hear the words spoken, but to hear them as they are located in a motivated and calculated discourse, uttered from a particular position. The ambivalent conclusion of the "Preludium" to *AMERICA a PROPHECY* suggests a Blake extremely self-conscious about his personae, perhaps also a Blake skeptical about the reality of a material social transformation to be brought about by the posturings of a Bard:

> The stern Bard ceas'd, asham'd of his own song; enrag'd he swung
> His harp aloft sounding, then dash'd its shining frame against
> A ruin'd pillar in glittering fragments; silent he turn'd away,
> And wander'd down the vales of Kent in sick & drear lamentings.
> (*A*2:18–21, E52)

To take the Bard here as a representation of Blake, and to claim that the presence or absence of the lines reveals his psychological state, is to take as confessional a poetry that is far removed from that mode.[13] Whatever psychological clues such evidence may provide can be seen to be compatible with the problematics of rhetoric and polemic that I have been identifying in Blake's work from the beginning. The non-effect of a series of carefully articulated voices on Thel has less to do with the Truth of what they say than it does with Thel's nonreceptivity that causes those voices to address her in vain. Oothoon's instantaneous response to the voice of the Marygold/Nymph, and Theotormon's non-response to her effusions point to the same thematic concerns.

For a final example, we can note that the famous assertion "every thing the lives is holy!" (8:10) is not Oothoon's unique formulation within the Blake *oeuvre*. It also concludes the chorus that follows "A Song of Liberty," and it is uttered by Orc in *AMERICA* (*A*8:13, E54). Both contexts seem to reach for a performative force in the utterance, claiming a historical transformation ("Empire is no more!" [*MHH*27, E44; *A*6:15, E53], "The times are ended" [*A*8:2, E54]), as a consequence of the denial of sexual pollution or defilement in any action. The conflation of political and sexual liberation is equally strong in Oothoon's assertion, but *VISIONS* emphasizes the futility rather than the power of her utterance.

The same words can be read a fourth time, in *The Four Zoas,* along with even more of Oothoon's verbal context:

> Arise you little glancing wings & sing your infant joy
> Arise & drink your bliss
> For every thing that lives is holy
> (*FZ*34:77–79, E324)

But this time the words are uttered by Enitharmon, in a carefully articulated state ("the God enraptured me infolds / In clouds of sweet obscurity my beauteous form dissolving" [*FZ*34:24–5, E323]), and the effects on her auditor, Los, are spelled out:

> Thus sang the Lovely one in Rapturous delusive trance
> Los heard reviving he siezd her in his arms delusive hopes
> Kindling She led him into Shadows & thence fled outstretchd
> Upon the immense like a bright rainbow weeping & smiling & fading
> (*FZ*34:93–96, E324)

My point here is to show that the same literal words can have quite a different effect depending on how they are framed and dramatized. Enitharmon's utterance does not prove the words are false (or that Blake thought them false) any more than Oothoon's utterance shows them to be (or to have been at that time) Blake's Truth. *The Four Zoas* dramatizes the effect of Enitharmon's words on Los who "siezd her in his arms," an effect comparable to that produced in many of

Oothoon's readers, who berate Theotormon for not reacting in the same manner. Indeed, in Oothoon's first appearance, on the title page of *VISIONS*, she is running toward the reader, arms outstretched, underneath a wash of rainbow coloring. David Erdman, who dedicated the 1967 *Concordance* "To Oothoon" helps us to see that her affective power over the reader can be comparable to Enitharmon's: "Oothoon's running under it [the "rainbow"] continues a journey that began in joy. . . . We are invited to help her sustain the faith whereby she still walks on the waves, despite the menaces of Bromion and Theotormon under the aegis of the selfish father-god Urizen."[14]

Eyes and Hearts

Le coeur a ses raisons que la raison ne connaît pas.
—Pascal, *Pensées*

What the eye can't see the heart can't grieve for.
—Joyce, *Ulysses*

> *She judges of refinement by the eye,*
> *He by the test of conscience, and a heart*
> *Not soon deceiv'd.*
—Cowper, *The Task*

It is appropriate that a poem entitled *VISIONS* begins with a "motto" about the eye as the instrument of knowledge: "The Eye sees more than the Heart knows." Title and motto call attention to the emphatically *scenic* (in the full theatrical sense) dimension of the poem, and to its specular thematics. We might well expect that the ambiguity of the title ("of" having the frequent Blakean ambiguity between the possessive and the objective genitive) be resolved by the motto, or that it provide a clue for us in our attempts to read the poem. But most attempts to explain the motto simply repeat it, as if its meaning were clear, in spite of Damon's interesting suggestion that by it Blake meant "that he could not understand the facts of this world."[15] On the face of it the oppositions between seeing and knowing, between eye and heart, packaged in a simple assertion, raise more questions than they answer. What is the difference between seeing and knowing, and is it better to see less and know more, or to know less and see more? Taken alone, the statement quickly becomes overdetermined, a pronouncement that means so much it means nothing. Taken in a larger context, the statement guides us to a basic *topos* of the eighteenth century, to a point of conflict in the discourse of Truth in which the eye and the heart have conflicting claims to dominate moral perception.

The opposition between the metaphoric eye as the figure for rational knowledge and the heart as the source of intuitive knowledge is at least as old as the Hebrew scriptures. As Alexander Cruden (the great biblical concordancer) observes, in the mid-eighteenth century the eye "is not only taken for the organ of sight but also for the understanding or judgment" and the heart is looked on "as the source of wit, understanding, love, courage, grief, and pleasure."[16] As a commonplace rhetorical *topos* in the Renaissance, the *débat* between eye and heart gave Shakespeare material for his wit to practice on: "Mine eye and heart are at a mortal war, / How to divide the conquest of thy sight."[17] Wherever we look in the eighteenth century we are reminded that its guiding epistemological concept was derived from Locke's image of the divided mind, one part operating unreflectively on signals from without, and one part observing those operations. The distinction divides the mind into a "feeling" self and a "reflective" self so that its rightfully controlling aspect can be identified with either the reflective reason or the private feelings of the moral sense or conscience. The two poles of the ongoing debate can be illustrated by the differences between Adam Smith's moral theory, where conduct is to be ruled by an internalized "impartial spectator" (whose existence comes from social conditioning) and Shaftesbury's insistence on the trustworthy primacy of innate principles of feeling. We can hear and see this issue inscribed among the many other basic conflicts between Blake's Urizen (your eyes "in two little caves" [*U*11:14, E76]) and Orc (*cor*).

In Blake's time advocates of the heart, with theorists of poetry prominent among them, placed the faculty of intuition above that of the physical organs and reflective reason. William Duff claimed the superiority of early poetry because "being the effusion of a glowing fancy and an impassioned heart [it] will be perfectly natural and ORIGINAL."[18] In his dissertation on Ossian, Hugh Blair claimed that the secret of Ossian's art was nothing more than "giving vent to the simple and natural emotions of the heart. . . . the Heart, when uttering its native language, never fails, by powerful sympathy, to affect the heart." Thus Ossian's poetry "deserves to be styled, *The poetry of the heart . . .* a heart that is full, and pours itself forth."[19] For Adam Ferguson, the authentic primitive poet was one who "delivers the emotions of the heart, in words suggested by the heart."[20] Richardson's Clarissa claims that "a feeling heart" is the "principle glory of the human nature," the source of "principles that *are* in my mind; that I *found* there; implanted, no doubt, by the first gracious Planter." But like the "wisest heart / Of Solomon . . . led by fraud" in *Paradise Lost* (1:400–401) her heart could be led astray: "And has not my own heart deceived me, when I thought it did not?"[21] Wordsworth reports having experienced his crisis of 1793 as a split into "A twofold Frame of body and of mind" in which "the most despotic of our senses," the eye, "was master of the heart."[22]

Given the possibility of delusion in both the physical eye and the feeling heart, the metaphoric eye of reason flourished in the tradition of the all-seeing blind poet Milton, and the "Philosophic Eye" of Newton's "scrutinous PHILOSOPHY" triumphed for many over the "vulgar stare" of those who could not "see" the rainbow they "saw."[23] When gendered, as in Kant, the rational eye tended to be masculine and the feeling heart feminine.[24] The tradition of the omnipotent eye culminated in the ideological-architectural fantasy of Blake's contemporary Bentham, whose Panopticon was a "rational" attempt to literalize the metaphor in a feat of social engineering. During the pamphlet war of the 1790s, the "cold" eye of reason was alternatively superior to the "heat" of passion and inferior to the "warmth" of the heart. Burke was critical of "that sort of reason which banishes the affections" and "is incapable of filling their place."[25] "In viewing this monstrous tragi-comic scene" of the French Revolution, he gauges its meaning by a different faculty, because "we are so made as to be affected at such spectacles" and "in those natural feelings we learn great lessons" (147). Priestley, surveying the same events, felt a different affect and a different version of what the heart knows: "Such events as these teach the doctrine of *liberty, civil and religious,* with infinitely greater clearness and force, than a thousand treatises on the subject. They speak a language intelligible to all the world, and preach a doctrine congenial to every human heart."[26] Still closer to Blake's own circle, and to the genesis of *VISIONS*, we find Mary Wollstonecraft seeking a more balanced perspective, critical of "sentiments and opinions current in conversation that have no root in the heart, or weight in the cooler resolves of the mind."[27] But when the amorous passions are at issue, she finds the heart a poor guide: "To speak disrespectfully of love is, I know, high treason . . . but I wish to speak the simple language of truth, and rather address the head than the heart. [Love] should not be allowed to dethrone superior powers, or to usurp the sceptre which the understanding should ever cooly wield."[28] This is the voice of that "reason" that Burke and Reynolds were convinced led to the atrocities of the French Revolution. Wollstonecraft's extended arguments in favor of rationality and against romantic love and sexuality helped the *Vindication of the Rights of Woman* to receive a favorable reception when it first came out, but might well have struck a jarring note to one like Blake who knew the details of her personal life and had a chance to observe at close quarters those "passions" that led to her attempted suicide, extramarital liaisons, and an illegitimate child.

Most Blake critics intuitively know to no the "knows" of the heart and to aye the "eye" in the poem's motto, suggesting that it "emphasizes the primacy of perception over the limited wisdom of the natural heart,"[29] convinced that "Oothoon sees more than the heart knows."[30] But for Blake "the Eye altering alters all" ("The Mental Traveller" 62, E485). The most variable and problematic of faculties, it seldom stays still, and seldom appears without qualification. "The Eye of Man a little narrow orb closed up and dark" (*M*5:21, E99) is not the standard of vision, and "A Fool's Eye is Not to be. a Criterion" (*E*638), nor is the "Lovesick eye" ("The Mental Traveller" 34 E484), nor the "Corporeal or Vegetative Eye" (*VLJ*95, E566) nor the eyes of the "Watchfiends" in *MILTON*. We need to see with the "visionary eye" (*M*39:33, E140) or the "Imaginative Eye" (*VLJ*70, E555) or the "inward Eye" (*E*721) if we are to see truly, and presumably this applies to the *VISIONS* as much as any other object of perception. If we were already "visionaries" we would not need its help to become such; and if we are not, there will always be the possibility of misperceiving it.

As so often with Blake, what we are invited to see in this poem is vision made the subject of vision. Oothoon presents herself as specialist of perception, critical of "the eyes of the envier" (4:11) and of the miser (8:1–4) and of the "lamplike eyes watching around the frozen marriage bed" (7:22) and of the eyes of love that "sicken at the fruit that hangs before his sight" (7:20), appreciative of "the eyes of honest morn" (6:15). Faced with Bromion's challenge ("behold this harlot" [1:18]), she presents herself both as the object to be seen correctly ("I am white and pure" [3:20]) and as a mirror in which Theotormon can see his own "image pure" (3:16). This image reflects the other role of Oothoon as first-person I-eye, exemplary subject of vision, transparent, not to be seen merely as object (for "Then is Oothoon a whore indeed!" [6:18]), urging Theotormon to see her, to see her eyes, to see himself in her eyes, and to see the world *through* her eyes: "Open to joy and to delight . . . my eyes are fix'd / In happy copulation" (6:23–7:1). Hers are the eyes that "shall view his dear delight" (7:28) with the girls she provides "& view their wanton play / In lovely copulation bliss on bliss with Theotormon" (7:25–26). "The moment of desire!" (7:3) thus offers two layers of copulatory pleasure (bliss on bliss), that of bodies in copulation, and that of eyes "In happy copulation" watching them. If Theotormon is to participate fully he must learn to follow her example, not keeping her "bound / In spells of law . . . in weary lust" (5:21–23) but free to pluck flowers where she finds them in "The clear heaven of her eternal spring" (5:24). This is her lesson of "free love" and of "vision," which leads the visionary eyes of readers to find in him a poor "pupil" for her, though a "good" one for Bromion: "Thou knowest that the ancient trees seen by thine eyes have fruit" (4:13).[31]

The emphasis on the seeing eye is echoed and reinforced by homophonic play on the first-person singular pronoun, beginning with the first six lines of the Argument: "I loved, I was, I trembled, I hid, I plucked, I rose." It sounds through the poem with cumulative force ("How can I be defild when I reflect thy image pure" [3:16]; "I cry arise" [2:23]; "Arise my Theotormon I am pure" [2:29]; "my eyes" [6:23]), and is reinforced by the treble echo of the Daughters of Albion with their "sighs toward America" (1:2) who "hear her woes, & eccho back her sighs" (2:20, 5:2, 8:13). Critical of the eye of the "cold miser" (8:1) and pitting its sound against Urizen, "Creator of men" (5:3) and "Father of Jealousy" (7:12), hers is a generous and outgoing I, not selfish or jealous like the tyrant god.

In conjunction with this homophonic emphasis and play on the first-person singular, there is a tendency Oothoon shares with Thel and Ahania to refer to herself by name—a device that manages to keep the speaking subject an object, and to keep the graphic form of her name present for our scrutiny. The source of this name has given rise to the usual speculations that result in an O-verdetermined result. In Macpherson's *Ossian* the character Oithona is raped by a lord of Orkney who carries her off to a cave. Raine points out that "Oithona comes from the Gaelic oi, a virgin, and thon, thona, a wave; she is a 'virgin of the wave' " (1:174). Those who prefer the Greek might remember the name Dionysus gave his ravished mother along with immortality: Thyone, or "the ecstatically raging." S. Foster Damon, as always confident of his ear, claims the name was "built upon Blake's favorite vowel, the long *u*" (329), and David Erdman goes to his favorite Stedman to find a source for the *oo–oo* doubling in African words ("apootoo, too-too, ooroocoocoo").[32]

However we choose to hear or pronounce her name, its double double O's are a striking feature, and the letter appears nine times in the twenty-four letters that spell the names of the three characters in the poem. As independent graphemes, these **O**'s become visual echoes of Oothoon's **O**'s as well as phonic echoes of her woes. In contrast with the **I** of subjective individuality, **O**'s as zeroes or ciphers hint at an absence of quantity that is nevertheless functional, the nothing within a system that allows it to work. In a plenum of eyes and **I**'s and ayes and knows and no's and **O**'s, of eyes and **I**'s in caves, suggesting eyeholes and I-holes, the poem develops a realm of phonographemic polysemy calling to our *yeux sonores*. As an O-riginal story from real life, Mary Wollstonecraft, vindicator of the rights of woman is implicated, that strong critic of the phantasy-woman Sophie, the cipher invented by Rousseau for his Emile. Both Blake and Wollstonecraft might have noticed Rousseau's snide exemplar in the little girl who refused to progress in her writing because she only wanted to make **O**'s. "She incessantly made big and little **O**'s, **O**'s of all sizes, **O**'s inside one another, and always drawn backward."[33] This incessant writing deserves comparison with Oothoon's "incessant writhing her soft snowy limbs" (2:12) in a constant state of w**o**e (2:20, 5:2, 8:13), and the numerous puns that reinforce the visual aspect of her name. As "one o'erflowed with woe" (3:22), Theotormon is also o'erflowed with **o**, undergoing The-**o**-torment of that "whole s**o**ul" who has come "over the waves" and "over Theotormon's reign" in order to "obey the scourge," still "**o**pen to virgin bliss," "**o**pen to j**o**y," bringing "with h**o**ly voice" the imperative mode ("**O** Man!") in the conviction that "everything that lives is h**o**ly!"

The reader too is in danger of being o'erflowed by Oothoon, as the poem opens itself implicitly to the readerly gaze. But where is the reader's eye in relation to the poetic scene? Does Oothoon know she has been "created" for us to see and hear, or is she oblivious to our voyeuristic gaze, totally absorbed in her personal drama? John Berger has shown at length how in the "average" European oil painting of the nude, the principle protagonist is never painted: "He is the spectator in front of the picture and he is presumed to be a man. Everything is addressed to him. Everything must appear to be the result of his being there."[34] In such paintings "women watch themselves being looked at. . . . The surveyor of woman in herself is male: the surveyed female. Thus she turns herself into an object—and most particularly an object of vision: a sight" (47). If the woman is involved with another man within the scene of the painting, the implicit dynamics are such that the viewer will in fantasy oust the other man or replace him through identification (56). Blake was certainly not an "average" painter in any sense of the word, but he was an artist who was also a critic of other paintings; and Berger's emphasis directs us to issues that are raised explicitly within the poem and implicitly by the presentation of the events of the poem to our readerly gaze, to that "moment of desire" that for the reader must be found in the act of looking itself.

The plate Blake used alternately as a frontispiece and tailpiece for *VISIONS* serves equally well as entrance or exit for a poem that articulates a stuck scene (illustration 6). The plate presents itself as a *scaena* and map of the seen and the seeing. Bromion (who says "Behold") is staring aghast at something to our left. Theotormon rejects Oothoon's invitation by covering his eyes with his arms, while Oothoon gazes downward at an area of dark shadow. Their lines of vision are such that they cannot see each other, and the composition emphasizes the impossibility for any one of them to see the scene they compose. Dominating the sky and background of the plate is a form that might be the sun shining through an opening in the clouds, but that looks to most viewers like a large eye ("Instead of morn arises a bright shadow, like an eye in the eastern cloud" [2:35–46]). It is the most enigmatic eyehole in a poem full of eyes and **I**'s and **O**'s. It has been taken as a representation of the eye of the reader by John Howard who identifies with it, but for many it creates an alienating effect: "We feel directly stared at," says David Erdman.[35] Whatever the sky-eye is or represents, the composition of the plate emphatically locates the reader's perspective in an eye *within* the cave, with the exit/entrance blocked by the naked trio who seem frozen like sculptures into postures congruent with their functions in the poem.

6. *Visions of the Daughters of Albion* (copy G), pl. i (frontispiece), Houghton Library, Harvard University.

This may suggest that as voyeur-readers we find ourselves in "Bromions caves" (2:5), or in the "religious caves beneath the burning fires / Of lust'" (2:9–10), or in the position of "cavern'd Man" (*Eur*3:1, E60) with our eyes like Urizen's "fixed in two little caves" (*U*11:14, E76). Perhaps we are even chained underground like the men in Plato's parable of the cave, seeing only shadows and hearing only echoes, mistaking these traces of "artificial objects" for reality.[36] If Oothoon is chained, or bound back to back with Bromion, how can she free us? If she is chained because we see her that way, then how can we see her differently, freeing her (as she would have Theotormon free her) through our accepting seeing of her? Can our vision of her vision free us to free her?

Erdman has called attention to the resemblance of the woman at the bottom of plate 1 to the woman in Fuseli's *Nightmare* (illustrations 7 and 8), a painting that Erasmus Darwin found room to praise as he described the vigorous sex life of his plants.[37] I find on plate 3 an even stronger reference to the *Nightmare* (illustration 9), and see both of them as glosses on the passive state of the Oothoon we see bound in the frontispiece-tailpiece.[38] In plate 3 the swan-bill of the "eagle" piercing Oothoon replaces the pressure of the incubus in the painting—an incubus squatting somewhat like Theotormon (though looking at the viewer), as the intense eyes of his "nightmare" remind us of Bromion's exaggerated gaze in the frontispiece-tailpiece. In all four cases we have the same dynamics, suggestive of an intense scopophilia, that provoked Jean Starobinski to claim *"le plaisir voyeuriste"* for the painter of the *Nightmare*.[39] Starobinski's evocation of *souffrance* (*"il voit souffrir; il fait souffrir"*) is applicable both to the viewer and the object of these scenes. *En souffrance*, unable to accomplish a first move toward change, what can we do in the presence of this eternal scene that challenges and tests our abilities to light Oothoon's "fires" by "the eyes of honest morn" (6:15)? As we gaze at that painting, or the echoes of it in Blake's representations of Oothoon, how can we be anything but voyeurs caverned in our culturally coded perceptions, viewing representations equally bound? We must look again at Oothoon.

7. Henry Fuseli, *The Nightmare* (1972), Goethe Museum, Frankfurt am Main.

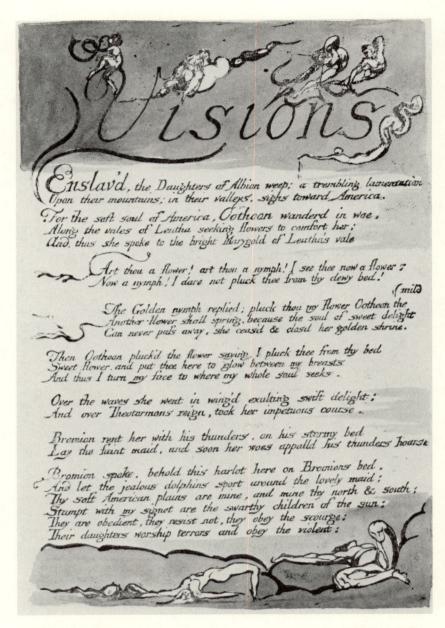

Enslav'd, the Daughters of Albion weep: a trembling lamentation
Upon their mountains; in their valleys, sighs toward America.

For the soft soul of America, Oothoon wanderd in woe,
Along the vales of Leutha seeking flowers to comfort her;
And, thus she spoke to the bright Marygold of Leutha's vale

Art thou a flower! art thou a nymph! I see thee now a flower;
Now a nymph! I dare not pluck thee from thy dewy bed!

                                                          (mild
The Golden nymph replied; pluck thou my flower Oothoon the
Another flower shall spring, because the soul of sweet delight
Can never pass away, she ceasd & closd her golden shrine.

Then Oothoon pluck'd the flower saying, I pluck thee from thy bed
Sweet flower. and put thee here to glow between my breasts
And thus I turn my face to where my whole soul seeks.

Over the waves she went in wing'd exulting swift delight;
And over Theotormons reign, took her impetuous course.

Bromion rent her with his thunders. on his stormy bed
Lay the faint maid, and soon her woes appalld his thunders hoarse

Bromion spoke. behold this harlot here on Bromions bed,
And let the jealous dolphins sport around the lovely maid:
Thy soft American plains are mine, and mine thy north & south:
Stampt with my signet are the swarthy children of the sun:
They are obedient, they resist not, they obey the scourge:
Their daughters worship terrors and obey the violent:

8. *Visions of the Daughters of Albion* (copy I), pl. 1, Paul Mellon Collection, Yale Center for British Art.

And none but Bromion can hear my lamentations.

With what sense is it that the chicken shuns the ravenous hawk?
With what sense does the tame pigeon measure out the expanse?
With what sense does the bee form cells? have not the mouse & frog
Eyes and ears and sense of touch? yet are their habitations.
And their pursuits, as different as their forms and as their joys:
Ask the wild ass why he refuses burdens: and the meek camel
Why he loves man: is it because of eye ear mouth or skin
Or breathing nostrils? No. for these the wolf and tyger have.
Ask the blind worm the secrets of the grave, and why her spires
Love to curl round the bones of death: and ask the ravenous snake
Where she gets poison: & the winged eagle why he loves the sun
And then tell me the thoughts of man, that have been hid of old.

Silent I hover all the night. and all day could be silent.
If Theotormon once would turn his loved eyes upon me;
How can I be defild when I reflect thy image pure?
Sweetest the fruit that the worm feeds on. & the soul preyd on by woe
The new washd lamb tingd with the village smoke & the bright swan
By the red earth of our immortal river: I bathe my wings.
And I am white and pure to hover round Theotormons breast.

Then Theotormon broke his silence. and he answered.

Tell me what is the night or day to, one oerflowd with woe?
Tell me what is a thought? & of what substance is it made?
Tell me what is a joy? & in what gardens do joys grow?
And in what rivers swim the sorrows, and upon what mountains

9. *Visions of the Daughters of Albion* (copy I), pl. 3, detail, Paul Mellon
Collection, Yale Center for British Art.

What Mov'd Oothoon?

Say first! what mov'd Milton, who walkd about in Eternity
One hundred years, pondring the intricate mazes of Providence
Unhappy tho in heav'n
—Blake, *MILTON*

For the soft soul of America, Oothoon wanderd in woe,
Along the vales of Leutha seeking flowers to comfort her
—Blake, *VISIONS of the Daughters of Albion*

Methought I heard, even from the silent spheres, a commanding call, to spurn
the abject earth, and pant after unseen delights. . . .
  I gaze, I ponder. I ponder, I gaze; and think ineffable things. I roll an eye
of awe and admiration. Again and again I repeat my ravished views, and can
never satiate either my curiosity or my enquiry. I spring my thoughts into this
immense field, till even fancy tires upon her wing.
—James Hervey, *Contemplations on The Starry Heavens*

Oothoon is moved twice in *VISIONS,* first by the speech of the Mary-
gold/flower/nymph to go to where her "whole soul seeks" (1:13),
then by the "rape" to enter the realm of speech where she attempts to
move her beloved Theotormon, "perswading him in vain" (2:22).
The "invitation" of the Marygold is conventionally taken to be a repetition of the mutable Lilly and other voices in *THE BOOK of THEL.*
But where Thel resists, Oothoon "suddenly wills the courage that Thel
could never achieve" in order "to enter without fear into the round of
generation."[40] The contrast here, between the few words of the flower/
nymph and the lengthy rhetorical exercises in *THEL* points to a receptivity in Oothoon quite different from that of her counterpart. Her
"will" is different (Thel is close to θέλω, "will") and it is this internal
state that "hears" what it wants to hear, a doctrine that corresponds to
the desire of her "whole soul" (10:13). Like Milton's Eve in her
propensity to follow a voice, she also raises the same problems about
the source and authority of the voice to be followed. In *Paradise Lost*
an angelic voice leads Eve away from her narcissistic self-love to a
new object of desire, a new mirror-relation ("hee / Whose image thou
art" [4:471–72]) and to a higher love. But another voice waits for her
in book 9 "hid among sweet Flow'rs and Shades" (408), a "human
voice" (561) strangely coming from one Eve thought "Created mute
to all articulate sound" (557)—a voice that will provide Eve with a
rationale to "pluck" the fruit of her desire, giving her a "message" to
bring home to Adam.

It is one thing to follow the voice of Nature, but quite another to be able to interpret what it is saying, and to be sure that the source of the message lies with divine Truth. If one gets the message right, then not only is one authorized for a certain mode of conduct, but one can become the conduit—both in action and speech—for the expression of that Truth; one can become a poet of Nature, and the eighteenth century saw many poets and meditative philosophers respond to this calling. The poetico-philosophical "flower-plucking" trope is as old as Lucretius, quoted early in the century by Swift on the title page of *A Tale of a Tub:*

> ————————————Juvatque novos decerpere flores,
> Insignemque meo capiti petere inde coronam,
> Unde prius nulli velarunt tempora Musae. Lucret.[41]

One of Swift's ironic ploys is to make his hack narrator a latter-day Lucretius, so the work's epigraph and numerous quotations from *De Rerum Natura* deliberately evoke the discourse of Epicurean materialism and atheism that Swift heard being given new voice in his own time. By deliberately taking on that voice, he achieves a reductio ad absurdum for the amusement of the reader who knew how to read his message.

How *not* to argue from Nature became almost as important in the following decades as how *to* argue, since its message could so readily be adopted by both parties. Cowper, in *The Task,* traces the inevitable downward slide of the soul whose "Reason . . . Takes part with appetite" participating in a "libidinous discourse" that bends nature to its purpose by repeating "shallow shifts and old devices, worn / And tatter'd in the service of debauch":

> Hath God indeed giv'n appetites to man,
> And stor'd the earth so plenteously with means
> To gratify the hunger of his wish:
> And doth he reprobate, and will he damn,
> The use of his own bounty? making first
> So frail a kind, and then enacting laws
> So strict, that less than perfect must despair?
> (5:630–36)

In the erotic finale to his "Spring," Thomson sings "the passion of the groves" (581) echoing the song of Nature and the creatures for whom "love creates their melody," which is "the voice of love" (614–15). In spite—or perhaps because—of this burning passion, the largest part of Thomson's conclusion is a warning about the "fevered rapture" that may betray the "aspiring youth":

> When on his heart the torrent-softness pours.
> Then wisdom prostrate lies, and fading fame
> Dissolves in air away; while the fond soul,
> Wrapt in gay visions of unreal bliss,
> Still paints the illusive form. . . .
>
> .   .   .   .
>
> And still, false-warbling in his cheated ear,
> Her siren voice enchanting draws him on
> (985–94)

And on and on, for 118 lines, to the appointed end in "a life / Of fevered rapture" with "all / His lively moments running down to waste" (1107–1112). This whole passage is adapted and expurgated from Lucretius 4 (1008–1208), where the Roman author shows how the tyrannic will to eject his seed leads the lover to strive toward the source of his wound, and outlines the "penalties" Venus imposes on those she has wounded. But whereas the lesson for Lucretius is to engage in promiscuous attachments to avoid the pain of a single grand passion, the lesson for Thomson is the opposite, a stable marriage and the "matchless joys of virtuous love" (1165). Different lessons can be learned from the same poet of Nature as well as from Nature herself.

Thel's impression of Nature might well have been formed by a reading of Blake's popular contemporary, Erasmus Darwin, whose *Loves of the Plants* provides a guide to the sexual life of flowers, where sexual organs are euphemized in mythical terms and ceaseless sexual encounters are dressed in conventional couplets and "flowery" poetic diction. Darwin's emphasis on personified sexuality, and especially on the violence of floral reproduction and the submission of the female to the aggressive force of the male's rape, are visually echoed in the title page of *THE BOOK of THEL*, which shows Thel witnessing such an encounter between two "flowers" as an unopened bud reaches toward her. The ambiguous reaction of the female "flower" (Erdman describes it as "joy—or horror"[42]) seems to pose the two options available to the female in this world, and to emphasize how "apt to pluck a sweet" (*Love's Labour's Lost*) Oothoon is, in contrast with Thel.

Oothoon's vision of the Marygold as "now a flower; / Now a nymph" (1:6–7) calls attention to the way in which Nature must be supplemented by a cultural code before it can give voice to a meaning, and "nymph" echoes the ancient practice of endowing natural objects with human attributes in order to give them meaning. Blake uses the term "nymph" to suggest what he elsewhere calls the "double vision" in which "With my inward Eye 'tis an old Man grey / With my outward a Thistle across my way" (E721). But the term "nymph" itself is subject to a double vision, ranging from an attribution of high praise ("O Helen, goddess, nymph, perfect, divine!" (*Midsummer Night's Dream* 3.2.137) to abuse: "To wanton with this queen, / This goddess, this Semiramis, this nymph" (*Titus Andronicus* 1.1.316).[43]

Other symbols or signs in the poem show a similar emphasis on the way natural signs must be supplemented or encoded before they can be used to produce meaning. Erdman's reaction to the rainbow coloring of the title page (which echoes Damon's reading of it as "the rainbow of hope") has already been mentioned. But in the symbolic codes of the eighteenth century, as Blake well knew, the rainbow became the signifier of error and deluded desire, redefined by the new scripture of Newton's *Opticks* (1704). Erdman's often-echoed suggestion that the impregnation of Oothoon "enhances her price" is another example of doubtful coding, ignoring the possibility that in context it intensifies the "violation" by Bromion and makes her less acceptable to Theotormon.[44] Raine narrows the mobility of the "swan" signifier on plate 3 (19–21) to a particular iconographic convention, as "Plato's emblem of the soul," which "has but dipped its wings in the 'red earth' of the natural body" and then "bathes its wings and is pure" (1:176). She ignores the fact observed by Erdman that the bill of the eagle on plate 3 is "rather like the bill of a swan" and that the "ingeniously ambiguous" mount for the naked female astride a "horse-like cloud" on plate 1 (illustration 10) can be seen as a pair of testicles and "a short round penis" to which a brown bill ("duck's or swan's") has been added in copy G.[45]

In what code can we read an "eagle" (the bird of sight and of Apollo, god of poetry) with a "swan" bill? Such a signifier calls conspicuous attention to itself as a signifier, a cultural symbolic product with a plurality of potential meanings, rather than the representation of a "natural" one. How can we ignore what Beryl Rowland refers to as "the customary phallicism of Apollo's bird," the swan? In a work

10. *Visions of the Daughters of Albion* (copy I), pl. 1, detail, Paul Mellon Collection, Yale Center for British Art.

dealing so conspicuously with a "rape," by an artist who would have known numerous graphic versions of the Leda myth, can we be satisfied with such reductive codifications in a context where the production of meaning from "natural signs" is so emphatically problematized?[46]

To identify Oothoon's "flower" as a "naiad of generation" or the flower "of imaginative experience" is to push for a clarity of coding in the service of a particular line of meaning, an interpretive plucking of the flower to serve the interpreter's desire.[47] The existence of a special term, "nymphology," for the branch of knowledge that treats of nymphs, suggests the range of possible connotations.[48] We might also remember that special disease or mania called "nympholepsy" (a state of rapture or trance, a frenzy inspired by having beheld a nymph), as we move to a consideration of the consequences for Oothoon of her plucking the nymph-flower. Although her journey to where her "whole soul seeks" is an interrupted failure, her entry into the realm of discourse proves a different matter, as the "moment of desire" in which her whole soul *speaks* is stretched out through the main body of the poem. Foucault has pointed out how "speech is not merely the medium which manifests—or dissembles—desire; it is also the object of desire."[49] If we expand our sense of the poem's libidinal and political economy to include the economy of speaking, we may hear a few things we would otherwise miss.

Did She Put on His Knowledge with His Power?

With holy raptures of adoration, rapd sublime in the Visions of God.
—Blake, *Jerusalem*

We must not think that by saying yes to sex, one says no to power; on the contrary, one tracks along the course laid out by the general deployment of sexuality.—Michel Foucault, *The History of Sexuality*

However we interpret Oothoon's response to the Marygold (the "plucking" and the "rape"), her next step is a move into the familiar world of discourse on sex and sexuality that occupies the greater part of the poem. On one level the "plot" of the poem provides sufficient cause for her to speak out; but there are other considerations that suggest we can take her eruption into speech as the consequence or effect of the rape by Bromion. David Punter has suggested that the "central imagining" of the dominant ideology of the eighteenth century "of course, is rape . . . the great unspoken theme of eighteenth-century fiction" that is increasingly disclosed as the century progresses.[50] More directly to the point of our concerns here is the frequency with which "rape" was used as a psychosexual metaphor for the effectiveness of the "sublime." The goal of the sublime is not to persuade, but to "transport" or "carry away" the reader-hearer; with its foundations in power and pain and terror, it is the masculine aesthetic mode in contrast to the feminine mode of Beauty. John Dennis provides a common formulation of the effect of a sublime that "Gives a noble Vigour to a Discourse, an invincible Force, which commits a pleasing Rape upon the very Soul of the Reader; that whenever it breaks out where it ought to do, like the Artillery of Jove, it thunders, blazes, and strikes at once."[51] In the Longinian sublime the poet's power to "rape" the reader depends on the ability to set an example, to evoke the transporting power so that first the poet is raped and then the reader, whose "ravish't ears" and "ravish't eyes" indicate the "rapture" of being carried away by the force of the poet. The poet's power of mastery, rhetorically exhibited, becomes sexually ambiguous as figurative "rape" becomes both cause and effect of this strange force of discourse. The reader's response copies that of the poet, as passive submission becomes its opposite, so that "uplifted with a sense of proud possession" we become "filled with joyful pride, as if we had ourselves produced the very thing we heard."[52]

The psychoaesthetics of rapture has an ancient history, with a key place in it for the god Dionysus, one of whose names is echoed in Blake's "Bromion." A god of sexually ambiguous origins, his mother was Semele, whose desire to see Zeus in the full manifestation of his power resulted in her simultaneous death and impregnation as the god ravished her in the form of a lightening bolt. Zeus sewed the embryo up in his thigh until ripe for birth, so that Dionysus was born from a "male womb," after which he was brought up hidden from the wrath of Hera in a "cave." In some ways an effeminate god, whom Ovid could call "a little fellow / As pretty as a girl" (*virginea puerum ducit per litora forma,* [*Metamorphoses* 3:607]), he became a second Zeus, "a Zeus of women," offering a "release" to women from the confinement and tedium of their restricted social roles.[53] As Guthrie notes, "the greatest gift of Dionysus was the sense of utter freedom, and in Greece it was the women, with their normally confined and straitened lives, to whom the temptation of release made the strongest possible appeal. . . .   Nothing is lacking which can serve to increase the sense of exaltation and of shedding the self of everyday existence."[54] Many instances of the myth, however, show that the liberation of Dionysus could be imposed against the resistance of the women (as in Ovid's "daughters of Minyas" section, *Metamorphoses* 4:1–412) or that it could have unforeseen consequences—as with Pentheus's mother Agave, who serves Dionysus and becomes his victim, showing that the release from ordinary consciousness could also include release of destructive impulses.

Philip Slater has suggested that the Dionysian cult functioned as part of the organization of the Greek psychological economy, providing "the ultimate fantasy solution to the torment which sex antagonism occasioned in Greek life by eliminating the exaggerated differentiation imposed by culturally defined sex roles."[55] Whether or not we agree with this particular formulation—or with Claude Lévi-Strauss's theory of the "function" of myth as the mediation of polarized tensions—it should be obvious that a myth is an elaborate cultural institution and that the production and circulation of myths dealing with sex and politics might well be one of the most regulated areas of cultural productions, coming under Foucault's hypothesis "that in every society the production of discourse is at once controlled, selected, organized and redistributed according to a certain number of procedures, whose role is to avert its powers and its dangers, to cope with chance events, to evade its ponderous, awesome materiality."[56]

In this view, we might expect the effect of a myth or mythic discourse to be not that of change but of accommodation in the service of stability. After all, the myth of Persephone (frequently cited as a "source" for VISIONS) does not show us how to change anything, but instead tells us a "story" of how things came to be that way, and of the crucial part erring woman's desire played in the story. I emphasize "story" here, because of Blake's early recognition of the power of "histories" when they constitute "Bibles or sacred codes" (MHH4). In THE MARRIAGE "Reason" and "Desire" have different perspectives, different "stories," competing in the "Abyss" to define "place" as heaven or hell. Explicitly in the background of this work is Paradise Lost, the "story" of how God put Satan in his place: "Him the Almighty Power / Hurl'd headlong flaming from th' Ethereal Sky / With hideous ruin and combustion down / To bottomless perdition. . . . Such place Eternal Justice had prepar'd / For those rebellious" (Paradise Lost 1:44–71). Milton's poem can be read as a carefully structured field of discursivity in which Satan is given a "place" as a speaking subject, the realm of sinful and erroneous discourse. Between Milton and Blake's MARRIAGE, with its witty play on links between "place" and speech, there was a growing attention in eighteenth-century narrative to what Nancy Miller aptly calls the "ideologically delimited space" of feminine narration.[57] Richardson's Lovelace notices that the house of his "mother," the whore-mistress Mrs. Sinclair, is not merely a brothel but is also a discursive site: "I think in my heart that I can say and write those things at one place [Mrs. Sinclair's] which I cannot at the other; nor indeed anywhere else" (3:178). In the male pornographic novel the brothel or the boudoir are represented emphatically as places of liberated female speech as well as sexual activity. John Cleland's Fanny notices this often, and describes her prostitute friends at Mrs. Cole's as women who enjoy exchanging their tales of female Bildung and "in the height of their humours style themselves the restorers of the golden age and its simplicity of pleasures, before their innocence became so unjustly branded with the names of guilt and shame."[58]

If we look at VISIONS as either a mapping of or a moment in a field of discursivity with a regulated economy, we can see that

Oothoon's "place" in that economy is the ambivalent focus of the work, as it was of much contemporary discussion and debate in Blake's time. As a fictional character in a work of art, she is conspicuously a representation. But can she be a representation of "desire" itself, purified from falsifying representations, the exemplar of true desire and the Truth of desire? How absolute is her truth? One is always in representation, but when a woman is asked to *take place* in a representation her function is to represent man's desire.[59] Oothoon seems to acknowledge that she occupies this place, that her goal is to "reflect. / The image of Theotormon on my pure transparent breast" (2:15–16). As a representation of speaking woman, she serves conveniently as a ventriloquating mirror for acts of narcissistic self-completion on the part of those male readers who like to have their truths of feminine desire come out of the mouths of "women." At the same time "woman," or "the feminine," has an ancient function of signifying those forces and processes that threaten to disrupt symbolic orders in Western discourse. How ironic, if the most effective means of neutralizing the potentially disruptive voice were to celebrate and affirm it, to give it a place in the economy of discourse where it can speak all it wants, or where what it wants can be spoken for it and through it by the ventriloquating male. Or if "woman," rather than being the essence of quiddity, the pole of Nature itself, were simply like Nature in being a place or site on and through which masculine meanings get spoken and masculine discursive desires enacted. As Foucault observes: "We like to believe that sexuality has regained, in contemporary experience, its full truth as a process of nature, a truth which has long been lingering in the shadows and hiding under various disguises—until now, that is, when our positive awareness allows us to decipher it so that it may at last emerge in the clear light of language."[60]

If we look again at Oothoon's Truth, we can see it riddled with the inevitable paradoxes that mark the systematization of discursive power. On the one hand, Eros is one of the most powerful of gods: "The Orphic and Narcissistic Eros awakens and liberates potentialities that are real in things animate and inanimate, in organic and inorganic nature—real but in the unerotic reality suppressed."[61] If only this god's power could be liberated, it would "necessarily operate as a destructive, fatal force—as the total negation of the principle which governs the repressive reality."[62] But that which can liberate this repressed god can only be imagined as "a libidinal break at a precise moment, a schiz whose sole cause is desire—which is to say the rupture with causality that forces a rewriting of history on a level with the real, and produces this strangely polyvocal moment when everything is possible."[63] Before we can be released, something must release the god of release so that it can release us. If Oothoon is "an exemplar of liberation, showing that the life of Energy is the way out" she is, at a deeper level, an exemplar showing that our fantasy of a "cure" may itself be a symptom of the disease, the result of what Foucault calls "a regulated and polymorphous incitement to discourse."[64]

Oothoon's Truth, as it emerges, is the larger Truth of a system that claims that authentic desire is repressed by the tyrant god Urizen, whose name first appears in this work, uttered by Oothoon. The idea of a transcendent god or power of Eros is simultaneously posited as existing outside all power regimes and as subject to repression and distortion by them, so that the category of repression functions as a form of intelligibility that allows the formulation of the relations of power and their analysis. The "moment of desire" is known through its inhibition or absence rather than through being acted out in fulfillment. The utterance of that desire is reduced to the trope of apostrophe, under a rule of interdiction that allows endless utterance of such empty wishes. In this system the structure of intelligibility doubles the structure of the libidinal economy, since the prohibitions and taboos, rather than setting a limit to already existing desires, actually enter into the primary stage of the formation of those desires. The story of Oothoon retraces the moves through which an eroticism that exceeds bonds is engendered in the very process of being bound, and a metaphoric "bondage" ("Bound back to back" [2:5]) reflects the existential situation of the kind of "liberation" that she represents.

> But there may be another reason that makes it so gratifying for us to define the relationship between sex and power in terms of repression: something that one might call the speaker's benefit. If sex is repressed . . . the mere fact that one is speaking about it has the appearance of a deliberate transgression. . . . We are conscious of defying established power. . . . We know we are being subversive, and we ardently conjure away the present and appeal to the future. . . . Something that smacks of revolt, of promised freedom, of the coming age of a different law, slips easily into this discourse on sexual oppression. Some of the an-

cient functions of prophecy are reactivated therein. . . . What sustains our eagerness to speak of sex in terms of repression is doubtless this opportunity to speak out against the powers that be, to utter truths and promise bliss, to link together enlightenment, liberation, and manifold pleasures; to pronounce a discourse that combines the fervor of knowledge, the determination to change the laws, and the longing for the garden of earthly delights.[65]

As a history, the story can be reduced to a synchronic system, endlessly repeating itself, anticipated by the poem's first word, "**ENSLAV'D**," which is appropriately engraved by Blake in extra large, extra bold letters. Equally bold on that plate is the name "**OOTHOON**," with its **O**'s suggesting eyes or **I**'s that are ciphers, as well as the links in a chain of mind-forged manacles. Is this the name of our liberator, or of an object of domination whose function is to reproduce its own repression? She is critical of the "nets & gins & traps" of the parson which bind virgins to the "chain / Of life, in weary lust" (5:18, 22–23); but she is ready to use her own "silken nets and traps of adamant" (7:23) to catch girls for Theotormon, and then to watch and supervise their "wanton play" like one of those libertines in Sade who "sets up the postures and directs the over-all progress of the erotic operation; there is always someone to regulate . . . the exercise, séance, orgy."[66] The law of the Law works equally well for both parties, whether in Sade, where one obeys the laws of nature by following the impulses of those passions that have been outlawed by society, or in Rousseau, where the inclination to excess is crucial for the economy of law:[67] "The limit and transgression depend on each other for whatever density of being they possess: a limit could not exist if it were absolutely uncrossable and, reciprocally, transgression would be pointless if it merely crossed a limit composed of illusions and shadows. . . . Their relationship takes the form of a spiral which no simple infraction can exhaust."[68]

Oothoon's story and her system reflect the same structure of suppression, in which an exterior alienating force is imposed on subjects that would otherwise presumably have their own free and liberated form. By telling the impossible story of how we could become free, it becomes a different kind of enabling discourse for the story we tell of ourselves as victims. "*If* Oothoon can reach Theotormon and give herself to him, and *if* that confused lover could accept the gift, *then* the fallen nature of the Atlantic would be raised to a golden status, and . . . there would be no more sea. The ethics of sexual release . . . would renovate mankind and end all mind-forg'd tyrannies, not just the political ones. *But* none of this is yet to be."[69] In the meantime there is still the sea, and our seeing, as we point our fingers at the scapegoat Theotormon, the tragi-comic cuckold, our always-defeated rival.

But it may well be that Theotormon is blamed for not looking and not listening by those who do not see or hear him. If Theotormon were at all well read in English and European literature, he would be trained to recognize in both how and what Oothoon says the signs of danger to his identity as a certain kind of male; and the more Oothoon goes on, the more those fears would be enhanced. There is a comic anticipation of *VISIONS* in chapter 8 of *An Island in the Moon*, where Steelyard shows his preference for Hervey's *Meditations* and Young's *Night Thoughts* while Miss Gittipin goes on at length about "her favorite topic," the desire for and lack of pleasure ("I might as well be in a nunnery"). Steelyard observes that "They call women the weakest vessel but I think they are the strongest A girl has always more tongue than a boy [who knows enough to] put his head into a hole & hide it" when asked a question; Scopprell plays the critic's role, chiming in with his "I think the Ladies discourses Mr Steelyard are some of them more improving than any book. that is the way I have got some of my knowledge" (E457).

On one level, Steelyard here is humorously echoing a commonplace observation, that "Women have flexible tongues; they talk sooner, more easily, and more attractively than men. They are also accused of talking more. Man says what he knows; woman says what pleases."[70] But on a deeper level, the stereotyped observations reflect another view of the place of woman, in which the rhetorical structure of femininity (the category of the feminine as an effect of language) becomes linked with "rhetoric" as a metaphorically gendered and unethical play of language. "Eloquence, like the fair sex, has too prevailing beauties in it to suffer itself ever to be spoken against," writes Locke gallantly, adding (rhetorically) that it is "in vain to find fault with those arts of deceiving, wherein men find pleasure to be deceived."[71] For Locke rhetoric is feminine because "it is deceitful, false, devious and over-adorned." In its appeal to the passions (or to the "heart") it becomes associated with carnal instincts, while logic and reason appeal to the godly instincts in man. The more rhetoric resists and subverts the rational faculties, the more it becomes an object for social control or exclusion from acceptable discourse, as when Sprat raving (quite rhetorically) about the "vanity" and "shallowness" and "vicious abundance" or "volubility of *Tongue*" asserts that it "ought to be banish'd out of all *civil Societies*" because it gives "the mind a motion too changeable, and bewitching, to consist with *right practice*."[72] The characteristics of this rhetorical mode incompatible with "*right practice*" of the mind threaten Sprat's desired economy of "Peace and good Manners" (111). The regulation of discourse, of society, of marriage, and of female sexuality within marriage, all come under the same organizing structure in which the male qualities are endangered by the female qualities. And while these rhetorical positions of feminity and masculinity are not necessarily limited to the biological male and female, certain pervasive metonymic associations seem inevitably linked to the differentiation of male and female sexual equipment. Danger and confusion at *that* level seem to inform the threats at every other level of discourse. Vicious volubility of "tongue" suggests not only a disorder in which discourse is not controlled by reason, but one in which the "tongue" is in the wrong place doing the wrong "practice," proliferating and eroticizing discourse rather than controlling and regulating it, with the passions, "its Slaves," in "open defiance against *Reason*" (Sprat 111). To describe the underlying sexual threat here as castration fear would be to oversimplify, since what is at issue is the loss of all aspects of identity that are figuratively (in discourse) and socially (in reality) built on the propriety of things being in their proper places.

The "tongue" in this context would seem to be a figure for libidinal energy and its control, with the "natural" distribution being unequal, man having a lot of control and little libido, woman having inexhaustible libido and no control at all. When the "volubility of tongue" rhapsodizes on endlessly renewed and renewable pleasure the content of discourse and its modality become one, equally threatening, equally based on the fantasy fear of woman's biological capacity for continuous sexual relations. From Capellanus to Castiglione to Rousseau to Sade, we can find the belief expressed that women "have far more violent desires than [men] for the pleasures of lust."[73] Rousseau dwells at length on the threat posed by woman's "natural" voracious sexual appetite and the possibility of controlling men by keeping them in a constant state of arousal, thanks to "an invariable law of nature which gives to woman more facility to excite the desires than man to satisfy them" (*Emile* 360). If "reserve" (*pudeur*) did not impose a restraint on the woman, balancing the "moderation which nature imposes on the other," then "men would be tyrannized by women. For, given the ease with which women arouse men's senses . . . men would finally be their victims and would see themselves dragged to death without ever being able to defend themselves" (*Emile* 358–59). Thus the Supreme Being, "while abandoning woman to unlimited desires," enjoins *pudeur* to provide the necessary restraint, without which she would be Rousseau's equivalent of Blake's "horrible thing / Not born for the sport and amusement of Man but born to drink up all his powers" (*FZ* IX:133:6–7, E401).[74]

In addition to fears fueled by Oothoon's appeals, Theotormon might well have reasons for staying in place that constitute part of his libidinal economy—a "painefull pleasure" and "pleasing paine" like that of Spenser's Malbecco, as complement to Oothoon's eroticized speech and cry. Although easily mockable by critics like Bloom as "wretchedly weak," he has the negative strength *not* to be moved from his place in the system, a position of power in which he (figuratively) stands like Joyce's "Ainsoph, this upright one with that noughty beside him zeroine."[75] In *Vindication of the Rights of Woman* Mary Wollstonecraft complained about a system that "made cyphers of women to give consequence to the numerical figure" (48), and we have already noticed that Oothoon's name "scans" visually as a string of ciphers as well as the round links in a chain and two pairs of eyes. Given this sense of a place occupied by Theotormon in a larger system, it may well be that nothing will change in this story until Oothoon pays more attention to why her proselytizing (whether for free love, prophecy, or imagination) is not working. Perhaps nothing will change in the critical discourse about the story until we do the same, or until we see ourselves seeing it.

Cosi Fan Tutti?

We are great watchers of each other's eyes.
—Clarissa Harlowe in Richardson, *Clarissa*

By dint of gazing, one forgets one can be gazed at oneself.
—Roland Barthes, "The Metaphor of the Eye"

She would follow her dream of love, the dictates of her heart that told her he was her all in all, the only man in all the world for her for love was the master guide. Nothing else mattered. Come what might she would be wild, untrammelled, free.—Gerty MacDowell in Joyce, *Ulysses*

In this quotation from *Ulysses*, where Joyce is giving us the interior monologue of Gerty MacDowell as she thrills under the gaze of Leopold Bloom ("the eyes that were fastened upon her . . . had made her his" [365]), few are tempted to take the words as anything but the pathetic thoughts of a lame girl who has read a few bad books that now speak themselves through her, fixing her place in an ironic text. But with Molly Bloom, that flow-er of affirmative rhetoric, we have a more difficult case that teases us to "accept" her as accurate exemplar of the eternal feminine, or as yet another example of "the speaking of female desire through a male pen."[76] Another touchstone for comparison with Oothoon, even more apropos for our concerns, is provided by Geli Tripping in *Gravity's Rainbow*, as she sets "off to find her gallant Attila," Tchitcherine. Presenting an intoxicated vision of a world free from history and individuation, "free as the mountain wind" (*VDA*7:16), is she ready for

> the shrieking-outward, into stone resonance, where there is no good or evil, out in the luminous spaces Pan will carry her to? Is she ready yet for anything so real? The moon has risen. She sits now, at the same spot where she saw the eagle, waiting, waiting for something to come and take her. Have you ever waited for *it*? wondering whether it will come from outside or inside? . . . Suddenly, Pan—leaping—its face too beautiful to bear, beautiful Serpent, its coils in rainbow lashings in the sky— . . . It is impossible in this moonlight to see if you are male or female now.[77]

Pynchon's text gives us several clues to help keep this passage at an ambiguous and ambivalent distance, with the reader unsure about Geli's status as witch and the purpose of her mission *"to promote death"* (720). In particular, we note the scene takes place "at night—

the strange canaried nights of the Harz (where canary hustlers are busy shooting up female birds with male hormones so they'll sing long enough to be sold to the foreign suckers who occupy the Zone)" (718). We can see that whatever the Harz knows, we know only our distance from that knowledge and the deceptive moonlight in which both suckers and visionaries lose track of conventional gender markings under the spell of an old, old song.[78]

Much of what I have done so far with *VISIONS* has been to indicate the possibility of a similar ambiguous distance between this text, its voices or personae, its author, and its readers. If we read it for its "message," how is that any different from the pornosophical message we can find in *Fanny Hill,* or in Sade's transformations of Oothoon into Juliette and Thel into Justine? Oothoon takes the course of Moll Flanders and Fanny Hill rather than Pamela or Clarissa, but there is a sameness beneath the differences of these works that links them parodically.[79]

I hope that my urging a resistance to the temptation to load conceptual content into Oothoon's words, in order to hear them with a difference and from a distance, will not seem merely an attempt to clothe the "naked truth" of her discourse with the French frock of critical jargon. For that too can simply become a new strategy of rhetorical persuasion in which substantial incentives are offered for ideological adherence if we succumb to the compulsion to constitute Blake's text as an allegory of some particular theoretical position. My unreading depends rather on a growing familiarity with those eighteenth-century discourses that help Blake achieve a sense of the intertextual economies of discursivity, and with those representational strategies that hide themselves while producing the effect of truth.

I have no doubt that the historical subject William Blake had aspirations to find a way to liberate his poetry from the shackles of previous literary practice. But I think he also had a canny sense of the power of discourse that seems to have a life of its own and the ability to speak itself through subjects without their knowing it. I think he sought a stance that would resist that power, without indulging the fantasy that he could ignore it or that it would ignore him, and without ignoring the necessity of borrowing his destructive materials from the system itself to achieve a practice of subversive bricolage, where repeating the already written with a difference might be the only way to "make it new."

I do not invest his text with an authority that depends on the literal truth of this historical subject, because I read it as a text that undercuts those interpretive bequests that recover from the text only the power first granted to it. A text without authority can still be an exemplary text, and a text with great utility, if it is engaged with issues that concern us. I also resist the temptation to imagine a Blake who was himself no more than an instance of institutionalized discourse, its victim, participating in his period's literary history as a symptomatic and epiphenomenal manifestation rather than its authoritative master and corrector. I resist that temptation because it only shifts the superiority denied Blake to the critic, while I can only claim to undertake the task of thinking historically about the larger history of discourses and the vocabularies, concepts, and ideological values embedded in and transmitted by them—a task in which I find Blake an eminently useful exemplar.

In particular, I have found his text useful in my attempts to understand how an interpretive discourse of "liberation" in our time continues to repeat itself in repeating Oothoon even though it continues to produce nothing more than its own echoes. Like hers, it is a discourse that claims to reveal a Truth while masking the process of its production and its source. Blake's text has spurred me to attempt to think historically—and I hope responsibly—about the values, concepts, and terms that we are using, and to attempt to locate the contemporary discourse of Blake in the larger history of discourses that we live in—and that live in us—whether we recognize them or not. Foucault claims that "there is barely a society without its major narratives, told, retold and varied; formulae, texts, ritualized texts to be spoken in well-defined circumstances; things said once, and conserved because people suspect some hidden secret or wealth lies buried within."[80] Ours is no exception.

"In the last ten years, at least in an English-speaking context, *jouissance* has become a doctrinal concept: singular, unambiguous, steady, and *de rigueur*."[81] Unless we limit ourselves to the specific word "*jouissance*," and its place in French feminist criticism, Gallop's historical perspective here is much too limited for one who has kept up with the interpretive discourse on *VISIONS*. Gallop is referring to the opposition so famously posed by Barthes in *The Pleasure of the Text*, between two affective modes of reading: *plaisir*, which is the comfortable pleasure of a reading recognized and legitimated by culture, and *jouissance*, which reflects the power of some texts—or some readings—to disrupt the cultural canons and classifications and shake up their ideologies. Barthes and Gallop both recognize the irony that once *jouissance* becomes stated doctrine it is nothing more than a new form of the comfortable old *plaisir*, a reading that comes from culture rather than breaking with it. As critics we live lives of allegory, and our works are comments on that life.

I would like to conclude with an allegory of reading drawn not from contemporary theory and its discourses, but from one of the West's oldest narratives, where we find the story of Odysseus who had himself securely tied to the upright mast of his ship before sailing close to the sirens' "noughty" song of desire, so he could experience the pleasure of hearing it without suffering the consequences. As readers of Blake's texts we may be bound in the same fashion to the male-stream mast of cultural discourse, saved from the dangers of a song that we love to hear and sing, self-righteous in our condemnations of Theotormon for having his ears sealed. If there is a disruptive and potentially liberating potential in Blake's *VISIONS*, it may be its ability to help us see ourselves seeing it.

Afterword

David Wagenknecht

All dualisms, all theories of the immortality of the soul or of the spirit, as well as all monisms, spiritualist or materialist, dialectical or vulgar, are the unique theme of a metaphysics whose entire history was compelled to strive toward the reduction of the trace. The subordination of the trace to the full presence summed up in the logos, the humbling of writing beneath a speech dreaming its plenitude, such are the gestures required by an onto-theology determining the archeological and eschatological meaning of being as presence, as parousia, as life without différance: another name for death, historical metonymy where God's name holds death in check.—Derrida, *Of Grammatology*

I know too well that a great majority of Englishmen are fond of The Indefinite which they Measure by Newton's Doctrine of the Fluxions of an Atom, a Thing that does not Exist. These are Politicians & think that Republican Art is Inimical to their Atom. For a Line or Lineament is not formed by Chance: A Line is a Line in its Minutest Subdivisions: Strait or Crooked It is Itself & Not Intermeasurable with or by any Thing Else. Such is Job, but since the French Revolution Englishmen are all Intermeasurable One by Another Certainly a happy state of Agreement to which I for One do not Agree. God keep me from the Divinity of Yes & No too, the Yea Nay Creeping Jesus, from supposing Up & Down to be the same Thing as all Experimentalists must suppose.—Blake, Letter to George Cumberland, 12 April 1827

Considering that their occasion is academic, many of the essays in this collection must seem to the uninitiated remarkably adventurous. They were spurred on, of course, by a remarkable combination of unusual subject (Blake) and an almost apocalyptic theoretical environment, but their occasional exorbitance will no doubt prove offensive to some, even excluding those who still find Blake himself insufferable in that department. The same sanction will, I am sure, befall the following remarks, themselves not a little exorbitant, which were inspired by my having observed in most of the essays, regardless of the points of view expressed and the levels of energy consumed, that there was energy left over and surplus point of view for signaling the author's attitude to poststructuralism. This was the case also with those authors who in a recent number of *Studies in Romanticism* discussed the future of Blake criticism.[1] Not everyone was hospitable to deconstructive readings, but it was apparent that deidealizing Blake's character or even questioning his total control over a redemptive meaning was less fraught with anxiety than having frankly to admit that to carry on with Blake might entail simply ignoring the new dispensation. So imperial seems to be the power of the latter.

Why this is so, in our culture just now, is an interesting question in the sociology of criticism. Derrida's reach into our imaginations has imponderably much to do, obviously, with his genius, and it is repulsive to pretend that the vogue may be attributable to some weakness in the collective imagination, but the durability of his appeal to Americans, which looks to survive reader-response theory and the revival of politics, begs some kind of question. It may not be a question best broached in the context of literary criticism (because whether it is useful to attempt the application of Derrida's methods to texts that are marginal to the history of the metaphysical assumptions he wants to dissolve—or whether it even makes sense to do so—is one of the questions I want to raise), and indeed it will be dealt with here in such a speculative way that, for both reasons, the place of these remarks "outside the book" is quite the most fitting. In what follows I will try not to dance with hypocritical tears in my eyes, but by the same token I hope not to be blamed if I fail to achieve what this tradition is pleased to call "*jouissance*." My purpose in any case is not therapy but to provide a vocabulary of imagery with which to figure the problem.

To begin with, then, is not the juxtaposition of my opening texts suggestive? Is Derrida, from Blake's point of view, the very embodiment of the effect of the French Revolution, or are the two of them, caught on the verge of anathematizing their enemies, not surprisingly unantithetical? Like Blake, Derrida, it has taken us a while to figure out, is the enemy of abstraction and dearly devoted to minute particulars. The worst thing he can say about Saussure's limitations is their tendency "not to recognize the rights of history . . . except in the form of the arbitrary and in the substance of naturalism."[2] And the resemblance to Blake does not end there either, for is not Derrida as well offering us a mysterious freedom of which the basis must be *imagined?* How often are we told, on the one hand, that the *trace "must be thought* [my emphasis] before the opposition of nature and culture, animality and humanity, etc., belongs to the very movement of signification" (70), and, on the other, "Arche-writing . . . cannot occur *as such* within the phenomenological experience of a *presence"* (68), i.e. that we cannot experience what he is talking about and that we cannot experience anything else? Are not Blake and Derrida, in certain respects, seeing each other through the wrong end of the other's telescope, antimystical mystics and iconophobic makers of icons?[3] Is their rhetoric not similar, their pleasure in genre-breaking? Are they both not margin-scrawlers and graffiti-masters, are they both not similarly overweening? The suggestion may seem a bit overenthusiastic, but whether or not Blake and Derrida take up their cudgels on opposite sides of the French Revolution (opposite historical sides of the same ideological side), their assaults on us, via contradiction but at the same time beyond contradiction, have a similar feel. Derrida's deconstruction of Saussure's distinction between speech and writing reminds us of Blake's similar play with the contraries in *The Marriage of Heaven and Hell,* where we seem less to unravel the scandal than to reconceive it and make it the unspoken assumption of all our speech.[4]

But I want to speak also in something other than the voice of reconciliation. Rodolphe Gasché, in a very rigorous review of the current situation, "Deconstruction as Criticism,"[5] argues that a great deal of what passes for deconstructive criticism is really a reduction of Derrida's position, and further that the reduction can best be understood as continuous with the previous formalist critical tradition in the United States. Deconstruction as a vogue merely contributes to the "purely aesthetic and a-historical vista of its academic antecedents" (179). It contributes to a vague idealism and a neglect of contingency with which Derrida would not sympathize. His point is not that the new dispensation hasn't taken us anywhere—he is reasonably generous in his recognition that it has drawn us closer to "the very object of literary criticism, the text" (178)—but he feels, rhetoric apart, that the "theoretical pretensions" of the new dispensation "end with the elaboration of the cognitive aspects of . . . texts" (179), and that there has been no "epistemological break" between the assumptions of this criticism and earlier modes of fetishizing and idealizing texts. Worse, Gasché argues, the newer poststructuralist criticism often falsifies the notion of écriture in Derrida by "the conviction that everything is literature, text or writing" (179). Here the difficulties are more serious, for they involve actual misreading in the application of Derrida's term:

> This precipitated application in question is made possible—as always—through a confusion of levels in a specifically philosophical debate with Husserl's phenomenology. These levels are in fact distinguished carefully by Derrida himself. The notion of *writing* (of text, and of literature, as well) as used by modern deconstructive criticism refers in general only to the *phenomenological experience of writing* as something present in all discourses and texts. Yet, in *Of Grammatology* Derrida clearly warned of mistaking writing (as arche-writing) for the colloquial meaning of writing. Indeed, writing as arche-writing "cannot occur *as such* within the phenomenological experience of a *presence.*" The notion of the trace, he adds, "will never be merged with a phenomenology of writing." (179–80)

To put it more succinctly, Gasché's argument is that the deconstructive critics have transferred to the immanence of the text aspects of it (such as *différance*) that appear not crossed out but erased, and that are beyond experience phenomenologically and beyond expression as immanent irony or contradiction. Although from Derrida's perspective perhaps an unhelpful analogy, it is as though someone failing to understand the Freudian distinction between the systems Ucs. and Cs. consulted the representations of the dream-work as if they were continuous in structure and affect and immanence with the dream-thoughts in the Ucs. Derrida's notion, I take it, is analogous to Freud's in that the evolution of post-Platonic philosophy, like the evolution of a personality, is in large measure a *history* of contingency that we can reconstruct on the basis of what we are told by consciousness not only about itself (reflexivity) but also, indirectly, about that of which consciousness is unaware. But here the model-analogy ceases to be useful, for in "deconstruction" what is repressed makes consciousness possible. "Deconstruction," Gasché remarks, "is an operation which accounts for and simultaneously undoes self-reflection" (194), and in this quite un-Freudian sense, therefore, "represents a critique of reflexivity and specularity" (183). Or, as Derrida puts it himself, "logocen-

tric repression is not comprehensible on the basis of the Freudian concept of repression; on the contrary, logocentric repression permits an
understanding of how an original and individual repression became
possible."[6]

Gasché's cautions may turn out to be a blessing for those burdened
by a fashion. The "litteral expressions" of post-Saussurean, poststructuralist criticism have a way of finding a place for themselves even in
writings that have no use for them, and the reminder we are not obliged to use the jargon except where distinct philosophical issues are
at risk can be a relief. Further, it is a curious aspect of the sociology
I refer to that the vogue for intransitive specularity (e.g. the enormous
development of interest in "romantic irony" and the popularity of de
Man's formulation of "blindness and insight") precludes discussions
founded upon intentionality or immanence even where questions of
metaphysical "presence," or intentionality as evocation of presence-to-
self seem to be philosophically irrelevant, and at such junctures the
evoked paraphernalia of *différance* and supplements begins to suggest
the charged atmosphere and aura of the fetish-object. It truly seems
that the reaction to poststructuralism is overdetermined, and if one recalls Freud's own, shall we say, blunt explanation of fetishes, and the
metaphysical quarrel between Derrida and Lacan as to whether the
missing phallus constitutes an inverted sign of a metaphysical presence
(in a kind of negative theology) or rather a supplement or trace (depending, I suppose, on your gender or where you come into the story)
various amusing games emerge, based on the analogies between Derrida's criticism of Lacan and Gasché's of the American poststructuralists.[7] But if the pleasures of play with the semiotic penis do not appeal, one can always console oneself with the reflection that the whole
business, according to this argument, can often be avoided.

However, letting go, even of a *différance*, can be hard to do. This
may be so (at least) because in Blake there are so many contexts that,
superficially considered, seem to recapitulate Derrida's mysticism of
différance:

> As when a man dreams, he reflects not that his body sleeps,
> Else he would wake; so seem'd he entering his Shadow: but
> With him the Spirits of the Seven Angels of the Presence
> Entering; they gave him still perceptions of his Sleeping Body;
> (*M*15:1–4, E109)

One yearns to argue that Milton is making of himself the divine *différ-ance*, but Gasché's rigor (i.e. "seem'd" and "perceptions") makes the indulgence impossible.

Still, one persists. In *Milton,* again, "Palamabron appeal'd to all Eden, and recievd / Judgement" (*M*9:9–10, E103), and as a consequence "Satan rag'd amidst the Assembly!" (*M*9:30, E103), but further down the line in the midst of some explanation on the part of the Eternals we are told, "And therefore Palamabron dared not to call a solemn Assembly / Till Satan had assum'd Rintrah's wrath" (*M*11:24–25, E105). If one is reasonably callous, one can dip into Derrida's essay "Différance" and discover oneself to have been treated to "adi-aphoristic reduction or repression": "not in order to see opposition erase itself but to see what indicates that each of the terms must appear as the *différance* of the other, as the other different and deferred in the economy of the same."[8]

Or—an even more attractive example (because less easily explained in other, better ways)—the contradiction between the first and last stanzas of "Holy Thursday" in the *Songs of Experience:*

Is this a holy thing to see,
In a rich and fruitful land,
Babes reducd to misery,
Fed with cold and usurous hand?

.   .   .   .

And where-e'er the sun does shine,
And where-e'er the rain does fall:
Babe can never hunger there,
Nor poverty the mind appall.
(*SE*33:1–4, 13–16, E19–20)

Instead of "Come again?" one has a whole vocabulary with which to figure the contradiction. But if Gasché is correct, alas, perhaps only an attractive but illicit windbag of misapplied analogy. Trop(e) de mal!

However that may be, the verbal play of deconstruction, specializing in double-entendres and an erotics of concealment, continues to be an almost irresistible methodology for figuring the daring flagrancy of Blakean contradiction. Gasché's technicalities to one side for the moment, there is also the more fundamental issue whether a sensibility offended by the scepticism of Voltaire and Rousseau is likely to have anything in common with Derrida, but the appeal of the comparison continues to stand even against such objections, and I mean to yield to it here. Still, we should not need to be reminded that more than formalism (or semiotics) is at issue. Blake's contradictions, and Derrida's as well, issue in religious attitudes and cultural perspectives, and in Blake's case at least it is surprising how buried in technicalities the question of his religion remains. (Does Blake really belong to the secular culture that made him a fad in the universities, or is he fundamentally at odds with that world? It is dispiriting how often we are told, with high degrees of confidence but on the basis of very generalized or oracular evidentiary procedures, that Blake "used" Gnostic imagery but was not a Gnostic, or how we must take with a grain of dramatizing salt this or that savage heterodoxy/orthodoxy.) I suppose this tendency has its counterpart in reading Derrida only as "method," i.e. for his technique, overlooking its odd but discernible *ethos* of restoration, and considering his capacity for aggression it may be useless to have expected us to do otherwise, but in Blake's case I don't think I am imagining a tendency to suppress generalist perspectives, and to evade those that emerge from philosophical perspectives. The following remarks, hoping—in the spirit of this collection—to atone for the tendency, proceed to speculate via two contexts, both of them, I believe, enriched by the problematic juxtaposition of Blake and Derrida which I am encouraging.

The first context emanates from the observation that Derrida encourages meditation upon iconography. The question of icon (or, in the semiotic jargon that modern semioticians have in common with earlier linguists, "motivated" or "natural" images)[9] is of course related to the issue of the sister arts. Derrida's scornful and ironic discussion of Saussure's "reduction of phonic matter" in *Of Grammatology* (53) reminds us, as do many details of his analysis, that his criticism of Saussure touches on issues that are as old as *ut pictura poesis* and Lessing, and Derrida's claim that he rises, in fact, above the fray ("This arche-writing would be at work not only in the form and substance of graphic expression but also in those of nongraphic expression" [60]) perhaps has its counterpart in an eighteenth-century artist who, outside the tradition of *ut pictura poesis*, expressed himself in a democracy of word and picture.[10]

The other context is Freud, whom I can conveniently reintroduce here via Derrida by recalling how the latter, after remarking "For the property of the sign is not to be an image," gratuitously carries on in the very next sentence of *Of Grammatology:* "By a process exposed by Freud in *The Interpretation of Dreams*, Saussure thus accumulates contradictory arguments to bring about a satisfactory decision: the exclusion of writing" (45). There is something inherently Freudian, it seems to me, in the very air of deconstruction, which comes from overlapping but distinguishable notions of repression, and by going so far out of his way for Freud in this passage Derrida is offering us a path to be explored rather than an obstacle in our way. Probably the most relevant and fundamental text for our purposes, hardly an obscure one, is the celebrated commentary on contradiction in the sixth chapter (Section C: "The Means of Representation") of *The Interpretation of Dreams:*

> The way in which dreams treat the categories of contraries and contradictories is highly remarkable. It is simply disregarded. "No" seems not to exist so far as dreams are concerned. They show a particular preference for combining contraries into a unity or for representing them as one and the same thing. Dreams feel themselves at liberty, moreover, to represent any element by its wishful contrary; so there is no way of deciding at a first glance whether any element that admits of a contrary is present in the dream-thoughts as a positive or a negative.[11]

No devotee of this liberty, Derrida hastens to deconstruct the presence in which it is to be found: "In this context, and beneath this guise, the unconscious is not, as we know, a hidden, virtual, or potential self-presence. . . . In this sense, contrary to the terms of the old debate full of the metaphysical investments that it has always assumed, the 'unconscious' is no more a 'thing' than it is any other thing, is no more a thing than it is a virtual or masked consciousness."[12] Derrida accomplishes this deconstruction somewhat circuitously via *Beyond the Pleasure Principle*, which of course was long antedated by the original conception (Freud might say the discovery) of the unconscious. The antinomies which Derrida uses as leverage against Freud's text exist in an economic vocabulary bringing together into one register the opposed ideas of the pleasure/reality principle and the death instinct: one economy always defers pleasure for collection later, whereas the other spends irreparably: "How are we to think *simultaneously*, on the one hand, *différance* as the economic detour which, in the element of the same, always aims at coming back to the pleasure or the presence that have been deferred by (conscious or unconscious) calculation and, on the other hand, *différance* as the relation to an impossible presence, as expenditure without reserve, as the irreparable loss of presence, the irreversible usage of energy, that is, as the death instinct?" (19).

What would happen to the potential implication of this passage were we to substitute in it Blake's text for Freud's unconscious? The ambiguity of Blake's text would find its way to the locus of the unconscious, and identify itself as a *choice*, between, on the one hand, a stock piling or accumulation of meaning, and, on the other, a tendency to ultimate undecidability or aporia that fascinated Blake critics long before the new New Criticism. In Blake the issues that find their way into this lacuna of undecidability are almost anagogically serious— they have a way of evoking the religious roots of his art—and by showing how high the stakes can be we go a long way toward explaining why Derrida is inspired to reach for his metaphysical revolver in the face of the undeciding unconscious. In the space we speak of, in the literature we write about, what is "at stake" is nothing less than the relationship between metaphorical capacity and divine analogy. If what Blake wants to show us, as Hazard Adams suggests by his phrase "(anti)system of metaphoricity" (above), is that there can be nothing more than this, Derrida's anxiety would seem to be to make the same point from the other side: "The outside, 'spatial' and 'objective' exteriority which we believe we know as the most familiar thing in the world, as familiarity itself, would not appear without the grammè, without differance as temporalization, without the nonpresence of the other inscribed within the sense of the present, without the relationship with death as the concrete structure of the living present. *Metaphor would be forbidden.*"[13]

Without the nonpresence of the other inscribed. At first I am going to turn away from Blake, to make the connection meaningful, to the, one would assume, less conflicted context of Italian Renaissance devotional painting. What do we find there? According to Leo Steinberg's astonishing study, *The Sexuality of Christ in Renaissance Art and in Modern Oblivion*, what we find is the sexual member of Christ.[14] Not always already there either (and hence overlooked)—"Normative Christian culture—excepting only this Renaissance interlude—disallows direct reference to the sexual member" (45)—but *there* with a vengeance (strange interlude) for roughly four centuries. After which effaced, excised, hidden. There is a remarkable range of pictorial representation, too, from the little widdler of many a baby Jesus being fondly manipulated by his family (where noticed this was referred to the unfortunate psychological hygiene of the Latin cultures!) all the way to truly astonishing and disturbing portrayals (most of these successfully repressed from public view) displaying the having-been-crucified Christ (e.g. Maerten van Heemskerck's *Man of Sorrows* [see illustration 11]) bearing such an enormous and unmistakable erection as to suggest an icon of masochism. "There exists," Steinberg remarks, "perhaps no more poignant proof of Renaissance openness to ancient mystery symbolism than the willingness of profound Christian artists to place this interdicted flesh at the center of their confessions of faith" (45–46).

This is not the place, nor do I have the competence, for a detailed review of Steinberg's findings. Suffice it to say, first, that he entertains no instinct at all for other than a normalizing interpretive procedure. Surely this is wise, because the phenomenon of representation is much too widespread historically and geographically to suggest subversive intent unless one were to assume that all such paintings were the function of some minority cult within Christianity, which is clearly not the case. Steinberg attempts interpretation, accordingly, within Christian norms, and his best guess is that the phallus functions iconographically, as do many other Christian symbols, as a reversal of the same sign in imperial or pagan contexts: "Christ's genitals contrast with the Bacchic phallus as the mystic Lamb contrasts with any fiercer heraldic beast; as the crown of thorns contrasts with conventional kingly regalia" (46–47). Or, even more plainly, "the penis of Christ, puissant in abstinence, would surpass in power the phalli of Adam or Dionysus" (46). Moreover, in order to understand the Renaissance emphasis on the mystery of Incarnation, it is important to see that Christ *has* a penis, emblem now of "God's assumption of human weakness" (48). It is nevertheless true that, especially in the more radical examples, certain aspects of what is being reversed would need to be written under erasure or repressed, and what shocks is that this need is not fulfilled. Commentary may remain tacit, but the image is all too clear, and it is precisely the lack of repression that makes this interesting.

Further, as already remarked, one of the interesting things about

11. Maerten van Heemskerck, *Ecce Homo* (also known as *Man of Sorrows*), Bob Jones University Collection, Greenville, S.C.

this tradition is that there seems to be no commentary, no writing. Far from being illustrations of an exegetical tradition, the paintings alone constitute the tradition (or inscription), and the ideas implicit emanate from no voice offstage (or off-canvas). For this show there is no prompter, for this display no frame. The paintings intrinsically suggest, however, remarkably intriguing sorts of exegetical "writing," teased out of them into speech by Steinberg in masterly fashion. For instance, one of the most telling instances of reversal or contradiction is the issuance of blood in Circumcision paintings: "The erstwhile symbol of the life force [the penis] yields not seed, but redeeming blood," Steinberg remarks, but then adduces a remarkably strange further instance: "We perceive a similar bond to the Passion in a painting by Joos van Cleve, where the coral cross of a rosary screens and jewels the privy parts" (47)—accomplishing the latter precisely by a sign of female enticement. In another instance the "terminal wounds" of Christ, that pertaining to the Circumcision and the wound in his side, are connected by a line of blood from latter to penis, prompting from Steinberg perhaps his most inspired remark, "a blood hyphen between commencement and consummation" (58). He suggests further that the formal symbolism of these pictures may be more like hieroglyphs or ideograms than traditional iconography: "Such pictures project a new iconography that is neither iconic nor narrative, nor linked to any liturgical feast. They are historiated emblems designed to enshrine the central mystery of the Creed. As Mina Bacci wrote of the Piero di Cosimo altarpiece at the Uffizi, they are direct 'visualizations of the dogma' " (121).

The sexual meaning of *The Man of Sorrows* is not repressed. The suppression of the painting proves this. What happens, rather, is that a very extended capacity for metaphorization is confidently introduced (or rather assumed), so that the rule of reversal of meaning can be applied, and sexual passion read in some fashion as a metaphor for Christ's. This is accomplished by iconicity (i.e. recognition of the sacred subject), but to a degree at the expense of it. What the allegorization (metaphorization) amounts to is the introduction into the reading of a principle of limit, a principle of exclusion. In terms of "motivated signs" (one definition of icon), it is almost as if the meaning were maximally motivated, whereas the representation had almost as radically escaped motivation, but it is hard to avoid seeing here a very particular interdiction: the divine meaning of the representation, itself a function of iconicity, extends to the idea that whatever the representation means it doesn't mean *that,* but *that* read in some other metaphorical way.

Some interesting paradoxes ensue. Iconicity on the face of it suggests a plenitude of immanent meaning, amounting almost to magic—though the meaning of "icon" and the culture of iconophobia remind us that this idea of immanence is subject to deconstruction. If the picture is a bearer of mana, it is literally (spiritually? materially?) what it represents. However, under the circumstances to which this particular icon has been exposed (a peculiar temptation), the following paradox occurs. Although usually the literal level of meaning would seem to be on a plane of opposition to metaphoricity, and the two ideas of meaning contradictory (i.e. the less literal the more metaphorical, and vice versa), here support of the picture's "original" iconicity by means of exclusion makes metaphoricity a support for, perhaps even a condition of, literal iconicity. Some analogous conundrum is at the center of what Derrida has to tell us. It is the contradiction between the following two contiguous sentences of *Of Grammatology:* "Without a retention in the minimal unit of temporal experience, without a trace retaining the other as other in the same, no difference would do its work and no meaning would appear. It is not the question of a constituted difference here, but rather, before all determination of the content, of the *pure* movement which produces difference" (62). Since the first sentence is the condition of the second as possibility (i.e. in theory), but the second is the condition of the first in experience, a mental bracketing has to occur within the terms of the syllogism implied by the first sentence that preempts the second sentence before it is theoretically experienced: "no difference [which I experience as constituted] would be able to appear in my argument as *unconstituted.*" Or, in other words, *without the nonpresence of the other inscribed* I could not uninscribe the presence (in my theoretical sentence: "grave the sentence deep"). Does this not bear some relationship, in the picture we are discussing, to the iconic paradox, expressible as (~~not that~~) that?

The second interesting paradox is that a sacrifice of iconicity undoubtedly nevertheless occurs. The principle of exclusion, while it preserves the "original" meaning of the icon, of this particular icon, does so at the expense of iconicity in general, for it puts into reserve, as it were, another kind of negativity—the possibility of different sorts of allegorical interpretation. The "real" allegory of the painting, therefore, may be the development of the analogy between Christ's sacrifice and this sacrifice of an apocalyptic plenitude beyond the reach of the exclusionary principle. (In fact my motivating idea, behind both this discussion and the Blake painting I take up below, is that the relationship between the semiotic or linguistic aspect of these pictures and their religious subject matter is integral rather than coincidental.) And yet the representation is struggling just as hard as it can in the opposite direction, to put on the visual record a suggestiveness (amounting almost to lewdness) that the gravity of the subject can steer by the censor. So a struggle is at work, the stakes in which appear to be on the one hand an apocalyptic plenitude of acceptance (a sort of endless stockpiling, like Hazard Adams's idea of synecdochal capacity), and on the other the necessary relationship between a world of judicious meaning (allegory) and a principle of exclusion or censorship.

One can see in this a formal principle interesting to apply to deconstruction. On one axis, contradiction and exclusion are similar (since both are negative), but on another (if one looks at contradiction as a system) exclusion is the negative of contradiction. Further, the systematic (or synecdochally hospitable) aspect of contradiction is always already based on the repression of exclusion, so in this sense exclusion is the *différance* of the acceptance of contradiction that Freud, very properly, locates in the unconscious. The reader represses or defers "that meaning," in a kind of "metaphysical" equivalent of the pleasure principle, noticing the meaning deferred more than the meaning of deferment. The opposition in this example, however, is not between speech and writing (and the silence of the unconscious need not beg questions of metaphysical presence) but between permissibility and impermissibility, and it is the achieved inaccessibility of exclusion in general that is problematic, inasmuch as consciousness of the effect of all allegorical readings on iconic immanence has been deferred. Looked at from this point of view, the rather grotesque hysteria of the metaphor (the Passion aligned with Christ's erection) may seem a necessary sacrifice to prevent the alternative, which is recognition that all divine meaning may only be human figuration, from rising to consciousness.

Derrida writes in "Différance":

> *Différance* maintains our relationship with that which we neces-
> sarily misconstrue, and which exceeds the alternative of presence
> and absence. A certain alterity—to which Freud gives the meta-
> physical name of the unconscious—is definitively exempt from
> every process of presentation by means of which we would call
> upon it to show itself in person. In this context, and beneath this
> guise, the unconscious is not, as we know, a hidden, virtual, or
> potential self-presence. It differs from, and defers, itself: which
> doubtless means that it is woven of differences, and also that it
> sends out delegates, representatives, proxies; but without any
> chance that the giver of proxies might "exist," might be present,
> be "itself" somewhere, and with even less chance that it might
> become conscious (20–21).

It is no criticism at all of this brilliant passage to suggest that in the
present instance we seem to have its polar opposite. By simple execu-
tive fiat ("not *that*") the Jesus of the picture becomes precisely the
presence that sends out proxies (even the ultimate proxy in a semiotics
of desire). Where Derrida's metaphysics fits into the picture I do not
know, but the expressive rhetoric of this picture exactly foregrounds
alterity, virtually rubs our nose in it (while suppressing its general
effect), and the price it pays for doing so is making "the process of
presentation by means of which we would call upon it to show itself in
person" the specific subject of the painting. The process, the exorbitant
daring of the metaphorical connection, sounds remarkably similar,
I'd guess, to what Hazard Adams is thinking of as ultimate synecdochal
possibility, or perhaps to what Blake enigmatically calls "Divine Analogy" (*J*85:7, E243). In any case, however, the reversal, in the Renaissance painting, of Derrida's argument suggests that it might be interesting to try the formula on a Blakean image.

The example I have in mind is also complex, and in fact an illustration
of the other "choice" of ambivalence discussed above, which it will be
recalled was undecidability. I want to consider briefly Blake's watercolor Crucifixion for Thomas Butts, *The Soldiers Casting Lots for
Christ's Garment*, which has the Crucifixion turning its collective back
(the three crosses are there) on the viewer while we regard the Romans
dicing for the robe at the foot of the central cross (see illustration 12).

12. *The Soldiers Casting Lots for Christ's Garments*, Fitzwilliam Museum, Cambridge University.

There are many minute particulars of this painting I have no time to discuss, but its principal conundrum, or presentation of contradiction, comes with the discovery that the central figure of the three dicing Romans (the one who is facing the viewer directly) is holding up his hand in a gesture resembling benediction, that he can be seen a representation of the Christ whose countenance overhead is so dramatically effaced. What could this mean?

At first the range of possibilities seems to lie comfortably within parameters of contradiction. There is perhaps a correction of the vertical axis of the picture (which had been promising a conventional protest: how *could* these men beneath the cross be doing *that* with the Crucifixion overhead?), saying, "The Christ you miss seeing is in fact right before you. Didn't you remember to seek him amidst thieves?" Or, in the second place, there may be a contradiction (alternative or correction?) of this Protestantism: "This Christ, whom you can see as you can't see the real one, is the antithesis of the other: a representation of the antitype. Here is the anti-Christ beneath the true." It is only a moment's reflection that carries us beyond this place also—to the brink of undecidability. For inasmuch as the first reading took us beyond the level of the primary literal protest of the picture (as recorded in its title), the second reading, without duplicating that level, nevertheless constitutes a return to it, but it is a return that cannot be accomplished without the "originary" contradiction of the first reading. This is a lot easier to "see" than to talk about, and with it we seem to have arrived, in the study of Blake, back also at a familiar aporia. Is this picture a show of radical iconic Protestantism or ironic play (something more available to modern consciousness)? Here, compared to the earlier picture, allegory works via a different paradox: the conflict between a wished-for, infinitely elastic "Divine Analogy" and a now-you-see-it-now-you-don't principle of interdiction is completely moot (mute)—there *is* no obvious "not *that*" (which is one source of the difficulty), and the idea of immanence or iconicity has perhaps been extended to everything we see, thereby mooting as well the all-important distinction between this-worldliness and otherworldliness. Since the contrast between these two dimensions, moreover, is at second glance the issue of the picture if not in fact its subject (can this Roman be Christ for me?), the denial of this difference extends to iconicity the capacity always to embrace contradictoriness as an allegory of system, of nonexclusion. Meaning is not motivated at all here, but representation is, if anything, overmotivated, and hence indistinct. Without begging any metaphysical questions, it would seem to be difference (with an *e*) which is under erasure in this instance, in order (to repeat) to extend the privilege of a positive "allegorical" meaning to the denial always lurking even in contradiction-as-system.

It is time, I think, to remark that an aesthetics of presence may not be convertible with a metaphysics of presence, and that Rodolphe Gasché's caution, which we evoked, applies to ourselves as well. But one final volley of speculation, please, before packing it in. The "unconscious" that Derrida prefers to Freud's (Blake's locus of undecidability: Beulah, I suppose, where it is not necessary to "go down with decision"), is it not a species of *possibility?*—a radical alterity that sends a never-ending series of proxies but that has no presence of its own? In *The Man of Sorrows* an alterity that was not ontological but affective (the unacceptable equation) created but held in check the dimension of allegory. It is true that the dimension of undecidability in Blake's picture manifests itself, in a way, by sending substitutes as well (a Roman for Christ), but what Blake is suppressing—and this helps to make reading him difficult—is not the possibility of allegory (because in his world that's all that was left), but the negative aspect of contradiction, the "not *that,*" the *need to choose.*

Expressed in this way (perfectly heretical to the way we usually think about Blake), it is hard not to see the difference between the two paintings, on some theoretical level, as suggesting the opposite ends or extremities of an historical era, and the alignment this notion encourages between Blake and Derrida places them very roughly together at the hither end of an iconic period in our culture. One hesitates, understandably, to offer at one extremity of an era so grotesque and lunatic an image as *The Man of Sorrows,* and Blake's painting, interesting as it is, is hardly a major work either. But marginal works can at the same time represent central tendencies, and while I am using these images as a machine for thought let me try one final exploitation of their strangeness.

On one axis, we argued, the negativity of contradiction is on the same level as allegorical exclusion, but on another axis (if we regard contradiction as system) exclusion denies contradiction. Blake (and I have been arguing Derrida as well, in his aesthetic application) would seem to be functioning on the second of these two axes, making exclusion (and choice) the *différance* of contradiction-as-system. It can be said of the Renaissance image that, having already made its choice, it invests (mistakenly) its repressive expenditure of energy on a single meaning, little noticing what has happened to the system as a whole (iconicity or "presence to self" has been turned into allegory). Blake's image, on the other hand, here "beyond the pleasure principle," seems bent on a nonexclusionary allegorical system of sacrifice, where the same religious purpose puts exclusion itself beyond the pale with respect to any number of particular meanings. This, if you will, is the Crucifixion as Orc on the Tree of Nature, but as expressive program it sounds exactly contrary to Blake's conscious intention. Choice and particularity are his avowed fetishes (the indefinite is "a Thing that does not Exist"), and surely, we may feel, Blake might not blink at *The Man of Sorrows* either if the alternative were an anarchy of ambiguity between Christ and anti-Christ, a field of polysemous possibility amounting (we may feverishly feel) to a death wish. (Nor would prudishness be a problem: Blake's *oeuvre* is replete with phalli, though, admittedly, a number fell under *some*one's erasure.) But he did blink.

I have withheld from my analysis so far one very interesting detail. Not only is the central cross turned away from us (and therefore erased), the facing Roman at the base of the cross also has his eyes cast down (at the dice) so that his countenance is effectually closed to us (crossed). If we were to pursue our "historical" thesis to the bitter end, could we not see this too as a sign of closure, including recondite reference to the other end of the scale? Could it be argued that the strange inwardness of the painting, which seems indeed to have contributed something to its visual lack of vitality, owes not a little to the implied "other end" of the scale? What we are *not* to see here, what the characters in the diversionary drama at the foot of the cross, have no possibility of seeing either, is the erect penis of Christ: in its place is an emblem of hazard, the dice. Is what we as well have no "chance" of seeing the trace Gasché cautions us about—superior to mere phenomenological experience? One risks such imagery, harsh and tactless though it is, because alongside a familiar bridge between Blake and Derrida (based on simultaneous but contradictory loyalties to the allegorical and the concrete) it begins to cast the shadow of a more mysterious and haunting connection between religious expression and an erotics of concealment and sacrifice.

Notes

Introduction

1 Johnson, *The English Romantic Poets: A Review of Research and Criticism*, ed. Frank Jordan, 4th ed. (New York: MLA, 1985), 249.

2 Webster, *Blake's Prophetic Psychology* (Athens: University of Georgia Press, 1983); George, *Blake and Freud* (Ithaca, N.Y.: Cornell University Press, 1980); Glen, *Vision and Disenchantment: Blake's* Songs *and Wordsworth's* Lyrical Ballads (Cambridge: Cambridge University Press, 1983); DiSalvo, *War of Titans: Blake's Critique of Milton and the Politics of Religion* (Pittsburgh: University of Pittsburgh Press, 1984); Aers, Cook, and Punter, *Romanticism and Ideology* (London: Methuen, 1981); Hilton, *Literal Imagination: Blake's Vision of Words* (Berkeley: University of California Press, 1983); Hilton and Vogler, eds., *Unnam'd Forms: Blake and Textuality* (Berkeley: University of California Press, 1986).

3 Keynes, *A Bibliography of William Blake* (New York: Grolier Club, 1921), *The Writings of William Blake* (London: Nonesuch Press, 1925), *Poetry and Prose of William Blake* (London: Nonesuch Press, 1927).

4 Keynes, *Complete Writings of William Blake with All the Variant Readings* (London: Nonesuch Press, 1957; reprint with new material, London: Oxford University Press, 1966).

5 Erdman, *Poetry and Prose of William Blake* (Garden City, N.Y.: Doubleday, 1965), *Complete Poetry and Prose of William Blake* (Garden City, N.Y.: Anchor Press–Doubleday, 1982).

6 Bentley, *William Blake's Writings* (Oxford: Clarendon Press, 1978).

7 Santa Cruz Study Group, *Blake: An Illustrated Quarterly* 18 (1984), 4–31.

8 Edwin J. Ellis and William Butler Yeats, *The Works of William Blake, Poetic, Symbolic and Critical* (London: 1893).

9 Damon, *William Blake: His Philosophy and Symbols* (1924; reprint, Gloucester, Mass.: Peter Smith, 1958); Sloss and Wallis, *William Blake's Prophetic Writings* (Oxford: Clarendon Press, 1925).

10 Damon, *A Blake Dictionary: The Ideas and Symbols of William Blake* (1969; reprint, Boulder, Colo.: Shambhala, 1979), x.

11 Harper, *The Neoplatonism of William Blake* (Chapel Hill, N.C.: University of North Carolina Press, 1961); Raine, *Blake and Tradition* (Princeton, N.J.: Princeton University Press, 1968).

12 Bronowski, *William Blake and the Age of Revolution* (1945; revised, New York: Harper and Row, 1965); Schorer, *William Blake: The Politics of Vision* (New York: Henry Holt, 1966).

13 Erdman, *Blake: Prophet against Empire* (1954; revised, Garden City, N.Y.: Doubleday, 1977).

14 Frye, *Fearful Symmetry: A Study of William Blake* (1947; reprint, Boston, Beacon Press, 1962), 420; *Anatomy of Criticism: Four Essays* (Princeton, N.J.: Princeton University Press, 1957).

15 Frye, *The Critical Path: An Essay on the Social Context of Literary Criticism* (Bloomington: Indiana University Press, 1971), 12–13.

16 Bloom, *Blake's Apocalypse: A Study in Poetic Argument* (Garden City, N.Y.: Doubleday, 1963); Fisher, *The Valley of Vision: Blake as Prophet and as Revolutionary*, ed. Northrop Frye (Toronto: University of Toronto Press, 1961).

17 *Studies in Romanticism* 21 (1982). Page citations to this issue will appear parenthetically in the text.

18 See Richard Robinson, *Plato's Earlier Dialectic* (Ithaca: Cornell University Press, 1941), 75. My abbreviated history of the concept of method draws on Robinson, on Kenneth M. Sayre, *Plato's Analytic Method* (Chicago: University of Chicago Press, 1969), and on Neal W. Gilbert, *Renaissance Concepts of Method* (New York: Columbia University Press, 1960).

19 See Gilbert, *Renaissance Concepts of Method*, 220–22.

20 Lately, historians of science and investigators of scientific method have pointed out that the objective, systematic, and stringently methodical character of science has been exaggerated. Thomas Kuhn and Paul Feyerabend are only two of many whose work has demonstrated the effectively rhetorical dimensions of scientific investigation.

21 Palmer, *Hermeneutics: Interpretation Theory in Schleiermacher, Dilthey, Heidegger, and Gadamer* (Evanston, Ill.: Northwestern University Press, 1969), 247.

22 Fry, *The Reach of Criticism: Method and Perception in Literary Theory* (New Haven: Yale University Press, 1983), 1.

23 De Man, *Blindness and Insight: Essays in the Rhetoric of Contemporary Criticism* (New York: Oxford University Press, 1971), ix.

24 More recently, in "The Resistance to Theory" (*Yale French Studies* 63 [1982], 3–20), de Man takes up the issue of method in a way that may seem to support Fry's position. De Man speaks of "a tension . . . between methods of understanding and the knowledge which those methods allow one to reach. If there is indeed something about literature, as such, which allows for a discrepancy between truth and method, between *Wahrheit* and *Methode*, then scholarship and theory are no longer necessarily compatible" (4). Scholarship, de Man argues, has proven "eminently teachable," while theory, as the "controlled reflection on the formation of method," ought to be equally teachable, unless truth and method are dis-

crepant, in which case "a method that cannot be made to suit the 'truth' of its object can only teach delusion" (3–4). Once again, however, the delusion is unavoidable: "such a difficulty is an inherent focus of the discourse about literature," so that opposition to theory (and, by extension, to method) "in the name of ethical and asthetic values" is fundamentally an act of evasion (5). De Man makes theory a paradoxical project, but he does not allow the possibility of extramethodological modes of understanding. His argument suggests that the flight from method aspires to a simplification of reading of the kind sought by the most reductive of methods.

25   Jacques Derrida, "Violence and Metaphysics: An Essay on the Thought of Emmanuel Levinas," in *Writing and Difference*, trans. Alan Bass (Chicago: University of Chicago Press, 1978), 117.

Methods and Limitations

1   Borges, *The Aleph and Other Stories: 1933–1969*, trans. Norman Thomas di Giovanni in collaboration with the author (New York: Dutton, 1970), 170.

2   In my discussion of falsification, the influence of Karl R. Popper should be evident. For a concise statement of his views, see "Philosophy of Science: A Personal Report," in *British Philosophy in the Mid-Century: A Cambridge Symposium*, ed. C. A. Mace (London: Allen and Unwin, 1957), 155–91—a discussion that is relevant not merely to interpretations in the natural sciences. Ideas somewhat similar to Popper's are developed by E. D. Hirsch, Jr., who adopts the concept of "corrigible schemata" (the phrase comes from Piaget) as an escape from facile positivism, naive perspectivism, and the dangers of hypnosis by the "hermeneutic circle": see *The Aims of Interpretation* (Chicago: University of Chicago Press, 1976), 17–35.

3   Adams, "Post-Essick Prophecy," *Studies in Romanticism* 21 (1982), 402.

4   Lewis, "Notes toward a Theory of the Referent," *PMLA* 94 (1979), 475.

5   Fischer, *Historians' Fallacies: Toward a Logic of Historical Thought* (New York: Harper, 1970), 91. Fischer's work, which analyzes in detail the problems of methodological assumptions, is a good example of a theoretical work that might be read with profit by students of several humanistic disciplines but that has been restricted in its audience by traditionally exaggerated notions about differences among the various kinds of interpretation performed in the several disciplines.

6   Because lack of efficiency is often synonymous with lack of effectiveness, critics should seek to identify the point at which an interpretation can work only by becoming so complicated that it is ripe for Occam's razor.

7   Fischer, 100. Cf. Hirsch, *Aims*, 21: "Linguistic interpretation cannot authenticate itself on the linguistic level alone."

8   Compare Hirsch's suggestion that "the hermeneutic hypothesis is not completely self-confirming since it has to compete with rival hypotheses about

the same text and is continuously measured against those components of the text which are least dependent on the hypothesis"—*Validity in Interpretation* (New Haven: Yale University Press, 1967), 261.

9   Hirsch, *Validity*, 40.

10   W. J. T. Mitchell poses an interesting political question about deconstructive criticism—a question that might be asked about many other methods: "If some of Blake's authority seems to be lost in [the critical] process, we will need to watch carefully where the power is being transferred—to a Nietzschean reader who imposes his will to power in critical texts which aspire to rival and surpass Blake's own?"—"Dangerous Blake," *Studies in Romanticism* 21 (1982), 416.

11   Hilton, *Literal Imagination* (Berkeley: University of California Press, 1983), 7–8.

12   Hilton, *Literal Imagination*, 7.

13   Raine, *Blake and Tradition* (Princeton, N.J.: Princeton University Press for Bollingen Foundation, 1968), 1:xxvi, xxvii.

14   Frye, *Fearful Symmetry: A Study of William Blake* (1947; reprint, Princeton, N.J.: Princeton University Press, 1969), 14. Complementary to Frye's assumption about the organization of Blake's text is his assumption about the a priori organization of knowledge: "The wise man has a pattern or image of reality in his mind into which everything he knows fits, and into which everything he does not know could fit" (87).

15   It should be noted, in preparation for what I say later about the assumption of Blake's success, that virtually all discussions of his dialectic assume that it adds great strength to his work. I know of only one substantial negative account: Peter L. Thorslev, Jr., "Some Dangers of Dialectic Thinking, with Illustrations from Blake and His Critics," in *Romantic and Victorian: Studies in Memory of William H. Marshall*, ed. W. Paul Elledge and Richard L. Hoffman (Rutherford, N.J.: Fairleigh Dickinson University Press, 1971), 43–74.

16   Arguments of special relevance to the current discussion can be found in two works of R. S. Crane, *The Languages of Criticism and the Structure of Poetry* (Toronto: University of Toronto Press, 1953), esp. 27–38, 126–28, 140; and *The Idea of the Humanities and Other Essays Critical and Historical* (Chicago: University of Chicago Press, 1967), esp. "Criticism as Inquiry; or, The Perils of the 'High Priori Road,'" 2:25–44; and "On Hypotheses in 'Historical Criticism': Apropos of Certain Contemporary Medievalists," 2:236–60 (here Crane brings forward Popperian notions of falsification).

17   But it is dismaying to consider how many of our contemporary methods would be damaged by the logical rigor of Chicago's attacks on the New Criticism in such essays as Crane's "Criticism as Inquiry" and Elder Olson's "William Empson, Contemporary Criticism, and Poetic Diction," in *On Value Judgments in the Arts and Other Essays* (Chicago: University of Chicago Press, 1976), 118–56.

18   And see Fischer, 36–38, on the importance of testing one's hypotheses in

person rather than simply identifying them and presenting them for others to debate.

19   Culler, *On Deconstruction: Theory and Criticism after Structuralism* (Ithaca, N.Y.: Cornell University Press, 1982), 9–10.

20   See, for example, Joseph Anthony Wittreich, Jr., *Angel of Apocalypse: Blake's Idea of Milton* (Madison: University of Wisconsin Press, 1975), 188–219; Stephen C. Behrendt, *The Moment of Explosion: Blake and the Illustration of Milton* (Lincoln: University of Nebraska Press, 1983), 69, 84, 196n.34.

21   Bloom, *Blake's Apocalypse: A Study in Poetic Argument* (Ithaca, N.Y.: Cornell University Press, 1963), 94.

22   Jackie DiSalvo, *War of Titans: Blake's Critique of Milton and the Politics of Religion* (Pittsburgh: University of Pittsburgh Press, 1983), 266–67. Non-Marxist readers—e.g., John Beer, *Blake's Humanism* (Manchester: Manchester University Press, 1968), 59, 246n.18—have also adopted the straight interpretation, looking for elements of agreement between *MHH*23 and other Blakean works, such as *The Everlasting Gospel*; one problem for such approaches is the apparent lack of agreement between *MHH*23 and other parts of *The Marriage*, when those parts are read straight.

23   Brenda S. Webster, *Blake's Prophetic Psychology* (Athens: University of Georgia Press, 1983), 86.

24   Ibid., 72.

25   Adams, "Post-Essick Prophecy," 401.

26   Mitchell, "Dangerous Blake," 411; Webster, *Blake's Prophetic Psychology*, 2.

27   For a review of relevant ideas of Jauss, see his "Literary History as a Challenge to Literary Theory," trans. Elizabeth Benzinger, *New Literary History* 2 (1970), 7–37. On the problems produced by the assumption of Blake's success, and on the power that sympathetic readers gain over their favorite texts, see Stephen D. Cox, "Adventures of 'A Little Boy Lost': Blake and the Process of Interpretation," *Criticism* 23 (1981), 301–16; this article draws on Jauss's concepts.

28   Todorov, "A Dialogic Criticism?", *Raritan: A Quarterly Review* 4, 1 (Summer 1984), 74.

29   Mitchell, "Dangerous Blake," 414.

30   Several interesting studies remain to be written concerning the relation of Blake's idea of an audience, at various times of his life, to his labor costs and the prices of his works.

31   Todorov, "A Dialogic Criticism?", 73.

32   David V. Erdman, ed., *A Concordance to the Writings of William Blake* (Ithaca, N.Y.: Cornell University Press, 1967), 2:2181.

33   Webster, *Blake's Prophetic Psychology*, 4.

34   See Crane, *Languages of Criticism*, 180.

35   The phrase is Blake's (J36:58, E183); the meaning is more mine than his.

36   Concerning the relation between literary experience, critical inquiry, and "the pre-scholarly experience of life," see Jauss, 31–37. Making use of

Popper's ideas, Jauss emphasizes the general importance of the kind of learning that is carried on through encounters with obstacles, limitations, and challenges to one's assumptions.

Synecdoche and Method

1 I employ the terms "myth" and "antimyth" as neo-Blakean contraries in *Philosophy of the Literary Symbolic* (Tallahassee: Florida State University, 1983).

2 Coleridge, *The Friend* [1818], ed. Barbara E. Rooke (London and Princeton, N.J.: Routledge and Kegan Paul and Princeton University Press, 1969), 1:449.

3 Jakobsen with Morris Halle, "The Metaphoric and Metonymic Poles," in *Fundamentals of Language* (1956), reprinted in *Critical Theory Since Plato*, ed. Hazard Adams (New York: Harcourt Brace Jovanovich, 1971), 1113–16.

4 Quinn, *Figures of Speech: 60 Ways to Turn a Phrase* (Salt Lake City: Gibbs M. Smith, 1982), 58.

5 Lévi-Strauss, *The Savage Mind* (Chicago: University of Chicago Press, 1962), 191–216; Leach, *Claude Lévi-Strauss* (New York: Viking Press, 1970), 47–52.

6 See, e.g., Lacan, "The Agency of the Letter in the Unconscious," in *Ecrits*, ed. Alan Sheridan (New York: W. W. Norton), 156.

7 Freud, *The Interpretation of Dreams*, trans. James Strachey (New York: Avon Books, 1965), 313.

8 Ricoeur, *Freud and Philosophy: An Essay on Interpretation*, trans. Denis Savage (New Haven: Yale University Press, 1970), 32–36 passim.

9 White, *Metahistory: The Historical Imagination in Nineteenth-Century Europe* (Baltimore: Johns Hopkins University Press, 1973), 36.

10 Vico, *The New Science*, trans. Thomas Goddard Bergin and Max Harold Fish (Ithaca, N.Y.: Cornell University Press, 1968), 129.

11 Adams, *Philosophy of the Literary Symbolic*, 5–12, 105–14.

12 De Man, *Blindness and Insight: Essays in the Rhetoric of Contemporary Criticism*, 2d ed., rev. (Minneapolis: University of Minnesota Press, 1983), 190.

13 Adams, *Philosophy of the Literary Symbolic*, 380.

14 Yeats, *A Vision* (New York: Macmillan, 1938), 33.

15 Goodenough, *An Introduction to Philo Judaeus* [1940] (New York: Barnes and Noble, 1962), 103.

16 Charles Bigg, *The Christian Platonists of Alexandria* [1913] (Oxford: Clarendon Press, 1968), p. 40.

17 Bloom, "Commentary," *The Complete Poetry and Prose of William Blake*, ed. Erdman, 903.

18 Jonas, *The Gnostic Religion* [1958] (Boston: Beacon Press, 1963), 93.

19 Bryant, *A New System, or An Analysis of Ancient Mythology* [1774]

(London: J. Walker, 1804). See Geoffrey Keynes, *Blake Studies* (London: Rupert Hart-Davis, 1949), 44.

20   Doberer, *The Goldmakers,* trans. E. W. Dickes (London and Brussels: Nicholson and Watson, 1949), 16.

21   Jung, *Psychology and Alchemy,* trans. R. F. C. Hull (New York: Pantheon Books, 1953); Seligmann, *The Mirror of Magic* (New York: Pantheon Books, 1948), 134, 138, 187.

22   Mellor, *Blake's Human Form Divine* (Berkeley and Los Angeles: University of California Press, 1974), 256–270.

23   Raine, "The Little Girl Lost and Found," *The Divine Vision,* ed. V. de S. Pinto (London: Gollancz, 1957), 19–49.

24   Hungerford, *Shores of Darkness* [1941] (Cleveland and New York: World, 1963); Todd, *Tracks in the Snow* (London: Grey Walls Press, 1943).

25   Stukeley, *Stonehenge, A Temple Restor'd to the British Druids* (London: W. Innys and R. Mamby, 1740); *Abury, a Temple of the British Druids* (London: n.p., 1743). Bryant, *A New System, or an Analysis of Ancient Mythology* (1774; London: J. Walker, 1807). Davies, *Celtic Researches* (London: J. Booth, 1804); *The Mythology and Rites of the British Druids* (London: J. Booth, 1809).

26   Burton Feldman and Robert D. Richardson, eds. *The Rise of Modern Mythology, 1680–1860* (Bloomington: Indiana University Press, 1972), 27.

27   Northrop Frye (*Fearful Symmetry* [Princeton: Princeton University Press, 1947], 173) has raised the issue. On Bryant see Nancy Warshaw Bogen, *Jacob Bryant and William Blake* (Master's thesis, Columbia University, 1962).

28   Hungerford, *Shores of Darkness,* 20.

29   Bryant, *A New System,* preface.

30   Feldman and Richardson, *The Rise of Modern Mythology,* p. 242.

31   See Hungerford, *Shores of Darkness,* where Blake's Albion is traced to Wilford, Pughe, Davies, Stukeley, and Bryant. See also Todd, *Tracks in the Snow,* where Bryant, Wilford, Stukeley, and Pughe are discussed in connection with Blake.

32   Stukeley, *Stonehenge,* preface. The supposed tradition Stukeley creates here may account for Blake's decision to have a Church of England funeral, even though he was buried in Bunhill Fields, a ground for dissenters.

33   Frye, *Fearful Symmetry,* 272.

34   Hungerford, *Shores of Darkness,* 47. This is not quite correct. They are Arthur, and he them; though corrupted myth and they in their myths do not know it.

35   Todd, *Tracks in the Snow,* 47.

36   Hungerford, *Shores of Darkness,* 56.

37   See especially A. L. Owen, *The Famous Druids: A Survey of Three Centuries of English Literature on the Druids* (Oxford: Clarendon Press,

1962), 224–36. According to Owen, Druidism for Blake, "was already ancient when it entered the ark." Druidism originated in Britain in its pristine visionary state, and the Jews received druidic traditions from there, but subsequently the Druids perverted their own traditions. In Blake's *Milton* and *Jerusalem*, Britain is the original Holy Land.

38　Quoted from Yeats's annotation to his copy of Saurat's *Blake and Modern Thought* (London: The Dial Press, 1929), 85, in *Blake and Yeats: The Contrary Vision*, by Hazard Adams (Ithaca, N.Y.: Cornell University Press, 1955), 123.

39　Owen, *The Famous Druids*, 236.

40　Yeats, "William Blake and His Illustrations to *The Divine Comedy*," *Ideas of Good and Evil* (London: A. H. Bullen, 1914), 127.

41　Erdman, *Blake: Prophet against Empire* (Princeton, N.J.: Princeton University Press, 1954), since revised.

42　Stukeley, *Abury: A Temple of the British Druids*, 55.

43　Stukeley seems to have been quite aware of Gnostic treatment of the serpent without perhaps understanding the Gnostic intent: "This figure of the circle and the snake, on which they [Avebury and Stonehenge] are founded, had obtained a very venerable regard, in being expressive of the most eminent and illustrious act of the deity, the multiplication of his own nature as the *Zorastrians and Platonists* speak; and in being a symbol of that divine person who was the consequence of it" (85).

44　Hilton, *Literal Imagination: Blake's Vision of Words* (Berkeley: University of California Press, 1983).

Blake's Revisionism

1　Jean-Pierre Mileur indicates that Bloom's theory is revisionary by focusing on Bloom in *Literary Revisionism and the Burden of Modernity* (Berkeley: University of California Press, 1985).

2　Like that of any other writer, Bloom's thought evolves. In the following I show his shift from Kabbalah to specifically Gnostic concerns and his shift in the recent *Agon* away from mechanical models of human experience. For the more mechanical Bloom, see *The Anxiety of Influence* (New York: Oxford University Press, 1973), which gives a skeletal description of Bloom's "ratios of revision," elaborated in subsequent works. Also see *A Map of Misreading* (New York: Oxford University Press, 1975); *Poetry and Repression* (New Haven: Yale University Press, 1976); *Kabbalah and Criticism* (New York: Seabury Press, 1975); *The Breaking of the Vessels* (Chicago: University of Chicago Press, 1982); *Agon* (New York: Oxford University Press, 1982).

3　Fite, *Harold Bloom: The Rhetoric of Romantic Vision* (Amherst: University of Massachusetts Press, 1985), 35–45.

4　Robinson's notes in *Blake Records*, by G. E. Bentley, Jr. (London: Oxford University Press, 1969), 545.

5　Mitchell, "Dangerous Blake," *Studies in Romanticism* 21 (1982), 410–16.

6 Mitchell, *Blake's Composite Art* (Princeton, N.J.: Princeton University Press, 1978), 131. Mitchell says: "It is tempting to label all this a Gnostic version of Genesis which identifies creation with fall and treats the entire created world of matter, time, space, the body, and the sexes as illusory and evil, but let us resist this temptation until we have examined the poem more closely" (123). Mitchell concludes that Blake is no Gnostic.

7 Rudolph cites this definition from "The Congress on the Origins of Gnosticism in Messina 1966," *Gnosis* (San Francisco: Harper and Row, 1983), 56.

8 Hans Jonas, *The Gnostic Religion* (Boston: Beacon Press, 1963). Jonas's most succinct description of Gnosticism can be found under "Gnosticism" in *The Encyclopedia of Philosophy*, vol. 3 (New York: Macmillan, 1967). See also Philip Merlan's description under "Plotinus," *Encyclopedia of Philosophy*, vol. 6.

9 Spector, "Kabbalistic Sources—Blake's and His Critics'," *Blake: An Illustrated Quarterly* (Winter 1983–84), 84–98.

10 Scholem, *Major Trends in Jewish Mysticism* (New York: Schocken Books, 1941), 322.

11 The present essay is in no way intended as a source study. For a larger evaluation of Gnostic sources available to Blake see chapter 2 of my "Blake's Gnosticism: The Material World as Allegory (Ph.D. diss., University of California, Los Angeles, 1978).

12 Curran, "Blake and the Gnostic Hyle: A Double Negative," *Blake Studies* 4 (1972), 122.

13 Pagels, *The Gnostic Gospels* (New York: Random House, 1979). Much of Pagels's work first appeared as a series of four articles in the *New York Review of Books*.

14 To date, Curran and Tannenbaum each have made the most fruitful examinations of Blake's Gnosticism. Curran, "Blake and the Gnostic Hyle"; Tannenbaum, "Blake's Art of Crypsis: *The Book of Urizen* and Genesis," *Blake Studies* 5 (1972), 141–64; Brown, "The Prophetic Tradition," *Studies in Romanticism* 21 (1982), 367–386.

15 Damon, *William Blake* (Boston: Houghton Mifflin, 1958), 116.

16 *The Hypostasis of the Archons*, in *The Nag Hammadi Library* (New York: Harper & Row, 1977), 152–160. Compare Urizen's repetition of "I" in chapter 2 and Satan's in *Paradise Lost*.

17 Bloom, *Blake's Apocalypse* (Ithaca: Cornell University Press, 1963), 23.

18 See *Hypostasis of the Archons*, 157. In Jonas, *The Gnostic Religion*, see discussions of Primal Man, First Man, Alien Man, and Adam. After *The Book of Urizen* Blake conflates such concepts first in his four Zoas and later in his Albion figure.

19 Derrida, "White Mythology," *Margins of Philosophy* (Chicago: University of Chicago Press, 1982), 213. This edition contains the following parenthetical remark: "translation modified: the last sentence reads: 'Their output is mythology, an anemic mythology'" (215).

20 For discussions of this darker side see Mario Praz, *The Romantic Agony*

(New York: Meridian, 1956); Ann Mellor, *English Romantic Irony* (Cambridge, Mass.: Harvard University Press, 1980); and Jerome Mc-Gann's view of these works in *The Romantic Ideology* (Chicago: University of Chicago Press, 1983).

21 For the definitive study of this, see Peter L. Thorslev, Jr., *The Byronic Hero* (Minneapolis: University of Minnesota Press, 1962).

22 See my "William Blake and the Problematic of the Self," in *William Blake and the Moderns,* ed. Robert J. Bertholf and Annette S. Levitt (Albany: State University of New York Press, 1982), 260–85.

23 Hume, *A Treatise of Human Nature* (London: Oxford University Press, 1975), 252.

24 The later Wordsworth is called a neo-Stoic in quite a different sense. See Jane Worthington Smyser, *Wordsworth's Reading of Roman Prose* (New Haven: Yale University Press, 1946, reprint 1970).

25 Miller, "Tradition and Difference," *Diacritics* 2 (1972), 6.

26 Shakespeare provides us with an equally "Romantic" account of humanity in Shylock's soliloquy: "I am a Jew. Hath not a Jew eyes? Hath not a Jew hands, organs, dimensions, senses, affections, passions? Fed with the same food, hurt with the same weapons, subject to the same diseases, healed by the same means, warmed and cooled by the same winter and summer as a Christian is? If you prick us, do we not bleed? If you tickle us, do we not laugh? If you poison us, do we not die? and if you wrong us, shall we not revenge?" (*The Merchant of Venice*, act 3, sc. 1, 60–69).

27 See *Kabbalah and Criticism*, 106. Also, in arguing against the extreme nominalism that denies the relational nature of our concepts E. P. Thompson quotes the following from Alasdair McIntyre: "You cannot characterise an army by referring to the soldiers who belong to it. For to do that you have to identify them as soldiers; and to do that is already to bring in the concept of an army. For a soldier just is an individual who belongs to an army. Thus we see that the characterisation of individuals and of classes has to go together. Essentially these are not two separate tasks." *The Poverty of Theory and Other Essays* (New York: Monthly Review Press, 1978), 30. Thompson's argument against the reifications of structuralism are close to the Blakean/Gnostic critique of reification that I outline in this paper.

28 Jaspers, "Existenzphilosophie," *Existentialism from Dostoevsky to Sartre* (New York: World, 1956), 166.

29 Freud, *Civilization and Its Discontents* (New York: W. W. Norton, 1961), 14.

Literal/Tiriel/Material

1 "The set (*Einstellung*) toward the MESSAGE as such, focus on the message for its own sake, is the POETIC function of language. . . . This function, by promoting the palpability of signs, deepens the fundamental dichotomy of signs and objects." Jakobson, "Closing Statement: Linguistics and

Poetics" (1960), reprinted in *Semiotics: An Introductory Anthology*, ed. Robert E. Innis (Bloomington: Indiana University Press, 1985): 145–76, 153.

2   An awareness to be gained, for example, in reading the following rough chronology of criticism on *Tiriel*: S. Foster Damon, *William Blake: His Philosophy and Symbols* (1924; rpt., Glouster, Mass.: Peter Smith, 1958), 71–73, 306–9; Mark Schorer, *William Blake: The Politics of Vision* (New York: Henry Holt, 1946), 227–30; Northrop Frye, *Fearful Symmetry: A Study of William Blake* (1947; rpt., Princeton, N.J.: Princeton University Press, 1969), 241–45; David V. Erdman, *Blake: Prophet against Empire*, 3d ed. (Princeton, N.J.: Princeton University Press, 1977), 132–39; Robert F. Gleckner, *The Piper and the Bard: A Study of William Blake* (Detroit: Wayne State University Press, 1959), 131–56; Harold Bloom, *Blake's Apocalypse: A Study in Poetic Argument* (1963; rpt., Ithaca, N.Y.: Cornell University Press, 1970), 30–35; G. E. Bentley, Jr., *William Blake['s] Tiriel: Facsimile and Transcript of the Manuscript, Reproduction of the Drawings, and a Commentary on the Poem* (Oxford: Clarendon, 1967); Kathleen Raine, *Blake and Tradition*, 2 vols., Bollingen Series 35, 11 (Princeton, N.J.: Princeton University Press, 1968), 1:34–66; John Beer, *Blake's Visionary Universe* (New York: Barnes and Noble, 1969), 60–67; Nancy Bogen, "A New Look at Blake's *Tiriel*," *Bulletin of the New York Public Library (BNYPL)* 74 (1970), 153–65; Mary S. Hall, "Blake's *Tiriel*: A Visionary Form Pedantic," *BNYPL* 74 (1970), 166–76; William F. Halloran, "Blake's *Tiriel*: Snakes, Curses, and a Blessing," *South Atlantic Quarterly* 70 (1971), 161–79; Robert N. Essick, "The Altering Eye: Blake's Vision in the *Tiriel* Designs," in *William Blake: Essays in Honour of Sir Geoffrey Keynes*, ed. Morton D. Paley and Michael Phillips, 50–65 (Oxford: Clarendon Press, 1973); Anne Kostelanetz Mellor, *Blake's Human Form Divine* (Berkeley: University of California Press, 1974), 28–39; David Bindman, *Blake as an Artist* (Oxford: Phaidon, 1977), 43–48; Stephen C. Behrendt, "'The Worst Disease': Blake's *Tiriel*," *Colby Library Quarterly* 15 (1979), 175–87; Brenda S. Webster, *Blake's Prophetic Psychology* (Athens: University of Georgia Press, 1983), 31–48; and Hans Ostrom, "Blake's *Tiriel* and the Dramatization of Collapsed Language," *Papers on Language and Literature* 19, 2 (1983), 167–82.

3   M. H. Abrams, *A Glossary of Literary Terms*, 4th ed. (New York: Holt, Rinehart and Winston, 1981), s.v. "allusion."

4   *Tiriel* numbers 393 lines in G. E. Bentley, Jr.'s *William Blake's Writings* (Oxford: Clarendon Press, 1978), as compared to 306 for *The French Revolution*, 265 for *Europe*, 226 for *America*; the double-columned *Urizen* has 517 eight-beat lines—still less total volume than *Tiriel's* 393 four-teeners.

5   See the selections from Peirce assembled under the title "Logic as Semiotic: The Theory of Signs" by Robert E. Innis in *Semiotics: An Introductory Anthology* (Bloomington: Indiana University Press, 1985): 4–23.

6   One notes at once the strange combination *Mne*, the Greek and Indo-European root for terms concerned with mind, memory, and mensuration, which appears most dramatically in the Greek goddess Mnemosyne, Memory, the mother of the Muses. Near anagram and consonantal association lead to "Athena," "Minerva," and, pertinent to a theme below, "anathema."

7   "Winged death" appears in Pope's *Odyssey* 21:16 and *Iliad* 20:508.

8   Ostriker, ed., *William Blake, The Complete Poems*, Penguin English Poets (Harmondsworth: Penguin, 1977), 881.

9   "Dreary plain": *Odyssey* 24:123; "sandy plain": *Iliad* 9:20, 13:425.

10   See Martin Butlin, *The Paintings and Drawings of William Blake*, 2 vols. (New Haven: Yale University Press, 1981), 1:79. See also the discussion and reproduction in William L. Pressly, *The Life and Art of James Barry* (New Haven: Yale University Press, 1981), 149–51. Blake was evidently involved enough with Barry to at least think of writing "Barry a Poem" (E515 and E872n.); the three instances of "bury" in *Tiriel* account for half of Blake's poetic uses of that word.

11   Blake would have read of the Norse Hela or Death in Thomas Gray or in Mallet's *Northern Antiquities*; the interpretation of Cordelia as Death is Freud's, in "The Theme of the Three Caskets" (cited in Raine, *Blake and Tradition*, 1:382n).

12   Barthes, *Mythologies*, selected and translated by Annette Lavers (New York: Hill and Wang, n.d.), 135.

13   John W. Derry, *The Regency Crisis and the Whigs: 1788–9* (Cambridge: Cambridge University Press, 1963), 9.

14   Irwin, *English Neoclassical Art: Studies in Inspiration and Taste* (Greenwich, Conn.: New York Graphic Society, 1966), 78.

15   The strange expression "vacant Orcus" might imply that Hades has been depopulated (spirits returning to earth, perhaps); but, corresponding with the Greek "Matha," "Orcus" strongly suggests the Greek "oath" (ὄρχυς— also "the object by which one swears," which for the Greek gods was the River Styx, hence the underworld connotations). Tiriel's house is then "false Learning. & as dark as empty Swearing" (which might be heard to make it as dark as "cant or curse").

16   Damon, *William Blake*, 72; Essick, "The Altering Eye," 65.

17   Late eighteenth-century English art could be experienced in a grating number of "great" locations: the Great Room of the Society of Arts— " 'the best Gallery in the Kingdom' "—was used by the Society of Artists in 1760 for the first major public art exhibition. In following years the exhibition was transferred to the Great Room in Spring Gardens, Charing Cross, evidently the same room hired by John Singleton Copley in 1781 for his hugely successful exhibition of *The Death of Chatham*. After selling its building in the Strand in 1776, the Society of Arts acquired a Great Hall in the Adelphi (the room Barry decorated with *The Progress of Human Culture* [1777–83]) (see Joseph Burke, *English Art: 1714–1800* [Oxford: Clarendon Press, 1976], 273, 250, 249). Beginning in 1780 the annual Royal Academy exhibition was held in its Great Room in Somerset House;

over the entrance was the inscription, in Greek (cited in the Ramberg and Martini design [illustration 1]), "Let no Stranger to the Muses enter" (see Sidney C. Hutchison, *The History of the Royal Academy: 1768–1968* [New York: Taplinger, 1968], 66). The Ramberg and Martini illustration shows Sir Joshua Reynolds, with ear trumpet, guiding the Prince of Wales. "The Great Style" was, of course, what Reynolds urged in his harangues to the harassed students at the Royal Academy.

18 Damon, *William Blake*, 72. Schorer, *William Blake*, identifies the cage as "the 'bounded' couplet, and the conventional forms of eighteenth-century verse" (228); for Alicia Ostriker, *William Blake*, the cage suggests "the heroic couplet" (880).

19 The topic of Blake's reading of Dryden is an open and promising field; one notes immediately, for instance, that Blake makes considerably more reference to Dryden than to Pope. Kathleen Raine, who would base *Tiriel* on Sophocles' *Oedipus at Colonus* using the contemporary translations of Potter and of Francklin, curiously neglects the other *Oedipus* and the notable translation of Dryden and Lee. In Act I of Dryden and Lee's version, for example, we encounter a Tiresias, "leaning on a staff, and led by his Daughter Manto," who can sound like Tiriel addressing Hela: "Thou wretched Daughter of a dark old man, / Conduct my weary steps" (Montague Summers, ed., *Dryden: The Dramatic Works*, 6 vols. [London: Nonesuch Press, 1932], 4:360).

20 See, for instance, C. G. Jung, *Mysterium Coniunctionis: An Inquiry into the Separation and Synthesis of Psychic Opposites in Alchemy*, 2d ed., trans. R. F. C. Hull, Bollingen Series 20, 14 (Princeton, N.J.: Princeton University Press, 1970), 501 and other references in the index under "Mercurius . . . as prima materia."

21 See Bogan, "A New Look at Blake's *Tiriel*," 157.

22 In Heva's arms, one might say, Tiriel finally gets to Heaven ("Heavn," as Blake sometimes has it), for, to draw on later associations, the traditional happy-ever-after image of heaven is what Blake terms "Beulah," which "to its Inhabitants appears within each district / As the beloved infant in his mothers bosom round incircled" (*M*30:10–11, E129).

23 Schneiderman, *Jacques Lacan: The Death of an Intellectual Hero* (Cambridge, Mass.: Harvard University Press, 1983), 77.

24 Franciscus Junius, *The Painting of the Ancients* (London 1638), 47. The importance of Junius's work is stressed by Lawrence Lipking in *The Ordering of the Arts in Eighteenth-Century England* (Princeton, N.J.: Princeton University Press, 1970), 23–37.

25 See Anika Lemaire, *Jacques Lacan*, trans. David Macey (London: Routledge and Kegan Paul, 1977), 83.

26 Ralph Waldo Emerson, *Essays and Lectures*, ed. Joel Porte (New York: The Library of America, 1983), 59.

Blake's De-Formation of Neo-Aristotelianism

1   Booth, *Now Don't Try to Reason with Me* (Chicago: University of Chicago Press, 1970), 115.

2   The complexity of the relationships (identities and differences in testing procedures, rules of correspondence, falsification, incommensurability, etc.) between theories and hypotheses has been explored exhaustively in a way I find quite congenial and usually brilliant in the two-volume collection of P. K. Feyerabend's *Philosophical Papers* (Cambridge: Cambridge University Press, 1981). Volume 1 is *Realism, Rationalism and Scientific Method;* volume 2 is *Problems of Empiricism.* "Theory" and "hypothesis" have lived through nearly inverse historical developments. "Theory" began as "a sight, a spectacle," from "to look on, view, contemplate" and has come to mean "a scheme or system of ideas or statements held as an explanation or account of a group of facts or phenomena"; as such, it is synonymous with "hypothesis" (*OED* s.v.). "Hypothesis" derives from the Greek for "foundation, base," but has generally come to mean "conjecture" or "speculation," and even "a groundless or insufficiently grounded supposition" (*OED* s.v.).

3   The legendary difficulty of Chicago criticism, which emphasized "method" long before it became fashionable to do so, has kept critics of more "popular" (what Crane called "a priori") methods at a distance. Northrop Frye claims direct descent from Aristotle in many ways, but his treatment focuses much more on an appropriation of Aristotle's *terms* than a real thinking through the causal hierarchies of Aristotelian categories in the formal way, for example, McKeon does. When "form" and "unity" were fashionably "in," the Chicago approach seemed to be too hierarchical and artificial to account for the "organic wholes" it attempted to explain. Now that unity and form are receding in fashion, Neo-Aristotelianism seems even more out of step with the desire to explain the resistance of texts to formal closure. At least one Chicago critic, Ralph Rader, has attempted to accommodate the interest in discrepancies in texts into a Neo-Aristotelian framework by developing the concept of *"unintended and unavoidable negative consequence[s] of the artist's positive constructive intention,"* in "Fact, Theory, and Literary Explanation," *Critical Inquiry* 1 (1974), 253.

4   Crane, *The Idea of the Humanities* (Chicago: University of Chicago Press, 1967), 2:236, n.1.

5   Crane, *The Languages of Criticism and the Structure of Poetry* (Toronto: University of Toronto Press, 1953), 140.

6   Crane "The Concept of Plot and the Plot of *Tom Jones,*" *Critics and Criticism* (Chicago: University of Chicago Press, 1952), 646.

7   Crane, *Idea of the Humanities,* 2:43.

8   Crane's insights into the limitations inherent in the exaggerated emphasis on linguistic and technical concerns of the New Critics should not be underestimated, because many of the current trends in critical practice involving, for example, "free play" and "transgression" could easily be

construed as subversive rewritings of New Critical ideology with the obsession for unity and form radically devalued if not completely erased. What Crane criticizes as the assumption of "plurisignation," for example (*The Idea of the Humanities*, 38–40), anticipates precisely a criticism that could be directed by methodological purists of Crane's school toward the "polysemous" readings of Blake's words by Nelson Hilton in *Literal Imagination: Blake's Vision of Words* (Berkeley and Los Angeles: University of California Press, 1983).

9   McKeon, "Philosophy and Method," *The Journal of Philosophy* 48 (1951), 653–82.

10   These methods are defined in some detail in the section, "How *The Book of Urizen* Rewrites Neo-Aristotelianism," below. In his comprehensive rewriting of Neo-Aristotelianism, Walter A. Davis analyzes McKeon's *four* "modes of thought" by reference to an unpublished essay by McKeon ("Philosophical Semantics and Philosophical Inquiry," Chicago, 1967), in *The Act of Interpretation: A Critique of Literary Reason* (Chicago: University of Chicago Press, 1978), esp. 92–115 and 176–78. Davis adds "operational" thought to the three methods noted in my text.

11   These principles are defined in the section, "How *The Book of Urizen* Rewrites Neo-Aristotelianism," below. Davis adds "actional" principles to those noted in my text.

12   Feyerabend, *Problems of Empiricism*, 197. Feyerabend's critique of Popper's "falsification" is especially acute in the essay "Popper's *Objective Knowledge*," 168–201.

13   Crane repeatedly makes this assumption. For example, in "Criticism as Inquiry" (*The Idea of the Humanities*, 2:41), Crane refers to "fact" justified "independently of speculation." Or again in "On Hypotheses in 'Historical Criticism'" (2:243), Crane says, "This is the objective fact, about which all disinterested interpreters of Swift's text must agree." Ralph Rader is one of the strongest proponents of the existence of facts independent of interpretation in "Fact, Theory, and Literary Explanation," *Critical Inquiry* 1 (1974), 245–72. Responses followed by Stanley Fish, Jay Schleusener, and Rader himself in *Critical Inquiry* 1 (1975): 883–911. Feyerabend's philosophically rigorous attack against the independent fact position is matched rhetorically by Stanley Fish's *Is There a Text in This Class? The Authority of Interpretive Communities* (Cambridge, Mass.: Harvard University Press, 1980).

14   McKeon's project seems aimed at developing totalizing incommensurable universes of discourse that (at some level) aim toward a unified existential real world. Feyerabend's project seems directed toward rigorously using the techniques of canonical science to undermine the possibility of a stable real world to which incommensurable discourses could refer.

15   Crane, "The Plot of *Tom Jones*."

16   Crane's account of the "working or power" as a writer's sequential solution to a series of problems is interestingly relegated to footnote 13 of "The Plot of *Tom Jones*," 631–32.

17 Examples of plot of technique might be self-reflexive fictions like Gilbert Sorrentino's *Mulligan Stew* or Italo Calvino's *If On a Winter's Night a Traveler*; plots of language might include Joyce's *Finnegans Wake.*

18 A clear exposition of Frye's position concerning the formal cause as simultaneous unity of theme appears in "Myth, Fiction, and Displacement," in *Fables of Identity: Studies in Poetic Mythology* (New York and London: Harcourt, 1963), 21–38.

19 In his essay on Hemingway's "The Killers," Crane posits a "plot" (in the sense of "necessary substrate of unified and probable action") that is present in the work primarily because of its absence, since the story is one of "treatment": "This is an action, and it is the only action in the story which we follow from beginning to end; the events and crises of the essential 'plot' all happen offstage, either before the beginning or after the end of the action involving the boys" (*The Idea of the Humanities*, 2:311).

20 Crane, *Languages of Criticism*, 141–44. Walter Davis relates Crane's concept of plot to Lévi-Strauss's "logistic method for analyzing the actions of 'plots' of narrative and dramatic structures," *The Act of Interpretation*, 109–10, in a way that makes my own move at this point seem more legitimate, though the convolutions through which this connection passes in the reading of Blake's departs significantly from Davis's characterization.

21 Two slightly different detailed accounts of perspective transformation appear in my *Narrative Unbound: Re-Visioning Blake's* The Four Zoas (Barrytown, N.Y.: Station Hill Press, 1987) and "Re-Visioning *The Four Zoas*," in *Unnam'd Forms: Blake and Textuality*, ed. Nelson Hilton and Thomas A. Vogler (Berkeley and Los Angeles: University of California Press, 1986), 105–39.

22 Blake organizes the material dimensions of the first four lines of the "Preludium" to *The Book of Urizen* in such a way that more and more options open up the closer we look at them:

> Of the primeval Priests assum'd power,
> When Eternals spurn'd back his religion;
> And gave him a place in the north,
> Obscure, shadowy, void, solitary ($U2$:1–4).

Space permits only a few suggestions of the subversive strategies Blake employs here, but these include situating an apostrophe in "assum'd" and leaving it out of "Priests." If the initial "Of" were deleted, it would be completely determinate that the "Priests" had "assum'd power"; the presence of the initial "Of," in conjunction with the absent apostrophe in "Priests" (to which attention is called by the unnecessary apostrophe in "assum'd," which seems to mark an absence), grammatically alters the perceptual field of the reader in such a way that it becomes indeterminate whether the Priests assumed (usurped? or believed they had acquired?) power, or whether the Priests' power had been "assum'd" by some other force, or whether the "Priest" is singular possessive (with the apostrophe having migrated to "assum'd") and thus refers to "Urizen," which the title tells us this is the "Book *of*," or whether the "power" is itself a being or character (referred to through the possessive "his" of the second line and confirmed by the reference to "Urizen" as "the dark power" in $U3:7$). Because the first two lines are connected by "When," the actions of assuming power and spurning religion are not causally related: the spurning is not a response to the assuming, even though the words follow one another in sequence on the page; rather, they are simultaneous aspects of one another. The primary agency for establishing the void is attributed to the Eternals, though when the poem begins the Eternals are horrified by the (apparently inexplicable) appearance of the void. In this brief glance at the "Preludium" we can see that Blake has already interlocked the Eternals and the "power" that will be objectified as Urizen, though the plot of the poem itself begins with a disruptive incommensurability between these apparently separate beings.

23 Blake's initial use of the term "Immortal" in *The Book of Urizen* seems designed to undermine the logistic calculus before it can get started. The "Immortal" of $U3:37$ embodies the characteristics one would like to attribute unequivocally to the Eternals (E_2); yet the term is singular and suggests either a nostalgic form of Urizen himself prior to his withdrawal from Eternity or a transitional term between Urizen and the Eternals. Either of these latter options invokes the kind of action plot-substructure that would make *The Book of Urizen* a rather confused conventional mimetic plot in Crane's sense. Blake seems to have anticipated a reading such as the one I am giving the poem and incorporated this term early in the plot to test the reader's willingness to attempt to sustain the logistic calculus in the face of a key falsifying textual "fact." Of course, just such a gesture is consistent with the reflexive principle that continually works to undermine the plot's logistic drive throughout the poem.

24 The term "Immortal" reappears in radically different contexts in *The Book of Urizen:* as the sensually expansive opposite of U_2 ($U3:37$); as the raging being of $U8:4$ who could be Los or Urizen or a form of the Eternals; as the "inchain'd" being of $U10:31$ who is both Urizen and Los (and the inverse of the repressed Eternals at this point); and as the multiple "Immortals" of $U15:11$ who seem to be the Eternals whose "eyes" expand in a limited way to see the female form separate. This modulation between the dialectical poles of the logistic calculus further reflects the subversive use of the materiality of language by the plot's reflexive principle to undermine the object of imitation as being formalized in a way that will unify or close it once and for all.

Blake and the Deconstructive Interlude

1 For some of the Miller/Abrams debate, see Miller's review of Abrams's *Natural Supernaturalism: Tradition and Revolution in Romantic Literature* (New York: W. W. Norton, 1971) titled "Tradition and Difference,"

Diacritics 2 (Winter 1976), 6–12, and Abrams's response, "The Deconstructive Angel," *Critical Inquiry* 3 (1977), 425–38.

2   See Said, "Roads Taken and Not Taken in Contemporary Criticism" and "Reflections on American 'Left' Literary Criticism" in *The World, the Text, and the Critic* (Cambridge, Mass.: Harvard University Press, 1983) 140–77; Lentricchia, "Paul de Man: The Rhetoric of Authority," *After the New Criticism* (Chicago: University of Chicago Press, 1980), 282–317, and *Criticism and Social Change* (Chicago: University of Chicago Press, 1983); Eagleton, *Literary Theory* (Minneapolis: University of Minnesota Press, 1983), 127–50.

3   The phrase is S. Foster Damon's in his introduction to *A Blake Dictionary: The Ideas and Symbols of William Blake* (1965; reprint, Boulder, Colo.: Shambhala, 1979), x. For discussion of Damon, Frye, Erdman, Bloom, and other Blake critics mentioned below, see my introduction to this collection. Bibliographic references are also found there.

4   Derrida, *Positions*, trans. and annotated by Alan Bass (Chicago: University of Chicago Press, 1972), 41; *Positions* (Paris: Minuit, 1972), 56. All parenthetical citations for Derrida's work list page numbers in the English translation followed by italicized page numbers from the French editions.

5   Derrida, *Of Grammatology*, trans. Gayatri Spivak (Baltimore: Johns Hopkins University Press, 1974), 158; *De la Grammátologie* (Paris: Minuit, 1967), 227.

6   Derrida, *Speech and Phenomena and Other Essays on Husserl's Theory of Signs*, trans. David B. Allison (Evanston, Ill.: Northwestern University Press, 1973), 70–104; *Of Grammatology*, 195–229; "Plato's Pharmacy" in *Dissemination*, trans. Barbara Johnson (Chicago: University of Chicago Press, 1981), 61–171.

7   Derrida, *Dissemination*, 63; *La Dissémination* (Paris: Seuil, 1972), 71.

8   Discussion following Derrida's presentation of "Structure, Sign, and Play in the Discourse of the Human Sciences" at Johns Hopkins University, in *The Structuralist Controversy: The Languages of Criticism and the Sciences of Man*, ed. Richard Macksey and Eugenio Donato (1970; reprint, Baltimore: Johns Hopkins University Press, 1972), 271.

9   In *Applied Grammatology: Post(e)-Pedagogy from Jacques Derrida to Joseph Beuys* (Baltimore: John Hopkins University Press, 1984), Gregory L. Ulmer misses the sense in which all deconstructive reading is already writing. Ulmer claims "that Writing, as Derrida practices it, is something other than deconstruction, the later being a mode of analysis, while the former is a mode of composition" (xi). Ulmer's is perhaps the most questionable current version of deconstruction. Ulmer makes Derrida the harbinger of a new, nondiscursive program of "Writing" (Ulmer's capitalization) that could in practice "overcome the logocentric limitations of discourse" (5). By ignoring the fact that Derrida's later style puts into practice exactly the methodological paradoxes set out in the earlier works, Ulmer distinguishes "deconstruction" from "grammatology" and treats

the latter as discourse based on image, pun, and metaphor for their own sakes.

10   Some versions of deconstruction indulge in the release from all constraints of method. These readings of Derrida tend to concentrate on the moment of inversion and forget its diagnostic and tactical purposes. The result is a deconstruction that simply subverts in the name of interpretive freedom. Vincent B. Leitch puts it very directly: "The formula for deconstructive reading is: repeat and undermine. . . . The subversion of the text, predicated on the rich possibilities of textuality and intertextuality, makes insecure the seemingly stable text and tradition through the *production* of undecidables" (*Deconstructive Criticism: An Advanced Introduction* [New York: Columbia University Press, 1983], pp. 177–78). Leitch goes so far as to posit, apparently without a trace of irony, this simple hierarchy: "For Derrida, there are two interpretations of interpretation. One seeks to decipher a stable center or truth, which escapes the transgressive activities of play and of the signifier. The other affirms play and the lawless signifier. It abjures transcendence. . . . Derrida promotes a joyous and free interpretation of the signifier, which neither demands nor promotes truth or center, escape or transcendence. . . . Instead of restricted play and filled spaces, deconstruction desires radical free play and exorbitantly overfilled spaces, aiming to subvert regulated and filtered interpretation" (237). Leitch's version of free play deconstruction is representative of many Anglo-American appropriations. The weakness is obvious: to glorify "radical free play" for its own sake amounts to elevating the subordinated term (in the oppositions restriction/freedom, limit/transgression, lawfulness/lawlessness), drawing back from the more difficult work of displacement, and hence remaining trapped within the same metaphysical field. The critic who reads in the spirit of "radical free play" will follow unacknowledged rules much more rigidly than the critic who suspects that rules for reading are inescapable.

11   Several accounts of deconstruction lack what might be called the proper tact, the right balance in definition. Usually, deconstruction is made into a manageable program. Here, for example, is J. Hillis Miller's description of the procedure: "The deconstructive critic seeks to find . . . the element in the system studied which is alogical, the thread in the text in question which will unravel it all, or the loose stone which will pull down the whole building. Deconstruction, rather, annihilates the ground on which the building stands by showing that the text has already annihilated the ground, knowingly or unknowingly. Deconstruction is not a dismantling of the structure of the text but a demonstration that it has already dismantled itself" ("Stevens' Rock and Criticism as Cure, II," *The Georgia Review* 30 [1976], 341).

Inversion-displacement is more than dismantling, more even than a demonstration that the text dismantles itself, for the Derridean operation shows more radically how the alogical textual elements have crafted the building as it stands. Miller does go on to acknowledge that deconstruction provides an analytic explanation, but he makes the construction of the text into a miraculous efflorescence from the void: "The uncanny moment in Derrida's criticism," he writes, "is the formulation and the reformulation of this non-existence of the ground out of which the whole textual structure seems to rise like the pleasure dome of Kubla Khan. Derrida has shown marvelous fecundity in finding or inventing new terms to express this generative non-source, absence, forking, or scattering beneath all appearances of presence" (341). Showing the non-existence of the ground without moving on to the next stage of analysis remains an act solely of inversion. Miller's "deconstruction-as-dismantling" is characteristic of much Yale School criticism.

12 Derrida, "Différance," in *Margins of Philosophy*, trans. Alan Bass (Chicago: University of Chicago Press, 1982), 7; *Marges de la philosophie* (Paris: Minuit, 1972), 7.

13 Derrida, "The Double Session," in *Dissemination*, 173–285; Genet and Hegel, *Glas* (Paris: Editions Galilee, 1974); Ponge, *Singéponge/Signsponge*, trans. Richard Rand (New York: Columbia University Press, 1984); Freud, *La Carte Postale: de Socrate à Freud et au-delà* (Paris: Aubier-Flammarion, 1980).

14 For a powerful critique of deconstruction as it is commonly understood and practiced in the American academy, see Rodolphe Gasché's "Deconstruction as Criticism" (*Glyph* 6 [1979], 177–215). Gasché points out that much recent criticism takes *écriture* to mean "the *phenomenological experience of writing*," a confusion that Derrida explicitly warns against (170–80). Gasché also explains, quite accurately, that deconstruction "is *not* a demolition or a dismantling to be opposed by or calling for a rebuilding or a reconstruction" nor a finding of "the moment where in a text the argument begins to undermine itself" (180–81). Deconstructive criticism, Gasché charges, is still largely based on the assumption that the literary text is autonomous and self-reflexive, the founding claim of New Criticism. Gasché argues "that deconstruction in the first place represents a critique of reflexivity and specularity" (183). In the terms used above, the text revealed by deconstruction can never be wholly or totally present to perception; its complexity eludes any single or systematic act of cognition.

15 "Différance," 19, *20–21*. Derrida refers here to "From Restricted to General Economy: A Hegelianism without Reserve," in *Writing and Difference*, trans. Alan Bass (Chicago: University of Chicago Press, 1978), 251–77.

16 Jameson, *The Political Unconscious: Narrative as Socially Symbolic Act* (Ithaca, N.Y.: Cornell University Press, 1981), 17.

17 See Raine, *Blake and Tradition* (Princeton, N.J.: Princeton University Press, 1968); Harper, *The Neoplatonism of William Blake* (Chapel Hill: University of North Carolina Press, 1961); Bloom, *Blake's Apocalypse: A Study in Poetic Argument* (Garden City, N.Y.: Doubleday, 1963), and

Poetry and Repression: Revisionism from Blake to Stevens (New Haven: Yale University Press, 1976) ; and Northrop Frye cited below.

18 Frye's immensely influential reading is fundamentally and overtly idealist. Frye begins his commentary by linking Blake's epistemology to Berkeley's assertion of "the mental nature of reality, expressed . . . in the phrase *esse est percipi*" (*Fearful Symmetry: A Study of William Blake* [1947; reprint, Boston: Beacon Press, 1962], 14). Frye treats Blake's metaphysics and poetics as consistently idealist: "Forms or images . . . exist only in perception" (15) ; "things are real to the extent that they are sharply, clearly, particularly perceived by themselves" (16) ; "the *esse-est-percipi* principle unites the subject and the object" (16–17).

We confront a strong critical consensus. George Mills Harper asserts that "Plato's Theory of Forms became the basis for Blake's aesthetic theory. The spiritual world, intuitively apprehended, was better organized than the material world" (*The Neoplatonism of William Blake*, 102). Peter F. Fisher holds that the "aim of Plato is also the aim of Blake: the vision of what eternally exists, but the means are different" (*The Valley of Vision: Blake as Prophet and Revolutionary*, ed. Northrop Frye [Toronto: University of Toronto Press, 1961], 48). Though Plato rejects what Blake celebrates—the imagination as means to transcendent knowledge—still Blake "is in agreement with what he is convinced Plato is actually talking about: the forms or ideas of eternal existence" (Fisher 50). Morton D. Paley's position is similar: for Blake, "imagination is intuitive, and its knowing is grounded not in materials of sensation but in innate ideas" (*Energy and the Imagination* [Oxford: Clarendon Press, 1970], 200). Paley links Blake to both Neoplatonic and Berkeleyan idealism (see his chapter 8, "The Sublime of Imagination," esp. 206–20).

19 Adams, *Philosophy of the Literary Symbolic* (Tallahassee: University Presses of Florida, 1983), 5.

20 Bloom, *Blake's Apocalypse: A Study in Poetic Argument*, 433.

21 Doskow, *William Blake's* Jerusalem: *Structure and Meaning in Poetry and Picture* (Rutherford, N.J.: Farleigh Dickinson University Press, 1982), 167–68.

Rouzing the Faculties

1 John Howard's recent *Infernal Poetics: Poetic Structure in Blake's Lambeth Prophecies* (Cranbury, N.J.: Associated University Presses, 1984) is an exception that focuses on the more lasting effects that Blake's poetry can have on a reader. Howard concentrates on the ways in which the poems and designs evoke multiple perspectives that, according to Howard, help release unconscious, repressed energies in the reader. The fundamental difference between Howard's position and mine is my conviction that alteration of perspective involves changes in the linguistic code that one inhabits, that release of "repressed energies" requires more than just an

alteration of perspective, and that Blake's poetry promotes not only the release of repressed energies but their transformation (displacement and sublimation) as well.

2   Because no one has yet formulated a theory of reader response based on Lacanian concepts, the present attempt to apply Lacanian concepts to Blake will of necessity be tentative and exploratory. For other applications of Lacanian concepts to reader-response theory, see Ellie Ragland-Sullivan, "The Magnetism between Reader and Text: Prolegomena to a Lacanian Poetics," *Poetics* 13 (1984), 381–406; Shoshana Felman, *Writing and Madness: Literature/Philosophy/Psychoanalysis* (Ithaca, N.Y.: Cornell University Press, 1985); Kaja Silverman, *The Subject of Semiotics* (New York: Oxford University Press, 1984); and Jane Gallop, *Reading Lacan* (Ithaca, N.Y.: Cornell University Press, 1985). Julia Kristeva's work, heavily influenced by Lacan, is also highly relevant here. See especially *Revolution in Poetic Language* (New York: Columbia University Press, 1984).

3   In the fourth memorable fancy, Blake shows us the way heaven and hell are already married. One of the functions of this fancy is to dramatize the relation between the traditional symbolic system (reason, heaven) and desire (energy, hell). Here the angel and Blake's persona go through the orthodox symbolic system (stable, Church, etc.) to explore the foundation of the system, which is revealed to rest on an abyss of repulsive, bestial and chthonic forces. The direct connection between these bestial forces and the spiritual, symbolic realm is indicated by the speaker's description of the supreme bestial force, the Leviathan, "advancing toward us with all the fury of a *spiritual existence*" (*MHH*18–19; emphasis added). This same point is dramatized more explicitly in the second tour, conducted by the speaker. Here the two enter the spiritual realm, and from there, the heart of the orthodox symbolic system, the Bible, where they discover bestial and aggressive forces, just as in the previous expedition. The message is clear: these impulses are at the basis of, and constitute the substance of, even the most spiritual and rational systems—Christianity and "Aristotles Analytics." Thought (reason) and spirituality (heaven) cannot be separated from instinctual energy and desire (hell). Heaven and hell are already married. In order for the marriage to be consummated, however, the reader must enact free intercourse between the two realms, and this is where the real difficulty lies. The angelic, devouring aspect of all humans occupies a dominant position, by virtue of its restrictive, bounding, directing power (the power of reason, the symbolic). Diminishing this tyranny thus requires that the symbolic be altered, opened up, and that repressed desire be allowed expression.

4   See Louis Althusser, "Ideology and Ideological State Apparatuses," in *Lenin and Philosophy*, trans. Ben Brewster (New York: Monthly Review Press, 1971), 127–86.

5   Howard claims that evoking such opposing perspectives "was Blake's con-

scious and perhaps ultimate strategy, for it is in changing perspective that one is set free from restrictions" (65). My argument is that such freedom depends on more than optics.

6 For an illuminating account of Blake's alteration of the given code, see Grahan Pechey, "*The Marriage of Heaven and Hell*: A Text and Its Conjuncture," *Oxford Literary Review* 3 (1979), 52–76.

7 Lacan finds an example of such modification in the phrase "fear of God"— a phrase that, he says, is by definition poetic. Observing that this phrase is not found everywhere, Lacan notes that someone had to invent it. And to do so was "to propose to men, as remedy for a world made of multiple terrors, to fear a being who can, after all, exercise his cruelties only by the evils that are there, multiply present, in human life. To replace the innumerable fears by the fear of a single being who has no other means of manifesting his power than by that which is feared behind these innumerable fears—that's impressive. . . . To invent such a thing, it is necessary to be a poet or a prophet" (*SJL*, 3:302).

8 In fact, one way to distinguish between poetry and philosophy might be to see philosophy as being more explicit and precise in its alterations of the code, and poetry as exerting greater force to get the reader to internalize the somewhat more ambiguous alterations that poetry embodies.

9 Fredric Jameson, *The Political Unconscious: Narrative as a Socially Symbolic Act* (Ithaca, N.Y.: Cornell University Press, 1981), 10, 19–20.

10 The radical force of the proverbs is enacted first in the powerfully interpellative "sentence now . . . read by [us] on earth" that introduces them: "How do you know but ev'ry Bird that cuts the airy way, / Is an immense world of delight, clos'd by your senses five?" (*MHH*7).

If we accept the question as addressed to us—and the previous "sentence" makes it difficult not to—we are interpellated out of our habitual code in which "bird" is given its signification as a relatively limited and insignificant creature. Instead of merely residing in this signification, we must now justify it in some manner. How? Perhaps in the way we normally attempt to justify our positions—by invoking experience. How do we know what a bird is? By our observation and experience of birds, we might say. The present question, however, has interpellated us into a position where such an answer is not acceptable, for the question posed here is not just an empirical one (How do you know what a bird is?) but also an epistemological one: How do you *know* that you know? That is, how do you know that your perception constitutes knowledge and not delusion; how do you know that "your senses five" are receptive to reality?

This instance of interpellation pressures us to seek a ground beyond not only our own sacred code, but all codes whatsoever. The groundlessness or relativity of "All Bibles or sacred codes" is driven home to us in plates 5–6, which point out how the key terms of the present argument—reason and desire—have no natural, univocal connection to any preexisting reality. Their significance is determined by their relation with other signifiers, which varies dramatically from one "history" (with its implicit code) to another. In *Paradise Lost,* for instance, "the Governor" is identical with "Reason," which is identified as the "Messiah." "But in the Book of Job Miltons Messiah is call'd Satan." Moreover, this discrepancy occurs between two "histories" that supposedly share the same code. The implication is thus that the code itself is ambiguous, and can lead to opposite conclusions. The Bible has an "infernal or diabolical sense" (*MHH*24), as Blake puts it at the end of the poem, and the sense one reads ultimately depends, perhaps, on what one desires, or on whether one's desire or one's reason is the stronger. We are thus left with the recognition that even if we were able to continue to dwell in the code, the code offers no final security or stability.

11 The Oedipal desire is evoked throughout the poem. As Brenda Webster notes, the general pattern of *The Marriage* is one "in which a previously subdued son triumphs over the father" (*Blake's Prophetic Psychology* [Athens: University of Georgia Press, 1983]).

12 I have provided an extended analysis of the way in which *Milton* alters the definition of being, particularly in relation to death, in *Being Form'd: Thinking through Blake's* Milton (Barrytown, N.Y.: Station Hill Press, 1985).

13 In addition to Hilton's essay in this volume, see his *Literal Imagination: Blake's Vision of Words* (Berkeley: University of California Press, 1983).

Blake, Women, and Sexuality

1 Robert Southey, cited in S. Foster Damon, *William Blake, His Philosophy and Symbols* (Gloucester, Mass.: Peter Smith, 1958), 246.

2 For example, H. M. Margoliouth in his edition of *William Blake's* Vala (Oxford: Clarendon Press, 1956), 144; or John E. Grant, "Visions in *Vala:* A Consideration of Some Pictures in the Manuscript," in *Blake's Sublime Allegory; Essays* on The Four Zoas, Milton, *and* Jerusalem, ed. Stuart Curran and Joseph Anthony Wittreich, Jr. (Madison: University of Wisconsin Press, 1973), 184.

3 S. Foster Damon, *A Blake Dictionary: The Ideas and Symbols of William Blake* (New York: Dutton, 1971), 196. Though Damon progresses from seeing Blake as a mystic to accepting his sexuality, in both cases he idealizes him.

4 Diana Hume George, *Blake and Freud* (Ithaca, N.Y.: Cornell University Press, 1980), 144.

5 See the quotation from Bernard Blackstone, *English Blake* (Hamden, Conn.: Archon Books, 1966), 294, cited by George in *Blake and Freud,* 245.

6 Jean Hagstrum, "Babylon Revisited, or the Story of Luvah and Vala," in *Blake's Sublime Allegory,* ed. Stuart Curran and Joseph Wittreich (Madison: University of Wisconsin Press, 1973), 105. Any doubts about the meaning of the line are cleared up by the variant in *Milton* where the fe-

male, repenting of her previous jealousy, begins "to give / Her maidens to her husband: delighting in his delight" (*M*33:17–18, E132).

7 During the time I was writing the book on which this paper is based (from 1972 to 1979), critics like Carolyn Heilbrun and Irene Tayler praised Blake's freedom from the prison of gender while Sandra Gilbert, Susan Gubar, and Diana Hume George compared him favorably to Milton. See Heilbrun in *Far Western Forum* 1 (1974), 284; Tayler, "The Woman Scaly," *Midwestern Modern Language Association Bulletin* 6 (1973), 87; Gilbert and Gubar, *The Madwoman in the Attic: The Woman Writer in the Nineteenth Century Literary Imagination* (New Haven: Yale University Press, 1979), 200; and Diana Hume George, "Is She Also the Divine Image? Feminine Form in the Art of William Blake," *Centennial Review* 23 (1979), 129–40, 137. Susan Fox is a notable exception. She points out that the difference between Blake's (seemingly benign) concepts and his consistently negative images of women must connote at least some uneasiness in the author's mind. See "The Female as Metaphor in William Blake's Poetry," *Critical Inquiry* 3 (1977), 519. Since my book was accepted by Macmillan in 1981 several new articles have appeared that point to Blake's antifeminism: Alicia Ostriker, "Desire Gratified and Ungratified: William Blake and Sexuality," *Blake* 16 (1982–83); Anne K. Mellor, "Blake's Portrayal of Women," *Blake* 16 (1982–83); and Margaret Storch, whose psychoanalytic approach resembles mine, "Blake and Women: Nature's Cruel Holiness," *American Imago* (1981).

8 James Reiger, "The Hem of Their Garments: The Bard's Song in *Milton*," in *Blake's Sublime Allegory*, 260.

9 Ricoeur, *Freud and Philosophy: An Essay on Interpretation*, trans. Denis Savage (New Haven: Yale University Press, 1970).

10 See Meredith Anne Skura, *The Literary Use of the Psychoanalytic Process* (New Haven: Yale University Press, 1981), 216, for a description of the ways the psychoanalytic process may be seen as a model for the literary text.

11 Frederick Crews, *Out of My System: Psychoanalysis, Ideology and Critical Method* (New York: Oxford University Press, 1975), 145.

12 David V. Erdman, *Blake: Prophet against Empire* (New York: Anchor Books, 1969), 228.

13 Melanie Klein, *Love, Guilt and Reparation and Other Works, 1921–1945* (New York: Delacorte Press, 1975), 114, 126.

14 Diana Hume George, *Blake and Freud*, 144.

Blake's Feminist Revision of Literary Tradition

1 Heilbrun, "Reply to Newman," *Signs* 10 (1985), 604.

2 I borrow Geoffrey Hartman's succinct summary of Showalter's definition. "The Challenge of Feminist Criticism: A Symposium," *Proceedings* (Evanston, Ill.: Program on Women, Northwestern University, 1983), 23.

3 Showalter, "Feminist Criticism in the Wilderness," *Signs* 8 (1981), 184–85.

4 Kolodny, "Dancing through the Minefield: Some Observations on the Theory, Practice, and Politics of a Feminist Literary Criticism," *Feminist Studies* 6 (1980), 19, 20.

5 Jehlen, "Archimedes and the Paradox of Feminist Criticism," *Signs* 6 (1981), 580.

6 The feminist analyses of Susan Fox, "The Female as Metaphor in William Blake's Poetry," *Critical Inquiry* 3 (1977), 507–19; and Alicia Ostriker, "Desire Gratified and Ungratified: William Blake and Sexuality," *Blake: An Illustrated Quarterly* 16 (1982–83), 156–65, have demonstrated the ambivalence in Blake's position on women. Ostriker has defined four distinct attitudes toward women in the poems and concludes that we find in Blake both a "richly developed anti-patriarchal and proto-feminist sensibility . . . and its opposite, a homocentric gynophobia" (233). She notes, too, that Blake believed that " 'To give Body to Error' was . . . an essential service performed by mighty intellects for posterity" (234). With such contradictions in his own work and such a disposition to recognize in great works the articulation of error, Blake clearly deserves a feminist hearing on bias in interpretation.

7 Hirsch, *Innocence and Experience: An Introduction to Blake* (New Haven: Yale University Press, 1964), 233, 234.

8 Harold Bloom, *Blake's Apocalypse: A Study in Poetic Argument* (New York: Doubleday, 1963), 135.

9 Brenda S. Webster, *Blake's Prophetic Psychology* (London: Macmillan, 1983), 107.

10 See, for example, Brian Wilkie, "Blake's *Innocence* and *Experience:* An Approach," *Blake Studies* 6 (1975), 119–37, who claims that "in the context of the *Songs* the reading [of the speaker as Blake or as a persona who is his direct spokesman] is inadequate, for it makes "The Sick Rose" a song *about* Experience rather than of it in the sense of *proceeding from* it, and the latter is the typical method on the volume" (131). He adds that Blake's poem "*is*, precisely, a depiction of an unhealthy attitude toward sexual love" (131). Other critics, like Michael Riffaterre, "The Self-Sufficient Text," *Diacritics* 3 (1975), 39–45, do not allegorize the worm and the rose along sexual lines. Riffaterre examines "The Sick Rose" using only internal evidence to refute the assumption that the poem's "symbolism cannot be understood without understanding them first as metaphors for man" (39).

11 I draw the term "reading as a feminist" from Elaine Showalter's review of Jonathan Culler's *On Deconstruction*. Her article, "Critical Cross-Dressing," *Raritan* 3 (1983), 139–43, responds to Culler's assertion that "reading as a man" versus "reading as a woman" will necessarily produce different results because of the inevitable differences of perspective and experience when a woman reads instead of a man. Elaine Showalter has revised Culler's "reading as a woman" to "reading as a feminist" in order to avoid making the reader's experience sex specific. "Feminist" is a perspective available to men and women; "woman" is biologically determined.

12 Paley, "Introduction," in *Twentieth Century Interpretations of Songs of Innocence and of Experience* (Englewood Cliffs, N.J.: Prentice-Hall, 1969), 7.

13 Mark Schorer, "Experience," in *Twentieth Century Interpretations of Songs of Innocence and of Experience*, ed. Paley, 100.

14 Hirsch, *Innocence and Experience*, 235.

15 Donald Ault, Vanderbilt University, in an unpublished article, "Un-Reading 'LONDON'," September 1986, has challenged the identification of the poem's speaker with Blake. His argument ultimately provides support for mine in demonstrating that we must avoid simple identifications of specific speakers with Blake.

16 Stevenson, ed., *The Poems of William Blake* (London: Longman, 1971), 217.

17 *The Illuminated Blake*, annotated by David V. Erdman (Garden City, N.Y.: Doubleday, 1974), 81. All subsequent comments by Erdman on the illustrations are taken from pages 81 and 82 of this text.

18 Keynes, "Introduction and Commentary," *William Blake: Songs of Innocence and of Experience*, by William Blake (New York: Oxford University Press, 1970), 147.

19 *The Notebook of William Blake: A Photographic and Typographic Facsimile*, ed. David V. Erdman (Oxford: Clarendon Press, 1973).

20 Bloom, *Blake's Apocalypse*, 135.

Representations of Revolution

1 Damrosch, *Symbol and Truth in Blake's Myth* (Princeton, N.J.: Princeton University Press, 1980), 9.

2 Mikhail Bakhtin, *The Dialogic Imagination* (Austin: University of Texas Press, 1981).

3 Bakhtin/Vološinov, *Marxism and the Philosophy of Language* (Cambridge, Mass.: Harvard University Press, 1986), 86.

4 Some forms of contemporary sociolinguistics are helpful here: see Bob Hodge and Gunther Kress, *Language as Ideology* (London: Routledge and Kegan Paul, 1979), and Roger Fowler, Bob Hodge, Gunther Kress, and Tony Trew, *Language and Control* (London: Routledge and Kegan Paul, 1979). The approach here is used and extended in David Aers, Bob Hodge, and Gunther Kress, *Literature, Language and Society in England 1580–1680* (Dublin: Gill and Macmillan, 1981).

5 Works I have in mind here include Chris Baldick, *Social Mission of English Criticism* (London: Oxford University Press, 1983); Tony Bennett, *Formalism and Marxism* (London: Methuen, 1979); Terry Eagleton, *Literary Theory* (Oxford: Blackwell, 1983); John Fekete, *The Critical Twilight* (London: Routledge and Kegan Paul, 1977); Jerome J. McGann, *The Romantic Ideology* (Chicago: University of Chicago Press, 1983); Francis Mulhern, *The Moment of Scrutiny* (London: New Left Books, 1979); Peter Widdowson, ed., *Re-Reading English* (London: Methuen, 1982); Frank Lentricchia, *After the New Criticism* (London: Methuen, 1982), and *Criticism and Social Change* (Chicago: University of Chicago

Press, 1983); R. Selden, *Criticism and Objectivity* (London: Croom Helm, 1984).

6 Glen, *Vision and Disenchantment: Blake's* Songs *and Wordsworth's* Lyrical Ballads (Cambridge: Cambridge University Press 1983), at 344.

7 Here his work converges with important developments in feminism still marginalized by the academic left, which, for reasons that cannot be unpacked here, are preoccupied with Lacanian traditions of psychoanalysis. See, for example, Carol Gilligan, *In a Different Voice* (Cambridge: Harvard University Press, 1982); Dorothy Dinnerstein, *The Rocking of the Cradle and the Ruling of the World* (London: Souvenir, 1978); Louise Eichenbaum and Susie Orbach, *What do Women Want?* (London: Fontana, 1984). See too Glen, cited above.

8 On hegemony, Antonio Gramsci, "Notes on Italian History," "The Modern Prince" and "State and Civil Society," in *Selections from the Prison Notebooks* (London: Lawrence and Wishart, 1971), esp. 245–53; also contrast Raymond Williams's account in *Marxism and Literature* (London: Oxford University Press, 1977), with what I see as Blake's more static version— cf. esp. 112–13.

9 For a haunting account of how such a society could be, see Colin Turnbull, *The Mountain People* (London: Colins, 1973).

10 Glen, *Vision and Disenchantment*, 95–109, 345.

11 The present essay is part of a larger project in which I take the questions it raises into comparative analysis of *Milton*, and *Jerusalem*, as well as considering *The Marriage of Heaven and Hell* (not discussed here because it does not project collective social revolution in the manner of the poems studied here). Limits of space entail great selectivity, but the justification, I hope, is the fundamental questions involved and the need to extend the area of current Blake studies to focus on such questions about the relations of literature, politics and history.

12 For example, *FR* 4:54; 10:186, 11:204, 206; 4:62, 15:286, E288–99.

13. On the Jacobins and the contexts see Albert Soboul, *The French Revolution* (London: New Left Books, 1974), parts 2 and 3; see Edmund Burke's extremely shrewd comments on English Jacobins in *Letters on the Proposals for Peace* . . . [1796–1797] in *The Works* vol. 6 (London: Oxford University Press, 1907), 129–31, 148–49, 203–9, 362–70, 375, 383–85.

14 I write "risk" because it is not inevitable: in grasping the key structures of any social formation, abstractions (class, modes, and forces of production) are essential: the problematic issue is how such abstractions are controlled and tested out against the empirical world. See E. P. Thompson, *The Poverty of Theory* (London: Merlin, 1978) and Perry Anderson's responses in *Arguments within English Marxism* (London: New Left Books, 1980). It should also be noted that in *The French Revolution* Blake does direct attention toward realities of political power and institutions (unlike *The Four Zoas*, Night IX and the merry endings of *Milton* and *Jerusalem*).

15 For contradictions and problems in this figure, see my essay "Blake: Sex,

Society and Ideology," in *Romanticism and Ideology*, Aers, Jon Cook, David Punter (London: Routledge and Kegan Paul, 1981).

16 See Glen, *Vision and Disenchantment*, passim, chapters 4 and 5.

17 Dworkin, *Pornography* (London: Womens' Press, 1981). Against Blake's texts should be set the approaches to desire in Mary Wollstonecraft, *Vindication of the Rights of Woman* and *Mary: A Fiction and the Wrongs of Women*, ed. Gary Kelly (London: Oxford University Press, 1976).

18 Despite marvelously sharp criticism of political economy and its moralizing, *The Song of Los*, 1795, concludes with a version of revolution like *America*'s: see *L7*:31–40, E69–70. This reflects the abstraction of sexuality discussed in the text here and perpetuates the same macho model of revolution and sex: revolution is a cosmic fuck, allegedly liberated sexuality an activity isolated from care, affection, reciprocity.

19 See also *FZIX*:126–131, E395–400 passim. On the "pastoral" in Night IX, see David Wagenknecht, *Blake's Night* (Cambridge, Mass.: Harvard University Press, 1973), 214–15.

20 See M. D. Paley, *Energy and Imagination* (London: Oxford University Press, 1970), 154.

21 The pre-Marxist traditions that emphasize the decisive nature of the sphere of production in social change would include the peasantry of 1381 (see R. Hilton, *Bond Men Made Free*, [London: Temple Smith, 1973], chapter 9), Winstanley in the seventeenth century, Spence and Owen in Blake's own time.

22 On work in Blake, see David Punter, "Blake: Creative and Uncreative Labour," *Studies in Romanticism* 16 (1977), 535–61.

23 E. P. Thompson, "Time, Work-Discipline and Industrial Capitalism," *Past and Present* 38 (1967).

24 The exception in Night VII[a], I discuss below. See *FZVI*:70:39–45, E347; *FZVI*:71:13–14, E348.

25 On the exterminist course of our culture, E. P. Thompson, "The Logic of Exterminism," *New Left Review* 121 (1980), 3–31; and Ronald Aronson, *Technological Madness: Towards a Theory of Impending Nuclear Holocaust* (London: Menard, 1983).

26 Frye, *Fearful Symmetry* (Boston: Beacon, 1962), 303; Bloom, "Commentary," E964.

27 A. K. Mellor, *Blake's Human Form Divine* (Berkeley and Los Angeles: University of California Press, 1974), 190; Paley, *Energy and Imagination*, 164. Contrast Paley's views in his recent study *The Continuing City* (London: Oxford University Press, 1983), 132, 136, 234: here the millennium is *this* worldly, although apparently confined to an autonomous aesthetic dimension.

28 B. Wilkie and M. L. Johnson, *Blake's Four Zoas* (Cambridge, Mass.: Harvard University Press, 1978), 213; B. Webster, *Blake's Prophetic Psychology* (London: Macmillan, 1983), 244.

29 D. V. Erdman, *Blake: Prophet against Empire* (Garden City, N.Y.: Doubleday–Anchor, Press, 1969), 352–53.

30 S. Crehan, *Blake in Context* (Dublin: Gill and Macmillan, 1984), 314.
31 T. R. Frosch, *The Awakening of Albion* (Ithaca, N.Y.: Cornell University Press, 1974), 141.
32 M. K. Nurmi, *Blake* (London: Hutchinson, 1975), 144–45.
33 This language has nothing to do with critical talk of "supreme fictions" or ahistorical archetypes. On Blake's period see E. P. Thompson, *The Making of the English Working Class* (London: Gollancz, 1963), esp. chapters 2 and 5; Clarke Garrett, *Respectable Folly* (Baltimore: Johns Hopkins University Press, 1975), chapters 6–9; J. F. C. Harrison, *The Second Coming: Popular Millenarianism 1750–1850* (London: Routledge and Kegan Paul, 1979).
34 The quotation comes from the fifth thesis on Feuerbach. On Marx's ideas about revolution an excellent starting place is John Elster's outstanding study, *Making Sense of Marx* (Cambridge: Cambridge University Press, 1985), 428–49.
35 Frye, *Fearful Symmetry*, 306.
36 On the wars and their effects, besides Erdman's *Blake* see Betty T. Bennett's introduction to *British War Poetry in the Age of Romanticism* (New York: Garland, 1976).
37 On the emerging northern working class see the study by John Forster, *Class Struggle and the Industrial Revolution* (London: Weidenfeld and Nicolson, 1974).
38 On the London radicals see part 1 of *The Making of the English Working Class* (I call it mistitled for some of the reasons offered by Perry Anderson in *Arguments*, 30–49). See too G. Williams, *Artisans and Sans-Culottes* (London: Arnold, 1968); C. B. Cone, *The English Jacobins* (New York: Scribner's, 1968).
39 See M. D. George, *London Life in the Eighteenth Century* (Harmonsworth: Penguin, 1966); G. Rudé, *Hanoverian London* (London: Secker, 1971); G. S. Jones, *Outcast London* (Oxford: Oxford University Press, 1971).
40 Jones, *Outcast London*, 344.
41 Another important area blurred in this approach is the one of fraternity/terror taken up in J.-P. Sartre's *Critique of Dialectical Reason* (London: New Left Books, 1982), 437–44, 468–70. This needs careful study and Blake's representations need to be considered in its light. Compare Michael Ferber, "Blake's Idea of Brotherhood," *PMLA* 93 (1978), 438–47. Since I wrote this Michael Ferber has published *The Social Vision of William Blake* (Princeton, N.J.: Princeton University Press, 1985), a book that will be of the greatest interest to anyone concerned with any of the issues I discuss.
42 Once more I should point out my acceptance of the main lines of Heather Glen's approach to the *Songs of Innocence and Experience*.
43 Coleridge, "A Moral and Political Lecture," in *Lectures 1795 On Politics and Religion*, ed. L. Patton and P. Mann, being vol. 1 of *The Collected Works of Coleridge* (London: Routledge and Kegan Paul, 1971), 18.
44 For the argument here, see my "Coleridge and the Egg that Burke Laid:

Ideological Collusion and Opposition in the 1790s," *Literature and History* 9 (1983), 152–63.

45 *FZIX*:131:19–22, E400; see *FZIX*:126–131, E395–400. The placement of the *Songs of Innocence* here is a topic I am currently working on. The harvesting is at *FZIX*:131:40–134, E400–403.

46 That the sources are biblical makes no difference to this analysis.

47 Bloom, "Commentary," E967.

48 Wickham, *The Writings*, ed. R. D. Smith (London: Virago, 1984), 366.

49 The shift to female cruelty (*FZVIII*:105:3–54, E378–79, developed obsessively in *Jerusalem*) raises issues too complex to take up here. I address them in the project mentioned above, also developing a discussion in *Romanticism and Ideology*, chapter 2.

50 See Richard Slotkin's *Regeneration through Violence* (Middletown: Wesleyan University Press, 1973). On the United States in Asia see Noam Chomsky: *At War with Asia* (London: Fontana, 1971), *American Power and the New Mandarins* (London: Chatto, 1969); *After the Cataclysm* (Boston: South End Press, 1979); *For Reasons of State* (London: Panther, 1973). On Central America, see Phillip Berryman, *Inside Central America* (London: Pluto, 1985) and *On Trial: Reagan's War against Nicaragua*, ed. M. Dixon (London: Zed Books, 1985).

51 Later I hope to explore the psychological and cultural pressures pushing Blake to ignore these possibilities.

52 The question of the order of composition of the parts of Nights VII[a] and [b] is not crucial here.

53 In my view even Blake's admirable ideal of collaborative male and female labor reproduces patriarchal power and sexual inequality of a rather traditional kind.

54 "Every Harlot was once a Virgin: every Criminal an Infant Love!" (*J*61:52, E212).

55 Gilligan, *In a Different Voice* (Cambridge, Mass.: Harvard University Press, 1982), 100.

56 In the project of which this essay is part, *Milton* and *Jerusalem* should be studied in this context.

"in vain the Eloquent tongue"

1 S. Foster Damon, *William Blake: His Philosophy and Symbols* (London: Dawsons of Pall Mall, 1969), 330. Kathleen Raine, *Blake and Tradition*, 2 vols. (Princeton, N.J.: Princeton University Press, 1968), 2:125.

2 Damrosch, *Symbol and Truth in Blake's Myth* (Princeton, N.J.: Princeton University Press, 1980), 198.

3 Northrop Frye, *Fearful Symmetry* (Princeton, N.J.: Princeton University Press, 1947), 239–40 passim.

4 Bloom and Lionel Trilling, eds. *Romantic Poetry and Prose* (New York: Oxford University Press, 1973), v, 44, 45.

5   Mark Anderson, "Oothoon, Failed Prophet," *Romanticism Past and Present* 8 (1984), 9.

6   George Mills Harper, *The Neoplatonism of William Blake* (Chapel Hill: University of North Carolina Press, 1961), 257.

7   Aers, "Blake: Sex, Society and Ideology," in *Romanticism and Ideology: Studies in English Writing 1765–1830* (London: Routledge and Kegan Paul, 1981), 31.

8   Susan Fox, *Poetic Form in Blake's* Milton (Princeton, N.J.: Princeton University Press, 1976); "The Female as Metaphor in William Blake's Poetry," *Critical Inquiry* 3 (1977), 507–20.

9   Mellor, "Blake's Portrayal of Women," *Blake: An Illustrated Quarterly* 16 (1982–83), 148, 154.

10   Alicia Ostriker, "Desire Gratified and Ungratified: William Blake and Sexuality," *Blake: An Illustrated Quarterly* 16, 3 (Winter 1982–83), 164.

11   Marilyn Butler, *Burke, Paine, Godwin, and the Revolution Controversy* (Cambridge: Cambridge University Press, 1984), 7.

12   Nelson Hilton's is the best discussion of these topics, both in its grasp of the complexities of the historical material and of their pertinence for a better understanding of Blake's text in its discursive context. See "An Original Story," in *Unnam'd Forms: Blake and Textuality* (Berkeley: University of California Press, 1986), 69–104.

13   The ambivalence is not only in the lines, but in their problematic status in the text. They were erased or masked in all but two of the printed versions. Erdman pushes the evidence to indicate "dismay" and momentary "despair." See David V. Erdman, *Blake: Prophet against Empire*, rev. ed. (Garden City, N.Y.: Anchor Books, 1969), 286, and E802.

14   David V. Erdman, ed., *The Illuminated Blake* (Garden City, N.Y.: Anchor Books, 1974, 126–27. This book is dedicated "To Enitharmon."

15   Damon, *William Blake: His Philosophy and Symbols*, 332.

16   Alexander Cruden, *Cruden's Unabridged Concordance* (Grand Rapids, MI: Baker Book House, 1977), 144, 221.

17   See J. H. Hanford, "The Debate of Eye and Heart," *Modern Language Notes* 26 (1911), 161–65. For a more recent discussion see Joel Fineman, "Shakespeare's 'Perjur'd Eye,' " in *Representations* 7 (1984), 59–86.

18   William Duff, *An Essay on Original Genius* (London, 1767), 270.

19   Blair, "A Critical Dissertation on The Poems of Ossian, the Son of Fingal," in *The Poems of Ossian* (Boston: Phillips, Sampson, 1854), 150, 175, 107.

20   Ferguson, *An Essay on the History of Civil Society*, 7th ed. (Boston, 1809), 285.

21   Samuel Richardson, *Clarissa: Or, The History of a Young Lady* (London: Dent, 1932), 2:466, 306, 438. Rousseau was fond of the image of an authentic "writing" or "engraving" on the heart, which could only be from Nature or God, and which could never be effaced. See Jacques Derrida, *Of Grammatology*, trans. Gayatri Chakravorty Spivak (Baltimore: Johns Hopkins University Press, 1976), 6–26.

22   Wordsworth, *The Prelude* (Text of 1805), ed. Ernest de Selincourt, rev. impression (London: Oxford University Press, 1960), 9:170–74, 210.

23   James Thomson, *The Seasons and The Castle of Indolence*, ed. James Sambrook (Oxford: Clarendon Press, 1972), "Spring," 203–21. Milton's Satan mounts a three-level eye attack on Eve, first by adopting a seductive appearance ("in sight of *Eve*, / To lure her Eye"), then by appealing to her vanity as one who should be seen by others, then to the human desire to see as gods. Throughout this section of *Paradise Lost* (9:495–780) with its focus on "The Eye of *Eve*" (9:528), the reader is frequently confronted with the graphic similarity of "Eye" and "Eve."

24   See, for example, Kant, *Observations on the Feeling of the Beautiful and Sublime*, trans. John T. Goldthwait (Berkeley: University of California Press, 1965). In section 3 Kant eroticizes the opposition, arguing that the "sex impulse" acting in the service of "the great goal of nature" results in a marriage that constitutes "a single moral person" uniting the pair. "In such a relation, then, a dispute over precedence (i.e. of 'eye' and 'heart') is trifling" (89–96).

25   Edmund Burke, *Reflections on the Revolution in France* (London, 1790), 145.

26   Joseph Priestly, *Letters to the Right Hon. Edmund Burke, Occasioned by his Reflections on the Revolution in France* (Birmingham, 1971), 146.

27   Mary Wollstonecraft, *A Vindication of the Rights of Men, in a Letter to the Right Hon. Edmund Burke, Occasioned by his Reflections on the Revolution in France* (London, 1790), 10.

28   Wollstonecraft, *A Vindication of the Rights of Woman, with Strictures on Political and Moral Subjects* (London, 1792), 38.

29   Harold Bloom, *Blake's Apocalypse* (New York: Doubleday, 1963), 101.

30   Anne Kostelanetz Mellor, *Blake's Human Form Divine* (Berkeley: University of California Press, 1974), 63.

31   The name "Bromion" echoes the Greek βρόμιος, used for the god Dionysus in Euripides' *Bacchae*, a play where the voyeuristic Pentheus—like Actaeon—sees what he should not see and becomes the "fruit" on his own visionary tree, plucked down and torn apart by his own mother. As the play opens, Dionysus has already "possessed" all the women, taking them from the city and from Pentheus into the "wild" forest, where he offers release from their women's work of looms and wombs. Pentheus' voyeuristic curiosity about the women is roused, and fueled by his fantasies, so that Dionysus finds it easy to manipulate his desire to see the maenads. E. R. Dodds has argued that the ecstatic communion of the Dionysiac *thiasos* or "holy band" should suggest a spiritual state of spontaneous fusion and communion (*Euripides' Bacchae*, 2d ed. [London: Oxford University Press, 1960]). But Pentheus can only imagine their revels as pretenses for the women to go "crouching into the wilderness, to serve the lechery of men— they profess to be maenads making sacrifice, but actually they put Aphrodite before the Bacchic god" (*Bacchae*, ll. 221–25). Pentheus' ready will-

ingness to be dressed like a maenad suggests his combined curiosity and desire to see them and be like them.

32 See Raine, 1:174; Damon, *William Blake: His Philosophy and Symbols*, 329; Erdman, *Prophet against Empire*, 233.

33 A modern avatar of this *O*-writing can be found in J. M. Coetzee's *Foe* (London: Secker and Warburg, 1985), a retelling of Defoe's *Robinson Crusoe*, where Crusoe becomes Cruso and Friday (his tongue has been cut out), given pen and paper, proceeds to produce an endless series of *O*'s. Dante provides a precedent for visual punning on *O*'s and eyes, in *Purgatorio* 23, which begins with an emphasis on eyes (*Mentre che li occhi*) and continues with a textual proliferation of the letter *O*, with special emphasis on double-*O* words (*odo, modo, odo, nodo*) leading up to: *chi nel viso delli uomini legge 'omo' | ben avria quivi conosciuta l'emme* ("He that reads 'omo' in men's faces might easily have made out the *M* there"), after which the emphasis shifts to *omo* words like *pomo* and *como*.

34 John Berger, *Ways of Seeing* (New York: Penguin Books, 1977), 54.

35 Erdman *The Illuminated Blake*, 126. John Howard's formulation is worth quoting in full: "This eye is the reader's, who sees more than his heart yet knows, as the motto tells him, but through the unfolding perspective his heart will discover the full extent of these caves." *Infernal Poetics* (Rutherford, N.J.: Fairleigh Dickinson University Press, 1984), 98. This opposition between reader identifications has been anticipated by Freud in his "Instincts and Their Vicissitudes," where he explores the dynamics of alternation between voyeurism and exhibitionism as they are staged textual positions. *The Standard Edition of the Complete Psychological Works of Sigmund Freud* 14 trans. James Strachey (London: Hogarth Press, 1955). Robert Con Davis discusses the structural positions inscribed in the text as a "profoundly paradoxical situation of reading, where the line of sight and the Gaze meet most dramatically. That is, we turn to and read a text as if, by giving attention to it, we look into it and master or possess it *as an object*. But while reading, in fact, we are focused upon and held by a Gaze that comes through the agency of the object text. Thus held in the act of reading . . . we are not masterful subjects; we—as readers—then become the object of the Gaze. The Gaze—which inscribes the Other's desire in a discourse of positioning—is trained on readers from the outside as they read, and through the willing surrender to the active/passive alternations of reading, readers (subjects who become objects) play within and also escape the confines of voyeurism and exhibitionism." *Lacan and Narrative* (Baltimore: Johns Hopkins University Press, 1985), 988.

36 Another caverned vision analogue pertinent here is that of Malbecco in book 3, canto 10 of the *Faerie Queene*. At the end of that episode, after having been forced to witness his wife Hellenore at revels and in bed with the satyrs, Malbecco is reduced to the eye of *"Gealosie,"* locked in "a caue with entrance small" (57:9) and in an oxymoronic affective state of "painefull pleasure" and "pleasing paine" (60:4).

37 Erasmus Darwin, *The Loves of the Plants*, part 2, vol. 2 of *The Botanic*

Garden: A Poem in Two Parts (Dublin: J. Moore, 1793), 95. The popularity of the poem and of Fuseli's painting led the publisher Johnson to commission another version, to be engraved as an illustration for a new edition of Darwin's poem, a project completed in 1792. Nelson Hilton has put these and other facts to interesting account in his discussion of *VISIONS;* his comments first drew my attention to Starobinski's discussion of the Fuseli painting.

38 Behind both Blake and Fuseli here is the classic posture Sir Joshua Reynolds described as the "figure of a Bacchante leaning backward, her head thrown quite behind her, which seems to be a favourite invention, as it is so frequently repeated in bas-relievos, camaeos and intaglios; it is intended to express an enthusiastick frantick kind of joy." He goes on to note that the same posture can "express frantick agony of grief," since the "extremes of contrary passions are with very little variation expressed by the same action." *Discourses on Art,* ed. Robert R. Wark (New Haven: Yale University Press, 1975), 221–22.

39 "Préférerais, pour ma part, attribuer au peintre non l'angoisse du cauchmare, mais le plaisir voyeuriste d'en être le spectateur, au moment du tourment le plus intense. Il voit souffrir; it fait souffrir. . . ." [For my part, I would prefer to attribute to the painter not the distress of the nightmare, but the pleasure the voyeur experiences watching it at its most intense moment. He watches the suffering; he causes the suffering. . . .] Starobinski, "La vision de la dormeuse," in *Trois Fureurs* (Paris: Editions Gallimard, 1974), 143.

40 Bloom, *Blake's Apocalypse,* 103; Raine, *Blake and Tradition,* 1:169.

41 In English these lines and the few following read: "I love to pluck fresh flowers, and to seek an illustrious chaplet for my head from fields whence ere this the Muses have crowned the brows of none, first because my teaching is of high matters and I proceed to unclose the mind from the close knots of religion." As Marx emphasized, it's a good idea to know what you're plucking: "Criticism has plucked the imaginary flowers from the chain, not in order that man shall bear the chain without caprice or consolation but so that he shall cast off the chain and pluck the living flower." Marx, "Contribution to the Critique of Hegel's *Philosophy of Right:* Introduction," in *The Marx-Engels Reader,* ed. Robert C. Tucker (New York: W. W. Norton, 1972), 11–12.

42 Erdman, *Illuminated Blake,* 34.

43 The range of connotations for the term reflects the range of male imaginations of female sexuality and their attitudes toward it. Some of the favorite epithets of the Roman poets for nymphs were *salaces, improbae,* and *procaces.* See Leo C. Curran, "Rape and Rape Victims in the Metamorphoses," in *Women in the Ancient World: The Arethusa Papers,* ed. John Peradotto and J. P. Sullivan (Albany: State University of New York Press, 1984), 278.

44 Erdman, *Prophet against Empire,* 233. "Confusion of Progeny constitutes the essence of the crime, and therefore a woman who breaks her marriage

vows is much more criminal than a man who does it." Samuel Johnson, in *Boswell's Life of Johnson*, ed. R. W. Chapman, new ed. corr. J. D. Fleeman (Oxford: Oxford University Press, 1970), 393.

45   Erdman, *The Illuminated Blake*, 131, 129.

46   Beryl Rowland, *Birds with Human Souls* (Knoxville: University of Tennessee Press, 1978), 174. Versions of Zeus's rape of Leda by Leonardo and Michelangelo are both lost, but they were widely copied and disseminated during the seventeenth and eighteenth centuries. Correggio, Tintoretto, and Veronese also treated the myth, but Michelangelo's was the most daring, depicting the actual moment of coition. Although probably not directly known by Blake, the erotic coding was emphasized in Greek art by the Pistoxenos Painter, whose cup from 460 B.C. represents Aphrodite riding on a swan. Other Greek artists depicted the swan with griffins or Bacchic revelry. I discuss the equivocal nature of Blake's representation of the eagle in "The Blake of That Already," *Romanticism Past and Present* 9 (1985), 1–33.

47   See Raine, *Blake and Tradition*, 1:169 and Frye, *Fearful Symmetry*, 239.

48   See G. S. Rousseau, "Nymphomania, Bienville and the Rise of Erotic Sensibility," in *Sexuality in Eighteenth-Century Britain*, ed. P. G. Boucé (Manchester: Manchester University Press, 1982), 95–119.

49   Foucault, *The Discourse on Language*, in *The Archaeology of Knowledge and The Discourse on Language*, trans. A. M. Sheridan Smith (New York: Harper and Row, 1976), 216–17.

50   David Punter, "Blake, Trauma and the Female," *New Literary History* 15 (1984), 478–79.

51   John Dennis, "The Grounds of Criticism in Poetry," in *Works*, ed. E. N. Hooker (Baltimore, 1939), 1:359.

52   Longinus, *On the Sublime*, in *Aristotle*, vol. 23, trans. W. H. Fyfe (Cambridge: Harvard University Library, 1973), 151. Suzanne Guerlac discusses this ambiguity in terms of the disruption of the identity of the subject, involving "a slippage among the positions of enunciation, as the *destinateur* gets 'transported' into the message and the *destinataire* achieves a fictive identification with the speaker." "Longinus and the Subject of the Sublime," *New Literary History* 16 (1985), 275–89.

53   Károly Kerényi, *The Gods of the Greeks*, trans. H. J. Rose (New York: Grove Press, 1959), 251. Among the Greek gods Dionysus is unique in the frequency with which he is defeated, bound, imprisoned, and the number of times he must be rescued. "It is almost as if the defeats and persecutions were the important part of the story and often dwelled upon more fully than his triumphs. . . . There is a masochistic sensuality about these tales—a voluptuous savoring of degradation and disintegration" (Philip Slater, *The Glory of Hera* [Boston: Beacon Press, 1968], 283). This is no doubt part of the reason why he was thought to be so suitable a deity for women.

54   W. K. C. Guthrie, *The Greeks and Their Gods* (Boston: Beacon Press,

1955), 225. Thus in the *Bacchae* the maenads sing joyously at their release from "the looms and shuttles" under the influence of the god's ecstasy (ll. 116–19). Pentheus's response is to reaffirm their status, threatening to sell the women as slaves or to possess them himself as "servants for his looms" (l. 514). In both cases they are regarded as domestic "property" (l. 514), which is enclosed within the house yet also part of the overall economy of the city. The trope of slavery for the status of women flourished throughout the eighteenth century, climaxing with Mary Wollstonecraft, who saw them as slaves *of* and *to* everything from injustice to their own senses (*A Vindication of the Rights of Woman*). Factory work in Blake's time made them "slaves" of "looms and shuttles" in a sense Euripides could not have anticipated.

55 Slater, *The Glory of Hera*, 283–84. This power to confuse sex roles, associated with the release of emotional energies usually controlled and channeled in the order of the polis, is the "fundamental quality of Dionysus in Greek literature . . . his dissolution and confusion of basic polarities." Charles Segal, "The Menace of Dionysus: Sex Roles and Reversals in Euripides' *Bacchae*," in *Women in the Ancient World: The Arethusa Papers*, ed. Peradotto and Sullivan, 197.

56 Foucault, *The Discourse on Language*, 216.

57 Miller, *The Heroine's Text: Readings in the French and English Novel, 1722–1782* (New York: Columbia University Press, 1980), xi.

58 Cleland, *Fanny Hill*, ed. Peter Quennell (New York: Putnam, 1963), 108.

59 For some more general observations on eighteenth-century practice see Nancy K. Miller, "I's in Drag: The Sex of Recollection," *The Eighteenth Century* 22 (1981), 47–57; and Peggy Kamuf, *Fictions of Feminine Desire* (Lincoln: University of Nebraska Press, 1982).

60 Michel Foucault, *Language, Counter-Memory, Practice*, ed. Donald F. Bouchard, trans. Donald F. Bouchard and Sherry Simon (Ithaca, N.Y.: Cornell University Press, 1977), 29.

61 Herbert Marcuse, *Eros and Civilization* (New York: Vintage Books, 1962), 165–66.

62 David Aers, "Blake: Sex, Society and Ideology," 30.

63 Gilles Deleuze and Félix Guattari, *Anti-Oedipus: Capitalism and Schizophrenia*, trans. Robert Hurley, Mark Seem, and Helen Lane (Minneapolis: University of Minnesota Press, 1983), 378.

64 Morton Paley, *Energy and the Imagination* (Oxford: Clarendon Press, 1970), 35. Foucault, *History of Sexuality, Volume I: An Introduction*, trans. Robert Hurley (New York: Random House, 1980), 34.

65 Foucault, *History of Sexuality*, 1:6–7.

66 Roland Barthes, *Sade, Fourier, Loyola*, trans. Richard Miller (New York: Hill and Wang, 1976), 5.

67 As Geoff Bennington suggests, the chains of law are admitted in Sade "precisely to the extent that they are broken." In the logic of Sade's system there is no *jouissance* except that which breaks a social law in the service of the higher laws of nature. "La volupté n'admet aucune chaîne,

elle ne jouit jamais mieux que quand elle les rompt toutes" Donatien Alphonse François, Marquis de Sade, *Oeuvres complètes*, édition définitive (Paris: Cercle du Livre Précieux, 1966–67), 8:62. Bennington: "Sade: Laying Down the Law," *Oxford Literary Review* 6 (1984), 38–56. Rousseau: "The Supreme Being wished to act graciously towards humanity; while he gave man boundless inclinations, he also gave him the law to regulate him, so that he might be free and self-controlled; while he abandoned man to immoderate passions, he also gave him reason to master them: while he abandoned woman to limitless desires, he also gave her pudicity to contain them" (*Emile*, 359).

68 Foucault, *Language, Counter-Memory, Practice*, 34–35.

69 Bloom, *Blake's Apocalypse*, 106. Italics added.

70 Rousseau, *Emile*, 376.

71 John Locke, *An Essay Concerning Human Understanding*, 2 vols, ed. Alexander Fraser (New York: Dover, 1959), 2:146–47.

72 Thomas Sprat, *The History of the Royal Society of London* (London, 1667), 111–13 passim.

73 "La Philosophie dans le boudoir," in *The Marquis de Sade: An Essay by Simone de Beauvoir*, trans. Annette Michelson, ed. Paul Dinnage (New York: Grove Press, 1973), 137. For discussions of the social engineering that transformed "woman" from the more to the less appetitive sex, see Thomas Laqueur, "Orgasm, Generation, and the Politics of Reproductive Biology," *Representations* 14 (Spring 1986), 1–41; Marlene Le Gates, "The Cult of Womanhood in Eighteenth-Century Thought," in *Eighteenth-Century Studies* 10 (1976), 21–39; Edmund Leites, *The Puritan Conscience and Modern Sexuality* (New Haven: Yale University Press, 1986).

74 Even if Theotormon had no fear of "Woman" and her "power over Man from Cradle to corruptible Grave" (*J*30:26) his reading would have provided an ample supply of alternative versions of restraint. Samuel Johnson held that "Man's chief merit consisted in resisting the impulses of nature" ("Recollections" of Miss Reynolds, in *Johnsonian Miscellanies*, ed. George B. Hill [New York: Barnes and Noble, 1897], 2:285). For Edmund Burke, "Men are qualified for civil liberty in proportion to their disposition to put on moral chains upon their own appetites," and for Kant the act of sensuous denial is precisely the "moral" act that uncovers the spiritual self and allows the "Pure Will" to shine through. For Burke, see "Letter to a Member," in *The Works of the Right Honourable Edmund Burke*, 6 vols. (London: G. Bell, 1884–90), 4:51–52. For Kant, see *Groundwork of the Metaphysics of Morals*, trans. H. J. Paton (New York: Harper and Row, 1964), 425–60.

75 Joyce, *Finnegans Wake* (New York: Viking Press, 1957), 261. Joyce is playing with the Cabalistic myth where the author of reality has 10 [i.e. 1 + 0] emanations that sustain the material universe.

76 Colin MacCabe, *James Joyce and the Revolution of the Word* (New York: Barnes and Noble, 1979), 131.

77 Thomas Pynchon, *Gravity's Rainbow* (New York: Viking Press, 1973), 720–21.
78 For an equally ambiguous example, closer to Blake in time, see the end of Fielding's *Jonathan Wild*, with Mrs. Heartfree's long narrative, where the "heartfree" triumphant conclusions are uttered by a speaker of dubious reliability, framed by a mock-biography written by an unreliable narrator who lacks control over the facts of his story and their possible significance.
79 The motto announced at the beginning of *Fanny Hill* is "Truth! stark, naked truth." Sade's *Philosophy in the Boudoir* had "truths" that could be extracted by the Saint-Simonians and republished during the revolution of 1848. Among them: "Must the diviner part of mankind be kept in chains by the other? Ah, break those bonds; nature wills it. Have no other curb than your tastes, no other laws than those of your own desires, no more morality than that of Nature herself." See Angela Carter, *The Sadeian Woman and the Ideology of Pornography* (New York: Harper and Row, 1980), 116–36, for some interesting observations on Sade and education.
80 Foucault, *The Discourse on Language*, 220.
81 Jane Gallop, "Beyond the *jouissance* Principle." *Representations* 7 (1984), 112.

Afterword

1 Morris Eaves, ed., *Homage to David Erdman*, "Inside the Blake Industry," *SiR* 21 (1982), 389–443.
2 Jacques Derrida, *Of Grammatology*, trans. Gayatri Chakravorty Spivak (Baltimore: Johns Hopkins University Press, 1976), 32–33.
3 Blake is called "that strangest of creatures, a Puritan painter, an iconoclastic maker of icons," by W. J. T. Mitchell in *Iconology: Image, Text, Ideology* (Chicago: University of Chicago Press, 1986), 115.
4 For an interesting analogous exploration, see Dan Miller, "Contrary Revelation: *The Marriage of Heaven and Hell*," *SiR* 24 (1985), 491–509.
5 Gasché, "Deconstruction as Criticism," *Glyph* 6 (Baltimore: Johns Hopkins University Press, 1979), 177–216.
6 "Freud and the Scene of Writing," in *Writing and Difference*, trans. Alan Bass (Chicago: University of Chicago Press, 1978), 197.
7 Freud, "Fetishism" (1927); reprint in *Sexuality and the Psychology of Love*, ed. Philip Rieff (New York: Collier Books, 1963), 214–19. The fetish is a substitute (ambivalently regarded) "for the woman's (mother's) phallus which the little boy once believed in and does not wish to forgo— we know why" (215). Derrida takes up the question of his "negative theology" in "Différance," in *Margins of Philosophy*, trans. Alan Bass (Chicago: University of Chicago Press, 1982), 6. The argument between Derrida and Lacan is redoubtably refereed by Barbara Johnson, "The Frame of Reference," in *Literature and Psychoanalysis: The Question of Reading: Otherwise*, ed. Shoshana Felman, *YFS* 55/56 (1977), 457–505.

8   Derrida, "Différance," 17.
9   Tzvetan Todorov, "Imitation and Motivation," in *Theories of the Symbol*, trans. Catherine Porter (Ithaca, N.Y.: Cornell University Press, 1982), 129–46.
10 This is the view made standard by W. J. T. Mitchell's *Blake's Composite Art* (Princeton, N.J.: Princeton University Press, 1978).
11 Freud, *The Interpretation of Dreams*, trans. James Strachey (New York: Avon Books, 1965), 353.
12 Derrida, "Différance," 20–21.
13 Derrida, *Of Grammatology*, 71. My emphasis.
14 Steinberg, *The Sexuality of Christ in Renaissance Art and in Modern Oblivion* (New York: Pantheon/October Book, 1983).

Index

Contributors

Hazard Adams is Professor of English and Comparative Literature at the University of Washington, and cofounder and Senior Fellow of the School of Criticism and Theory. His publications include *Blake and Yeats: The Contrary Vision; The Interests of Criticism; William Blake: A Reading of the Shorter Poems; Joyce Cary's Trilogies;* and *Philosophy of the Literary Symbolic.*

David Aers is currently Reader in English Literature at the University of East Anglia, Norwich, England. His publications include *Chaucer, Langland, and the Creative Imagination; Romanticism and Ideology* (with Jon Cook and David Punter) ; *Literature, Language and Society in England 1580–1680* (with Bob Hodge and Gunther Kress) *Chaucer;* and *Medieval Literature: Criticism, Ideology, and History* (ed.).

Donald Ault is Associate Professor at Vanderbilt University and author of *Visionary Physics: Blake's Response to Newton* and *Narrative Unbound: Re-Visioning Blake's* The Four Zoas, as well as articles and reviews on Blake and on popular culture.

Mark Bracher is Assistant Professor of English and Associate Director of the Center for Literature and Psychoanalysis at Kent State University. He is the author of *Being Form'd: Thinking through Blake's Milton* and several articles on Blake and psychoanalytic approaches to reading.

Stephen D. Cox is Associate Professor of Literature at the University of California, San Diego. He is the author of *"The Stranger Within Thee": Concepts of the Self in Late Eighteenth-Century Literature* and of essays on Blake and other literary figures.

Nelson Hilton is Associate Professor of English at the University of Georgia and serves as review editor of *Blake: An Illustrated Quarterly.* He is coeditor (with Thomas A. Vogler) of *Unnam'd Forms: Blake and Textuality,* editor of *Essential Articles for the Study of Blake, 1970–1984,* and author of *Literal Imagination: Blake's Vision of Words.*

William Dennis Horn is Associate Professor of Technical Communication at Clarkson University, where he develops computer authoring systems and language analysis programs. He has written articles on English Romanticism and on computer applications in humanities education.

Elizabeth Langland, Associate Professor of English at the University of Florida, is the author of *Society and the Novel* and coeditor of *The Voyage In: Fictions of Female Development*, and *A Feminist Perspective in the Academy: The Difference It Makes*. She has also written numerous articles and is currently engaged in writing a book on Anne Brontë and a broader study setting out a poetics of women's fiction in the nineteenth century.

Dan Miller is Assistant Professor of English at North Carolina State University and has published articles and reviews on Blake and literary theory.

Thomas A. Vogler is Professor of English Literature and Fellow of Cowell College at the University of California, Santa Cruz. A member of the Santa Cruz Blake Study Group, he is author of *Preludes to Vision* and coeditor (with Nelson Hilton) of *Unnam'd Forms: Blake and Textuality*. In addition to numerous essays on Blake and the other English Romantics, he has written on various literary figures from Thomson to Ralph Ellison.

David Wagenknecht is Associate Professor of English at Boston University and Editor of *Studies in Romanticism*. He is the author of *Blake's Night: William Blake and the Idea of Pastoral*.

Brenda S. Webster is a free-lance writer. In addition to her books, *Yeats: A Psychoanalytic Study* and *Blake's Prophetic Psychology*, she has translated poetry from Italian for three anthologies of women's poetry, reviewed fiction for the Oakland *Tribune*, and written articles, the latest of which concerns Helene Deutsche.

Library of Congress Cataloging-in-Publication Data
Critical paths.
Includes bibliographies and index.
1. Blake, William, 1757–1827—Criticism and interpretation. 1. Miller, Dan, 1949–   . II. Bracher, Mark, 1950–   . III. Ault, Donald D.
PR4147.c75   1987   821'.7   87–13514
ISBN 0–8223–0751–0